Advanced Oxidation Processes: Applications and Prospects, 2nd Volume

Advanced Oxidation Processes: Applications and Prospects, 2nd Volume

Topic Editors

Gassan Hodaifa
Antonio Zuorro
Joaquín R. Dominguez
Juan García Rodríguez
José A. Peres
Zacharias Frontistis
Mha Albqmi

MDPI

Basel • Beijing • Wuhan • Barcelona • Belgrade • Novi Sad • Cluj • Manchester

Topic Editors

Gassan Hodaifa
University of Pablo de Olavide
Dos Hermanas
Spain

Antonio Zuorro
Sapienza—University of Rome
Rome
Italy

Joaquín R. Dominguez
Universidad de Extremadura
Badajoz
Spain

Juan García Rodríguez
Complutense University of Madrid
Madrid
Spain

José A. Peres
University of Trás-os-Montes and Alto Douro
Vila Real
Portugal

Zacharias Frontistis
University of Western Macedonia
Kozani
Greece

Mha Albqmi
Jouf University
Sakaka
Saudi Arabia

Editorial Office
MDPI AG
Grosspeteranlage 5
4052 Basel, Switzerland

This is a reprint of the Topic, published open access by the journals *Catalysts* (ISSN 2073-4344), *Processes* (ISSN 2227-9717), *Sci* (ISSN 2413-4155) and *Water* (ISSN 2073-4441), freely accessible at: https://www.mdpi.com/topics/KH49X32SG7.

For citation purposes, cite each article independently as indicated on the article page online and as indicated below:

Lastname, A.A.; Lastname, B.B. Article Title. *Journal Name* **Year**, *Volume Number*, Page Range.

ISBN 978-3-7258-7773-7 (Hbk)
ISBN 978-3-7258-7774-4 (PDF)
https://doi.org/10.3390/books978-3-7258-7774-4

Contents

About the Editors

Gassan Hodaifa

Gassan Hodaifa (Web of Science H-index: 27) holds degrees in Food Engineering from the University of Albaath (Syria) and Chemical Engineering from the University of Granada (Spain). He earned his PhD in 2004 from the University of Jaén. He is a member of the Bioprocesses Research Group TEP-138 (Junta de Andalucía), where his research focuses on microalgae, wastewater treatment, chemical oxidation, membrane technology, adsorption, pesticide removal, olive oil processing, enzyme biotechnology, and nematode biotechnology. Prof. Hodaifa has participated in 27 research projects, serving as Principal Investigator (PI) in 8 of them, as well as in 4 European programmes, including 1 PRIMA project and 3 projects developed in collaboration with M.A.P.A. and the companies INFAOLIVA and UNAPROLIVA. He has also been involved in 16 research contracts, acting as PI in 4. In addition, he has twice been appointed as an advisor to the Japanese multinational Asahi Kasei Corporation. His funded research includes six projects supported by the Junta de Andalucía (including two as PI), five projects under the Spanish National Research Plan, one project funded by the Community of Madrid, and several additional projects carried out in collaboration with industry. His scientific output includes 79 articles published in JCR-indexed journals and 21 publications indexed in other databases. More than 10 of these publications were produced through international collaborations with researchers from countries across all continents. He is also the co-inventor of two patents related to the purification of olive mill wastewater. In addition, he has served as editor of several books, Guest Editor of Special Issues and thematic topics, and author of book chapters published by leading international publishers, such as Academic Press (Elsevier), CRC Press, Taylor and Francis Group, and Springer International Publishing. He has also participated in more than 125 scientific conferences.

Antonio Zuorro

Antonio Zuorro is the Scientific Coordinator of GreenSapiens (bit.ly/GreenSapiens), author of more than 160 scientific papers and 5 national and international industrial invention patents (H-index 44), Professor and Researcher at the Department of Chemical, Materials and Environmental Engineering of Sapienza, University of Rome, in Principles of Chemical Engineering. He is also a Circular and Bio-economy Expert, and in 2017 won a European project Horizon 2020, BBI JU (€ 7.2 million), as Project Manager and Scientific Coordinator, leading an international consortium of 13 partners, including public institutions and multinational private companies. Now he coordinates for EU projects. For decades, he has worked on the enhancement of agro-industrial residues through the extraction of bio-active compounds of interest in the cosmetic, nutraceutical and pharmaceutical sectors, participating in several research projects leading the unit or the project as a whole. With consultancy and research projects for third parties in the Circular Economy and Green Chemistry fields, his activity has developed in various sectors, including advanced oxidation processes (AOPs), catalysis, chemical thermodynamics, enzyme kinetics, protein engineering and transport phenomena in microencapsulated systems. His current research is mainly focused on the treatment and re-use of agro-industrial residues, especially through the recovery of high-added-value bioactive compounds, and the degradation of pollutants by advanced oxidation processes, the development of functional products with antioxidant and/or antibacterial and anti-quorum sensing properties. With the collaboration of important industrial partners, he recently targeted the production of "green" nanoparticles of cosmetic and biomedical interest and the optimization of new-generation biorefineries operating with microalgae.

Joaquín R. Dominguez

Joaquín R. Dominguez holds a degree (1996) and a PhD (2000) in Chemistry from the University of Extremadura (Spain), both with honours, and received the University's Research Excellence Award in 2001. Between 1997 and 2000, he held an MEC FPU Predoctoral Fellowship, including research stays at Instituto Superior Técnico (Lisbon, Portugal). In 2001, he joined the Department of Chemical Engineering at the University of Extremadura as an Assistant Lecturer, becoming Associate Professor in 2007 and Full Professor in 2023. His research focuses on water and wastewater treatment, particularly on the removal of micropollutants and emerging contaminants using advanced oxidation processes (AOPs), including ozone, Fenton's reagent, hydrogen peroxide, persulphate, and UV/VIS radiation, as well as their combinations. Since 2007, he has also developed electrochemical treatment methods, especially anodic electrooxidation using boron-doped electrodes, with highly productive outcomes. More recently, he has incorporated a new line on sonochemical oxidation using high-frequency ultrasonic waves (MHz range). Prof. Domínguez has participated in 25 research projects in Environmental Engineering, mainly related to water treatment and contaminant removal. He has chaired the biannual International Conference on Water, Waste and Energy Management (WWEM) since 2015. He has co-authored approximately 85 scientific papers, 9 book chapters, and 8 books, with an H-index of 35 (WoS). He has supervised or co-supervised 50 research works, including 20 B.Sc. and 5 PhD theses, and presented about 90 communications at national and international conferences. He is a member of the Editorial Board of the journals *Processes* and *Open Chemistry*, and has served as Guest Editor of nine Special Issues in leading international journals.

Juan García Rodríguez

Juan García Rodríguez has been a Full Professor of Chemical Engineering in the Department of Chemical and Materials Engineering of the Complutense University of Madrid since 2018. He received a PhD in Chemical Engineering in 2000 and has carried out research stays in Chile, Portugal, and the United Kingdom. Since 2002, he has belonged to the CyPS (UCM) research group, first as a member and then as director in 2022. The research group CyPS was recognized with the Excellent mark by Agencia Estatal de Investigación in the last evaluation, 2023. His research interests have focused on the synthesis and characterization of carbon materials with enhanced properties and their catalytic application in adsorption and environmental catalysis, and biomass valorization. He has published more than 140 papers in JCR journals (2/3 in Q1) (H-index: 46 and more than 7000 citations). He has sent more than 150 communications to congresses (2/3 international) and written 18 book chapters. He has supervised 9 doctoral theses (2 with Extraordinary Award, 4 with International Mention and 2 with Industrial PhD Mention), more than 30 master's theses and 18 supervisions of international students. So far, he has participated in more than 25 research projects financed by public funds, the National Plan, European and Community of Madrid (in 12 of them as main researcher) and in more than 35 research and consulting projects funded by companies (Art. 83 LOU, Art. 60 LOSU) (in 16 of them as main researcher). He is co-author of one industrial property product and the recipient of the 5th Technology and Knowledge Transfer Award at Complutense University for the project of the research group entitled "Development of cyclic adsorption processes applied in the chemical industry". He has four recognized six-year research periods (4 sexenios).

José A. Peres

José A. Peres (H-index of 37 in Web of Science) graduated in Chemical Engineering at the University of Coimbra, Portugal. He completed his PhD degree in Chemistry at the University of Trás-os-Montes and Alto Douro (UTAD), Vila Real, Portugal, in 2002 and obtained a Habilitation degree in 2011 at UTAD. He was Director of the Chemistry Department (2017–2021) and Director of the PhD course in Chemical and Biological Sciences (2021–2023). Currently, he is an Associate Professor with habilitation at UTAD and a member of the Chemistry Research Centre of Vila Real, where he is the Scientific Coordinator of the Environmental Chemistry Research Group. He is author and co-author of more than 300 scientific publications, including 110 papers published in SCI journals, which received more than 5200 citations, 2 patents, and more than 200 communications in conference abstracts and proceedings. He has been involved in 25 research and development projects and 7 enterprise projects. His main research interests focus on environmentally friendly strategies for pollution control, including the development of Advanced Oxidation Processes (AOPs) such as Fenton reagent, homogeneous and heterogeneous photo-Fenton, ozonation, ferrioxalate/solar radiation and heterogeneous photocatalysis. He also studies combined treatments (physical–chemical and biological) particularly for agro-industrial wastewaters and water reuse. He was the Conference Chair of the 6th International Conference on Green Chemistry and Sustainable Engineering (GreenChem-24) which took place in Lisbon (Portugal) from 24 to 26 July 2024 and II International Meeting of Molecules4Life and Sustainable Development which was organized in Vila Real (Portugal) from September 10 to 12, 2025.

Zacharias Frontistis

Zacharias Frontistis is a Full Professor specializing in water and wastewater process engineering in the Department of Chemical Engineering at the University of Western Macedonia. He previously served as the chairman of the Department of Environmental Engineering (2018–2019) and the Department of Chemical Engineering (2019–2021) at the same university. Dr. Frontistis holds a Diploma in Environmental Engineering (2005), a Master's Degree (2007), and a PhD (2011), all from the Technical University of Crete. Before joining the University of Western Macedonia, he worked as a Postdoctoral Researcher at several institutions, including the Department of Civil and Environmental Engineering at the University of Cyprus and the International Water Research Centre, NIREAS, the Department of Civil and Environmental Engineering at Namik Kemal University, and the Department of Chemical Engineering at the University of Patras. His research focuses on catalysis for environmental and energy applications, the development of new physicochemical processes for water treatment (Advanced Oxidation Processes), combining physicochemical and biological processes for agro-industrial wastewater treatment, and simulating these processes. He has supervised and co-supervised a large number of diploma and postgraduate theses. Dr. Frontistis has a significant publishing record, with over 175 articles in high-impact international journals, an H-index of 51, and approximately 7,000 citations according to Scopus. He has also contributed to international conference proceedings more than 60 times and authored two book chapters on advanced wastewater treatment and reuse. Dr. Frontistis has reviewed over 1,200 papers for more than 100 high-impact scientific journals. He serves as an editor for the *Journal of Environmental Chemical Engineering* (Elsevier), sits on the Editorial Board of six international journals, and has been a Guest Editor for 15 Special Issues in his fields of interest.

Mha Albqmi

Mha Albqmi currently holds the position of Assistant Professor at Jouf University, Saudi Arabia. Her educational background includes a Ph.D. in Chemistry from Oklahoma State University, Stillwater, Oklahoma, USA, a Master of Science degree in Chemistry from Lamar University, Texas, USA, and a Bachelor of Science degree in Chemistry from Taif University, Taif, Saudi Arabia. A portion of Dr. Mha Albqmi's research has been dedicated to supporting the olive sector, reflecting her previous role in the Olive Research Center at Jouf University. Throughout her duration, she contributed to enhancing research activity in this field, which focuses on improving the utilization of olive processing by-products and valorizing them on certain plants experiencing heavy-metal toxicity. Additionally, her work explores treatment approaches aimed at reducing the environmental impact associated with the olive oil mill wastewater. Her current research interests focus on the design and synthesis of advanced inorganic and hybrid nanomaterials for environmental and energy-related applications. She works on developing functional materials such as porous frameworks and nanocomposites with enhanced physicochemical properties. A key aspect of her research is understanding structure–property relationships to optimize performance in adsorption, catalysis, and electrochemical systems. She is particularly interested in applying these materials for water treatment, pollutant removal, and energy storage technologies. Her work also explores coordination chemistry and the role of metal-based systems in improving material functionality. Overall, her research aims to develop efficient and sustainable materials that address challenges in environmental remediation and energy applications.

Preface

This Topic brings together recent scientific contributions on advanced oxidation processes and related developments in process engineering. Its subject is the design, optimization, and application of advanced oxidation-based technologies for water and wastewater treatment, environmental protection, resource recovery, and improved industrial performance. The scope of the Topic extends from established methods to emerging hybrid systems that combine treatment efficiency with operational practicality, monitoring, and predictive tools. Its main aim is to present current knowledge, highlight common research directions, and show how these technologies are moving from laboratory study toward broader commercial use. The purpose of this scientific work is to provide researchers, engineers, and professionals with a coherent view of recent progress, present challenges, and future opportunities in the field. This Topic is addressed to academics, practitioners, and decision-makers interested in sustainable treatment strategies and modern process design. It was developed to support knowledge exchange at a time when effective and scalable solutions for complex environmental problems are increasingly needed.

Gassan Hodaifa, Antonio Zuorro, Joaquín R. Dominguez, Juan García Rodríguez, José A. Peres, Zacharias Frontistis, and Mha Albqmi
Topic Editors

catalysts

MDPI

Editorial

From Oxidation Chemistry to Intelligent Water Systems: Emerging Directions in Process Optimization and Environmental Engineering

Gassan Hodaifa [1,*], Antonio Zuorro [2], Joaquín R. Dominguez [3], Juan García Rodríguez [4], José A. Peres [5], Zacharias Frontistis [6] and Mha Albqmi [7]

1 Department of Molecular Biology and Biochemical Engineering, Chemical Engineering Area, Universidad Pablo de Olavide, Avenida Rectora Rosario Valpuesta 1, 41089 Dos Hermanas, Spain
2 Department of Chemical Engineering, Materials and Environment, Sapienza-University of Rome, Via Eudossiana 18, 00184 Rome, Italy; antonio.zuorro@uniroma1.it
3 Chemical Engineering and Physical Chemistry Department, Universidad de Extremadura, Av. Elvas s/n, 06006 Badajoz, Spain; jrdoming@unex.es
4 Department of Chemical and Materials Engineering, Complutense University of Madrid, 28040 Madrid, Spain; jgarciar@ucm.es
5 Department of Chemistry, Chemistry Research Centre—Vila Real, University of Trás-os-Montes and Alto Douro, UTAD, Quinta de Prados, 5000-801 Vila Real, Portugal; jperes@utad.pt
6 Department of Chemical Engineering, University of Western Macedonia, 50100 Kozani, Greece; zfrontistis@uowm.gr
7 Department of Chemistry, College of Science, Jouf University, Sakaka 72341, Aljouf, Saudi Arabia; maalbgmi@ju.edu.sa
* Correspondence: ghodaifa@upo.es

Advanced oxidation processes (AOPs) are treatment technologies designed to generate highly reactive oxidizing species, mainly hydroxyl radicals and, in some systems, sulfate radicals, for the degradation of refractory organic pollutants that are difficult to remove by conventional biological or physicochemical treatment. Globally, AOPs are now recognized as an important part of advanced water and wastewater treatment, particularly for the removal of micropollutants, toxic organics, color, odor, and residual toxicity. However, the field shows a clear gap between commercially mature technologies and emerging research-stage technologies [1,2].

The current global situation of AOPs can be described as scientifically mature but industrially selective. Established systems such as ozonation, UV/H_2O_2, and Fenton-based processes are already used in real treatment practice, while many other variants remain largely confined to laboratory and pilot scales. Recent reviews emphasize that AOP research has expanded rapidly, but full-scale implementation is still limited by operating cost, oxidant consumption, energy demand, water-matrix effects, by-product control, and scale-up difficulties [1,2].

The papers gathered in this Topic entitled "Advanced Oxidation Processes: Applications and Prospects, 2nd Volume" illustrate the breadth of process engineering while revealing a shared scientific direction: the move toward more selective, efficient, and operationally relevant technologies for environmental protection, resource recovery, and product-quality enhancement. Although the studies cover distinct application domains, namely, tannery wastewater, landfill leachate, municipal effluents, natural water, aquaculture, gold tailings, soybean oil processing, and dissolved oxygen forecasting, they are united by a common commitment to process intensification, optimization, and decision support under realistic conditions.

A dominant theme across the collection is the central role of oxidation-based technologies in water and wastewater treatment. Urbina-Suarez et al. [3] examined an enhanced UV/H_2O_2 system for tannery effluents and showed that a carefully optimized combination of acidic pH, elevated temperature, ultraviolet power, and hydrogen peroxide can simultaneously reduce multiple pollution indicators, including ammonium, chromium, BOD, COD, and color. Their study is notable because it addresses a complex real industrial effluent rather than a simplified laboratory matrix, thereby reinforcing the practical value of statistically optimized advanced oxidation processes.

A complementary perspective is offered by Becerra-Moreno et al. [4], who evaluated catalytic ozonation with magnetite for landfill leachates. Their results showed substantial COD removal and, importantly, improved biodegradability, evidenced by increases in the BOD_5/COD ratio. This contribution underscores a key strength of catalytic ozonation: it can function not only as a polishing technology but also as a transformation step that renders recalcitrant mixtures more amenable to downstream biological treatment. At the same time, the gradual decrease in catalyst efficiency after repeated cycles reminds us that catalyst stability and regeneration remain decisive issues for scale-up.

Dominguez et al. [5] extended the oxidation discussion into the electrochemical domain through boron-doped diamond anodic oxidation of wastewater treatment plant effluents. Their work demonstrated the strong capacity of EO-BDD to eliminate neonicotinoid pesticides and other emerging contaminants from real effluents intended for reuse. Particularly relevant is the authors' simultaneous consideration of degradation efficiency, kinetics, mineralization, and specific energy consumption. Such multidimensional evaluation is essential if advanced treatment technologies are to move beyond proof-of-concept and become credible tools for water regeneration.

Shen et al. [6] addressed another pressing water-quality issue by comparing several UV-activated advanced oxidation systems for humic acid removal from natural water. Their identification of UV/peroxymonosulfate (UV/PMS) as the most effective option highlights how oxidant selection can decisively alter process performance. Beyond the high mineralization achieved, this study is significant because humic substances are closely linked to color, heavy-metal transport, and disinfection by-product formation. In this respect, the paper contributes not only to oxidation science but also to safer drinking-water treatment strategies.

The broader conceptual and technological framework for many of these studies is supplied by Zhang et al. [7] in their review of ozone technology. By surveying ozone generation methods and applications in water treatment, air pollution control, soil remediation, food preservation, medicine, and the power industry, the review demonstrates the continuing versatility of ozone as a platform technology. It also highlights a persistent tension in ozone research and deployment: ozone is simultaneously mature in many industrial uses and still evolving through innovations in generation efficiency, reactor design, coupling with other processes, and application-specific integration.

The coupling of oxidation chemistry with aquaculture management appears in the paper by Afif et al. [8], who proposed a lime-based composite integrating calcium peroxide, titanium dioxide, and peracetic acid encapsulated in Fe-alginate granules. Their system was designed to provide in situ oxygenation while promoting advanced oxidation at the sediment–water interface in shrimp ponds. The reported maintenance of dissolved oxygen and the removal of ammonia, sulfide, and turbidity suggest that this strategy may offer a practical route for improving pond-bottom conditions in traditional aquaculture systems. The work is especially timely because it frames advanced treatment not as an isolated laboratory exercise but as a farmer-oriented technology requiring safety, simplicity, and operational resilience.

https://doi.org/10.3390/catal16040333

If Afif et al. [8] focused on intervention, Wang et al. [9] focused on anticipation. Their deep learning-based rolling forecasting of dissolved oxygen in coastal waters demonstrates the growing role of artificial intelligence in water-quality management. By comparing several forecasting architectures and building an ensemble-based early-warning system, the authors moved beyond model benchmarking to deployment-oriented decision support. This is an important signal for the field: future environmental engineering will increasingly combine treatment technologies with predictive analytics, enabling a shift from reactive management to proactive control.

The Topic collection also broadens the notion of process optimization beyond water treatment. Kenzhaliyev et al. [10] investigated the use of trichloroisocyanuric acid as an oxidizer in the leaching of gold-containing concentrate derived from tailings. By showing improved gold recovery following oxidative pretreatment, the paper contributes to the sustainable valorization of technogenic raw materials and reminds us that oxidation processes can serve both environmental remediation and resource recovery objectives. In a different industrial context, Mohammadi-Moghaddam et al. [11] optimized stripping and drying parameters in soybean oil extraction, demonstrating how relatively targeted adjustments in temperature and pressure can substantially influence quality indicators such as acidity, color, peroxide value, moisture, and oxidative stability. This paper underscores that process engineering advances are not confined to pollutant destruction; they also include the refinement of manufacturing conditions for better product quality and improved industrial efficiency.

Taken together, these papers suggest several directions for future work. First, optimization remains indispensable, but it must increasingly be linked to realistic matrices, lifecycle performance, and techno-economic constraints. Second, hybridization—whether between ozone and catalysts, oxygen release and AOPs, electrochemical oxidation and water reuse, or forecasting and early warning—has emerged as a defining strategy for improving robustness and applicability. Third, future progress will depend on connecting chemistry with systems thinking: treatment performance, energy use, catalyst durability, digital monitoring, and end-use requirements must be considered together rather than in isolation.

In summary, this Topic collection captures a field in productive transition. Advanced oxidation processes continue to evolve from single-process laboratory studies into integrated solutions for complex environmental and industrial challenges. Meanwhile, process optimization, materials design, and machine learning are expanding the disciplinary boundaries of process engineering. The papers assembled here, therefore, do more than report individual results; collectively, they show how modern process research is becoming more interdisciplinary, more application-driven, and more closely aligned with the demands of sustainability.

The scientific contributions to this Topic have shed light on the state of the art of emerging advanced oxidation technologies, which show promise for being incorporated into the industrial sector in the not-too-distant future.

Acknowledgments: We would like to express our gratitude to MDPI Editorial, through the journals Catalysts, Processes, Sci, Sustainability, and Water, for offering us the opportunity to serve as Guest Editors and contribute to this detailed exploration of advanced oxidation technologies. In addition, we would like to thank all the authors who shared their research and the referees for their invaluable contributions.

Conflicts of Interest: The authors declare no conflicts of interest.

https://doi.org/10.3390/catal16040333

References

1. Mukherjee, J.; Lodh, B.K.; Sharma, R.; Mahata, N.; Shah, M.P.; Mandal, S.; Ghanta, S.; Bhunia, B. Advanced oxidation process for the treatment of industrial wastewater: A review on strategies, mechanisms, bottlenecks and prospects. *Chemosphere* **2023**, *345*, 140473. [CrossRef] [PubMed]
2. Hübner, U.; Spahr, S.; Lutze, H.; Wieland, A.; Rüting, S.; Gernjak, W.; Wenk, J. Advanced oxidation processes for water and wastewater treatment—Guidance for systematic future research. *Heliyon* **2024**, *10*, e30402. [CrossRef] [PubMed]
3. Urbina-Suarez, N.A.; Lopez-Barrera, G.L.; Garcia-Martinez, J.B.; Barajas-Solano, A.F.; Machuca-Martinez, F.; Zuorro, A. Enhanced UV/H_2O_2 System for the Oxidation of Organic Contaminants and Ammonia Transformation from Tannery Effluents. *Processes* **2023**, *11*, 3091. [CrossRef]
4. Becerra-Moreno, D.; Machuca-Martinez, F.; Ramirez-Rios, L.F.; Garcia-Martinez, J.B.; Barajas-Solano, A.F. Synergistic Degradation of Organic Contaminants in Landfill Leachates Using Catalytic Ozonation with Magnetite. *Sci* **2025**, *7*, 31. [CrossRef]
5. Dominguez, J.R.; Gonzalez, T.; Correia, S.E.; Nunez, M.M. Emerging Contaminants Decontamination of WWTP Effluents by BDD Anodic Oxidation: A Way towards Its Regeneration. *Water* **2023**, *15*, 1668. [CrossRef]
6. Shen, Q.; Song, X.; Fan, J.; Chen, C.; Li, Z. UV/Advanced Oxidation Process for Removing Humic Acid from Natural Water: Comparison of Different Methods and Effect of External Factors. *Water* **2024**, *16*, 1815. [CrossRef]
7. Zhang, K.; Liu, J.; Lv, H.; Zeng, X.; Ling, Z.; Ding, L.; Jin, C. Advances in Ozone Technology for Environmental, Energy, Food and Medical Applications. *Processes* **2025**, *13*, 1126. [CrossRef]
8. Afif, M.I.; Astuti, H.W.; Pratiwi, N.T.M.; Widigdo, B.; Khotib, M.; Rosiana, N.; Faisal, M. Synergistic Coupling of In Situ Oxygenation and Advanced Oxidation Processes Using a Novel Lime-Based Composite for Water Quality Management in *Litopenaeus vannamei* Ponds. *Water* **2026**, *18*, 296. [CrossRef]
9. Wang, Y.; Song, J.; Li, X.; Zhong, G. Deep Learning-Based Rolling Forecasting of Dissolved Oxygen in Shandong Peninsula Coastal Waters. *Water* **2025**, *17*, 3102. [CrossRef]
10. Kenzhaliyev, B.K.; Tussupbayev, N.K.; Abdykirova, G.Z.; Koizhanova, A.K.; Fischer, D.Y.; Baltabekova, Z.A.; Samenova, N.O. Evaluation of the Efficiency of Using an Oxidizer in the Leaching Process of Gold-Containing Concentrate. *Processes* **2024**, *12*, 973. [CrossRef]
11. Mohammadi-Moghaddam, T.; Bakhshabadi, H.; Bojmehrani, A.; Valdes, M.E.; Morshedi, A. The Effect of Optimizing the Stripping and Drying Parameters During Industrial Extraction on the Physicochemical Properties of Soybean Oil. *Processes* **2025**, *13*, 541. [CrossRef]

https://doi.org/10.3390/catal16040333

processes

MDPI

Article

Enhanced UV/H_2O_2 System for the Oxidation of Organic Contaminants and Ammonia Transformation from Tannery Effluents

Néstor A. Urbina-Suarez [1,2], German L. López-Barrera [1], Janet B. García-Martínez [1], Andrés F. Barajas-Solano [1], Fiderman Machuca-Martínez [3] and Antonio Zuorro [4,*]

1 Department of Environmental Sciences, Universidad Francisco de Paula Santander, Av. Gran Colombia No. 12E-96, Cúcuta 540003, Colombia; nestorandresus@ufps.edu.co (N.A.U.-S.); lucianolb@ufps.edu.co (G.L.L.-B.); janetbibianagm@ufps.edu.co (J.B.G.-M.); andresfernandobs@ufps.edu.co (A.F.B.-S.)
2 School of Natural Resources and Environment, Universidad del Valle, Ciudad Universitaria Meléndez, Calle 13 # 100-00, Cali 760015, Colombia
3 Center of Excellence in New Materials—CENM, School of Chemical Engineering, Universidad del Valle, Ciudad Universitaria Meléndez, Calle 13 # 100-00, Cali 760015, Colombia; fiderman.machuca@correounivalle.edu.co
4 Department of Chemical Engineering, Materials and Environment, Sapienza University, Via Eudossiana 18, 00184 Roma, Italy
* Correspondence: antonio.zuorro@uniroma1.it

Abstract: In this work, a UV/H_2O_2 system in real tannery wastewater was evaluated by an experimental design with optimal stage 2-level I-optimal reaction surface using Design Expert software to analyze the effects of temperature, pH, UV lamp power (W), and H_2O_2 concentration on COD removal and nitrification. It was found that pH and temperature were the variables that affected the process the most. It was found that an acidic pH of 4.5–5.5 and temperatures between 50 and 70 °C favored improved COD and ammonium oxidation. The process conditions—temperature 54.6 °C, pH 4, pW-UV 60 W and hydrogen peroxide 0.5—were confirmed in the next phase of the study using a one-way statistical analysis ANOVA. Under these conditions, the nitrite removal rate was 98.4%, ammonium 94.53%, chromium 92.3%, chlorides 62.4%, BOD 67.4%, COD 44.5%, and color 48%.

Keywords: tannery wastewater; advanced oxidation processes; COD; nitrification; photocatalysis

1. Introduction

Tanneries are significant businesses that create high-quality leather goods utilized in various industries, including apparel, automobiles, footwear, and furniture. However, since the production process uses a lot of water, wastewater with high levels of organic and inorganic pollutants, including heavy metals, salts, and tannins, is produced. Due to its detrimental effects on aquatic life and human health, this wastewater from tanneries is a significant environmental issue [1]. In a global context, Asia, Latin America and Europe are the leading leather producers in the world; Italy is the leading leather producer in the European continent, owning 60% of the companies and exporting more than 70% of the total production in Europe; in Latin America, Brazil and Argentina stand out in the sector; they have a significant number of emerging companies with great competitiveness in the market, exporting their products to countries such as China, Hong Kong, Vietnam and the United States. Colombia has a 5% share in the production of the tanning industry worldwide and is the sixth largest producer in this sector in Latin America [2]. Production in the tanning industry consumes an average of 10–25 m^3 of water in its various stages and can generate an average of 8 to 20 m^3 of wastewater; this amount can vary depending on the technological development of each industry. According to estimates, the tanning industry produces roughly 22 billion liters of wastewater annually, most of which takes place in underdeveloped nations because the process requires little technological advancement. These effluents are reported to typically contain biodegradable substances such as fats, proteins, and carbohydrates as well as contaminants such as solvents, additives, and toxic heavy metals that are typical of the process and, in addition to changing the characteristics of the ecosystems into which they are discharged, also influence human health. They also contain pollutants such as solvents, additives, and toxic heavy metals [3], which, in addition to altering the properties of the ecosystems into which they are discharged, also impact human health by causing, among other things, liver and kidney damage, skin irritation, chronic bronchitis, nasal irritation, cancer, and DNA damage [4,5].

Several studies have described using physical, chemical, biological, and advanced oxidation processes (AOPs) to treat tannery wastewater. Concerning physical treatment systems, processes such as sedimentation, filtration, and centrifugation have been used to remove suspended solids and other particulates from tannery wastewater. The advantages of physical treatment systems are low cost and ease of use, but their effectiveness in removing dissolved contaminants is limited [6]. Chemical processes have shown that chemicals such as coagulants and flocculants are used to remove suspended solids and dissolved organics from tannery wastewater. The advantages of chemical treatment systems include their effectiveness in removing pollutants, but they can generate large amounts of sludge and require careful handling of the chemicals [7]. The use of micro-organisms to biodegrade organic matter in tannery wastewater has been reported; studies of these processes have used biological agents, including bacteria, microalgae, and some fungi. Batch reactor (SBR) systems have been used to treat tannery wastewater, reducing concentrations of COD and BOD by 70–88% [8,9]. Activated sludge systems show exciting results in BOD_5 and COD removal of 90% and 80%, respectively, with specific suspended solids in the mixed liquor (MLVSS) operating requirements of 3500 mg/L while maintaining an aeration time of 12 h [10]. The advantages of biological treatment systems include their efficiency in removing pollutants and their potential for energy recovery. Still, they require longer treatment times and are sensitive to variations in wastewater composition, especially concentrations of fats and oils and recalcitrant compounds that can lead to cell death of the micro-organisms used in these processes [11].

AOPs have become very important in recent years in treating wastewater-containing dyes [12], especially from the tanning industry [13]. Strongly oxidizing radicals, primarily the free hydroxyl radical (OH), are produced and used in these procedures with the goal of selectively reducing stubborn contaminants to a less hazardous state. One of the most crucial processes is the Fenton process, which employs iron ($Fe_2{}^+$) to break down hydrogen peroxide and create an OH radical before it is reduced again. According to reports, this system can remove up to 62% chromium, 98% BOD, and 93% COD from effluent from tanneries. A photo-Fenton system, a cyclic mechanism that regenerates the $Fe_2{}^+$ ion, might be used to address this technique's fundamental limitation—the disposal of significant amounts of iron ions in the sludge—even if it raises treatment costs [14,15]. Because of its capacity to reduce dyes, synthetic aromatic compounds, and persistent organic pollutants, ozone oxidation is another method used in the treatment of tannery wastewater; removal rates of 90–98% COD, 96% dyes, and 90% ammonium have been reported, though the effectiveness of the process primarily depends on pH. Molecular ozone dominates the reaction and is selective at acidic values (pH 4.5) where the process is direct; however, at pH > 7, the reaction decomposes and creates OH, which is less selective and has a greater oxidation potential [16]. As for photocatalytic processes, photo-Fenton is one of the most studied processes in tannery effluents and achieves a removal rate of 70–90% of COD, 86–98% of color and 90% of Cr. The efficiency of the process depends largely on the pH of the solution, with the optimal range for higher catalytic activity being 2.8–3.0. Iron hydroxides are formed at a pH of >5, which reduces the reactivity of OH, while at values below 2, complex iron species are formed, which react more slowly with H_2O_2 and reduce the efficiency of the process [17,18].

The UV/H_2O_2 system is very important for treating tannery effluents, as it allows no sludge production and significant COD removal in short reaction times [19]. Recent studies have brought significant insight into the treatment of wastewater with this process, evaluating individually the effects of pH, peroxide dosage, and UV intensity [20]; the use of catalysts such as TiO_2 and Fe_2O_3 has been employed to improve the performance of the UV/peroxide system. Although these catalysts increase the degradation rate and reduce the amount of peroxide to be used, the cost of the process rises, and its use in large-scale applications may limit its use, the UV absorption range is limited, and finally, the recovery of the catalyst from the treated wastewater is still a challenge [21]. As can be seen, the UV/H_2O_2 system is of great importance in treating tannery effluents. However, the effects of parameters such as temperature, pH, and UV intensity and their correlation with peroxide concentration still need to be determined, as they have yet to be analyzed in depth in real tannery effluents. This work sought to contribute scientifically to the optimization of operating conditions of the UV/peroxide photocatalytic process for the treatment of real tannery wastewater using a statistical design with response surface analysis, where the effect of temperature, pH, peroxide concentration and lamp potential was evaluated. The optimization conditions were validated with 10 replicates. This research contributes to the scientific understanding of advanced photocatalytic oxidation processes on the role of pH, temperature, UV lamp potential, and peroxide concentration in the generation of reactive species such as hydroxyl radical and their role in pollutant degradation contributing to the development of sustainable tannery wastewater treatment strategies that can be adapted to specific pollutants and environmental regulations.

2. Materials and Methods

2.1. Tannery Wastewater

The effluent came from a cattle hide tannery in the city of Cúcuta (Norte de Santander, Colombia). The samples were collected 60 min apart during the working day (by duplicate), with a volume of 300 mL per sample up to a total volume of 20 L. The samples were slightly acidified with H_2SO_4 and kept at 4 °C before COD analysis.

2.2. Physicochemical Characterization of the Tannery Effluents

The tannery wastewater was physiochemically characterized according to the 23rd edition of Standard methods for examining water and wastewater (Table 1).

Table 1. Physicochemical characterization.

Parameter	Units	Standard Methods Number
COD	$mg{\cdot}L^{-1}$	5220C
BOD		5210B-4500-OG
Nitrates		4500-NO_3 B
Nitrites		4500-NO_2 B
Ammonia nitrogen		4500-NH_3 F
Phosphates		4500-P C
Total Suspended Solids		2540D
Cr		3111D
Sulfides		4500-S2 F
Chlorides		4500-ClB
pH	pH units	4500B
Conductivity	$\mu S{\cdot}cm^{-1}$	2510B

2.3. Experimental Analysis

An experimental design with three levels of I-optimal reaction area (Table 2) was used and analyzed with Design-Expert® software version 22.0.2 (Stat-Ease, Inc., Minneapolis, MN, USA). The variables evaluated were temperature, initial pH, UV lamp power, and hydrogen peroxide concentration, and the reaction variables were COD, NO_3, and color. The experimental design resulted in 40 experiments performed in triplicate, giving 120 experiments.

Table 2. Experimental design.

Parameter	Factor		
	Lower Lever (−1)	**Medium Level (0)**	**Higher Level (+1)**
H_2O_2 (M)	0.3	0.5	0.7
Lamp power (W)	30	45	60
pH	4	5	6
Temperature (°C)	50	65	80

The wastewater was passed through a grease trap for 10 min and then segmented for 30 min in a pilot plant located at the laboratory of operational units of Universidad Francisco de Paula Santander (Cúcuta, Colombia). A photocatalytic reactor with a 500 mL overall volume and an operating volume of 200 mL was used, with temperature and pH control (Figure 1). Circulation was performed at 550 rpm. HCl and NaOH at a concentration of 0.1 M were used for pH control. The H_2O_2 concentration was 35%, from which the concentrations used in the experimental design were calculated. Finally, 254 Nm UVC lamps with a power of 15 W were used, providing a light intensity of 44 $\mu W \cdot cm^{-2}$.

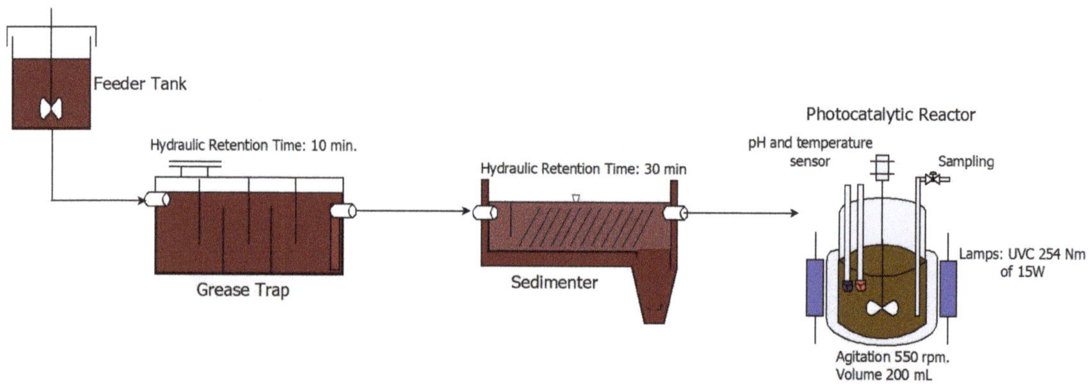

Figure 1. Experimental setup for the UV/Hydrogen Peroxide process.

2.4. Analytical Methods

Total organic carbon (TOC) was determined using a TOC analyzer (Thermo Fisher Scientific, Waltham, MA, USA). Operating conditions were a sample volume of 0.5 mL, water chase volume 1.0 mL, injection line purge on, injection line purge of 0.5 mL, acid volume of 0.5 mL, ICS loading flow 200 mL·min^{-1}, carrier gas delay time of 0.40 min, ICS loading time 50 min, detector sweep flow 500 mL·min^{-1}, oven sweep time 1.0 min, and system flow 200 mL·min^{-1} The measurement of nitrates was carried out according to the method described (SM-4500-NO_3-C), following the standard procedure indicated in the commercial kits for these compounds of HANNA Instruments UK; a calibration curve was elaborated from 0 to 10 mg·L^{-1}, obtaining the Equation (1) with which the concentrations were determined.

$$C = \frac{A - I}{S} \quad (1)$$

where:

C = concentration (mg·L^{-1})
A = absorbance

I = intercept of the regression line.
S = slope of the regression line.

The quantification of the COD was determined by the method 5220 C-Closed reflux of the standard methods edition 23, using potassium dichromate as an oxidant agent in an acid medium. For this, its digestion was carried out by adding 1.5 mL of digester solution and 3.5 mL of catalyst solution to 2.5 mL of sample; it was stirred in the vortex, heated for 2 h at 150 °C, and allowed to cool to room temperature (25 °C). The sample was then transferred to a larger vessel, and 0.05 to 0.10 mL (1 to 2 drops) of ferroin indicator was added and stirred rapidly on a magnetic stirrer while titrating with standardized 0.10 mol L^{-1} FAS. The endpoint was an abrupt color change from blue–green to reddish brown. The calculation was performed using the Equation (2). The COD calibration curve was generated from five patterns of potassium acid phthalate, made up of five concentrations: 0, 50, 100, 250, and 500 mol·L^{-1}. Each experiment was carried out in triplicate.

$$COD\ mg\ O_2/L = \frac{(B - A) * M * 8000}{mL\ sample} \quad (2)$$

where:
B = mL FAS used for sample
A = mL FAS used for blank
M = molarity of FAS
8000 = milliequivalent weight of oxygen × 1000 mol·L^{-1}

To determine color removal, a spectrophotometric scan was performed using a THERMO GENESYS10 spectrophotometer from the Environmental Quality Laboratory, Bayamon, PR, USA. The scan was performed for each sample in a wavelength range from 200 to 750 nm at a temperature of 25 °C, and the peaks of the absorbance values in the curve were determined. The separation interval of the measurement was calibrated to 1 nm. Deionized water was used to measure the baseline of the sweeps.

3. Results and Discussions

3.1. Physicochemical Characterization of Tannery Wastewaters

Table 3 shows the physicochemical characterization of the tannery effluents evaluated in this study. The results of the physicochemical characterization show that the COD concentration is 6180.45 ± 3.24 mg·L^{-1} and the BOD is 2128.27 ± 2.86 mg·L^{-1}, which allows detection of a high pollutant load of these effluents, as well as a high concentration of total suspended solids 1184.65 ± 1.12 mg·L^{-1}, chlorides 2100.38 ± 1.73 mg·L^{-1} and conductivity 1102 ± 0.56 μS·cm^{-1}. The pH of the effluents evaluated showed an acid pH (5.18 ± 0.1); the concentration of chromium was 1.2 ± 0.04 mg·L^{-1}, a value close to the levels allowed by current regulations for Colombia. It has been reported that tannery effluents have a pollutant organic load resulting from the chemicals used in the tanning and dyeing process, a higher number of suspended solids (SS), a fluctuating pH (4–7), and a high concentration of COD [22,23]; these characteristics are similar to those found in this study. Studies have reported that a BOD/COD ratio > 0.6 shows that effluents are biodegradable and, therefore, can be degraded by biological processes; lower values imply recalcitrant wastewater that must be treated by other oxidative processes such as those found in this study [24]. BOD shows biodegradable organic compounds, unlike the COD value related to organic and inorganic constituents [25]; changes in the BOD/COD ratio may be related to the degree of changes in the structure of organic compounds after oxidation [3].

Table 3. Physicochemical characterization of tannery effluents.

Parameter	Units	Average Value
COD	$mg{\cdot}L^{-1}$	6180.45 ± 3.24
BOD		2128.27 ± 2.86
Nitrates		74.56 ± 0.67
Nitrites		0.64 ± 0.08
Ammonia nitrogen		18.32 ± 0.23
Phosphates		21.8 ± 0.48
Total Suspended Solids		1184.65 ± 1.46
Cr		1.2 ± 0.04
Sulfides		47.34 ± 0.54
Chlorides		2100.38 ± 1.73
pH	pH units	5.18 ± 0.03
Conductivity	$\mu S{\cdot}cm^{-1}$	928.5 ± 1.12

3.2. COD

The results of the ANOVA analysis for COD removal (Table 4) using the UV/H_2O_2 system show that the model F-value of 2.78 implies that the model is significant. There is only a 1.34% chance that such a large F-value is due to noise. *p*-values less than 0.0500 indicate that the model terms are significant. It can be demonstrated that pH, temperature-pW, and pH-pW interactions are significant terms in the model. Finally, the F-value for lack of fit of 0.22 implies that the lack of fit is not significant relative to the pure error. There is a 97.62% chance that such a large F-value of lack of fit is due to noise.

Table 4. ANOVA analysis of 2-level I-optimal Response Surface design for COD removal.

Source	Sum of Squares	Df	Mean Square	F-Value	*p*-Value	
Model	188.50	14	13.46	2.78	0.0134	significant
A-Temperature	2.09	1	2.09	0.4321	0.5172	
B-pH	64.75	1	64.75	13.38	0.0012	
C-Hydrogen Peroxide	1.01	1	1.01	0.2091	0.6516	
D-pW	0.2136	2	0.1068	0.0221	0.9782	
AB	1.66	1	1.66	0.3427	0.5637	
AC	8.94	1	8.94	1.85	0.1867	
AD	76.36	2	38.18	7.89	0.0023	
BC	20.37	1	20.37	4.21	0.0513	
BD	50.94	2	25.47	5.26	0.0127	
CD	7.10	2	3.55	0.7338	0.4906	
Residual	116.16	24	4.84			
Lack of Fit	9.54	7	1.36	0.2174	0.9762	not significant
Pure Error	106.62	17	6.27			
Cor Total	304.66	38				

Figure 2 shows the effects of pH and temperature on COD removal. Studies have reported high COD levels in tannery effluents, a typical average characterization may be in the range of 1500–12,000 ppm, a product of the various dyes used in the process as well as salts, organic acids, and other compounds that interfere with treatment and degradation [26–29]. COD, the removal of pollutants, depends on the amount of OH available for oxidation; therefore, the generation of OH is crucial, and this process is affected by the pH of the wastewater. As observed in this work, an acidic pH favors the generation of OH and its reaction with the oxidation of the pollutant load, while high pH values decrease the COD removal rate; studies have shown that at high pH (9–12) the dissociated form of hydrogen peroxide acts as a scavenger of the generated OH*, which affects the reduction of COD removal due to the loss of carbon oxidation potential [20,30]. Temperature affects the rate of peroxide degradation, the generation of hydroxyl radicals, and the solubility of the target impurity, among other factors that contribute to the effectiveness of the UV/H_2O_2 oxidation process. Studies have shown that the ideal temperature for tannery fluids can vary from 30 to 70 °C to eliminate organic contaminants. Generally, higher temperatures favor quicker reactions but can also result in the peroxide degrading itself [31]; similar values were found in this study. Another factor that can affect the efficiency of the UV peroxide oxidation process is the concentration of contaminants in the tannery effluent. Chen et al. [32] revealed that greater starting COD concentrations resulted in a slower removal rate for organic pollutants from tannery effluent by UV/peroxide oxidation; this aspect may account for the removal findings attained in our investigation.

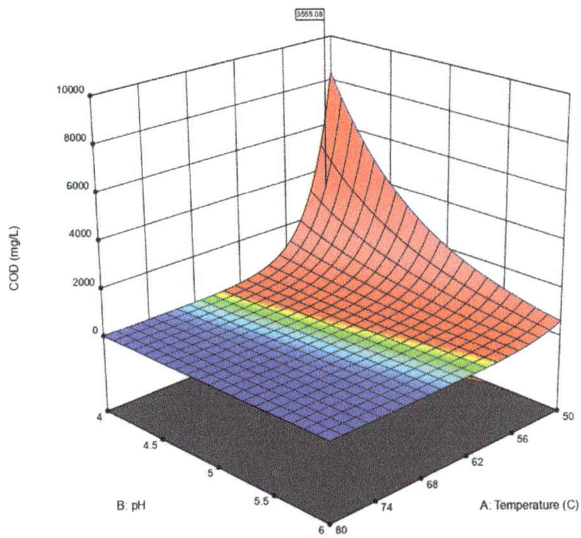

Figure 2. Response Surface Graphical for COD removal. Red color show high COD removal, while blue color shows low COD removal.

3.3. *Nitrification*

The results of the ANOVA analysis on nitrification (Table 5) using the UV/H_2O_2 system show that the model F-value of 8.65 is significant; there is only a 0.01% chance that such a large F-value is due to noise. *p*-values less than 0.0500 indicate that the model terms are significant. In this case, pH is the significant variable in the model; the remaining variables evaluated are not significant as they obtained values greater than 0.1000. Finally, the F-value of 0.53 implies that the lack of fit is not significant concerning the pure error; there is an 89.49% chance that such a large F-value of lack of fit is due to noise.

Table 5. ANOVA analysis of 2-level I-optimal Response Surface design for Nitrification.

Source	Sum of Squares	Df	Mean Square	F-Value	*p*-Value	
Model	158.33	5	31.67	8.65	<0.0001	significant
A-Temperature	1.77	1	1.77	0.4825	0.4921	
B-pH	119.48	1	119.48	32.63	<0.0001	
C-Hydrogen Peroxide	6.22	1	6.22	1.70	0.2014	
D-pW	15.91	2	7.95	2.17	0.1300	
Residual	120.84	33	3.66			
Lack of Fit	40.18	16	2.51	0.5293	0.8949	not significant
Pure Error	80.66	17	4.74			
Cor Total	279.17	38				

Figure 3 shows the response surface analysis of the interaction between pH and temperature on nitrate generation. Nitrification is a crucial step in wastewater treatment [11]; pH and temperature can significantly impact the efficiency of the nitrification process in a UV/H_2O_2 system. The pH affects the availability of hydroxyl radicals, which are the vital oxidizing species in the process. Singh et al. [33] reported that at low pH values (lower than 3.5), the concentration of hydroxyl radicals could decrease, resulting in lower nitrification rates; similarly, at higher pH values (higher than 9.5), the concentration of hydroxyl radicals is also reduced due to the formation of peroxide radicals, which are less reactive than hydroxyl radicals. Similarly, it was pointed out that at an initial pH above 9, photo-oxidation converts ammonium to NO_2 and NO_3, and it is also possible that at a pH above 9 and in the presence of UV, photoreduction of NO_3 to NO_2 occurs. The inability of natural waters to convert NO_3 to NO_2 by UV photolysis may be due to the rates of NO_2 photo-oxidation being significantly quicker in the presence of H_2O_2 than those of NO photo-oxidation, NO_3 photoreduction, and NO_2 photo-oxidation in the absence of H_2O_2 [34], a situation demonstrated in this study. In this work, the optimal pH range was found to be 4.5–5.8. Temperature is another critical factor affecting the nitrification process in the UV/H_2O_2 system [26]; the reaction rate usually increases with increasing temperature, up to a certain point, after which it starts to decrease; it has been reported that the optimum temperature range for the UV/peroxide nitrification process is between 35 °C and 60 °C for tannery wastewater [13], similar to those found in this study; at room temperature or below 35 °C the reaction rate decreases, requiring thermal boosting, while at higher temperatures (above 80 °C), the reaction rate decreases due to OH* recombination, and the scavenging effect (OH* acts as an antioxidant) dominates over the thermal decomposition of H_2O_2 present in tannery waste effluents [30].

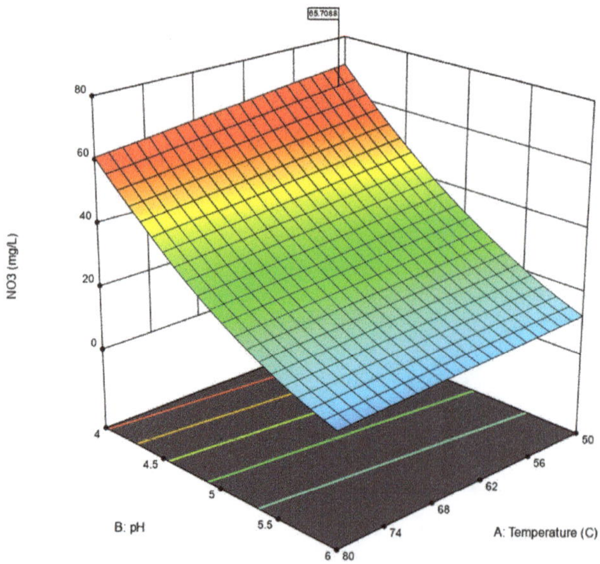

Figure 3. Surface response of the interaction between pH and hydrogen peroxide concentration. Red shows high NO_3 content, while blue shows low content.

3.4. Optimization and Validation of UV/H_2O_2 Operating Conditions

To optimize the operational variables, a new experimental design was developed based on the findings of the previous experimental design, and an ANOVA analysis was developed with a 2-stage I-optimal response surface design (Table 6).

Table 6. 2-level I-optimal response surface design.

Factor	Parameter	Units	Minimum	Maximum
A	H_2O_2	M	0.2000	0.8000
B	Lamp Power	W	30.00	60.00
C	pH		4.50	7.50
D	Temperature	°C	50.00	80.00

Table 7 shows the result of the ANOVA design for the removal of COD, the conditions were volume: 300 mL, reaction time 1 h, stirring 550 rpm, and the lamps were UVC 254 nm.

Table 7. ANOVA Results of COD removal.

Source	Sum of Squares	Df	Mean Square	F-Value	*p*-Value	
Model	1428.27	14	102.02	19.12	<0.0001	significant
A-H_2O_2	98.85	1	98.85	18.52	0.0016	
B-Lamp Power	642.49	1	642.49	120.40	<0.0001	
C-pH	62.48	1	62.48	11.71	0.0065	
D-Temperature	51.80	1	51.80	9.71	0.0110	
AB	10.53	1	10.53	1.97	0.1904	
AC	10.91	1	10.91	2.04	0.1832	
AD	0.2993	1	0.2993	0.0561	0.8176	
BC	14.75	1	14.75	2.76	0.1274	
BD	17.68	1	17.68	3.31	0.0988	
CD	5.26	1	5.26	0.9864	0.3441	
A^2	15.26	1	15.26	2.86	0.1218	
B^2	165.37	1	165.37	30.99	0.0002	
C^2	106.68	1	106.68	19.99	0.0012	
D^2	8.14	1	8.14	1.52	0.2451	
Residual	53.36	10	5.34			
Lack of Fit	31.86	5	6.37	1.48	0.3383	not significant
Pure Error	21.50	5	4.30			
Cor Total	1481.63	24				

As for the removal of COD, the model results show that it is significant, as the F value of the model is 19.12. There is only a 0.01% chance that such a large F value is due to noise. *p*-values of less than 0.0500 indicate that the model terms are significant. In this case, the linear behaviors of H_2O_2, lamp power, pH, and temperature are not significant. Similarly, the quadratic behaviors of lamp power and pH are also significant. Values above 0.1000 indicate that the model terms are not necessary. The F-value for the lack of fit of 1.48 means that the lack of fit is not significant relative to the pure error. There is a 33.83% chance that such a large F-value for lack of fit is due to noise.

Table 8 shows the result of the ANOVA design for nitrate formation; the conditions were: volume 300 mL, reaction time (1 h), stirring 550 rpm, and the lamps were UVC 254 nm.

The model's F-value of 80.79 indicates that the model is significant; there is only a 0.01% chance that such a large F-value is due to noise. *p*-values less than 0.0500 indicate that the model terms are significant. In this case, the variables with linear behavior: H_2O_2, lamp power, pH, and temperature are significant; likewise, the linear interactions of H_2O_2—lamp power, lamp power—temperature, pH-temperature, as well as the quadratic behavior of lamp power, pH and temperature are significant terms in the model. The F-value for the lack of fit of 4.13 implies a probability of 7.28% that such a significant F-value is due to noise.

Table 8. ANOVA Results for nitrification.

Source	Sum of Squares	Df	Mean Square	F-Value	*p*-Value	
Model	5457.47	14	389.82	80.79	<0.0001	significant
A-H_2O_2	327.04	1	327.04	67.78	<0.0001	
B-Lamp Power	2380.42	1	2380.42	493.36	<0.0001	
C-pH	123.41	1	123.41	25.58	0.0005	
D-Temperature	298.50	1	298.50	61.87	<0.0001	
AB	107.82	1	107.82	22.35	0.0008	
AC	12.03	1	12.03	2.49	0.1454	
AD	2.96	1	2.96	0.6126	0.4520	
BC	23.82	1	23.82	4.94	0.0505	
BD	32.10	1	32.10	6.65	0.0275	
CD	113.57	1	113.57	23.54	0.0007	
A^2	1.65	1	1.65	0.3418	0.5717	
B^2	706.58	1	706.58	146.44	<0.0001	
C^2	172.05	1	172.05	35.66	0.0001	
D^2	88.53	1	88.53	18.35	0.0016	
Residual	48.25	10	4.82			
Lack of Fit	38.85	5	7.77	4.13	0.0728	not significant
Pure Error	9.40	5	1.88			
Cor Total	5505.72	24				

Figure 4 shows the response surface plots for COD removal and nitrate formation (nitrification). Treatment of tannery effluent is a complex process and may require combining multiple treatment techniques to achieve effective contaminant removal [12]. According to the study's experimental methodology, various parameters affect how well the UV/H_2O_2 process removes COD. (Figure 4a). The H_2O_2 concentration, the temperature, the pH of the process, the UV radiation applied, and the contact time between the wastewater and the light are variables that need to be optimized for each type of tannery wastewater [31]. The amount of organic pollutants in the effluent, including phenols, aromatics, dyes, and other organic compounds, may increase competition for the hydroxyl radicals produced by the UV/H_2O_2 process, which could lower the effectiveness of pollutant removal because some organic pollutants might not receive enough -OH radicals for oxidation [30]. The major source of OH* formation is H_2O_2, hence the higher the COD concentration, the more peroxide must be used; however, too much H_2O_2 contributes to effluent COD since any remaining H_2O_2 acts as an OH* scavenger, which reduces the effectiveness of COD removal [1]. UV light intensity also affects the UV/H_2O_2 reaction to decolorize dyes in tannery effluents. It has been reported that decolorization efficiency is very low when only H_2O_2 without UV is used, and that the use of UV light causes degradation of the pollutants but requires too long exposure times; the rates of dyeing and degradation of the pollutants increase with increasing lamp intensity, with pseudo-first order reaction rates occurring in relation to UV power [35]; However, the disadvantage of the UV/H_2O_2 process is the low absorption of H_2O_2 in the UV range, so the amount of UV radiation is reduced. In this study, it was discovered that both the degradation rate of COD and the oxidation of ammonium to nitrate increased with increasing lamp power, which is explained by the fact that theoretically higher pollutant discoloration and oxidation rates occur at higher UV powers due to the faster formation of free radicals and also depend on the initial conditions [36]. Concerning the photo-oxidation of ammonium to nitrate, it has been pointed out that an optimal concentration of H_2O_2 is required to achieve effective photo-oxidation [12]. There have been no reports demonstrating direct photolysis of NH_3/NH_4 to NO_3 by UV254nm, thus requiring the addition of H_2O_2; in this study, the low concentrations of H_2O_2 were found to have a better effect on the photo-oxidation of nitrogen compounds to nitrate than high concentrations. It has been reported that high concentrations of H_2O_2 do not always increase the photo-oxidation of ammonium to nitrate because UV and OH can rapidly degrade H_2O_2. High amounts of H_2O_2 may be ineffective for the photo-oxidation of ammonium and increase COD concentrations in wastewater [34].

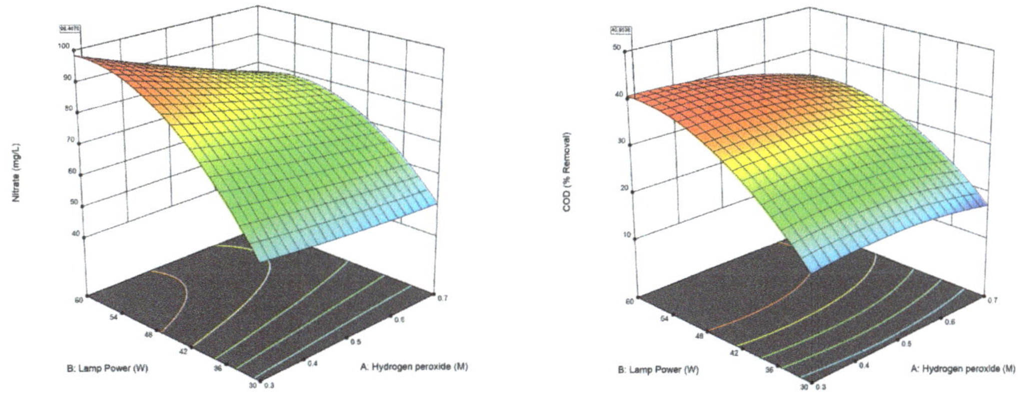

(a) (b)

Figure 4. Surface response of optimization and validation of UV/H_2O_2 operating conditions (**a**) nitrate formation. (**b**) COD removal. Red color shows high removal, while blue color shows low removal.

The findings from the response surface and experimental design in this study enabled the identification of the variables needed to validate the process conditions. Temperature, pH, and pW values were 65.5 0.2 °C, 5.5 0.1, and 0.3 M, respectively, of peroxide. Experiments were repeated 10 times to verify these conditions. The results were analyzed using a One-sample t-test on GraphPad Prism software version 10.1.0 for Mac (GraphPad Software, Boston, MA, USA). Figure 5 shows the results of the verification of the optimal conditions. In the case of DOC, there are no significant differences between the observed and expected values. In contrast, in the case of nitrates, there are significant differences between the experimentally determined value and the expected value, although the predicted value was higher.

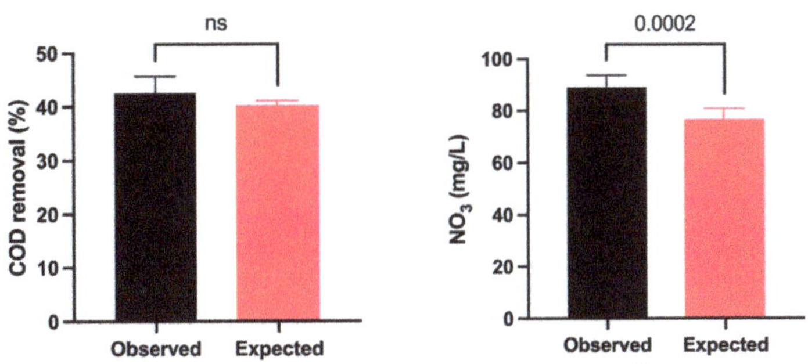

(a) (b)

Figure 5. The One sample *t*-test between predicted and expected results of (**a**) COD removal and (**b**) nitrate generation.

Figure 6 shows the removal percentages achieved using the optimum values with the UV/H_2O_2 process. Most of the pollutant parameters evaluated had removal rates above 70%; COD achieved a removal rate of 44.5%, BOD 67.4%, chromium 92.3%, and color 48%.

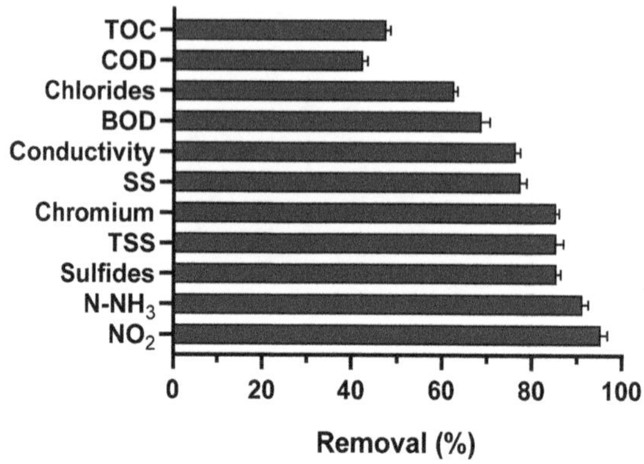

Figure 6. Removal of contaminants. Process conditions: reaction time: 60 min., temperature: 52.5 ± 0.2 °C, pH: 4.2 ± 0.1, and pW: 60.

In a UV/peroxide process, the removal of COD and BOD occurs through a combination of oxidation and biodegradation processes. The hydroxyl radicals produced by the UV/peroxide reaction attack and oxidize the organic pollutants, breaking them down into simpler, biodegradable compounds [37], yielding an effluent that microorganisms can potentially use as the pollutant load has decreased to a level where biodegradation processes can occur, further reducing the pollutant load [38]. Table 9 shows the removal percentages achieved in this research compared to other AOPs used for tannery water treatment.

Table 9. Pollutant removal rates of the UV/H_2O_2 process compared to other AOPs.

Parameters (% Removal)	This Research (UV/H_2O_2)	[39]	[40]	[41]		[19]	
				UV/H_2O_2	$TiO_2/H_2O_2/UV$	FENTON	UV/H_2O_2
COD	43.34 ± 1.04	64.3	30.2	18.8	68.3	63.06	45.2
TOC	46.5 ± 0.67	n.r	n.r	n.r	n.r	60	57.7
BOD	68.65 ± 1.35	n.r	30.2	n.r	n.r	52.5	46.18
Color	43.4 ± 0.16	56	n.r	67.36	91.5	n.r	
$N\text{-}NH_3$	77.5 ± 0.28	16.45	n.r	78.8	90.7	12	0.5
Cr	85.23 ± 0.78	68.02	65.7	n.r	n.r	n.r	n.r
TSS	83.5 ± 1.55	9.21	49	n.r	n.r	n.r	n.r
Chlorides	62.5 ± 0.84	n.r	43	n.r	n.r	n.r	n.r

n.r.: no register.

According to studies, COD and BOD removal rates typically range from 40 to 80%. In this study, COD and color removal results were relatively lower than those of Saranya et al. [39], while removal rates for Cr, $N\text{-}NH_3$, and TSS were lower than those attained in this study; [40] applied a $UV//H_2O_2$ process in the fluxes of a tannery and found COD removals of 18.8%, BOD 30.2%, TSS 49%, Cr 65.7%, and chlorides 43%, which were lower than those reported in this study; nevertheless, color removal was greater compared to that achieved in this research; [41] reported the implementation of two AOPs (UV/H_2O_2 and $TiO_2/H_2O_2/UV$) in which they evaluated the removal of COD, color, and $N\text{-}NH_3$ showing removals of 18.8%, 67.36%, and 78.8%, respectively, for the UV/H_2O_2 process and 68.3% for COD, 91.5% for color and 90.7% for $N\text{-}NH_3$ in the $TiO_2//H_2O_2/UV$ system, it can be seen that comparing the results with this study, the $UV//H_2O_2$ process obtained lower efficiencies while the TiO_2 mediated system obtained removals above the system evaluated in this study. Finally, Schrank et al. [19] examined the removal rates of a Fenton system with a UV/H_2O_2 photocatalytic system and discovered that the Fenton system performs better. However, there are not many noticeable changes between them. When comparing those results to the ones from this study, it was also discovered that the Fenton system performs marginally better in terms of COD and TOC removal, whereas the UV/H_2O_2 system in this study performed marginally better in terms of BOD removal. Although systems such as Fenton or photo-Fenton can have removals above the range established in this research, the results reported in the literature for various AOPs for the treatment of tannery wastewater clearly show that the photocatalytic system implemented in this research is within the established ranges for the removal of different pollutants, given the expense of employing reagents and other equipment, the UV/peroxide system has a lower energy cost than Fenton, ozone, and photo-Fenton [8,42]. The concentration of the pollutant load and the physicochemical characteristics of the wastewater determine the clearance rate [43]. As observed in this study, chlorides can also be removed by the UV/peroxide system. This process can occur because chlorides can react with -OH to form hypochlorous acid (HOCl) and hydrochloric acid (HCl), which are subsequently oxidized to chloride ions and water [44]. Concerning chromium, removal in a UV/peroxide system can be achieved by oxidation followed by precipitation. Chromium in wastewater can exist in various oxidation states, with hexavalent chromium (Cr (VI)) being the most toxic. -OH, can oxidize Cr (VI) to trivalent chromium (Cr (III)), which can then precipitate as hydroxide or oxide salts [45].

4. Conclusions

A UV peroxide system can effectively remove various pollutants from wastewater, including organic pollutants, COD, BOD, chlorides, chromium and ammonium. The removal efficiency of each pollutant depends on several factors, such as the initial concentration of the pollutant, the pH of the system, and the amount of H_2O_2 used. According to this study, the degradation process is influenced by the pH, temperature, and UV radiation intensity, and their optimization results in faster degradation rates. The application of a catalyst can increase removal rates; integrating bicarbonate or carbonate in the UV/peroxide system as a catalyst can be a promising strategy to improve the removal times, removal efficiency, and oxidation rates of the organic compounds. However, it is necessary to investigate additional strategies to improve the removal of COD and TOC using the photocatalytic process examined in this work. The results of the final physicochemical properties allow evaluation of the potential of the UV/peroxide system's integration with the cultivation of microalgae and cyanobacteria as a culture medium and as a source of biomass with industrially relevant metabolites that would allow development of a sustainable strategy for the implementation of these treatments for the tanning industry in the future.

Author Contributions: Conceptualization, F.M.-M. and A.Z.; Data curation, A.F.B.-S., J.B.G.-M., N.A.U.-S., G.L.L.-B. and A.Z.; Funding acquisition, F.M.-M.; Investigation, N.A.U.-S.; Resources, A.F.B.-S. and F.M.-M.; Software, N.A.U.-S., J.B.G.-M. and A.Z.; Supervision, A.F.B.-S., F.M.-M. and A.Z.; Writing—original draft, N.A.U.-S.; Writing—review and editing, A.F.B.-S., F.M.-M., J.B.G.-M. and A.Z. All authors have read and agreed to the published version of the manuscript.

Funding: This research was supported by Universidad del Valle (Colombia) with the project "Evaluation of a coupled system for advanced oxidation of industrial effluents and production of microalgae to obtain high value-added metabolites. ID CI 21144", Newton Fund Institutional Links, ID 527624805. FINU projects 016 and 017, and Sapienza University for Academic Mid Projects 2021 n. RM12117A8B58023A.

Institutional Review Board Statement: Not applicable.

Informed Consent Statement: Not applicable.

Data Availability Statement: Not applicable.

Acknowledgments: We would like to express our sincere gratitude to Universidad del Valle, Universidad Francisco de Paula Santander, and Sapienza University of Rome for the equipment for this research.

Conflicts of Interest: The authors declare no conflict of interest.

References

1. Sivagami, K.; Sakthivel, K.P.; Nambi, I.M. Advanced Oxidation Processes for the Treatment of Tannery Wastewater. *J. Environ. Chem. Eng.* **2018**, *6*, 3656–3663. [CrossRef]
2. Urbina-Suarez, N.A.; Machuca-Martínez, F.; Barajas-Solano, A.F. Advanced Oxidation Processes and Biotechnological Alternatives for the Treatment of Tannery Wastewater. *Molecules* **2021**, *26*, 3222. [CrossRef]
3. Hansen, É.; de Aquim, P.M.; Hansen, A.W.; Cardoso, J.K.; Ziulkoski, A.L.; Gutterres, M. Impact of Post-Tanning Chemicals on the Pollution Load of Tannery Wastewater. *J. Environ. Manag.* **2020**, *269*, 110787. [CrossRef]
4. Chhikara, S.; Hooda, A.; Rana, L.; Dhankhar, R. Chromium (VI) Biosorption by Immobilized Aspergillus Niger in Continuous Flow System with Special Reference to FTIR Analysis. *J. Environ. Biol.* **2010**, *31*, 561–566.
5. Daneshvar, E.; Zarrinmehr, M.J.; Kousha, M.; Hashtjin, A.M.; Saratale, G.D.; Maiti, A.; Vithanage, M.; Bhatnagar, A. Hexavalent Chromium Removal from Water by Microalgal-Based Materials: Adsorption, Desorption and Recovery Studies. *Bioresour. Technol.* **2019**, *293*, 122064. [CrossRef]
6. Zhao, J.; Wu, Q.; Tang, Y.; Zhou, J.; Guo, H. Tannery Wastewater Treatment: Conventional and Promising Processes, an Updated 20-Year Review. *J. Leather Sci. Eng.* **2022**, *4*, 1–22. [CrossRef]
7. Achouri, O.; Panico, A.; Bencheikh-Lehocine, M.; Derbal, K.; Pirozzi, F. Effect of Chemical Coagulation Pretreatment on Anaerobic Digestion of Tannery Wastewater. *J. Environ. Eng.* **2017**, *143*, 04017039. [CrossRef]
8. Lofrano, G.; Meriç, S.; Zengin, G.E.; Orhon, D. Chemical and Biological Treatment Technologies for Leather Tannery Chemicals and Wastewaters: A Review. *Sci. Total. Environ.* **2013**, *461–462*, 265–281. [CrossRef]
9. Urbina-Suarez, N.A.; Ayala-González, D.D.; Rivera-Amaya, J.D.; Barajas-Solano, A.F.; Machuca-Martínez, F. Evaluation of the Light/Dark Cycle and Concentration of Tannery Wastewater in the Production of Biomass and Metabolites of Industrial Interest from Microalgae and Cyanobacteria. *Water* **2022**, *14*, 346. [CrossRef]
10. Haydar, S.; Aziz, J.; Saeed, M. Biological Treatment of Tannery Wastewater Using Activated Sludge Process. *Pak. J. Eng. Appl. Sci.* **2007**, *1*, 61–66.
11. GracePavithra, K.; Jaikumar, V.; Kumar, P.S.; Sundar Rajan, P.S. A Review on Cleaner Strategies for Chromium Industrial Wastewater: Present Research and Future Perspective. *J. Clean. Prod.* **2019**, *228*, 580–593. [CrossRef]
12. Urbina-Suarez, N.A.; Rivera-Caicedo, C.; González-Delgado, D.; Barajas-Solano, A.F.; Machuca-Martínez, F. Bicarbonate-Hydrogen Peroxide System for Treating Dyeing Wastewater: Degradation of Organic Pollutants and Color Removal. *Toxics* **2023**, *11*, 366. [CrossRef]
13. Korpe, S.A.; Landge, V.; Hakke, V.S.; Rao, P.V.; Sonawane, S.H.; Sonawane, S.S. Advanced Oxidation Processes for Tannery Industry Wastewater Treatment. In *Novel Approaches towards Wastewater Treatment and Resource Recovery Technologies*; Elsevier: Amsterdam, The Netherlands, 2022; pp. 253–276. [CrossRef]
14. Jessieleena, A.A.; Priyanka, M.; Saravanakumar, M.P. Comparative Study of Fenton, Fe^{2+}/NaOCl and $Fe^{2+}/(NH_4)_2S_2O_8$ on Tannery Sludge Dewaterability, Degradability of Organics and Leachability of Chromium. *J. Hazard. Mater.* **2021**, *402*, 123495. [CrossRef] [PubMed]
15. Borba, F.H.; Pellenz, L.; Bueno, F.; Inticher, J.J.; Braun, L.; Espinoza-Quiñones, F.R.; Trigueros, D.E.G.; de Pauli, A.R.; Módenes, A.N. Pollutant Removal and Biodegradation Assessment of Tannery Effluent Treated by Conventional Fenton Oxidation Process. *J. Environ. Chem. Eng.* **2018**, *6*, 7070–7079. [CrossRef]
16. Di Iaconi, C. Biological Treatment and Ozone Oxidation: Integration or Coupling? *Bioresour. Technol.* **2012**, *106*, 63–68. [CrossRef]
17. Arslan-Alaton, I.; Gurses, F. Photo-Fenton-like and Photo-Fenton-like Oxidation of Procaine Penicillin G Formulation Effluent. *J. Photochem. Photobiol. A Chem.* **2004**, *165*, 165–175. [CrossRef]
18. Vaiano, V.; Iervolino, G. Facile Method to Immobilize ZnO Particles on Glass Spheres for the Photocatalytic Treatment of Tannery Wastewater. *J. Colloid Interface Sci.* **2018**, *518*, 192–199. [CrossRef]
19. Schrank, S.G.; José, H.J.; Moreira, R.F.P.M.; Schröder, H.F. Applicability of Fenton and H_2O_2/UV Reactions in the Treatment of Tannery Wastewaters. *Chemosphere* **2005**, *60*, 644–655. [CrossRef]
20. Souza, E.A.; Cerqueira, U.M.; Silva, L.A. Comparative Study of Various Advanced Oxidation Processes for the Treatment of Tannery Wastewater. *Desalination Water Treat.* **2020**, *181*, 88–97. [CrossRef]
21. Li, R.; Li, T.; Zhou, Q. Impact of Titanium Dioxide (TiO_2) Modification on Its Application to Pollution Treatment—A Review. *Catalysts* **2020**, *10*, 804. [CrossRef]
22. Assémian, A.S.; Kouassi, K.E.; Drogui, P.; Adouby, K.; Boa, D. Removal of a Persistent Dye in Aqueous Solutions by Electrocoagulation Process: Modeling and Optimization Through Response Surface Methodology. *Water Air Soil Pollut.* **2018**, *229*, 1–13. [CrossRef]

23. Gomes, A.I.; Soares, T.F.; Silva, T.F.C.V.; Boaventura, R.A.R.; Vilar, V.J.P. Ozone-Driven Processes for mature Urban Landfill Leachate Treatment: Organic Matter Degradation, Biodegradability Enhancement and Treatment Costs for Different Reactors Configuration. *Sci. Total. Environ.* **2020**, *724*, 138083. [CrossRef]
24. Rosales, A.G.; Rodríguez, C.D.; Ballen-Segura, M. Remoción de Contaminantes y Crecimiento Del Alga *Scenedesmus* Sp. En Aguas Residuales de Curtiembres, Comparación Entre Células Libres e Inmovilizadas. *Ing. Y Cienc.* **2018**, *14*, 11–34. [CrossRef]
25. Zhou, L.; Zhang, W.; De Costa, Y.G.; Zhuang, W.-Q.; Yi, S. Assessing Inorganic Components of Cake Layer in A/O Membrane Bioreactor for Physical-Chemical Treated Tannery Effluent. *Chemosphere* **2020**, *250*, 126220. [CrossRef]
26. Urbina-Suarez, N.A.; Barajas-Solano, A.F.; Zuorro, A.; Machuca, F. Advanced Oxidation Processes with Uv-H_2O_2 for Nitrification and Decolorization of Dyehouse Wastewater. *Chem. Eng. Trans.* **2022**, *95*, 235–240. [CrossRef]
27. Tolkou, A.K.; Katsoyiannis, I.A.; Zouboulis, A.I. Removal of Arsenic, Chromium and Uranium from Water Sources by Novel Nanostructured Materials Including Graphene-Based Modified Adsorbents: A Mini Review of Recent Developments. *Appl. Sci.* **2020**, *10*, 3241. [CrossRef]
28. Selvan, S.T.; Velramar, B.; Ramamurthy, D.; Balasundaram, S.; Sivamani, K. Pilot Scale Wastewater Treatment, CO_2 Sequestration and Lipid Production Using Microalga, *Neochloris aquatica* RDS02. *Int. J. Phytoremed.* **2020**, *22*, 1462–1479. [CrossRef]
29. Katsoyiannis, I.A.; Xanthopoulou, M.; Zouboulis, A.I. Cr(VI) Femoval from Ground Waters by Ferrous Iron Redox-Assisted Coagulation in a Continuous Treatment Unit Comprising a Plug Flow Pipe Reactor and Downflow Sand Filtration. *Appl. Sci.* **2020**, *10*, 802. [CrossRef]
30. Korpe, S.; Rao, P.V. Application of Advanced Oxidation Processes and Cavitation Techniques for Treatment of Tannery Wastewater—A Review. *J. Environ. Chem. Eng.* **2021**, *9*, 105234. [CrossRef]
31. Iqbal, M.; Muneer, M.; Hussain, S.; Parveen, B.; Javed, M.; Rehman, H.; Waqas, M.; Abid, M.A. Using Combined UV and H_2O_2 Treatments to Reduce Tannery Wastewater Pollution Load. *Pol. J. Environ. Stud.* **2019**, *28*, 3207–3213. [CrossRef]
32. Guan, Y.-H.; Chen, J.; Chen, L.-J.; Jiang, X.-X.; Fu, Q. Comparison of UV/H_2O_2, UV/PMS, and UV/PDS in Destruction of Different Reactivity Compounds and Formation of Bromate and Chlorate. *Front. Chem.* **2020**, *8*, 581198. [CrossRef]
33. Goutam, S.P.; Saxena, G.; Singh, V.; Yadav, A.K.; Bharagava, R.N.; Thapa, K.B. Green Synthesis of TiO_2 Nanoparticles Using Leaf Extract of *Jatropha curcas* L. for Photocatalytic Degradation of Tannery Wastewater. *Chem. Eng. J.* **2018**, *336*, 386–396. [CrossRef]
34. Wang, J.; Song, M.; Chen, B.; Wang, L.; Zhu, R. Effects of pH and H_2O_2 on Ammonia, Nitrite, and Nitrate Transformations during UV254nm Irradiation: Implications to Nitrogen Removal and Analysis. *Chemosphere* **2017**, *184*, 1003–1011. [CrossRef]
35. Shu, H.-Y.; Chang, M.-C. Decolorization and Mineralization of a Phthalocyanine dye C.I. Direct Blue 199 Using UV/H_2O_2 Process. *J. Hazard. Mater.* **2005**, *125*, 96–101. [CrossRef] [PubMed]
36. Rajagopal, S.; Paramasivam, B.; Muniyasamy, K. Photocatalytic Removal of Cationic and Anionic Dyes in the Textile Wastewater by H_2O_2 Assisted TiO_2 and Micro-Cellulose Composites. *Sep. Purif. Technol.* **2020**, *252*, 117444. [CrossRef]
37. Farzanehsa, M.; Vaughan, L.C.; Zamyadi, A.; Khan, S.J. Comparison of UV-Cl and UV-H_2O_2 Advanced Oxidation Processes in the Degradation of Contaminants from Water and Wastewater: A Review. *Water Environ. J.* **2023**, *37*, 1–11. [CrossRef]
38. Nidheesh, P.V.; Couras, C.; Karim, A.V.; Nadais, H. A Review of Integrated Advanced Oxidation Processes and Biological Processes for Organic Pollutant Removal. *Chem. Eng. Commun.* **2021**, *209*, 390–432. [CrossRef]
39. Saranya, D.; Shanthakumar, S. An Integrated Approach for Tannery Effluent Treatment with Ozonation and Phycoremediation: A Feasibility Study. *Environ. Res.* **2020**, *183*, 109163. [CrossRef]
40. Hussain, Z.; Arslan, M.; Shabir, G.; Malik, M.H.; Mohsin, M.; Iqbal, S.; Afzal, M. Remediation of Textile Bleaching Effluent by Bacterial Augmented Horizontal Flow and Vertical Flow Constructed Wetlands: A Comparison at Pilot Scale. *Sci. Total. Environ.* **2019**, *685*, 370–379. [CrossRef] [PubMed]
41. Sauer, T.P.; Casaril, L.; Oberziner, A.L.B.; José, H.J.; Moreira, R.d.F.P.M. Advanced Oxidation Processes Applied to Tannery Wastewater Containing Direct Black 38—Elimination and Degradation Kinetics. *J. Hazard. Mater.* **2006**, *135*, 274–279. [CrossRef] [PubMed]
42. Mahamuni, N.N.; Adewuyi, Y.G. Advanced Oxidation Processes (AOPs) Involving Ultrasound for Waste Water Treatment: A Review with Emphasis on Cost Estimation. *Ultrason. Sonochem.* **2010**, *17*, 990–1003. [CrossRef]
43. Saravanathamizhan, R.; Perarasu, V.R.; Dhandapani, B. Advanced Oxidation Process for Effluent Treatment in Textile, Pharmaceutical, and Tannery Industries. In *Photocatalytic Degradation of Dyes: Current Trends and Future Perspectives*; Elsevier: Amsterdam, The Netherlands, 2021; pp. 719–745. [CrossRef]
44. Khuzwayo, Z.; Chirwa, E.M.N. Analysis of Catalyst Photo-Oxidation Selectivity in the Degradation of Polyorganochlorinated Pollutants in Batch Systems Using UV and UV/TiO_2. *S. Afr. J. Chem. Eng.* **2017**, *23*, 17–25. [CrossRef]
45. Josué, T.G.; Almeida, L.N.B.; Lopes, M.F.; Santos, O.A.A.; Lenzi, G.G. Cr (VI) Reduction by Photocatalyic Process: Nb_2O_5 an Alternative Catalyst. *J. Environ. Manag.* **2020**, *268*, 110711. [CrossRef]

Sci

MDPI

Article

Synergistic Degradation of Organic Contaminants in Landfill Leachates Using Catalytic Ozonation with Magnetite

Dorance Becerra-Moreno [1,2,*], Fiderman Machuca-Martínez [3], Luisa F. Ramírez-Rios [4], Janet B. García-Martínez [1] and Andrés F. Barajas-Solano [1,*]

1 Department of Environmental Sciences, Universidad Francisco de Paula Santander, Av. Gran Colombia No. 12E-96, Cúcuta 540003, Colombia; janetbibianagm@ufps.edu.co
2 School of Natural Resources and Environment, Universidad del Valle, Ciudad Universitaria Meléndez, Calle 13 # 100-00, Cali 760015, Colombia
3 Center of Excellence in New Materials—CENM, School of Chemical Engineering, Universidad del Valle, Ciudad Universitaria Meléndez, Calle 13 # 100-00, Cali 760015, Colombia; fiderman.machuca@correounivalle.edu.co
4 School of Engineering, Universidad De Los Llanos, km 12, Vda. Barcelona, Villavicencio 500003, Colombia; lfernandaramirez@unillanos.edu.co
* Correspondence: dorancebm@ufps.edu.co (D.B.-M.); andresfernandobs@ufps.edu.co (A.F.B.-S.)

Abstract: This study evaluated the efficiency of catalytic ozonation with magnetite (Fe_3O_4) in degrading recalcitrant organic compounds in leachates from two sanitary landfills in Colombia. The optimum treatment conditions were also analyzed by means of a response surface design, resulting in 6 g O_3/h, 2.5 g/L Fe_3O_4, and pH 9, which resulted in COD removal rates of 85.3% in El Guayabal and 75.8% in La Madera. Moreover, the BOD_5/COD ratio increased from 0.26 to 0.38 and from 0.23 to 0.32, respectively, suggesting increased effluent biodegradability. The most efficient ozone consumption (2.7 g O_3 per gram of COD removed) was obtained under alkaline conditions with a high catalyst concentration. Magnetite demonstrated structural stability, although its catalytic efficiency progressively decreased after three cycles of use, with COD removal decreasing from 85.3% to 73.6%. These findings validate catalytic ozonation with magnetite as an efficient alternative for advanced leachate treatment, with the potential to optimize contaminant removal in industrial effluents and strengthen environmental remediation strategies.

Keywords: catalytic ozonation; magnetite (Fe_3O_4); leachates; contaminant degradation

1. Introduction

A challenging problem in the management of urban solid waste is represented by leachates generated in sanitary landfills, which have heterogeneous compositions and high recalcitrant contaminant loads. Their chemical complexity—compounded by heavy metals, difficultly degrading organic matter, and emerging pollutants—has underscored the shortcomings of conventional treatment methods. Although such processes are based on biological or physicochemical strategies, they are limited to certain efficiencies, and they often do not comply with more stringent environmental regulations [1]. This has, in turn, put more pressure on the development of feasible solutions that promote the development of new technologies for optimizing contaminant removal and for making any process sustainable.

In this context, significant knowledge concerning the degradation of recalcitrant compounds has been obtained via advanced oxidation processes (AOPs). Among them, catalytic ozonation has proven to be a promising option, as it synergistically improves the oxidizing ability of ozone through contact with selective catalytic materials [2]. This method aids in the conversion of difficult organic materials to biodegradable intermediates, greatly increasing the overall treatment efficiency [3]. Moreover, its use has been confirmed in multiple contexts, enabling deployment within different operating states and guaranteeing performance in practical systems [4].

One of the most studied and efficient catalysts in this process is magnetite (Fe_3O_4), which promotes the decomposition of ozone into hydroxyl radicals—highly reactive species that play a key role in the oxidation of hard-to-degrade organic contaminants [5]. In addition to its structural stability, its physicochemical properties make it a valuable tool for the effective removal of contaminants from leachates. Furthermore, its active surface serves as an efficient adsorption site, improving reaction kinetics and maximizing process efficiency [3]. Recent research has shown that magnetite can enhance organic matter removal efficiency when combined with other catalysts, such as iron nanoparticles and cerium compounds, expanding the possibilities for process optimization [6]. Moreover, doping magnetite with transition metals has been found to improve its catalytic activity and material stability [7]. The combination of these catalysts enhances process efficiency by increasing reaction rates and reducing the formation of undesirable byproducts.

Catalytic ozonation for leachate treatment is a new advancing topic. Multiple studies have confirmed that this approach not only facilitates the degradation of stubborn contaminants but also increases the biodegradability of the leachate after treatment. The process proved to be highly efficient for the removal of persistent organic compounds when it was coupled with electrocoagulation and adsorption, as demonstrated by recent research. [8]. In a related study, hybrid processes such as synergizing catalytic ozonation with membrane bioreactors (MBRs) have exhibited great potential for the removal of toxic constituents and also effectively lead to great reductions of chemical oxygen demand (COD) for optimal remediation levels [9]. Another promising approach has been the use of advanced catalysts, such as magnetite doped with transition metals, which has improved the efficiency of converting ozone into hydroxyl radicals while minimizing the formation of undesirable secondary byproducts. Research has reported that incorporating materials such as manganese ferrite ($MnFe_2O_4$) and Fe-N_4 nano-catalysts within carbon structures yields enhanced long-term stability and catalytic activity, facilitating their application under more demanding operational conditions [2]. Likewise, the inclusion of EDTA-Fe-based complexes has enhanced ozonation efficiency under neutral pH conditions, a key factor for implementation in industrial scenarios without requiring additional chemical adjustments [10].

Regarding process optimization, recent studies have explored the implementation of catalysts supported on activated carbon and porous structures, which has significantly reduced metal leaching and improved catalyst reusability over multiple treatment cycles [11]. Such innovations are fundamental to ensuring the economic and environmental viability of the process on an industrial scale. Moreover, integrating catalytic ozonation with photo assisted processes (O_3/UVC and O_3/H_2O_2/UVC) has been evaluated as a complementary strategy for degrading high-molecular-weight organic compounds, enhancing the conversion of contaminants into biodegradable products, and reducing the generation of toxic byproducts [12].

Various studies have demonstrated that the application of catalytic ozonation with magnetite not only facilitates organic matter removal but also significantly reduces leachate toxicity and improves its biodegradability [13]. This technology has proven particularly effective in eliminating aromatic compounds, humic substances, and other refractory contaminants that conventional methods fail to degrade efficiently [14]. Additionally, recent studies have shown that integrating catalytic ozonation with other processes, such as electrochemical treatment and biofiltration, can further improve treatment efficiency and reduce chemical reagent demand [15]. Moreover, optimizing the ozone concentration and incorporating hybrid catalysts, such as Fe_3O_4 combined with fly ash, have led to enhanced degradation of persistent compounds and increased leachate biodegradability [2]. Another critical aspect is the reusability of the catalyst. Magnetite has shown high stability after multiple reaction cycles, maintaining its catalytic capacity and reducing the operational costs associated with the process [5]. However, the efficiency of catalytic ozonation depends on multiple factors, including the medium pH, ozone concentration, and presence of other substances in the leachate matrix. Therefore, optimizing operating conditions is essential to maximize process effectiveness and ensure feasibility at an industrial scale [1]. Exploring different reactor configurations and adjusting ozone and catalyst concentrations could provide practical solutions to these challenges.

In this context, the present study evaluated the performance of catalytic ozonation with magnetite for the treatment of leachates from two sanitary landfills in Colombia, aiming to determine the optimal operating conditions and their impact on the removal of recalcitrant contaminants. Key variables such as ozone dosage, catalyst concentration, and pH were analyzed to maximize process efficiency. Additionally, catalyst stability after multiple usage cycles was assessed, identifying potential modifications in catalyst structure and composition. Through this analysis, the study seeks to establish technical criteria for large-scale implementation, contributing to the development of sustainable strategies for landfill leachate remediation and the optimization of advanced effluent treatment technologies.

2. Materials and Methods

2.1. Leachate Sampling and Characterization

Two sanitary landfills located in Norte de Santander, Colombia, were sampled for leachate. The first is Regional La Madera, which has been in function since 2001 in Ocaña (8°14′ N, 73°21′ W). Waste collected at the site comes mainly from municipalities, with the largest share of agricultural activity and no major industrial impact. On the other hand, the Environmental Technology Park El Guayabal has been operating since 2007; it is in the city of Cúcuta (8°05′ N, 72°30′ W) and receives waste from municipalities with industrial activities, which modifies the chemical characteristics of their leachates (CORPONOR, 2000; 2015).

Sampling was conducted following the methodology described by [16], employing a stratified scheme at three depth levels: surface (0–50 cm), intermediate (50–150 cm), and deep (>150 cm). This strategy allowed for the evaluation of contaminant distributions at different depths in the storage ponds, ensuring a representative characterization. To prevent sample alteration, sterile borosilicate bottles were used, preserved with 0.2% sodium azide, and stored at 4 °C immediately after collection [17]. Additionally, transportation was carried out in insulated containers with cold packs, maintaining a temperature between 2 and 4 °C to preserve the physicochemical and microbiological properties of the samples [18].

Table 1 summarizes the physicochemical parameters and heavy metals analyzed and the analytical methods used for the samples collected for this study. The standards used for all procedures were based on Standard Methods for the Examination of Water and Wastewater, 23rd Edition [19].

2.2. Catalyst Characteristics

The selection of the catalyst used in this study followed the criteria described by [20]. Synthetic magnetite (Fe_3O_4) was chosen because of its high purity and chemical stability, making it suitable for advanced oxidation processes. Its interaction with ozone facilitates the generation of hydroxyl radicals, which are essential for the degradation of organic contaminants in leachates, thereby optimizing treatment efficiency. Additionally, its homogeneous morphology enhances dispersion in aqueous media, ensuring greater surface contact and improving catalytic activity. The characterization of the commercial magnetite used, presented in Table 2, details the distribution of its main elements, highlighting its low impurity content and the presence of oxides such as magnesium oxide (MgO), titanium dioxide (TiO_2), and aluminum oxide (Al_2O_3), which may influence its stability and catalytic performance.

Table 1. Analytical methods for physicochemical characterization of leachates.

Parameter	Method
pH	SM 4500 H^+ B
Temperature (°C)	SM 2550 B
Conductivity (μS/cm)	SM 2510 B
Chemical Oxygen Demand (COD) (mg/L)	SM 5220 D
Biochemical Oxygen Demand (BOD_5) (mg/L)	SM 5210 B
Total Suspended Solids (mg/L)	SM 2540 D
Cadmium (mg/L)	SM 3030 E, SM 3111 B
Chromium (mg/L)	SM 3030 E, SM 3111 B
Lead (mg/L)	SM 3030 E, SM 3113 B
Mercury (mg/L)	SM 3112 B

Table 2. Chemical composition of synthetic magnetite.

Component	Concentration	Units
Fe_3O_4	>98	%
MgO	0.9	
Mn	0.3	
TiO_2	0.25	
Zn	0.1	
Al_2O_3	0.1	
SiO_2	0.05	
Pb	5	ppm
Cd	5	
As	10	
Hg	0.5	

Source: (Alpha Chemicals, Karachi, Pakistan, N.D.).

2.3. Ozonation Process

The ozonation process was conducted in a 500 mL glass reactor designed to maximize ozone mass transfer in the liquid phase. As shown in Figure 1, the reactor features an internal concentric tube for gas injection, facilitating the uniform dispersion of ozone through microbubbles generated by an aeration system with 0.45 μm holes. This configuration was employed to increase the efficiency of contact between ozone and leachate.

During operation, the system temperature was maintained at 20 ± 2 °C under controlled conditions. The ozone used in the experiment was generated from pure oxygen via a model O1 generator (Pacific Ozone, Lenntech, Delfgauw, The Netherlands) with a production capacity of 6 g/h and an adjustable flow rate between 3.3 and 4.7 L/min. The ozone concentration was regulated through a voltage controller, ensuring precise dosing throughout the experiment. Finally, residual gases were directed into a 30% potassium iodide (KI) solution to neutralize unreacted ozone and prevent its release into the atmosphere.

To avoid errors associated with the operation of the ozone generator and to ensure stable dosing, the gaseous ozone was continuously monitored by a BMT 964 BT ozone analyzer. This equipment employs a double-beam UV photometer (254 nm) and pressure and temperature compensations, ensuring high-precision measurements with an error margin of less than 0.5%. Thanks to this monitoring, it was possible to detect and correct deviations in the ozone concentration supplied to the reactor, improving the reliability of the process. Also, to evaluate the efficiency of ozone transfer to the liquid phase, dissolved ozone was measured using a multi-parameter photometer HI 83300 (Hanna Instruments, Smithfield, RI, USA), based on the DPD (N,N-diethyl-p-phenylenediamine) reagent method. This technique makes it possible to quantify ozone in solution by the formation of colored complexes whose absorbance is measured spectrophotometrically. In this way, it was possible to determine precisely the amount of ozone dissolved in the medium and to evaluate its availability for the catalytic reaction with magnetite.

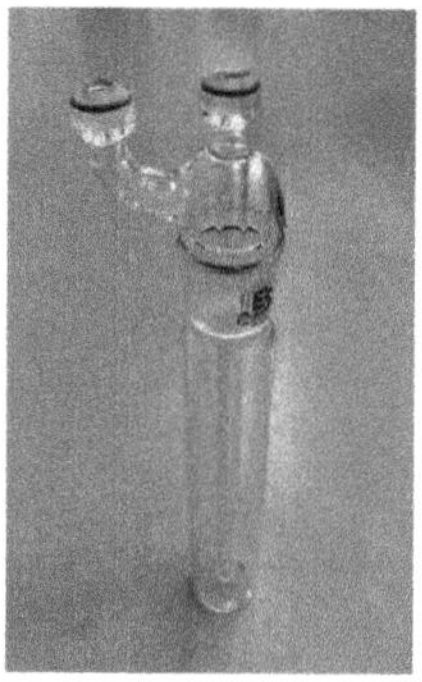

Figure 1. Schematic of glass reactor used in ozonation process.

2.4. Optimization of Catalytic Ozonation with Magnetite

Evaluation of Factors via Box–Behnken Design

Ozonation process optimization was performed according to the Box–Behnken design with three factors (15 experiments) through Design Expert software (v22. 02, StatEase, Minneapolis, MN, USA). The study used untreated samples from two landfills (La Madera and El Guayabal). For case (a) and case (b), the ozone dosage (g/h—flow rate of 3.3 L/min) was provided as a variable in accordance with the ranges that were investigated by [21–25]; the magnetite concentration (g/L) was obtained from [5,25–27]; and the pH values were obtained on the basis of the results of [21,23,28–30] (Table 3). The response variable was the percentage removal of chemical oxygen demand (COD) compared with the initial value. COD removal was measured at time intervals of 0, 20, 40, 60, and 120 min for each experiment. In addition, three control runs were incorporated into the experimental design: (i) ozone (6 g/h), magnetite (0 g/L), and pH (9), (ii) ozone (0 g/h), magnetite (2.5 g/L), and pH (9), and (iii) ozone (0 g/h), magnetite (0 g/L), and pH (9). The data collected after 120 min were analyzed via variance analysis (ANOVA) based on the software settings to determine which of the independent variables and their interactions had a significant effect on COD elimination.

Once the variables with the most significant impact on COD removal were identified, a central composite design (CCD) was applied via Design Expert software (v22.02, StatEase, Minneapolis, MN, USA). This approach allowed for the determination of an optimal region for maximizing the selected response variables.

2.5. Assessment of Recoverability of the Catalyst

After ozonation treatment, the magnetite was recovered via magnetic separation with a neodymium N35 magnet (10 mm × 2 mm). After that, it was rinsed with distilled water to wash away leachate residues and put in an oven to dry at 105 °C for 24 h, in accordance with [5,31]. The structural and morphological properties of the catalyst were evaluated after each cycle via Fourier transform infrared spectroscopy (FTIR, FTIR-Jasco 4100 spectrometer, KBr pellet, Thermo Fisher Scientific, Waltham, MA, USA) to detect probable changes in the functional groups. Furthermore, to characterize the morphology and structure of the retrieved particles, scanning electron microscopy (SEM) was carried out with a Phenom Pro X microscope (Thermo Fisher Scientific, Waltham, MA, USA). In the United States with a backscattered electron detector. Finally, the catalytic capacity of the recovered magnetite was analyzed for COD removal in three consecutive ozonation cycles, as was the mass recovery of the material after each cycle.

Table 3. Resolved Box–Behnken experimental design.

Run	Factor A O_2 g/h	Factor B Fe_3O_4 g/L	Factor C pH pH
1	4	0.5	9
2	6	1.5	9
3	6	0.5	6
4	2	2.5	6
5	2	1.5	3
6	2	1.5	9
7	4	2.5	9
8	4	2.5	3
9	4	1.5	6
10	6	2.5	6
11	6	1.5	3
12	4	0.5	3
13	4	1.5	6
14	2	0.5	6
15	4	1.5	6

2.6. Evaluation of the Efficiency of Ozone Dosing and Transfer in Organic Matter Removal

The ozone utilization efficiency (EO_3, expressed in mg COD/mg O_3) was evaluated based on the amount of chemical oxygen demand (*COD*) removed relative to the transferred ozone dose (*TOD*, in mg). This calculation determines the effectiveness of ozone in degrading the organic matter present in leachates, according to the methodology established by [32,33]. The relationship is expressed by the following Equation (1):

$$EO_3 = \frac{COD_{removal}}{TOD} \quad (1)$$

To determine the transferred ozone dose, a mass balance of ozone in the gas and liquid phases was employed. This method quantifies the amount of ozone dissolved in the system and distinguishes it from losses due to volatilization. The balance is described by the following Equation (2) [33]:

$$TOD = \int_0^t [O_3]_{gas\ in} Q_{gas} dt - \int_0^t [O_3]_{gas\ out} Q_{gas} dt \quad (2)$$

where $[O_3]_{gas\ in}$ is the ozone concentration in the gas phase (mg/L), $[O_3]_{gas\ out}$ is the ozone concentration in the aqueous phase at a specific moment during the reaction (mg/L), and Q_{gas} corresponds to the gas flow rate (L/min). The ozone concentration in the aqueous phase was measured via a multiparameter photometer (model HI 83300, Hanna Instruments, Smithfield, RI, USA) via the DPD (N,N-diethyl-p-phenylenediamine) method, which uses the HI 93757-0 reagent, where DPD reacts with ozone to produce colored complexes, the measurement of which was conducted photometrically. To avoid errors associated with the operation, the gas phase ozone concentration was continuously monitored by a BMT 964 BT ozone analyzer. This equipment employs a double-beam UV photometer (254 nm) and pressure and temperature compensations, ensuring high-precision measurements with an error margin of less than 0.5%.

3. Results

3.1. Chemical Caracterization of Landfill Leachates

The physicochemical characteristics of the analyzed leachates are shown in Table 4, as reflected by the variability of the measured parameters. In El Guayabal, the highest values for conductivity, pH, and temperature were recorded, along with an elevated concentration of chromium. In contrast, La Madera presented the highest organic load, as evidenced by its elevated chemical oxygen demand (COD) and biochemical oxygen demand (BOD_5) values, coupled with lower conductivity and mercury detection. Chromium was detected in El Guayabal, whereas mercury was detected in La Madera, indicating differences in waste sources and leaching dynamics at each site. Moreover, the BOD_5/COD ratio was low in both cases, suggesting limited biodegradability.

Table 4. Characteristics of evaluated leachates.

Parameter	El Guayabal	La Madera	Units
pH	8.5	7.57	pH units
Temperature (°C)	30.1	29.4	°C
Conductivity (µS/cm)	18.740	1.128	µS/cm
Chemical Oxygen Demand (COD) (mg/L)	1.664	1.933	mg O_2/L
Biochemical Oxygen Demand (BOD_5) (mg/L)	6.295	8.421	mg O_2/L
Total Suspended Solids (mg/L)	8.309	5.151	mg/L
Cadmium (mg/L)	<0.050	<0.014	mg/L
Chromium (mg/L)	0.294	n/a	mg/L
Lead (mg/L)	<0.10	<0.10	mg/L
Mercury (mg/L)	<0.001	0.28	mg/L

3.2. Ozonation Process

The results revealed variations in chemical oxygen demand (COD) removal efficiency between the leachates from the two sanitary landfills (Figure 2). In El Guayabal, a maximum removal of 85.3% was achieved, whereas in La Madera, the highest recorded removal was 75.8%. However, the removal rates within the first 20 min were similar for both leachates, with removal values ranging between 30% and 40%, indicating that the initial stage of the process is critical to the degradation kinetics. After 60 min, the removal curve begins to stabilize, showing a trend toward a decrease in process efficiency over time.

Analysis of the extreme values indicated that, in both leachates, the highest removal rate occurred within the first 40 min, with a significant increase in the COD removal level. In contrast, in the control experiments conducted without the catalyst, COD removal remained below 42%, underscoring the contribution of magnetite to the generation of active oxidizing species. Additionally, variations in efficiency among the catalytic tests can be attributed to the influence of the initial composition and physicochemical conditions of the leachates.

3.3. Results of Design of Experiments Proposed

The effects of light O_2 (A), Fe_3O_4 (B), and pH (C) on COD removal were statistically assessed via an ANOVA model (Table 5) for samples from El Guayabal and La Madera. Metrics such as the coefficient of determination (R^2), adjusted R^2, forecast R^2, and Adeq

Precision, which gauges the signal-to-noise ratio in the data, were used to evaluate the model's validity. In the case of the samples from El Guayabal, the findings show that the Model F value of 21.93 implies that the model is significant, with only a 0.01% chance that an F value that this large could occur due to noise. In this case, A, B, C, AC, and C^2 are significant model terms with p-values lower than 0.05. Finally, the lack of fit F value of 3.03 implies that the lack of fit is not significant relative to the pure error. There is a 27.07% chance that a lack of fit F value for this large value could occur due to noise. The predicted R^2 of 0.7344 is in reasonable agreement with the adjusted R^2 of 0.8820. Additionally, an Adeq Precision of 14.633 indicates an adequate signal.

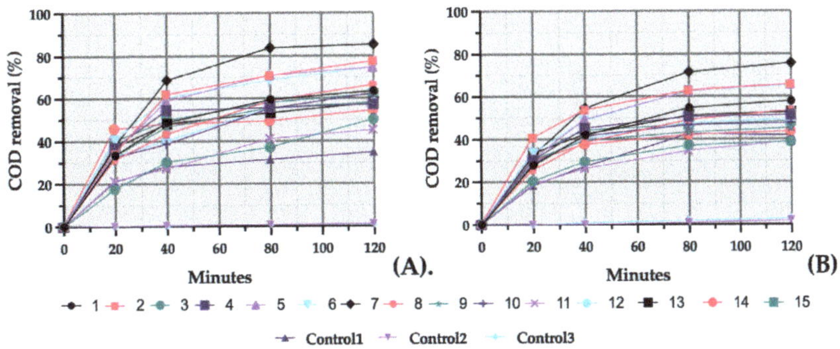

Figure 2. COD removal by catalytic ozonation (Fe_3O_4): (**A**) El Guayabal sanitary landfill, (**B**) La Madera sanitary landfill.

In the case of the samples from La Madera, the Model F value of 54.01 implies that the model is significant. There is only a 0.02% chance that an F value that is this large could occur due to noise. In this case, A, B, C, AC, BC, and C^2 are significant model terms. The lack of fit F value of 1.88 implies that the lack of fit is not significant relative to the pure error. There is a 36.56% chance that a lack of fit F value for this large value could occur due to noise. Finally, the predicted R^2 of 0.8737 is in reasonable agreement with the adjusted R^2 of 0.9715. An adequate precision of 28.047 indicates an adequate signal.

The response surface analysis highlights the influence of operational variables on the removal of chemical oxygen demand (COD) from the leachates of the El Guayabal and La Madera sanitary landfills. In El Guayabal (Figure 3A), pH and magnetite concentration were the factors with the greatest impact on process efficiency. The highest removal was achieved under alkaline conditions (pH 9), where the interaction between ozone and magnetite promoted the generation of hydroxyl radicals. The response surface exhibited significant curvature, suggesting that the combination of magnetite and pH had a synergistic effect on advanced oxidation. As the pH decreases, the removal efficiency decreases markedly, confirming the reduced production of oxidizing species under acidic conditions.

In La Madera (Figure 3B), the response patterns differ, with a greater dependence on the ozone dose. The linear trend of the surface suggests that increasing the ozone concentration progressively enhances COD removal, with no evident saturation within the evaluated ranges. Although magnetite contributes to this process, its impact is less pronounced than that of El Guayabal. This behavior indicates that the recalcitrant compounds present in this leachate respond more favorably to direct ozone oxidation than to the catalytic action of magnetite. The optimal combination of ozone and magnetite achieved a removal efficiency of approximately 76%, although at very high ozone concentrations, the trend began to stabilize, possibly because of excessive oxidant self-decomposition. For both leachates, the process demonstrates optimal performance under alkaline conditions; however, the specific composition of the leachate determines the relevance of each variable. While in El Guayabal, magnetite plays a key role in degradation, in La Madera, the predominant effect is that of direct ozone oxidation. This underscores the need to adjust the treatment conditions according to the nature of the leachate to optimize process efficiency.

Table 5. ANOVA of experimental data from El Guayabal and La Madera.

Sample	Source	Sum of Squares	Df	Mean Square	F Value	p-Value
El Guayabal	Model	1509.16	5	301.83	21.93	<0.0001 *
	A-O_2	143.65	1	143.65	10.43	0.0103 *
	B-Fe_3O_4	356.44	1	356.44	25.89	0.0007 *
	C-pH	404.70	1	404.70	29.40	0.0004 *
	AC	257.60	1	257.60	18.71	0.0019 *
	C^2	346.76	1	346.76	25.19	0.0007 *
	Residual	123.90	9	13.77		
	Lack of Fit	113.21	7	16.17	3.03	0.2707 **
	Pure Error	10.69	2	5.34		
	Total Cor	1633.06	14			

Sample	R^2	Adj R^2	Pred R^2	Acq Pr	Std. Dev.	Mean	CV%
El Guayabal	0.9241	0.8820	0.7344	14.6328	3.71	63.64	5.83

Sample	Source	Sum of Squares	Df	Mean Square	F Value	p-Value
La Madera	Model	1924.28	9	213.81	54.01	0.0002 *
	A-O_2	228.98	1	228.98	57.85	0.0006 *
	B-Fe_3O_4	267.96	1	267.96	67.69	0.0004 *
	C-pH	401.86	1	401.86	101.52	0.0002 *
	AB	20.25	1	20.25	5.12	0.0732 **
	AC	182.25	1	182.25	46.04	0.0011 *
	BC	49.70	1	49.70	12.56	0.0165 *
	A^2	12.13	1	12.13	3.06	0.1404 **
	B^2	9.31	1	9.31	2.35	0.1858 **
	C^2	719.82	1	719.82	181.84	<0.0001 *
	Residual	19.79	5	3.96		
	Lack of Fit	14.61	3	4.87	1.88	0.3656 **
	Pure Error	5.18	2	2.59		
	Total Cor	1944.07	14			

Sample	R^2	Adj R^2	Pred R^2	Acq Pr	Std. Dev.	Mean	CV%
La Madera	0.9898	0.9715	0.8737	28.0471	1.99	52.43	3.79

* Significant. ** Not significant.

3.3.1. Evaluation of Organic Matter Removal

The ozone consumption per unit of chemical oxygen demand (COD) removed exhibited significant variability depending on the evaluated operational conditions, reflecting the impact of ozone dosage, magnetite concentration, and pH on process efficiency (Figure 4). In this context, optimizing the system is essential to minimize reagent usage and maximize organic matter degradation. Among all the tested conditions, treatment with 4 g O_3/h, 2.5 g/L Fe_3O_4, and pH 9 was the most efficient, with a minimum consumption of 2.7 g O_3 per gram of COD removed. This behavior can be attributed to the formation of highly reactive hydroxyl radicals in an alkaline medium, where the catalyst facilitates the conversion of ozone into more effective oxidizing species. Moreover, the high concentration of Fe_3O_4 enhances the generation of these radicals, thereby promoting the degradation of recalcitrant organic compounds.

Conversely, the least favorable conditions were observed under acidic pH and low magnetite concentrations, where higher ozone consumption values were recorded. A clear example is the treatment with 6 g O_3/h, 0.5 g/L Fe_3O_4, and pH 6, in which ozone consumption increased to 4.8 g O_3 per gram of COD removed. In this case, the reduced availability of catalyst limits hydroxyl radical production, implying that oxidation occurs primarily through direct ozone attack, a mechanism that is less efficient in terms of energy consumption and contaminant degradation.

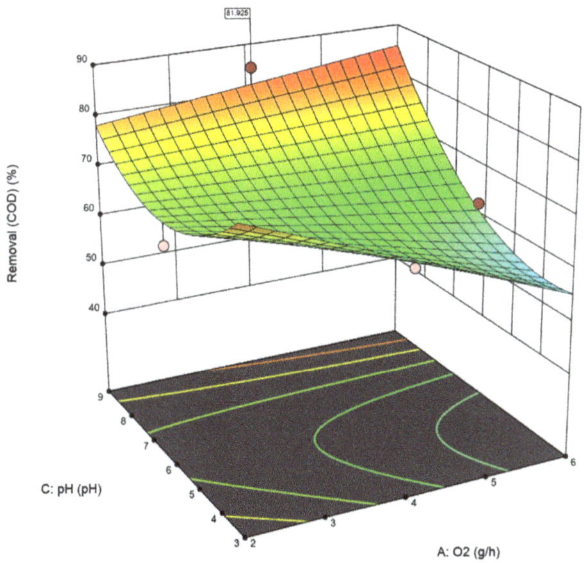

(**A**)

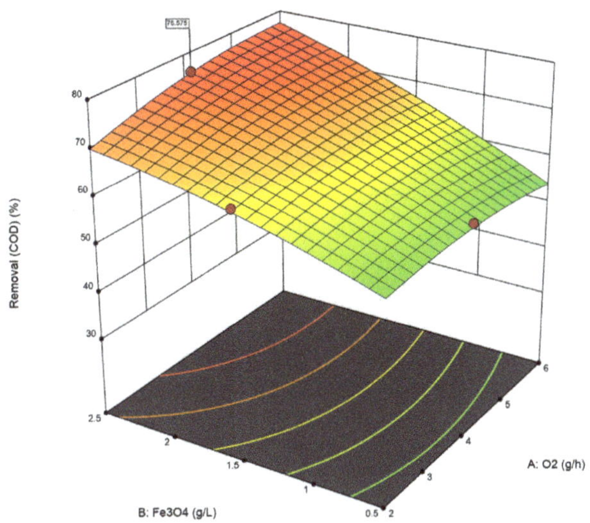

(**B**)

Figure 3. Surface response for COD removal using landfill leachate from El Guayabal (**A**) and La Madera (**B**).

Furthermore, experiments conducted without magnetite demonstrated markedly lower process efficiency, with an extreme ozone consumption of 7.7 g O_3 per gram of COD removed under conditions of 6 g O_3/h and pH 9. These values underscore the importance of the catalyst in optimizing the ozonation process, as its absence prevents the effective conversion of ozone into hydroxyl radicals, thereby significantly reducing treatment efficiency.

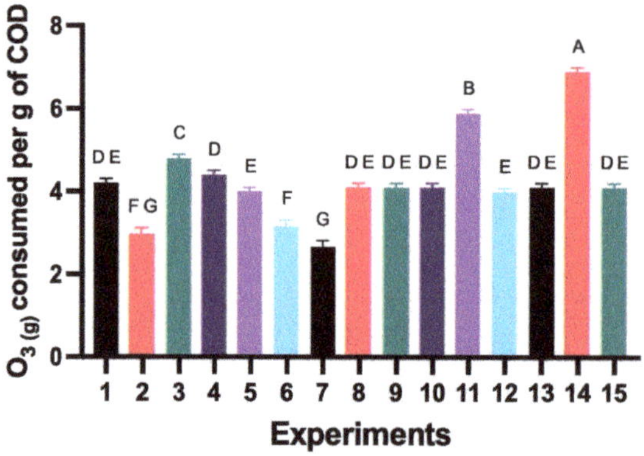

Figure 4. Ozone consumption efficiency in organic matter degradation. Different letters mean statistical significance.

3.3.2. CCD Optimization

Based on the results of the Box–Behnken experimental design, the variables with the greatest influence on COD removal were identified. Consequently, a central composite design (CCD) was implemented to optimize the process and determine the parameter combination that maximizes treatment efficiency for the leachates from La Madera and El Guayabal. The CCD considers the ozone dosage (O_2) and magnetite concentration (Fe_3O_4) as the main variables while maintaining the pH at 9 because of its role in hydroxyl radical generation. A total of 13 experimental runs were conducted with expanded variable combinations to assess the system response and develop a predictive optimization model. The resolved experimental design is presented in Table 6.

Table 6. Central composite design (CCD) experimental runs.

Run	Factor A O_2 g/h	Factor B Fe_3O_4 g/L
1	6	5.33
2	2	0.5
3	11.66	2.5
4	6	−0.33
5	6	2.5
6	10	0.5
7	2	4.5
8	10	4.5
9	0.34	2.5
10	6	2.5
11	6	2.5
12	6	2.5
13	6	2.5

The data obtained after 120 min of treatment were analyzed via ANOVA in Design Expert v22.02 (StatEase, Minneapolis, MN, USA) to evaluate the significance of each variable and interaction, enabling the determination of optimal conditions for future applications in leachate treatment.

The effects of light O_2 (A) and Fe_3O_4 (B) on COD removal were assessed statistically via an ANOVA model (Table 7). Metrics such as the coefficient of determination (R_2), adjusted R_2, predicted R_2, and Adeq Precision (which gauges the signal-to-noise ratio in the data) were used to evaluate the model's validity. The findings show that the Model F value of 1690.10 implies that the model is significant. There is only a 0.01% chance that an F value that is this large could occur due to noise. In this case, A, B, AB, A^2, and B^2 are significant model terms. The lack of fit F value of 2.40 implies that the lack of fit is not significant relative to the pure error. There is a 20.81% chance that a lack of fit F value for this large value could occur due to noise. Finally, the predicted R^2 of 0.9958 is in reasonable agreement with the adjusted R^2 of 0.9986. An Adeq Precision of 100.462 indicates an adequate signal.

Table 7. ANOVA anlysis for optimization data from El Guayabal and La Madera.

Sample	Source	Sum of Squares	Df	Mean Square	F Value	p-Value
El Guayabal	Model	8.826×10^5	5	1.765×10^5	1690.10	<0.0001 *
	A-O_2	1.052×10^5	1	1.052×10^5	1007.71	<0.0001 *
	B-Fe_3O_4	2.062×10^5	1	2.062×10^5	1974.04	<0.0001 *
	AB	1616.25	1	1616.25	15.47	0.0056 *
	A^2	2.570×10^5	1	2.570×10^5	2460.37	<0.0001 *
	B^2	3.849×10^5	1	3.849×10^5	3685.68	<0.0001 *
	Residual	731.10	7	104.44		
	Lack of Fit	470.23	3	156.74	2.40	0.2081 **
	Pure Error	260.87	4	65.22		
	Total Cor	8.833×10^5	12			
	R^2	Adj R^2	Pred R^2	Acq Pr	Std. Dev.	Mean	CV%
	0.9992	0.9986	0.9958	100.4622	10.22	462.77	2.21
La Madera	Model	5774.09	5	1154.82	937.58	<0.0001 *
	A-O_2	462.32	1	462.32	375.35	<0.0001 *
	B-Fe_3O_4	669.77	1	669.77	543.78	<0.0001 *
	AB	9.00	1	9.00	7.31	0.0305 *
	A^2	3326.14	1	3326.14	2700.46	<0.0001 *
	B^2	1880.45	1	1880.45	1526.72	<0.0001 *
	Residual	8.62	7	1.23		
	Lack of Fit	4.51	3	1.50	1.47	0.3505 **
	Pure Error	4.11	4	1.03		
	Total Cor	5782.71	12			
	R^2	Adj R^2	Pred R^2	Acq Pr	Std. Dev.	Mean	CV%
	0.9985	0.9974	0.9933	72.2616	1.11	53.55	2.07

* Significant. ** Not significant.

In the case of the La Madera samples, the Model F value of 937.58 implies that the model is significant. There is only a 0.01% chance that an F value that is this large could occur due to noise. In this case, A, B, AB, A^2, and B^2 are significant model terms. The lack of fit F value of 1.47 implies that the lack of fit is not significant relative to the pure error. There is a 35.05% chance that a lack of fit F value for this large value could occur due to noise. The nonsignificant lack of fit is good; we want the model to fit. The predicted R^2 of 0.9933 is in reasonable agreement with the adjusted R^2 of 0.9974. Finally, the Adeq Precision of 72.262 indicates an adequate signal.

Response surface analysis provides a visual representation of the interaction between the operational variables and their impact on chemical oxygen demand (COD) removal.

Figure 5 shows that the process efficiency is maximized at medium to high concentrations of magnetite (Fe_3O_4), ranging from 2.5 to 3.5 g/L, combined with a high ozone dosage (6 to 7 g/h). This pattern is consistent in the leachates from both sanitary landfills, El Guayabal (Figure 5A) and La Madera (Figure 5B), suggesting that the interaction between these two factors plays a key role in process optimization. In the response surface for El Guayabal (Figure 2A), a pronounced curvature is evident, indicating a parabolic relationship between the Fe_3O_4 concentration and COD removal. At low magnetite concentrations, removal is limited, whereas at optimal levels, the efficiency reaches values close to 90%. However, at excessively high concentrations, the trend begins to stabilize, suggesting possible catalyst saturation and a reduction in process efficiency due to particle agglomeration.

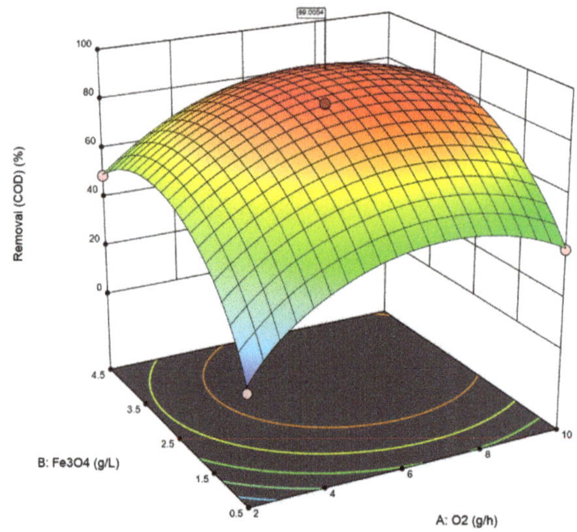

(A)

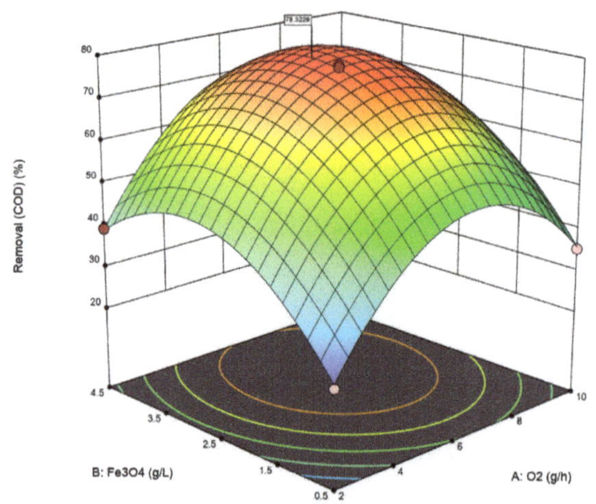

(B)

Figure 5. Surface response for COD removal using landfill leachate from El Guayabal (**A**) and La Madera (**B**).

In contrast, the response surface for La Madera (Figure 5B) shows a similar trend, albeit with a less pronounced slope, indicating greater process stability with respect to variations in magnetite concentration. The optimal response was also observed within the 2.5–3.5 g/L range of Fe_3O_4, with an ozone dosage of at least 6 g/h. However, in this case, the maximum efficiency does not reach the values observed in El Guayabal, suggesting differences in leachate composition and reactivity to advanced oxidation mechanisms.

The optimization of the experimental parameters via the Design Expert module enabled the identification of operating conditions that maximize chemical oxygen demand (COD) removal in the evaluated leachates. As reported in Table 8, the optimal conditions for El Guayabal included an ozone dosage of 7 g/h, a magnetite (Fe_3O_4) concentration of 3.47 g/L, and a pH of 9, achieving an estimated removal efficiency of 89%. For La Madera, the optimal conditions consisted of an ozone dosage of 6 g/h, a magnetite concentration of 2.94 g/L, and a pH of 9, with an expected removal efficiency of 78% (GraphPad Prism version 10.4.1 for Mac, GraphPad Software, Boston, MA, USA).

Table 8. Optimized conditions for maximum COD removal.

Sample	Code	Variable	Unit	Value
Guayabal	A	O_2	g/h	7
	B	Fe_3O_4	g/L	3.47
	C	pH	-	9
	Z_1	COD Removal	%	89
La Madera	A	O_2	g/h	6
	B	Fe_3O_4	g/L	2.94
	C	pH	-	9
	Z_2	COD Removal	%	78

To validate the model's predictions, additional tests were conducted with five replicates, and the experimental results were compared with the estimated values via a paired *t*-test in GraphPad Prism (version 10.2.3). As shown in Figure 6, no statistically significant differences were observed between the expected and actual values, confirming the robustness of the predictive model and the suitability of the established conditions for optimizing treatment efficiency.

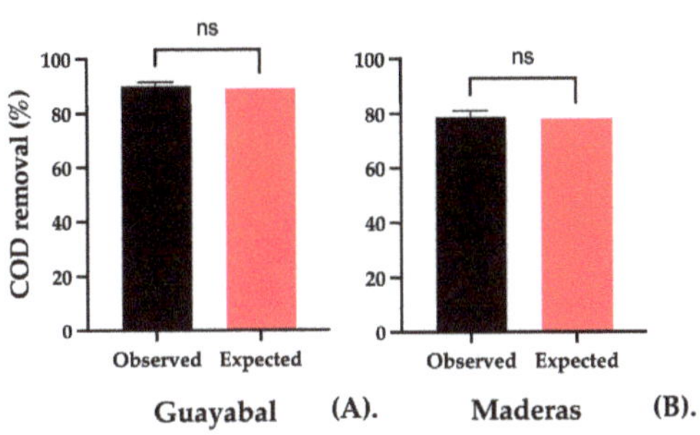

Figure 6. Results of one-sample t-test between expected and observed COD removal for leachates from El Guayabal (**A**) and La Madera (**B**).

The leachates were characterized after treatment to evaluate the effects of this process on their physicochemical properties. The final concentrations of COD in El Guayabal and La Madera were 925.8 mg/L and 2038 mg/L, respectively; the corresponding removal efficiencies were 85.3% and 75.8%, respectively (Table 9). The observed decrease in biodegradable organic load indicates successful elimination of recalcitrant compounds through treatment.

Table 9. Characteristics of treated leachates.

Parameter	El Guayabal	La Madera	Units
pH	9.4	9.1	pH units
Temperature (°C)	20.2	21.3	°C
Conductivity (μS/cm)	21.636	1663.28	μS/cm
Chemical Oxygen Demand (COD) (mg/L)	925.8	2038	mg O_2/L
Biochemical Oxygen Demand (BOD_5) (mg/L)	351.8	652.2	mg O_2/L
Total Suspended Solids (mg/L)	<4.0	<4.0	mg/L

The conductivity increased in both leachates, reaching 21,636.55 μS/cm in El Guayabal and 1663.28 μS/cm in La Madera. This behavior has been linked to the initial formation of ionic species such as sulfates, carbonates, and nitrates (known byproducts of advanced oxidation processes). This increase was more pronounced in El Guayabal, which indicates greater mineralization of preexisting inorganic compounds in this leachate.

The final pH slightly increased, stabilizing at 9.4 in El Guayabal and 9.1 in La Madera. This shift suggests the formation of bicarbonates and carbonates, contributing to the chemical stability of the medium. Finally, total suspended solids (TSS) were reduced to nearly undetectable levels (<4 mg/L), demonstrating the effective removal of suspended particles and an improvement in the clarity of the treated effluent.

Figure 7 illustrates the evolution of the leachate color during different phases of the treatment process. A significant reduction in color intensity was observed as catalytic ozonation progressed, confirming the degradation of organic compounds responsible for coloration. In comparison, treatment with ozone alone resulted in a lower color reduction under the same operating conditions.

(A)

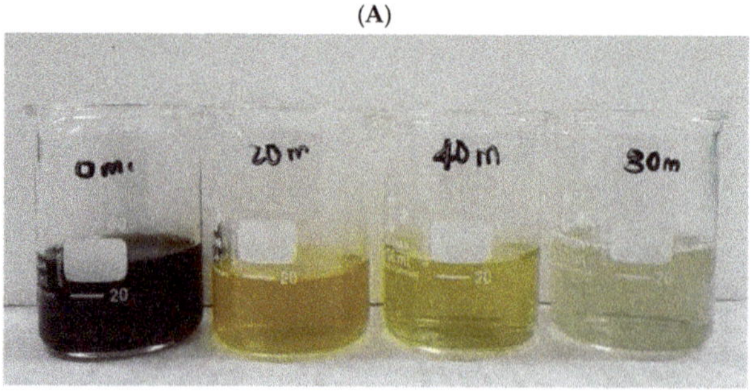

(B)

Figure 7. Evolution of leachate color during treatment: (**A**) ozone alone and (**B**) ozone + magnetite.

3.4. Catalyst Recoverability

Figure 8 presents scanning electron microscopy (SEM) images used to assess the structure and composition of magnetite at different stages of use. Image (A) depicts unused synthetic magnetite, which is characterized by a homogeneous surface and a composition consisting entirely of Fe_3O_4 (100%). Image (B) corresponds to magnetite after one treatment cycle of leachate under optimal conditions (6 g O_3/h, 2.5 g/L Fe_3O_4, and pH 9), showing a reduction in the Fe_3O_4 concentration to 74.80%, along with the appearance of elements such as silicon (Si, 21.53%), suggesting possible adsorption of contaminants. Finally, image (C) of magnetite after two cycles of use shows an additional decrease in the concentration of Fe_3O_4 (65.12%) and new compounds, including TiO_2 (11.04%) and Ca (1.45%), indicating the progressive degradation of the material, as well as a possible interaction with the species present in the leachate. Images were taken at 22,500×, 22,000×, and 25,000× with a 15 kV acceleration voltage, and backscattered electron detectors for surface alterations corresponded to the catalytic use in ozonation.

3.5. Fourier Transform Infrared Spectroscopy (FTIR) Analysis

The structure and chemical properties of magnetite before and after catalytic ozonation were studied via Fourier transform infrared (FTIR) spectroscopy. The absorption spectra of the magnetite samples in three states are shown in Figure 9: (A) unused, (B) after the first treatment cycle, and (C) after the second treatment cycle. In the FTIR spectrum of unused magnetite (Figure 9A), characteristic absorption bands of Fe_3O_4 are observed, with a prominent peak at approximately 570 cm^{-1}, corresponding to Fe–O stretching vibrations. This finding confirms the high initial purity of the material and its unaltered crystalline structure. Furthermore, the absence of bands associated with foreign functional groups suggests that the material was free of surface contaminants prior to treatment.

After one cycle of use (Figure 9B), a reduction in the intensity of the primary Fe_3O_4 peak is observed, indicating structural modifications in the magnetite. Additionally, secondary bands emerge in the 1200–1600 cm^{-1} region, suggesting the presence of adsorbed compounds, possibly carbonates or organic residues from the leachate. This observation aligns with previous scanning electron microscopy (SEM) images, which revealed changes in the surface texture of magnetite after its first cycle of use. Following two treatment cycles (Figure 9C), a further decrease in the Fe_3O_4 peak intensity is evident, along with an increase in the number of bands associated with secondary compounds. These changes indicate the accumulation of adsorbed residues on the catalyst surface, potentially limiting the availability of active sites for future interactions. Additionally, the progressive alteration in the intensity and position of the bands confirms that magnetite undergoes structural modifications with continued use, impacting its catalytic efficiency in subsequent treatments.

To evaluate the catalyst's stability after use, additional tests were performed to measure the amount of material recovered after each cycle and its performance in chemical oxygen demand (COD) removal. In the first test, when 2.5 g of initial magnetite was used, a COD removal efficiency of 85.3% was achieved. In the second cycle, with 2.275 g of recovered magnetite, the removal efficiency decreased to 79.4%. Finally, in the third cycle, with 2.0175 g of remaining material, the efficiency decreased to 73.6%. This trend suggests that, in addition to material loss, the decrease in catalytic activity may be associated with contaminant adsorption and saturation of the active sites.

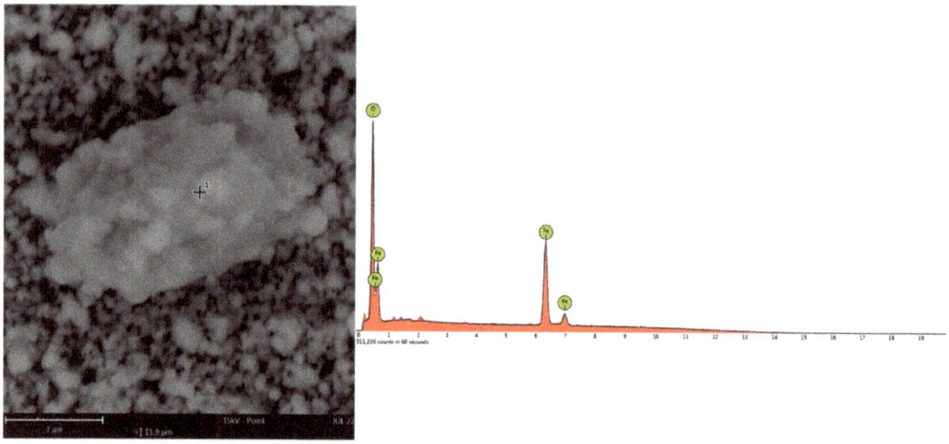

(A)

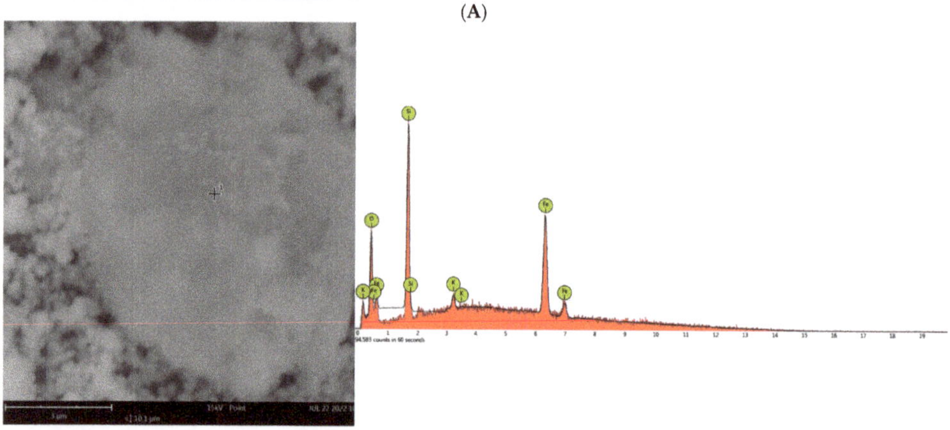

(B)

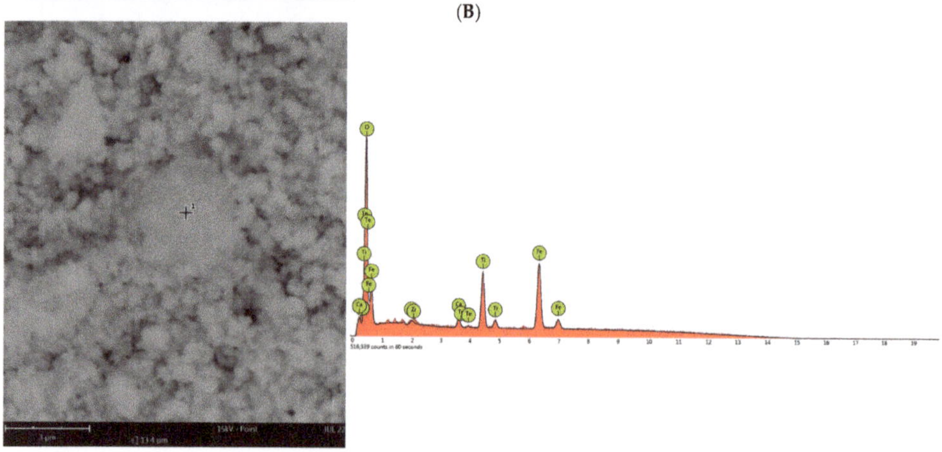

(C)

Figure 8. Scanning electron microscopy (SEM) images. (**A**) Unused synthetic magnetite, (**B**) synthetic magnetite after one cycle of use, and (**C**) magnetite after two cycles of use.

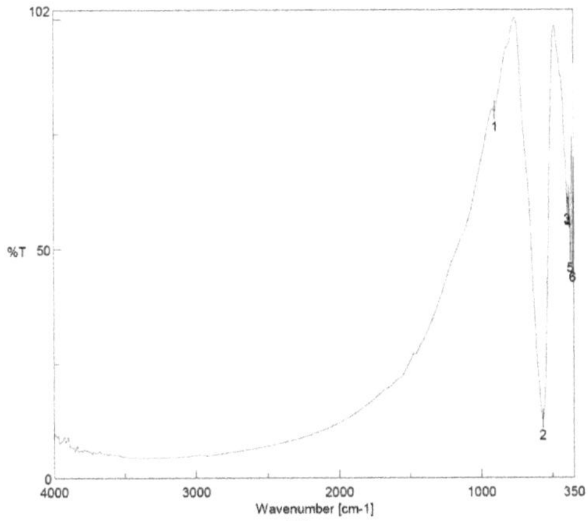

(**A**)

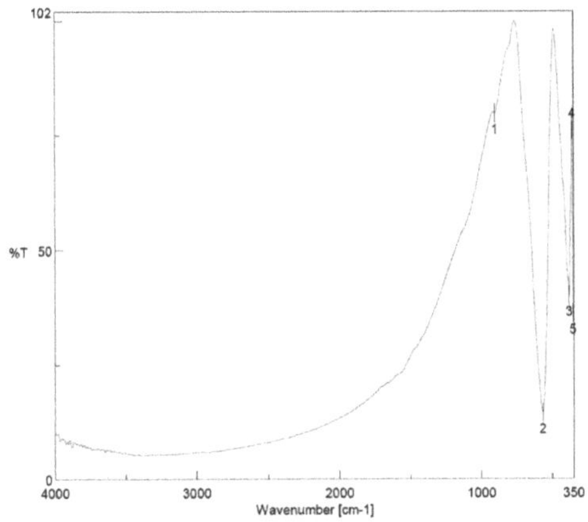

(**B**)

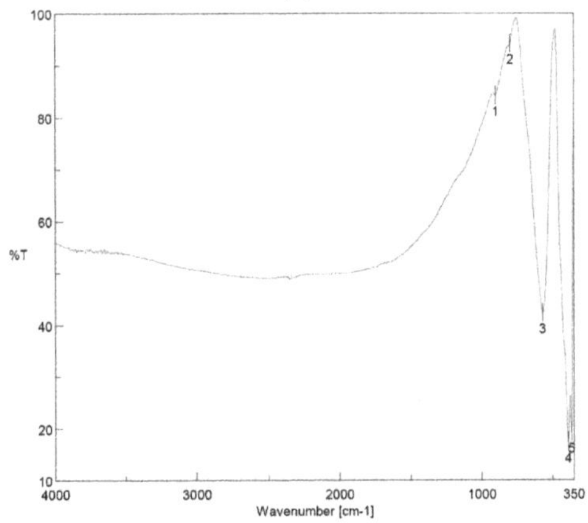

(**C**)

Figure 9. FTIR spectra of magnetite: (**A**) unused synthetic magnetite, (**B**) magnetite after one cycle of use, and (**C**) magnetite after two cycles of use.

4. Discussion

The observed variations in the evaluated leachates are directly related to the composition of the waste disposed of in each sanitary landfill (Table 5). First, the high conductivity in El Guayabal (18,740 μS/cm) indicates a greater concentration of dissolved salts, a characteristic of leachates generated at sites with a high presence of industrial and urban waste [34–36]. In contrast, La Madera exhibited considerably lower conductivity (1128.56 μS/cm), suggesting a lower load of ionic compounds and a predominance of biodegradable waste.

In addition, the organic load also differed between the landfills. La Madera had the greatest increase in chemical oxygen demand (COD) of 8421.4 mg/L, indicating the concentration of recalcitrant organic matter, whereas El Guayabal presented 6295.6 mg/L COD, indicating a lower concentration of undecomposed compounds. Many studies have shown that when the COD concentration is very high (generally above 5000 mg/L), the leachate contains a high quantity of refractory substances, thus limiting the feasibility of biologically based treatment [4,22,37]. Hence, the utilization of technologies such as advanced oxidation processes, adsorption, and electrocoagulation has been suggested as a potential solution to eliminate these compounds [38]. Additionally, the pH behavior of both leachates reflects the influence of microbial activity on the chemical stabilization of the leachate. El Guayabal recorded a relatively high pH (8.5), whereas La Madera presented a pH of 7.57. This phenomenon has been documented in previous studies, where methanogenic activity produces carbonates and bicarbonates that stabilize the pH in sanitary landfills during prolonged operational periods [39–41]. For leachates with these characteristics, techniques such as membrane filtration and adsorption using advanced materials have improved the contaminant removal efficiency.

The presence of heavy metals in the leachates highlights differences in the composition of the waste disposed of in each landfill. The detection of chromium in El Guayabal (0.294 mg/L) can be attributed to the disposal of industrial waste containing heavy metals, whereas the presence of mercury in La Madera (0.28 mg/L) suggests the disposal of electronic waste or batteries. Research has demonstrated that strategies such as adsorption on activated carbon and chemical precipitation can be highly effective for removing these metals [42]. In this regard, the development of emerging techniques such as bioadsorption and photocatalysis may represent promising alternatives to optimize the removal of heavy metals and other persistent contaminants in leachates from similar sanitary landfills.

Recent studies were found to determine the combination of advanced processes, besides traditional adsorption and chemical precipitation, for the effective removal of heavy metals from landfill leachates. Catalytic ozonation in the presence of functionalized adsorbents, e.g., metallic-nanoparticles-modified activated carbon, has been reported to offer improved retention of metallic cations, which reduces their mobility within the aqueous phase [11]. Similarly, investigations on the use of magnetite supported on a porous structure have shown its ability for the adsorption and oxidation of metals, including lead, chromium, and mercury, largely diminishing their toxicity in aqueous media [10]. Emerging technologies will provide new alternatives for removing heavy metals from leachates and improving the quality of the treated effluent.

The results obtained for the removal of chemical oxygen demand (COD) from the leachates of El Guayabal and La Madera reveal differences in treatment efficiency when ozone catalyzed by magnetite is used (Figure 2). The greater removal observed in El Guayabal (85%) than in La Madera (76%) underscores the influence of the leachate composition on the oxidation kinetics. The nature of the compounds present, as well as their degree of recalcitrance, can affect both the rate and extent of organic matter degradation. Previous studies have reported that the presence of humic substances and fulvic acids in mature leachates limits ozone effectiveness and reduces overall process efficiency [3,4,43].

The process behavior suggests that catalytic ozonation is governed by a combination of direct and indirect oxidation. While molecular ozone preferentially attacks compounds containing double bonds and specific functional groups, the hydroxyl radicals generated on the surface of magnetite exhibit broader and nonselective reactivity [5]. This difference in reaction mechanism is crucial for explaining the variability in process efficiency between the two leachates. Recent studies have demonstrated that the capacity to generate hydroxyl radicals depends on the structural stability of the catalyst and its interaction with the leachate matrix [8]. Moreover, the temporal evolution of COD removal indicates that the most significant degradation occurs within the first 60 min, followed by gradual deceleration. This behavior is partly due to the decreasing concentration of available ozone and the possible adsorption of intermediates onto the catalyst surface. Competition among compounds in the medium may reduce the availability of active sites on magnetite, thereby affecting the generation of hydroxyl radicals during the later stages of treatment [15].

Another key aspect influencing process efficiency is the effect of pH. The conversion of ozone into hydroxyl radicals is relatively efficient in alkaline media because of the increased stability of these species in high-pH solutions [44]. However, extremely high pH values can promote the premature decomposition of ozone before it interacts with target compounds, thereby reducing treatment efficiency. In the present study, the leachates presented slightly alkaline pH values, which may have contributed to the improved degradation of recalcitrant compounds without adversely affecting oxidant stability [33]. Control tests confirmed that the synergy between ozone and magnetite is fundamental for achieving high contaminant removal efficiency. COD removal in tests using ozone alone was considerably lower, indicating that Fe_3O_4 not only facilitates the decomposition of ozone into reactive species but also stabilizes the process by maintaining the constant generation of hydroxyl radicals. In summary, these results reinforce the applicability of catalytic ozonation in the treatment of leachates with high organic loads and refractory compounds. Nevertheless, the optimization of key variables—such as ozone dosage and catalyst concentration—remains an area of interest.

In this context, various studies have demonstrated that the efficiency of catalytic ozonation can be enhanced through the incorporation of advanced catalysts and process optimization strategies. The use of magnetite modified with transition metal ions has shown an increase in the conversion of ozone into reactive oxygen species, thereby facilitating the degradation of recalcitrant compounds with reduced formation of secondary byproducts [12]. Additionally, the implementation of Fe-N_4-based catalysts supported on carbon structures has improved the selectivity of oxidation reactions without requiring drastic modifications to the pH of the medium [2]. These enhancements have been validated through advanced spectroscopic techniques, confirming the structural stability of the catalysts and their efficacy over multiple operational cycles.

For the first phase of optimization, statistical analysis via analysis of variance (ANOVA) (Table 6) confirmed the robustness of the predictive model, demonstrating that the evaluated variables have a significant effect on the removal of chemical oxygen demand (COD). The results indicate that the model has a coefficient of determination (R^2) of 0.9241 for El Guayabal and 0.9898 for La Madera, indicating that the model adequately explains the observed variability. Furthermore, the F values obtained for each factor were high, with p-values less than 0.05, reinforcing the statistical significance of the independent variables on the system response. This is supported by the significance values obtained in the analysis, where the model presented an F value of 21.93 for El Guayabal and 54.01 for La Madera, indicating that the evaluated variables account for a large portion of the variability in the results. Additionally, the R^2 values of 0.9241 and 0.9898, respectively, demonstrate a high explanatory capacity of the model, whereas Adeq Precision values greater than 14 ensure a strong signal in the data, allowing for proper interpretation [21]. These findings are consistent with previous studies where the optimization of ozonation processes has shown similar levels of fit and precision in advanced leachate treatments [4].

pH was established as the most influential factor in COD removal, exerting a significant effect on both leachate matrices (Figure 3). The relationship between pH and hydroxyl radical generation has been extensively documented in the literature [4], and these results underscore the importance of operating under alkaline conditions to maximize oxidation efficiency. However, in El Guayabal, magnetite had a more pronounced influence, suggesting that the catalytic interaction with ozone was decisive in generating reactive oxygen species. In contrast, in La Madera, ozone plays a predominant role, implying that the organic fraction of the leachate is more susceptible to direct oxidation [15]. These results agree with the findings of [28], who reported that an alkaline pH favors the formation of highly reactive radicals, thereby increasing the degradation of recalcitrant organic contaminants. Response surface analysis demonstrated that the interactions among pH, ozone dose, and magnetite concentration play a key role in process efficiency. In El Guayabal, the impact of magnetite is more significant, likely because of the presence of a higher fraction of organic compounds resistant to direct oxidation, necessitating a catalytic process for effective degradation. In La Madera, the response surface indicates a greater influence of ozone, suggesting that the compounds present are more amenable to oxidation by ozone alone, without the need for additional catalytic assistance [25].

From a mechanistic perspective, COD removal in both leachates results from a mixed process involving direct and indirect oxidation. In El Guayabal, the presence of magnetite promoted the generation of hydroxyl radicals, which non-selectively attack recalcitrant compounds, whereas in La Madera, ozone primarily acted through direct oxidation mechanisms targeting specific chemical bonds [5]. The nature of these mechanisms has been widely explored in recent studies, which have demonstrated that combining ozone with iron-based catalysts significantly enhances process efficiency [8].

The continuous development of new catalysts facilitated the process efficiency by improving the interaction between ozone molecules and the organic materials which are included in leachates. Doping of magnetite has been shown to enhance the generation of reactive oxygen species and facilitate the degradation of recalcitrant compounds through radical and non-radical oxidation mechanisms [8]. Likewise, recent work had been focused on the combination of ozonation and electrochemical processes, leading to an effective removal of aromatic compounds and phenolic derivatives which minimizes the effect of humic substances in treatment performance [7]. The results suggest that differences in the chemical composition of the leachates directly influence treatment effectiveness, reinforcing the need to optimize operating conditions based on the type of leachate treated. Recent research has shown that leachates with higher metal contents may exhibit distinct removal kinetics due to the possible interference of cations in the generation of reactive oxygen species [28]. These differences could also explain why magnetite played a more relevant role in El Guayabal, whereas ozone demonstrated greater efficiency in La Madera.

Statistical analysis via analysis of variance (ANOVA) was conducted to evaluate the influence of independent variables on chemical oxygen demand (COD) removal in leachates from El Guayabal and La Madera (Table 7). The high statistical significance of the model in both cases (F = 1690.10 for El Guayabal and F = 937.58 for La Madera) confirms that oxygen (O_2) and magnetite (Fe_3O_4), along with their interactions and quadratic terms, have a significant effect on process efficiency. These findings align with previous studies demonstrating the relevance of operational parameters in optimizing advanced oxidation processes through statistical design [5]. Additionally, the adjusted coefficients of determination (adjusted $R^2 = 0.9986$ for El Guayabal and 0.9974 for La Madera) and adequate precision values (Adeq Precisions of 100.462 and 72.262, respectively) indicate that the model accurately describes data variability and is suitable for predicting system behavior, which is consistent with recent studies on wastewater treatment optimization [45].

In terms of interactions, both the ozone dosage and the magnetite concentration have a substantial effect on the removal efficiency, but their effects vary depending on the leachate composition (Figure 4). In El Guayabal, magnetite has a more pronounced influence, suggesting a greater dependence on hydroxyl radical (•OH) generation for organic matter degradation. This observation is consistent with previous studies indicating that leachates with a higher content of recalcitrant compounds respond more effectively to catalytic processes [5]. Conversely, in La Madera, COD removal is more strongly controlled by ozone dosage, implying that direct oxidation is the dominant mechanism in this leachate [4]. Response surface analysis reinforced these observations. In El Guayabal, the removal efficiency is maximized at medium to high magnetite concentrations (2.5–3.5 g/L), whereas in La Madera, there is a greater dependence on ozone dosage. The pronounced curvature of the response surface in El Guayabal indicates the existence of an optimal magnetite concentration, beyond which no significant improvements in efficiency are observed. This phenomenon has been reported in studies where catalyst saturation reduces the availability of free ozone for reactions [46] and has been validated in heterogeneous advanced oxidation systems [47].

From a mechanistic perspective, the interaction between ozone and magnetite under alkaline pH conditions promotes high production of hydroxyl radicals (•OH), which are primarily responsible for the advanced degradation of persistent organic compounds [4]. Ozone adsorption on the active sites of magnetite, followed by its catalytic decomposition, facilitates the generation of highly reactive oxidizing species. The combination of these mechanisms explains the high efficiency observed in this study and has been documented in other advanced oxidation systems [8]. Additionally, recent studies have highlighted the influence of catalyst surface structure on ozone adsorption and decomposition. Active sites, such as oxygen vacancies and hydrated hydroxyl groups, increase process efficiency by facilitating the formation of atomic oxygen and hydroxyl radicals. This effect is amplified under alkaline conditions, where the increased availability of hydroxide ions (OH^-) enhances the generation of oxidizing species, improving the removal of recalcitrant contaminants [46]. This combination of mechanisms not only enables the mineralization of complex organic compounds but also broadens the applicability of the system to heterogeneous aqueous matrices, further establishing catalytic ozonation with magnetite as a viable and highly efficient alternative for leachate treatment [5].

The validation of the optimal parameters via the *t*-test confirmed the reliability of the predictive model, demonstrating that the selected conditions can be accurately replicated to maximize chemical oxygen demand (COD) removal (Table 8). This result aligns with previous studies in which statistical modeling of advanced oxidation processes has proven essential for predicting and optimizing wastewater treatment efficiency [8]. Moreover, the co-application of magnetite with ozone effectively removed TSS to levels very close to the detection limits, demonstrating that ozone actively causes chemical oxidation as well as coagulation and flocculation and aids in effluent clarification (Figure 5). This phenomenon has been reported in recent studies on advanced leachate treatments and the presence of metal catalysts to increase the removal efficiency for particulate matter [27].

Moreover, the increase in conductivity indicates enhanced mineralization of organic matter, which is consistent with the formation of inorganic ions such as sulfates, carbonates, and nitrates, common byproducts of oxidative degradation [4]. Likewise, the stabilization of pH at alkaline levels after treatment agrees with findings from studies in which ozonation facilitates the formation of carbonates and bicarbonates, buffering pH fluctuations and enhancing the chemical stability of the treated medium [48].

The optimization of operational parameters has been supported by studies that have identified specific conditions to maximize the efficiency of the catalytic ozonation process. Applications of the Box–Behnken design have demonstrated high coefficients of determination ($R^2 > 0.98$) for predictive models of organic contaminant removal, confirming the direct relationship between operational variables and treatment efficiency [13]. Similarly, response surface analysis has allowed for the evaluation of the interaction among pH, ozone concentration, and catalyst dosage, establishing optimal conditions for the generation of hydroxyl radicals in the aqueous phase [12]. The characterization of intermediate products through chromatographic techniques has evidenced the transformation of refractory compounds into biodegradable species, thereby reinforcing the effectiveness of the process in removing persistent contaminants. The observed color change in the leachates (Figure 6) further confirms the degradation of chromophoric compounds, with a more pronounced reduction in trials involving ozone and magnetite, underscoring the catalytic effect in breaking down conjugated structures responsible for coloration. This effect has been widely documented in studies demonstrating that hydroxyl radical formation enhances the removal of aromatic and polyphenolic compounds [5].

Additionally, the reduction of total suspended solids (TSS) to nearly undetectable levels suggests that the combination of ozone and magnetite not only promotes chemical oxidation but also induces coagulation and flocculation, facilitating effluent clarification. This phenomenon has been described in recent research on advanced leachate treatments, where the presence of metal catalysts improved the particulate matter removal efficiency [27]. Overall, these findings reinforce the potential of catalytic ozonation with magnetite as an effective strategy for reducing the organic load and improving the quality of treated leachate, supporting its viability for integration into wastewater treatment systems with high chemical complexity.

The changes in magnetite composition following its use in the catalytic ozonation process reflect both physical and chemical modifications in the catalyst structure (Figure 7). The reduction in the Fe_3O_4 concentration after multiple treatment cycles suggests possible partial dissolution of the material or surface transformation induced by prolonged exposure to ozone and reactive oxygen species. Previous studies have reported that continuous exposure to oxidative conditions can lead to iron ion (Fe) leaching and the formation of secondary compounds on the catalyst surface [8]. The presence of elements such as silicon (Si) and titanium dioxide (TiO_2) in the samples used suggests an adsorption process involving components from the leachates, which may alter the catalyst's reactivity in subsequent applications (Figure 8). This phenomenon has been documented in prior studies, where the accumulation of contaminants on catalytic surfaces affects the distribution of active sites and the capacity to generate reactive oxygen species [48]. However, the catalyst's crystalline structure remains stable after multiple cycles, allowing for its reuse with relatively high performance in the degradation of organic compounds. This structural stability is crucial for ensuring the feasibility of the process for long-term industrial applications [45].

Given the progressive deterioration observed in magnetite composition, regeneration strategies to extend its lifespan and maintain catalytic efficiency are essential. Some studies suggest that washing with mildly acidic solutions or thermal treatments can partially restore the material's activity by removing surface impurities and regenerating active sites [49]. In this context, the recoverability of magnetite over multiple cycles will depend on the implementation of appropriate maintenance strategies to minimize catalytic activity loss and optimize performance in the treatment of complex leachates.

According to Nisticò et al. [46], magnetite (Fe_3O_4) may require treatment to maintain its catalytic activity over multiple use cycles. It explores strategies such as calcination in an oxidizing atmosphere and washing with mild acid solutions, as well as methods that restore the material's crystalline structure and magnetic properties. It points out that the conversion of magnetite to hematite (α-Fe_2O_3), which occurs at temperatures above 600 °C, can be reversed by reduction treatments, enabling the recovery of the catalyst. This was corroborated by Bona et al. [47], who describe a method based on a two-step process that allows the complete recovery of the catalyst while maintaining its efficiency. Initially, the spent magnetite is subjected to calcination in an oxidizing atmosphere at 800 °C for 4 h, which allows the removal of residual organic compounds and the conversion of partially reduced magnetite (Fe_3O_4) into hematite (α-Fe_2O_3). Subsequently, this calcined material is digested with 6 M HCl at 60 °C for 4 h, dissolving the Fe (III) in aqueous solution, which is neutralized with 6 M NaOH for subsequent re-synthesis of the catalyst by co-precipitation. The regenerated magnetite nanoparticles showed structural, physicochemical, and magnetic properties comparable to those of the fresh catalyst, which was reflected in their performance in the photo-Fenton degradation of paracetamol in water, reaching a removal of 96–98% after 120 min of UV irradiation, results superimposable to those obtained with magnetite without previous use. Similarly, Gautam and Tiwari [50] evaluated the regeneration and reuse of magnetite nanoparticles functionalized with humic acid (Fe_3O_4/HA) used as nanosorbents in the remediation of water contaminated with malachite green dye. For the regeneration of the material, different solvents were explored for the desorption of the adsorbed pollutant, finding that the treatment with 0.1 M HCl was the most effective, achieving a recovery of 95.8% of the adsorption capacity. The regeneration process consisted of immersion of the saturated material in the acid solution, followed by washing with distilled water to remove dye and acid residues before reuse. Recycling tests confirmed that the Fe_3O_4/HA nano sorbents could be reused for up to five cycles, maintaining a decolorization efficiency of over 85% for the first four uses. These results indicate that chemical regeneration with HCl can extend the catalyst's lifetime, reducing operational costs and contributing to the sustainability of the adsorption process for the treatment of contaminated water.

The results obtained demonstrate the key role of magnetite in optimizing ozone consumption and maximizing organic matter degradation (Table 9). The highest efficiency observed under alkaline conditions with elevated Fe_3O_4 concentrations aligns with previous studies that have shown that a high pH promotes the production of hydroxyl radicals, thereby increasing the rate of contaminant degradation without requiring an increased ozone dosage [32]. This effect has been widely reported in advanced wastewater treatments, where the alkalinity of the medium enhances the conversion of ozone into reactive species and improves the efficiency of oxidation processes [32].

Conversely, treatments conducted under acidic conditions and with low catalyst concentrations exhibit lower efficiency and higher ozone consumption, as also reported in previous leachate treatment studies. Under these conditions, the generation of hydroxyl radicals is more limited, resulting in a greater reliance on direct ozone oxidation, a less selective and less efficient mechanism for degrading recalcitrant compounds [45]. Comparisons with prior research indicate that optimal ozone consumption for organic matter removal falls within the range of 2.8–4.5 g O_3 per gram of COD removed, values that are consistent with those obtained in this study under optimal conditions [32].

The increased ozone consumption and lower removal efficiency due to the absence of a catalyst indicate the crucial role of the synergistic effect of ozonation with magnetite in enhancing the performance of the treatment process. Ozone utilization leads to a significant increase in hydroxyl radicals through the combination of ozone and iron-based catalysts, thus increasing the degradation rate of contaminants and shortening the effective treatment time [8]. The coupling between the catalyst and ozone is essential for making the process technologically feasible at an industrial scale, as it leads to a decrease in costs linked with the consumption of reagents and increased efficiency in the elimination of organic matter.

The increase in conductivity observed during the ozonization process is an expected and technically justifiable result. This increase is due to the oxidation of organic and inorganic compounds in the leachate, leading to more oxidized species, such as soluble ions and salts. During ozonation, complex molecules can be degraded into smaller, highly ionized fragments, which increases the concentration of conductive species in the solution. Oxidizing nitrogenous and sulfurous compounds can generate nitrates, sulfates, and other anions, increasing electrical conductivity. This behavior is, therefore, consistent with the process's chemistry and confirms the contaminants' transformation during treatment. This behavior was observed by Maharaja et al. [51] in ozone treatment applied to reverse osmosis reject stream derived from tannery effluents, where an increase in the conductivity of the treated water occurred. This effect is due to the fragmentation of organic compounds and the generation of ionized byproducts, such as sulfates, chlorides, and nitrates, which increase the concentration of conductive species in solution. Electrochemical impedance spectroscopy (EIS) analysis confirmed that the decrease in charge transfer resistance after the ozonation process is correlated with an increased electrical conductivity of the system. In the Nyquist plots, a reduction in the semicircle diameter and an increase in the linearity of the curve were observed after ozone application, indicating an increased availability of ionic species in solution.

Furthermore, the combined treatment of ozonation with hydrogen peroxide (H_2O_2) showed an even more pronounced effect on the increase in conductivity due to increased mineralization of the compounds present. This is corroborated by Wang et al. [52], who evaluated the treatment of saline wastewater from a reverse osmosis (RO) concentrate of a coal-fired chemical plant in Hebei, China. Two technologies were compared: electron beam (EB) radiation and ozonation for organic pollutant degradation and organic load reduction. The results indicated that ozone treatment impacted the conductivity of the treated water, increasing its value compared to the original wastewater. This increase is attributed to the oxidation of organic compounds into more oxidized products, such as ions and inorganic salts, which contribute to the conductivity. A comparable result was obtained by Santos et al. [53] for ozone treatment applied to dairy effluent, which showed variations in electrical conductivity depending on the presence of an activated carbon filter. During the experiments without the filter, a decrease in electrical conductivity was observed at 60 min of ozonation, remaining stable until 120 min. However, in the tests with the charcoal filter, the electrical conductivity remained constant for the first 60 min, increasing at the 90 min interval and decreasing again at 120 min. This suggests that depending on its configuration and the filter material used, ozonation can induce changes in electrical conductivity, probably associated with the release or retention of salts and ions in the treated medium.

5. Conclusions

The catalytic ozonation process with magnetite (Fe_3O_4) demonstrated high efficiency in degrading organic matter, achieving chemical oxygen demand (COD) removal rates of 85.3% in El Guayabal and 75.8% in La Madera. These differences in efficiency reflect the influence of the leachates' chemical composition, where the presence of recalcitrant compounds affects the oxidation kinetics. In both cases, the highest removal rate was observed during the first 60 min of treatment, which was attributable to the generation of hydroxyl radicals promoted by the interaction between ozone and magnetite. However, in later stages, degradation slowed, suggesting a reduced availability of easily oxidizable compounds and possible saturation of the catalyst's active sites.

Optimal condition analysis revealed that the combination of 6 g O_3/h, 2.5 g/L Fe_3O_4, and pH 9 maximized the process efficiency, with pH being the most influential variable. The alkalinity of the medium favored the production of hydroxyl radicals, thereby enhancing the removal of recalcitrant organic compounds. In contrast, tests conducted without magnetite revealed an increase in ozone consumption without a significant improvement in COD removal, confirming the catalyst's critical role in optimizing the treatment. Furthermore, the process response varied according to the specific composition of the leachate, indicating that while the catalytic effect of magnetite was decisive in El Guayabal, the predominant mechanism in La Madera was direct oxidation by ozone.

Regarding catalyst recoverability, structural and morphological analyses revealed progressive modifications on the magnetite surface after each cycle of use. A decrease in the Fe_3O_4 concentration and the adsorption of contaminants were observed, suggesting a partial loss of active sites and a potential deterioration in catalytic performance. Nevertheless, the material's structural stability allowed for its reuse over multiple cycles, albeit with a gradual decline in COD removal efficiency. The loss of material and surface changes could affect long-term performance, underscoring the need to implement regeneration strategies to prolong its service life.

Finally, the evaluation of ozone consumption confirmed that the optimal conditions minimized oxidant use, reaching a consumption of 2.7 g O_3 per gram of COD removed. In contrast, less favorable conditions, such as low magnetite concentrations or the absence of a catalyst, resulted in higher ozone demand and lower removal efficiency. These results highlight the synergy between ozone and magnetite as a key factor in optimizing the process and reducing operating costs. Based on these findings, it is recommended to explore catalyst regeneration strategies and assess their performance in continuous systems at pilot and industrial scales to ensure their viability and sustainability in managing leachates from sanitary landfills.

Author Contributions: Conceptualization, F.M.-M., A.F.B.-S. and D.B.-M.; methodology, L.F.R.-R. and J.B.G.-M.; software, A.F.B.-S. and D.B.-M.; validation, D.B.-M., L.F.R.-R. and J.B.G.-M.; formal analysis, F.M.-M. and A.F.B.-S.; investigation, D.B.-M. and L.F.R.-R.; resources, F.M.-M., A.F.B.-S. and J.B.G.-M.; data curation, F.M.-M., A.F.B.-S. and D.B.-M.; writing—original draft preparation, D.B.-M.; writing—review and editing, A.F.B.-S. and J.B.G.-M.; visualization, A.F.B.-S.; supervision, F.M.-M.; project administration, D.B.-M.; funding acquisition, F.M.-M. and A.F.B.-S. All authors have read and agreed to the published version of the manuscript.

Funding: This research was funded by Universidad Francisco de Paula Santander (Colombia) (FINU 011-2023), the Ministry of Science and Technology of Colombia, and the Colombian Institute of Educational Credit and Technical Studies Abroad (MINCIENCIAS-ICETEX) under the project titled "FOTOLIX" with ID 2023-0686.

Institutional Review Board Statement: Not applicable.

Informed Consent Statement: Not applicable.

Data Availability Statement: Data are contained within the article.

Acknowledgments: We would like to express our sincere gratitude to Universidad del Valle, Universidad del Llano, and Universidad Francisco de Paula Santander (Colombia) for providing the equipment for this research. We also thank the Colombian Ministry of Science, Technology, and Innovation MINCIENCIAS for supporting national Ph.D. Doctorates through the Francisco José de Caldas scholarship program.

Conflicts of Interest: The authors declare no conflicts of interest.

References

1. Ren, T.; Zhang, X.; Chen, S.; Huang, X.; Zhang, X. Hydrogen Peroxide and Peroxymonosulfate Intensifying Fe−doped C−Al_2O_3−framework−based Catalytic Ozonation for Advanced Treatment of Landfill Leachate: Performance and Mechanisms. *Sci. Total Environ.* **2022**, *843*, 156904. [CrossRef]
2. Ren, T.; Yin, M.; Chen, S.; Ouyang, C.; Huang, X.; Zhang, X. Single-Atom Fe-N_4 Sites for Catalytic Ozonation to Selectively Induce a Nonradical Pathway toward Wastewater Purification. *Environ. Sci. Technol.* **2023**, *57*, 3623–3633. [CrossRef] [PubMed]
3. Wang, H.; Zhang, S.; He, X.; Yang, Y.; Yang, X.; Van Hulle, S.W.H. Comparison of Macro and Micro-Pollutants Abatement from Biotreated Landfill Leachate by Single Ozonation, O_3/H_2O_2, and Catalytic Ozonation Processes. *Chem. Eng. J.* **2023**, *452*, 139503. [CrossRef]
4. Zhang, R.; Liu, J.; Gao, B.; Sillanpää, M. The Effect of Autochthonous Metal Ions and Humic Substances on Landfill Leachate Ozonation: Reactive Oxygen Species and 3D Fluorescence Analysis. *Sep. Purif. Technol.* **2025**, *354*, 129433. [CrossRef]
5. Moussavi, G.; Khosravi, R.; Omran, N.R. Development of an Efficient Catalyst from Magnetite Ore: Characterization and Catalytic Potential in the Ozonation of Water Toxic Contaminants. *Appl. Catal. A Gen.* **2012**, *445*, 42–49. [CrossRef]
6. Dong, S.; Ding, Y.; Feng, H.; Xu, J.; Han, J.; Jiang, W.; Xia, Y.; Wang, A. Source Preventing Mechanism of Florfenicol Resistance Risk in Water by VUV/UV/Sulfite Advanced Reduction Pretreatment. *Water Res.* **2023**, *235*, 119876. [CrossRef]
7. Li, S.; Lü, F.; Zhang, H.; Shao, L.; He, P. Electron Exchange Capacities of Colloidal Biochar: Affected by Spatial Structure Distribution Instead of Particle Size. *Chem. Eng. J.* **2023**, *455*, 140567. [CrossRef]
8. Ghahrchi, M.; Rezaee, A. Electrocatalytic Ozonation Process Supplemented by EDTA-Fe Complex for Improving the Mature Landfill Leachate Treatment. *Chemosphere* **2021**, *263*, 127858. [CrossRef]
9. Ma, C.; Ma, P.; He, Z.; Mi, X. A Combined Catalytic Ozonation-MBR Approach to Remove Contaminants from the Mature Landfill Leachate in the Yellow River Basin. *Toxics* **2022**, *10*, 505. [CrossRef]
10. Segundo, I.D.B.; Gomes, A.I.; Souza-Chaves, B.M.; Park, M.; dos Santos, A.B.; Boaventura, R.A.R.; Moreira, F.C.; Silva, T.F.C.V.; Vilar, V.J.P. Incorporation of Ozone-Driven Processes in a Treatment Line for a Leachate from a Hazardous Industrial Waste Landfill: Impact on the Bio-Refractory Character and Dissolved Organic Matter Distribution. *J. Environ. Chem. Eng.* **2021**, *9*, 105554. [CrossRef]
11. Braga, W.L.M.; de Melo, D.H.A.; de Morais, D.; Samanamud, G.R.L.; França, A.B.; Finzi Quintão, C.M.; Loures, C.C.A.; de Urzedo, A.P.F.M.; Naves, L.L.R.; de Freitas Gomes, J.H.; et al. Optimization of the Treatment of Sanitary Landfill by the Ozonization Catalysed by Modified Nanovermiculite in a Rotating Packed Bed. *J. Clean. Prod.* **2020**, *249*, 119395. [CrossRef]
12. Jin, X.; Wu, C.; Tian, X.; Wang, P.; Zhou, Y.; Zuo, J. A Magnetic-Void-Porous $MnFe_2O_4$/Carbon Microspheres Nano-Catalyst for Catalytic Ozonation: Preparation, Performance and Mechanism. *Environ. Sci. Ecotechnology* **2021**, *7*, 100110. [CrossRef] [PubMed]
13. Ghahrchi, M.; Rezaee, A. Electro-Catalytic Ozonation for Improving the Biodegradability of Mature Landfill Leachate. *J. Environ. Manag.* **2020**, *254*, 109811. [CrossRef] [PubMed]
14. de Brito, R.A.; Filho, H.J.I.; Aguiar, L.G.; de Alcântara, M.A.K.; Siqueira, A.F.; da Rós, P.C.M. Degradation Kinetics of Landfill Leachate by Continuous-Flow Catalytic Ozonation. *Ind. Eng. Chem. Res.* **2019**, *58*, 9855–9863. [CrossRef]
15. Tang, X.; Zhu, S.; Quan, X.; Huang, X.; Qiu, F.; Feng, C. Degradation Treatment of Concentrated Landfill Leachate by Catalytic Ozonation in a Microbubble Reactor. *Ozone Sci. Eng.* **2021**, *43*, 476–489. [CrossRef]
16. Yang, X.; Meng, L.; Meng, F. Combination of Self-Organizing Map and Parallel Factor Analysis to Characterize the Evolution of Fluorescent Dissolved Organic Matter in a Full-Scale Landfill Leachate Treatment Plant. *Sci. Total Environ.* **2019**, *654*, 1187–1195. [CrossRef]
17. Teng, C.; Zhou, K.; Peng, C.; Chen, W. Characterization and Treatment of Landfill Leachate: A Review. *Water Res.* **2021**, *203*, 117525. [CrossRef]
18. Caroline Baettker, E.; Kozak, C.; Knapik, H.G.; Aisse, M.M. Applicability of Conventional and Non-Conventional Parameters for Municipal Landfill Leachate Characterization. *Chemosphere* **2020**, *251*, 126414. [CrossRef]
19. American Public Health Association; American Water Works Association. *Water Environment Federation Standard Methods for the Examination of Water and Wastewater*, 24th ed.; Lipps, W.C., Braun-Howland, E.B., Baxter, T.E., Eds.; APHA Press: Washington, DC, USA, 2023.
20. Liu, M.; Ye, Y.; Ye, J.; Gao, T.; Wang, D.; Chen, G.; Song, Z. Recent Advances of Magnetite (Fe_3O_4)-Based Magnetic Materials in Catalytic Applications. *Magnetochemistry* **2023**, *9*, 110. [CrossRef]
21. Feng, H.; Mao, W.; Li, Y.; Wang, X.; Chen, S. Characterization of Dissolved Organic Matter during the O_3-Based Advanced Oxidation of Mature Landfill Leachate with and without Biological Pre-Treatment and Operating Cost Analysis. *Chemosphere* **2021**, *271*, 129810. [CrossRef]
22. Gu, Z.; Yang, Z.; Song, B.; Li, Q. Treatment of Landfill Leachate MBR Effluent by Ozone Combined with a Semi-Aerobic Aged Refuse Bioreactor. *J. Water Process Eng.* **2025**, *69*, 106625. [CrossRef]
23. Ricky, R.; Shanthakumar, S.; Gothandam, K.M. A Pilot-Scale Study of the Integrated Phycoremediation-Photolytic Ozonation Based Municipal Solid Waste Leachate Treatment Process. *J. Environ. Manag.* **2022**, *323*, 116237. [CrossRef] [PubMed]

24. Duan, Y.; Gao, B.; Liu, J.; Wang, X.; Sillanpää, M. Treatment of Landfill Leachate in the MBR and Catalytic Ozonation Coupled System Based on Mn Ni Catalyst: Efficiency and Bio/Chemical Mechanism. *J. Water Process Eng.* **2024**, *66*, 106033. [CrossRef]
25. Yang, Y.-Z.; Zhang, Y.; Zhan, Y.; Liu, J.-Q.; Yan, C.-C.; Zhang, Y.; Zhang, H.-L. Synergistic Enhancement of UASB Reactor for Leachate Treatment Using Fe2O3 Nanomodified Pumice and Ozone Oxidation. *Chem. Eng. J.* **2024**, *497*, 154891. [CrossRef]
26. Ma, C.; Yuan, P.; Jia, S.; Liu, Y.; Zhang, X.; Hou, S.; Zhang, H.; He, Z. Catalytic Micro-Ozonation by Fe_3O_4 Nanoparticles @ Cow-Dung Ash for Advanced Treatment of Biologically Pre-Treated Leachate. *Waste Manag.* **2019**, *83*, 23–32. [CrossRef]
27. Ma, C.; Jia, S.; Yuan, P.; He, Z. Catalytic Ozonation of 2, 2′-Methylenebis (4-Methyl-6-Tert-Butylphenol) over Nano-Fe_3O_4@cow Dung Ash Composites: Optimization, Toxicity, and Degradation Mechanisms. *Environ. Pollut.* **2020**, *265*, 114597. [CrossRef]
28. Bai, F.; Liu, S.; Zhang, Y.; Ma, J. Effective and Mechanistic Insights into Reverse Osmosis Concentrate of Landfill Leachate Treatment Using Coagulation-Catalytic Ozonation-Bioaugmentation-Based AnMBR. *Chem. Eng. J.* **2023**, *463*, 142430. [CrossRef]
29. Mu, S.; Chen, X.; Song, B.; Wu, C.; Li, Q. Enhanced Performance and Mechanism of the Combined Process of Ozonation and a Semiaerobic Aged Refuse Biofilter for Mature Landfill Leachate Treatment. *Chemosphere* **2022**, *308*, 136432. [CrossRef]
30. Yuan, Y.; Liu, J.; Gao, B.; Sillanpää, M. Landfill Leachate Treatment In-Depth by Bio-Chemical Strategy: Microbial Activation and Catalytic Ozonation Mechanism. *Chem. Eng. J.* **2022**, *444*, 136464. [CrossRef]
31. Zhu, Y.; Luo, H.; Wang, T.; Zhou, J.; Zhu, Y.; Hou, J. Advanced Treatment of Landfill Leachate by Catalytic Ozonation with MnCeOx/γ-Al_2O_3 Catalyst. *Surf. Interfaces* **2024**, *46*, 104113. [CrossRef]
32. Pophali, G.R.; Hedau, S.; Gedam, N.; Rao, N.N.; Nandy, T. Treatment of Refractory Organics from Membrane Rejects Using Ozonation. *J. Hazard Mater.* **2011**, *189*, 273–277. [CrossRef] [PubMed]
33. Yang, Y.; Demeestere, K.; Van Hulle, S. Ozone-Based Advanced Oxidation of Biologically Treated Landfill Leachate: Oxidation Efficiency, Mechanisms, and Surrogate-Based Monitoring for Bulk Organics. *J. Environ. Chem. Eng.* **2021**, *9*, 106459. [CrossRef]
34. Scott, M.; Millar, G.J.; Altaee, A. Process Design of a Treatment System to Reduce Conductivity and Ammoniacal Nitrogen Content of Landfill Leachate. *J. Water Process Eng.* **2019**, *31*, 100806. [CrossRef]
35. Sabba, F.; Kassar, C.; Zeng, T.; Mallick, S.P.; Downing, L.; McNamara, P. PFAS in Landfill Leachate: Practical Considerations for Treatment and Characterization. *J. Hazard Mater.* **2025**, *481*, 136685. [CrossRef]
36. Jolaosho, T.L. Characterization of Potentially Toxic Elements in Leachates from Active and Closed Landfills in Nigeria and Their Effects on Groundwater Systems Using Spatial, Indexical, Chemometric and Health Risk Techniques. *Chemosphere* **2024**, *369*, 143678. [CrossRef] [PubMed]
37. Clemente, E.; Domingues, E.; Quinta-Ferreira, R.M.; Leitão, A.; Martins, R.C. European and African Landfilling Practices: An Overview on MSW Management, Leachate Characterization and Treatment Technologies. *J. Water Process Eng.* **2024**, *66*, 105931. [CrossRef]
38. Parida, B.; Dash, A.K.; Verma, A.K. Technologies for Treatment of Landfill Leachate: A Brief Review. *Recent Innov. Chem. Eng. (Former. Recent Pat. Chem. Eng.)* **2023**, *16*, 260–284. [CrossRef]
39. Torres-Herrera, S.; Palomares-Cortés, J.; González-Cortés, J.J.; Cubides-Páez, D.F.; Gamisans, X.; Cantero, D.; Ramírez, M. Start-up and Long-Term Operation of the Nitrification Process Using Landfill Leachates in a Pilot Sequencing Batch Bioreactor. *J. Water Process Eng.* **2025**, *70*, 106895. [CrossRef]
40. Liu, C.; Li, D.; Li, J.; Zhao, C.; Liu, X.; Huang, X.; Yin, F.; Shi, W.; Yu, J.; Wu, J.; et al. Treatment of Landfill Leachate by Two-Stage Electrochemical Combination Technology. *J. Environ. Chem. Eng.* **2025**, *13*, 115355. [CrossRef]
41. Das, R.; Raj, D. Sources, Distribution, and Impacts of Emerging Contaminants—A Critical Review on Contamination of Landfill Leachate. *J. Hazard. Mater. Adv.* **2025**, *17*, 100602. [CrossRef]
42. Bilardi, S.; Calabrò, P.S.; Greco, R.; Moraci, N. Selective Removal of Heavy Metals from Landfill Leachate by Reactive Granular Filters. *Sci. Total Environ.* **2018**, *644*, 335–341. [CrossRef] [PubMed]
43. Song, B.; Wang, Q.; Ali, J.; Wang, Z.; Wang, L.; Wang, J.; Li, J.; Glebov, E.M.; Zhuang, X. Biochar-Supported Fe_3C Nanoparticles with Enhanced Interfacial Contact as High-Performance Binder-Free Anode Material for Microbial Fuel Cells. *Chem. Eng. J.* **2023**, *474*, 145678. [CrossRef]
44. Zhe, J.; He, H.; Yi, Z.; Guo, Z.; Xu, H.; Huang, B.; Pan, X. Mechanism and Molecular Level Insight of Refractory Dissolved Organic Matter in Landfill Leachate Treated by Electroflocculation Coupled with Ozone. *Sep. Purif. Technol.* **2025**, *356*, 129812. [CrossRef]
45. Wang, F.; Liu, Y.; Yin, J.; Xiang, Y.; Yuan, Y.; Zhang, J.; He, C.; Zhang, H.; Xiong, Z.; Lai, B. Critical Role of Oxygen Vacancies in Catalytic Ozonation: Non-Radical Pathways and Enhanced Hydroxyl Groups. *Chem. Eng. J.* **2024**, *500*, 156952. [CrossRef]
46. Nisticò, R. A Synthetic Guide toward the Tailored Production of Magnetic Iron Oxide Nanoparticles. *Boletín Soc. Española Cerámica Y Vidr.* **2021**, *60*, 29–40. [CrossRef]
47. Bona, G.; Viganò, L.; Cantoni, M.; Mantovan, R.; Di Credico, B.; Mostoni, S.; Scotti, R.; Nisticò, R. An Experimental Demonstration on the Recyclability of Hybrid Magnetite-Humic Acid Nanoparticles. *Sustain. Mater. Technol.* **2025**, *43*, e01275. [CrossRef]
48. Zhou, L.; Liu, Y.; Shi, H.; Qing, Y.; Chen, C.; Shen, L.; Zhou, M.; Li, B.; Lin, H. Molecular Oxygen Activation: Innovative Techniques for Environmental Remediation. *Water Res.* **2024**, *250*, 121075. [CrossRef]

49. Bi, Z.; Wang, W.; Zhao, L.; Wang, X.; Xing, D.; Zhou, Y.; Lee, D.-J.; Ren, N.; Chen, C. The Generation and Transformation Mechanisms of Reactive Oxygen Species in the Environment and Their Implications for Pollution Control Processes: A Review. *Environ. Res.* **2024**, *260*, 119592. [CrossRef]
50. Gautam, R.K.; Tiwari, I. Humic Acid Functionalized Magnetic Nanomaterials for Remediation of Dye Wastewater under Ultrasonication: Application in Real Water Samples, Recycling and Reuse of Nanosorbents. *Chemosphere* **2020**, *245*, 125553. [CrossRef]
51. Maharaja, P.; Athithyan, I.; Karthiyayini, C.; Kameswari, K.S.B. Evaluation of Ozonation and Electro Oxidation Treatment for the Removal of Organics and Salt Recovery from RO Reject from Leather Industries: Sustainable Approach for the Management of Contaminated Salt in CETPs. *Appl. Catal. O Open* **2025**, *200*, 207028. [CrossRef]
52. Wang, S.; Hu, J.; Wang, J. Comparative Study of Saline Industrial Wastewater Treatment by Electron Beam Radiation and Ozonation Oxidation. *Chem. Eng. J.* **2025**, *505*, 159438. [CrossRef]
53. dos Santos, M.S.; de Mello Mattos, C.; de Mendonça, H.V. Dairy Effluent Treatment with Ozone Reactor, Zeolite and Porous Membrane in Sequential Filtration. *J. Water Process Eng.* **2025**, *71*, 107184. [CrossRef]

water

MDPI

Article

Emerging Contaminants Decontamination of WWTP Effluents by BDD Anodic Oxidation: A Way towards Its Regeneration

Joaquin R. Dominguez [1,2,*], Teresa González [1,2], Sergio E. Correia [1] and Maria M. Núñez [1]

1 Chemical Engineering Department, Universidad de Extremadura, Av. Elvas s/n, 06006 Badajoz, Spain
2 Instituto Universitario de Investigación del Agua, Cambio Climático y Sostenibilidad (IACYS), Avda. de la Investigación s/n, 06006 Badajoz, Spain
* Correspondence: jrdoming@unex.es; Tel.: +34-924289300 (ext. 86888); Fax: +34-924289385

Abstract: Electrochemical oxidation using a boron-doped diamond anode (EO-BDD) was tested to remove emerging contaminants commonly present in wastewater treatment plant effluents (WWTPe). The main objective of the work was the regeneration of this water for its possible reuse in high-quality demanding uses. In the first part of the work, we investigated the potential of this technique for removing a group of neonicotinoid pesticides (thiamethoxam (TMX), imidacloprid (ICP), acetamiprid (ACP), and thiacloprid (TCP)) in a WWTP effluent. The influence of operating variables, such as current density, the conductivity of media, supporting electrolyte type (Na_2SO_4, NaCl or $NaNO_3$), or the natural aqueous matrix on target variables were fully established. Selected target variables were: (1) the percentage of pollutant removal, (2) the kinetics (apparent pseudo-first-order kinetic rate constant), (3) total organic carbon (TOC) removal, and (4) the specific energy consumption (SEC). A response surface methodology (RSM) was applied to model the results for all cases. In the paper's final part, this technology was tested with a more broad group of common emerging pollutants, including some azole pesticides (such as fluconazole (FLZ), imazalil (IMZ), tebuconazole (TBZ), or penconazole (PNZ)), antibiotics (amoxicillin (AMX), trimethoprim (TMP), and sulfamethoxazole (SMX)), and an antidepressant (desvenlafaxine (DVF)). The results confirm the power of this technology to remove this emerging contamination in WWTP effluents which supposes an interesting way towards its regeneration.

Keywords: anodic oxidation; BDD electrodes; emerging contaminants; neonicotinoid pesticides; azole pesticides; wastewater treatment plant effluent

1. Introduction

Water resources worldwide, in general, and in the European Union (EU) are under increasing pressure, leading to water scarcity problems and quality deterioration. Furthermore, climate change and droughts contribute significantly to a decrease in the volume of fresh water available. For specific uses, wastewater treatment plant (WWTPe) effluents have been subjected to a further treatment process (tertiary), allowing them to adapt their quality to different potential uses.

In this context, the European Commission has specified the minimum quality of regenerated water for agricultural use (EU Decision 2020/741). This regulation considers that reusing adequately treated water (from WWTP effluents) has less environmental impact than other water supply alternatives. This regulation aims to guarantee regenerated, safe water for agricultural irrigation and ensure a high level of protection for the environment, humans, and animals. Concerning organic contamination, this regulation is completed with EU Decision 2020/1161, which establishes a list of priority contaminants which includes: neonicotinoid pesticides (thiamethoxam, imidacloprid, acetamiprid, and thiacloprid), antibiotics (amoxicillin, sulfamethoxazole, trimethoprim, and ciprofloxacin), antifungals (clotrimazole, fluconazole, and imazalil), or antidepressants (such as venlafaxine). The final aim of this work is to provide a feasible technology to remove these micropollutants from WWTP effluents.

Among these organic contaminants, neonicotinoid pesticides represent the most widely used insecticide worldwide [1,2], accounting for >25% of the global insecticide market. Essential, since their properties include a broad spectrum of insecticidal activity, a persistent effect, and a systemic nature [3], their use is gradually increasing over the years, and they are currently one of the best-selling insecticides in the world [4]. These pollutants are relatively persistent and mobile and are easily transported through surface and groundwater [5]. Recent works have confirmed the presence of neonicotinoids in aquatic ecosystems [6] in concentrations that exceed the reference values established to protect these ecosystems. They exhibit slow dissipation rates (half-life = 0.5 to 0.7 years) [7]. The main transport routes to aquatic ecosystems are runoff, soluble or insoluble fractions transported by melting ice, contaminated dust, and leaching into groundwater [5]. Additionally, we include in this work the emerging pollutants present in the mentioned EU Decision, which are the group of azole pesticides (fluconazole (FLZ), imazalil (IMZ), tebuconazole (TBZ), and penconazole (PNZ)), antibiotics (such as amoxicillin (AMX), trimethoprim (TMP), and sulfamethoxazole (SMX)), and antidepressants (desvenlafaxine (DVF)).

In this context, studying more efficient technologies than the conventional ones used in wastewater treatment plants (WWTPs) is necessary. Among these processes, advanced oxidation processes (AOPs) may be a great alternative. For example, we can mention ozonation [8], UV photo-oxidation [9], UV/H_2O_2, UV/Persulphate [10], sonochemical oxidation [11], and electrochemical oxidation (EO) [12,13]. EO constitutes an attractive alternative to other systems due, fundamentally, to two factors: firstly, chemical reagents are not added in the medium, and secondly, there is a greater mineralization capacity. Some authoritative reviews about mechanisms and involved species of this oxidation system have been recently published [14–16].

The EO process allows the generation of hydroxyl radicals (•OH) for organic matter oxidation to CO_2, H_2O, and inorganic salts. Some of these studies have already been published with the prospect of applying them shortly in pilot plants [14]. Due to its main properties, the boron-doped diamond (BDD) covering has emerged as a new anodic treatment. It has become the best-known electrode for degrading toxic and refractory organic compounds [17]. For this electrochemical technique, it is convenient to use an inert electrolyte that does not produce reactive species during electro-oxidation or generate them under specific conditions and that is harmless concerning the electrodes used. Various studies have verified that Na_2SO_4 is the supporting electrolyte that best degrades different pollutants/drugs [18,19]. On the other hand, due to the considerable energy costs associated with this technique, it is necessary to evaluate their viability and efficiency by determining the specific energy consumed (SEC) (amount of energy consumed per unit mass of pollutant removed (kW h g^{-1})) [19].

Regarding the potential of this technique, some exciting results were obtained in ultrapure-water (UPW), removing pharmaceuticals [20], neonicotinoid pesticides [13], and some antidepressants [21]. However, no results were found about the group of azole pesticides (present in the last EU Decision 2020/1161). Additionally, all the works mentioned here were carried out in UPW. In this case, all the experiments were carried out in natural water matrices.

The present work was divided into two parts. In the first part of the work, the EO of a mixture of neonicotinoid pesticides was carried out in the Badajoz-WWTP effluent. A design of experiments (DoE) was developed, taking as its target variables: (1) the percentage of removal of each pollutant (E, %), (2) the kinetics of the reaction (k_i, min^{-1}), (3) the removal of total organic carbon (TOC, %), and (4) the specific energy consumption (SEC, kWh μM^{-1}). The influence of different supporting electrolytes (Na_2SO_4, $NaNO_3$, and NaCl) and different aqueous matrices (Almendralejo-WWTP effluent, Peña del Águila-reservoir, and Guadiana-river) on target variables was also established. In the second part of the work, the potential of this technique was evaluated with one more broad group of emerging contaminants (azole pesticides, antibiotics, and antidepressants) in the same aqueous matrix (Badajoz-WWTP effluent).

2. Materials and Methods

2.1. Materials

The neonicotinoid pesticides (NCTs), thiamethoxam (TMX), imidacloprid (ICP), acetamiprid (ACP), and thiacloprid (TCP), added to natural water matrices were supplied by Sigma-Aldrich, Madrid, Spain, with a purity of >98% for all cases. The support electrolyte used was anhydrous sodium sulfate (Na_2SO_4) with a purity of >99%. Sodium chloride (NaCl) and sodium nitrate ($NaNO_3$) were provided by Panreac Química, Barcelona, Spain (purity >99%). The mobile phase used in the HPLC analysis was a mixture of acetonitrile (Panreac Química) and ultrapure water (Milli-Q Millipore, Madrid, Spain) acidified with formic acid (CH_2O_2) with a purity of 98–100% (supplied by Merck, Madrid, Spain).

The pharmaceutical products added to real water matrices were amoxicillin (AMX), trimethoprim (TMP), and sulfamethoxazole (SMX); all were provided by Sigma-Aldrich with a purity of 98%. Across Quimica, Madrid, Spain, supplied Desvenlafaxine (DVF) in 97% purity. The azole products, fluconazole (FLZ), imazalil (IMZ), tebuconazole (TBZ), and penconazole (PNZ), were all supplied by Sigma-Aldrich.

Electrochemical oxidation runs were carried out in a circular single-cell reactor consisting of two circular electrodes with a geometric area of 78 cm^2, with an electrode gap of 9 mm. Boron-doped diamond material (BDD) and a stainless-steel electrode (AISI 304) were used as anode and cathode, respectively. The BDD electrode was supplied by CSEM (Switzerland). Before experiments, the electrodes were polarised and cleaned with a 10 mM Na_2SO_4 solution at a current density (j) of 20 $mA \cdot cm^{-2}$ for 15 min. The electrolysis was carried out using the equipment detailed and shown in Figure 1.

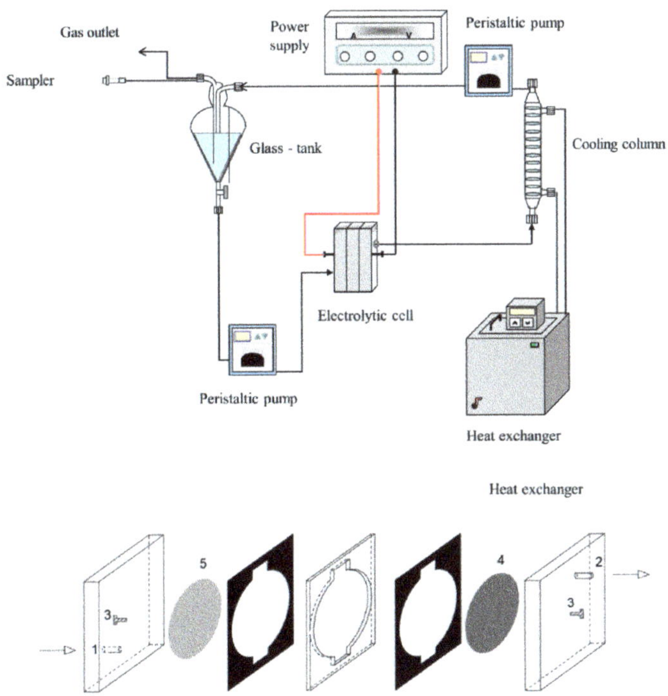

Figure 1. Electrochemical installation scheme for NCTs degradation (**top**) and electrolytic cell details (**bottom**): (1) gas inlet, (2) gas outlet, (3) power supply-electrodes connections, (4) Stainless Steel cathode, and (5) BDD anode.

2.2. Methods

The degradation of NCTs in a natural water matrix (Badajoz WWTP effluent) by electrochemical oxidation was followed by reverse-phase high-performance liquid chromatography (HPLC) using a method previously used [13,22].

Quantifications for azole pharmaceuticals (FLZ, IMZ, TBZ, and PNZ) were performed at 205 nm, 210 nm for AMX and TMP, 224 nm for DVF, and 265 nm for SMX. In all cases, we injected aliquots of 100 μL into the system. Well-defined peaks were obtained for FLZ, IMZ, TBZ, and PNZ at 7.68, 15.06, 24.24, and 25.17 min, respectively. Peaks were obtained for AMX, TMP, DVF, and SMX at 2.69, 4.86, 5.47, and 7.88 min, respectively. TOC content was determined using an Analytikjena Multi N/C® 3100 analyzer.

Real water matrices used in this investigation (Badajoz-WWTP effluent, Almendralejo-WWTP effluent, Peña del Águila-reservoir, and Guadiana-river) were thoroughly characterized (physicochemical characterization) in previous work [13]. The samples were filtered through a 0.45 μm filter and stored in the dark at 4 °C for later use. Before their use, these water matrices were dopped with the corresponding mixture of contaminants (concentration of each = 1 μM).

The study of the influence of variables on the electro-oxidation process was planned and statistically analyzed using Statgraphics Plus 5.1 for Windows with a randomized central composite orthogonal and rotatable design (CCORD). The target variables were the percentage of pollutant removal (Ei, %) (Equation (1)), the apparent pseudo-first-order kinetic rate constant (k_i) (Equation (2)), TOC removal (TOC, %), and the specific energy consumption (SEC, kWh μM^{-1}) (Equation (3)). After determining the essential factors, a response surface methodology model (RSM) was used. This method fits a second-order equation (Equation (4)) for predicting a theoretical response, where the quadratic terms model the curvature. The validity of the applied model was supported by the analysis of the variance (ANOVA test).

$$Ei = \left(\frac{N_o - N}{N_o}\right)100 \tag{1}$$

$$In\left(\frac{N_o}{N}\right) = k_i \cdot t \tag{2}$$

$$SEC = \frac{E_{cell} \cdot I \cdot t}{3600 \cdot V \cdot (N_o - N)} \tag{3}$$

N_o is the initial concentration of each contaminant (μM), N is the concentration at different reaction times (μM), t is the reaction time (min), E_{cell} is the applied cell potential (V), I is the supplied current intensity (A), and V is the volume of solution (dm^3).

$$Y = a + b\,C + c\,j + d\,C^2 + e\,C\,j + f\,j^2 \tag{4}$$

Y is the predicted response (E, k_i, TOC, or SEC) and a, b, c, d, e, and f are the polynomial coefficients of the fitting equation for the linear, quadratic, and second-order terms. The experimental conditions (coded variables-experimental variables) used for each run are shown in Table 1.

Table 1. Experimental conditions for electrochemical oxidation of neonicotinoid mixture (1 μM each). Aqueous matrix = Badajoz WWTP effluent.

Experiment	Coded Variables		Real Variables	
			j ($mA \cdot cm^{-2}$)	C ($mS \cdot cm^{-1}$)
EO-1	0	0	20	3.5
EO-2	0	0	20	3.5
EO-3	1.41	0	34.14	3.5
EO-4	1	−1	30	2.0
EO-5	0	0	20	3.5

Table 1. *Cont.*

Experiment	Coded Variables		Real Variables	
			j ($mA \cdot cm^{-2}$)	C ($mS \cdot cm^{-1}$)
EO-6	1	1	30	5.0
EO-7	0	0	20	3.5
EO-8	−1.41	0	5.6	3.5
EO-9	−1	1	10	5.0
EO-10	0	0	20	3.5
EO-11	0	−1.4142	20	1.4
EO-12	−1	−1	10	2.0
EO-13	0	0	20	3.5
EO-14	0	0	20	3.5
EO-15	0	1.4142	20	5.6
EO-16	0	0	20	3.5

3. Results and Discussion

3.1. *Influence of Operating Variables on the Electrochemical Oxidation of Neonicotinoid Pesticides in a WWTP Effluent*

The response surface methodology (RSM) has been used according to a Central Composite Design (DCC) [23]. The target variables were the percentage of pollutant removal (E, %) (Equation (1)), the apparent pseudo-first-order kinetic rate constant (k_i) (Equation (2)), TOC removal (TOC, %), and the specific energy consumption (SEC, kWh μM^{-1}) (Equation (3)).

3.1.1. Neonicotinoids Removal as the Target Variable

In this section, the influences of the current density (j) and the conductivity of the media (C) on neonicotinoids removal (TMX, ICP, ACP, and TCP) were evaluated. The conductivity of the media was adjusted by adding Na_2SO_4 for all cases. The removal percentages achieved for each contaminant at different reaction times (60 and 120 min) are shown in Table 2 (Ei, %). Obtained results agree with those obtained by Meijide et al. [24] for TMX degradation using Na_2SO_4 (0.01 M), BDD anode, and carbon-felt cathode. However, improved levels of degradation were obtained by Brahim et al. [25] for ICP oxidation using the same electrolyte with a Ta/PbO_2 anode and a Pt cathode.

Table 2. NCTs removal (%) at 60 and 120 min of electrochemical treatment time. Aqueous matrix = Badajoz WWTP effluent. See the experimental conditions for each experiment in Table 1.

Exp.	$E_{TMX,60}$ (%)	$E_{ICP,60}$ (%)	$E_{ACP,60}$ (%)	$E_{TCP,60}$ (%)	$E_{TMX,120}$ (%)	$E_{ICP,120}$ (%)	$E_{ACP,120}$ (%)	$E_{TCP,120}$ (%)
EO-1	96.0	97.3	85.1	99.0	100	100	97.5	100
EO-2	96.9	97.6	85.8	99.1	100	100	98.2	100
EO-3	100	100	97.8	100	100	100	100	100
EO-4	98.6	98.6	93.5	100	100	100	100	100
EO-5	97.1	98.2	88.1	100	100	100	98.4	100
EO-6	100	99.6	96.7	100	100	100	100	100
EO-7	95.9	97.5	84.1	99.0	100	100	97.3	100
EO-8	73.7	75.9	45.0	75.0	92.6	94.1	72.0	94.4
EO-9	86.9	89.6	65.4	94.2	98.0	98.7	87.9	100
EO-10	95.5	96.8	82.2	98.6	100	100	96.5	100
EO-11	95.6	96.3	82.1	98.5	100	100	96.1	100
EO-12	83.4	85.0	58.6	91.0	96.4	98.5	81.4	97.8
EO-13	95.7	97.1	85.3	99.1	100	99.6	97.7	100
EO-14	97.1	97.5	85.7	99.0	100	100	98.4	100
EO-15	98.8	98.9	93.2	100	100	100	100	100
EO-16	96.7	97.7	86.8	100	100	100	97.7	100

Figure 2 shows the response surface and level curves corresponding to ACP removal at 60 min of reaction time. These surfaces are convex within the study region. The percentage of neonicotinoids removal increases with current density (j). However, the curvature has an asymptotic tendency (less influential at longer treatment times), whereas conductivity's influence is positive but moderate.

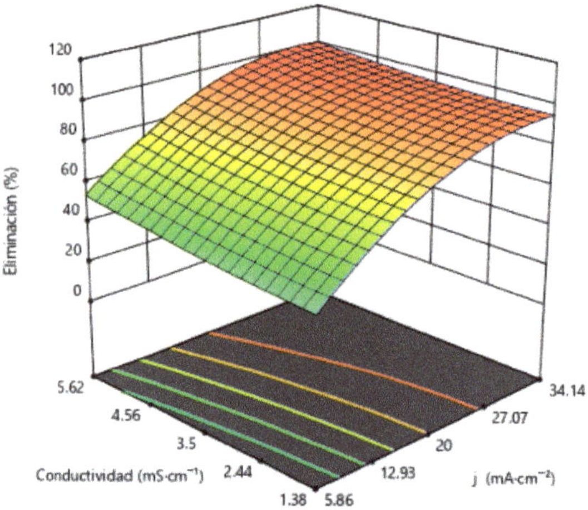

Figure 2. Estimated response surface and level curves for ACP removal at 60 min of reaction time. Aqueous matrix = Badajoz WWTP effluent.

The above trend was attributed to the proportional relationship between the hydroxyl radicals concentration (·OH) generated on the electrode surface and the applied current density (*j*). Thus, these hydroxyl radicals can react with the neonicotinoid molecules and break them down. High *j* values increase the hydroxyl radical production rate and, thus, the pollutant removal rate [24]. However, the removal efficiency does not increase proportionally with the current density. The observed asymptotic trend (see Figure 2) is due to radical deactivation (see Equation (5)) at high current densities and other oxidation (parasite) reactions with other NCT oxidation intermediates (see Equation (6)) [25]. Additionally, at higher current densities, the high generation of hydrogen bubbles at the cathode negatively affects the oxidation process in the aqueous phase.

$$OH + \cdot OH \rightarrow H_2O_2 \tag{5}$$

Concerning the influence of reaction time, at low current density values (experiment EO-8, $j = 5.6\ mA \cdot cm^{-2}$), ACP removal increases from 45% (at 60 min) to 72% (at 120 min). In contrast, for high-density values (EO-1 experiment, $j = 20\ mA \cdot cm^2$), the pollutant removal increased softly from 85.1% to 97.5% (see Table 2). This was also attributed to secondary reactions with other oxidation intermediates.

$$OH + \cdot Pox1 \rightarrow Pox2 \tag{6}$$

3.1.2. Kinetics as the Target Variable

In this case, the target variable was the reaction kinetics measured by the pseudo-first-order kinetic rate constant (k_i) (see Equation (2)). The conductivity adjustment was carried out by adding Na_2SO_4 for all cases. The results after 120 min of reaction time are shown in Table 3 (see the experimental conditions in Table 1).

Table 3. Pseudo-first-order kinetic rate constant for the electrochemical oxidation of the different neonicotinoids. (Experimental conditions in Table 1). Aqueous matrix = Badajoz WWTP effluent.

Experiment	k_{TMX} (min^{-1})	k_{ICP} (min^{-1})	k_{ACP} (min^{-1})	k_{TCP} (min^{-1})
EO-1	0.0536	0.0593	0.0310	0.0800
EO-2	0.0560	0.0609	0.0330	0.0803
EO-3	0.0920	0.1062	0.0625	0.1438
EO-4	0.0731	0.0840	0.0457	0.1153
EO-5	0.0564	0.0638	0.0345	0.0911
EO-6	0.0894	0.0981	0.0523	0.1389
EO-7	0.0534	0.0592	0.0308	0.0804
EO-8	0.0220	0.0237	0.0104	0.0265
EO-9	0.0332	0.0368	0.0176	0.0451
EO-10	0.0542	0.0566	0.0285	0.0730
EO-11	0.0491	0.0531	0.0277	0.0750
EO-12	0.0287	0.0351	0.0143	0.0352
EO-13	0.0536	0.0611	0.0314	0.0819
EO-14	0.0574	0.0604	0.0336	0.0786
EO-15	0.0696	0.0755	0.0433	0.0885
EO-16	0.0544	0.0626	0.0325	0.0846

The experimental results of the design were fitted to an equation of type 4. Equations (7)–(10) show the adjustment coefficients for each factor for TMX, ICP, ACP, and TCP contaminants, respectively. These equations show a positive effect on the degradation rate of all operative variables (j and C), including their interactions.

$$k_{TMX} = 0.0549 + 0.0249 \cdot j + 0.0062 \cdot C + 0.0005 \cdot j^2 + 0.0029 \cdot j \cdot C + 0.0017 \cdot C^2 \quad (7)$$

$$k_{ICP} = 0.0605 + 0.0284 \cdot j + 0.0059 \cdot C + 0.0019 \cdot j^2 + 0.0031 \cdot j \cdot C + 0.0016 \cdot C^2 \quad (8)$$

$$k_{ACP} = 0.0319 + 0.0175 \cdot j + 0.0040 \cdot C + 0.0014 \cdot j^2 + 0.0008 \cdot j \cdot C + 0.0009 \cdot C^2 \quad (9)$$

$$k_{TCP} = 0.0812 + 0.0425 \cdot j + 0.0066 \cdot C + 0.0020 \cdot j^2 + 0.0034 \cdot j \cdot C + 0.0003 \cdot C^2 \quad (10)$$

For all cases, the values of the regression coefficients of k_i plots presented in Table 3 were greater than 0.990. As is shown in this Table, k_i values increase with current density, implying a more significant generation of •OH radicals [12]. On the other hand, it is observed that the values of k_i corresponding to runs EO-1, EO-11, and EO-15 are very similar, indicating that the conductivity poorly influences the degradation rate (at least in this study region) in this aqueous matrix. However, a higher current density (see experiments EO-3 and EO-8) conducts a higher kinetic rate constant because of a higher •OH radicals concentration on the electrode's surface [26].

3.1.3. TOC Removal as the Target Variable

In this section, the results are analyzed, taking as the target variable the removal of total organic carbon (TOC) expressed as a percentage (% E_{COT}) after 120 min of reaction time. As shown in Table 4, higher percentages of TOC removal were obtained when the current density increased. According to other authors, higher mineralization was reached under a higher current density [27]; however, the influence of the conductivity was softly positive in this study range (54.8–62.5%).

As shown the Figure 3, TOC removal efficiency depends more firmly on the current density (j). This fact is fundamental because we aim to degrade the pollutants and mineralize them to CO_2 and H_2O.

Table 4. Elimination of TOC in the electrochemical oxidation of the neonicotinoid mixture at 120 min of reaction time. Aqueous matrix = Badajoz WWTP effluent. (Experimental conditions see Table 1).

Experiment	E_{TOC} (%)	Experiment	E_{TOC} (%)
EO-1	58.37	EO-09	45.39
EO-2	59.11	EO-10	58.00
EO-3	77.09	EO-11	54.85
EO-4	74.91	EO-12	42.67
EO-5	60.00	EO-13	60.80
EO-6	75.47	EO-14	58.12
EO-7	60.26	EO-15	62.55
EO-8	27.33	EO-16	58.33

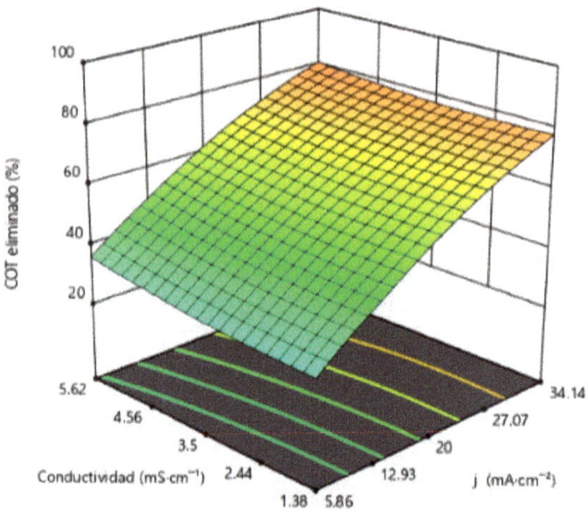

Figure 3. Response surface and contour curves for TOC removal in the electrochemical oxidation of the neonicotinoid mixture. Aqueous matrix = Badajoz WWTP effluent.

3.1.4. Energy Efficiency as the Target Variable

The specific energy consumed (SEC) was determined to evaluate the energetic and economic viability of the process (see Equation (3)). Table 5 shows the average values obtained after 120 min of treatment under different experimental conditions (see Table 1).

Table 5. Specific energy consumed (SEC) in the electrochemical oxidation process. Aqueous matrix = Badajoz WWTP effluent. Experimental conditions in Table 1.

Experiment	SEC ($kW{\cdot}h{\cdot}g^{-1}$)	Experiment	SEC ($kW{\cdot}h{\cdot}g^{-1}$)
EO-1	0.0107	EO-9	0.0052
EO-2	0.0107	EO-10	0.0108
EO-3	0.0172	EO-11	0.0144
EO-4	0.0163	EO-12	0.0064
EO-5	0.0105	EO-13	0.0103
EO-6	0.0131	EO-14	0.0107
EO-7	0.0102	EO-15	0.0090
EO-8	0.0046	EO-16	0.0107

As is shown in Table 5, in the experiments carried out with a constant electrolyte conductivity (experiments EO-1, EO-3, and EO-8) (see Table 1), an increase in current intensity produces an increase in the SEC parameter (which measures energy efficiency), increasing the costs associated with the process. For the experiments carried out with a constant applied current intensity (experiments EO-1, EO-11, and EO-15) (see Table 1), the cell's potential increases inversely proportional to the conductivity of the electrolyte, negatively influencing the energy efficiency of the process. Thus, we can constate a positive influence of the conductivity of media (C) on the SEC parameter, reducing the associated energy costs by up to 38%.

3.2. *Influence of Supporting Electrolyte Type on WWTPe Treatment*

The supporting electrolyte type is essential in the electrochemical treatment. The presence of these electrolytes increases conductivity, decreases resistance, and, therefore, reduces the energy cost of the process. In several cases, the electrochemistry of the electrolytes plays an essential role in the process due to the possible formation of secondary products that can increase or decrease the process's efficiency. Chloride and sulfate salts are two of the most widely used electrolytes. Rabaaoui et al. [18] stated that anodic oxidation of aqueous chloride or sulphate solutions promotes hypochlorite and persulfate species. Adding these electrolytes to the effluent should improve conductivity and increase electron mass transfer [28]. In this context, Na_2SO_4 is often used as a supporting electrolyte because it generates species of peroxy-disulfate ($S_2O_8{}^{2-}$) (see Equations (11)–(13)), a potent oxidant. Anions, in low concentrations, can trap photogenerated electrons more efficiently than O_2 and hinder the recombination of electrons and holes. A very detailed mechanism for the production of persulphate was proposed by Araujo et al. [29].

$$2SO_4{}^{2-} \rightarrow S_2O_8{}^{2-} + 2e^- \quad (11)$$

$$2H_2SO_4{}^{-} + 2 \cdot OH \rightarrow S_2O_8{}^{2-} + 2H_2O \quad (12)$$

$$SO_4{}^{-} + SO_4{}^{-} \rightarrow S_2O_8{}^{2-} \quad (13)$$

On the other hand, the case of NaCl was related to the existence of soluble Cl_2 and HClO, generated from the oxidation of chloride anions on the anode, which is shown in the following Equations (14)–(18) [16,19]:

$$2Cl^- \rightarrow Cl_2 + 2e^- \quad (14)$$

$$Cl_2 + H_2O \rightarrow HOCl + H^+ + Cl^- \quad (15)$$

$$HOCl \rightarrow ClO^- + H^+ \quad (16)$$

$$Cl^- \rightarrow Cl\cdot + e^- \quad (17)$$

$$ClO_2{}^- \rightarrow ClO_2\cdot + e^- \quad (18)$$

Other studies analyzed the influence of $NaNO_3$ as a supporting electrolyte, concluding that it is an inert reagent in the chemical electro-oxidation process [30].

In the present work, three sodium salts (NaCl, Na_2SO_4, and $NaNO_3$) were used to investigate the influence of the electrolyte type on the process (in the Badajoz WWTP effluent). The removal percentages achieved for each pollutant (at 60 min of reaction time) are shown in Table 6 for experiment EO-4 (see conditions in Table 1). The conductivity adjustment has been made by adding the necessary amount of supporting electrolyte until it reaches 2 mS cm^{-1}. As shown in Table 6, the pollutant removal at 60 min was maximum when Na_2SO_4 was used as a supporting electrolyte.

These results are confirmed by the pseudo-first-order kinetic rate constants obtained for NCTs removal (experiment EO-4) using different electrolytes (see Table 7). The influence of the supporting electrolyte on TOC removal (EO-4 experiment) at 120 min of reaction time (Badajoz WWTP effluent) is practically negligible. These results follow the results of Velappan et al. [31] for other contaminants in other complex aqueous matrices.

Table 6. Neonicotinoids removal at 60 min of reaction time for experiment EO-4. Aqueous matrix = Badajoz WWTP effluent.

Electrolyte	$E_{TMX,60}$ (%)	$E_{ICP,60}$ (%)	$E_{ACP,60}$ (%)	$E_{TCP,60}$ (%)
EO-NaCl	83.1	91.1	64.8	100
EO-$NaNO_3$	92.0	91.4	79.7	90,6
EO-Na_2SO_4	98.6	99.3	93.5	100

Table 7. Pseudo-first-order kinetic rate constants for NCTs removal (experiment EO-4) with different supporting electrolytes. Aqueous matrix = Badajoz WWTP effluent.

Experiment	k_{TMX} (min^{-1})	R^2	k_{ICP} (min^{-1})	R^2	k_{ACP} (min^{-1})	R^2	k_{TCP} (min^{-1})	R^2
EO-NaCl	0.0312	0.99	0.0395	1.00	0.0216	0.976	0.0334	0.99
EO-$NaNO_3$	0.0410	1.00	0.0402	1.00	0.0259	0.999	0.0387	1.00
EO-Na_2SO_4	0.0731	1.00	0.0840	1.00	0.0457	0.999	0.1153	1.00

3.3. *Influence of the Real Aqueous Matrix*

Different aqueous matrices, such as surface water, groundwater, and WWTP effluents, contain different concentrations of inorganic and organic species. Species can interfere with or potentiate electrochemical treatment [12]. The role of chloride in the anodic oxidation of organics is of particular interest, as it is commonly present in wastewater [32]. In this sense, the aqueous matrix's complexity affects the process's efficiency.

NCTs removal was carried out in four real water matrices, that is, Guadiana-river (RW-1), Villar del Rey-reservoir (RW-2), Almendralejo-WWTP effluent (RW-3), and Badajoz WWTP effluent (RW-4). Aqueous matrices were filtered through a 0.45 μm filter and stored in the dark at 4 °C for later use. A complete physicochemical characterization of these different water matrices was carried out (see Table 8) [13]. The mixture of NCTs (concentration of each = 1 μM) was added to each real matrix.

Table 8. Physico-chemical characterization of different real aqueous matrices.

Parameter	RW-1 (Guadiana River)	RW-2 (Reservoir Villar del Rey)	RW-3 (Almendralejo WWTP)	RW-4 (Badajoz WWTP)
pH	7.95	8.11	8.72	7.57
Conductivity ($\mu S \cdot cm^{-1}$)	641	151	2332	538
Turbidity (NTU)	0.58	0.44	0.98	0.61
TOC ($mg \cdot L^{-1}$)	7.04	8.69	20.04	9.66
COD (mg $O_2 \cdot L^{-1}$)	22.4	26.8	60.7	29.7
Total phosphorus (mg $P \cdot L^{-1}$)	0.06	0.05	0.99	1.27
Total nitrogen (mg $N \cdot L^{-1}$)	2.3	1.6	11.6	12.1
Nitrate (mg $NO_3^- \cdot L^{-1}$)	8.5	1.3	30.5	23.7
Nitrite (μg $NO_2^- \cdot L^{-1}$)	51	634	57	621
Ammonium (mg $NH_4^+ \cdot L^{-1}$)	0.23	0.78	1.17	3.87
A_{254nm} (cm^{-1})	0.135	0.140	0.559	0.183
Total solids ($mg \cdot L^{-1}$)	360	250	1690	410
Fixed solids ($mg \cdot L^{-1}$)	285	175	1390	325
Volatile solids ($mg \cdot L^{-1}$)	75	75	300	85

Table 9 shows the elimination percentage of each neonicotinoid (Ei, %) in each aqueous matrix (RW-1, RW-2, RW-3, and RW-4) at 60 min of reaction time. The experiments were carried out under the same conditions (see EO-4 experiment in Table 1). The conductivity adjustment was carried out by adding the amount of Na_2SO_4 (supporting electrolyte) necessary to reach 2.0 $mS \cdot cm^{-1}$. A significant increase in the degradation level for all neonicotinoids was found with the following sequence: RW-1 > RW-4 > RW-2 > RW-3.

This fact is attributable to anionic species acting as ·OH radical scavengers (such as NO_3^-, HPO_4^{2-}, or HCO_3^-) [13]. Another factor that can influence efficiency is pH. All the experiments were carried out with the natural pH of the sample (pH_o), which presented a basic initial pH, obtaining similar pH values at the end of each experiment.

Table 9. NCTs removal at 60 min in different real aqueous matrices.

Exp.	$E_{TMX,60}$ (%)	$E_{ICP,60}$ (%)	$E_{ACP,60}$ (%)	$E_{TCP,60}$ (%)
RW-1	100	100	97.4	100
RW-2	97.1	97.6	88.7	99
RW-3	74.9	86,0	55.4	100
RW-4	98.6	98.6	93.5	100

This reactivity sequence was also corroborated by the pseudo-first-order kinetic rate constants obtained for this experiment (EO-4) in the different aqueous matrices (see Table 10).

Table 10. Pseudo-first-order kinetic constant in the electro-oxidation of neonicotinoids for different aqueous matrices.

Experiment	k_{TMX} (min^{-1})	R^2	k_{ICP} (min^{-1})	R^2	k_{ACP} (min^{-1})	R^2	k_{TCP} (min^{-1})	R^2
RW-1	0.0908	1.00	0.1005	1.00	0.0600	1.00	0.1745	1.00
RW-2	0.0567	1.00	0.0577	1.00	0.0353	1.00	0.0765	1.00
RW-3	0.0202	1.00	0.0376	0.99	0.0126	0.99	0.3643	0.96
RW-4	0.0731	1.00	0.084	1.00	0.0457	1.00	0.1153	1.00

Regarding TOC removal, after 120 min of reaction in the different aqueous matrices, we reached values of 17.91%, 28.21%, 78.43%, and 74.91% for RW-1, RW-2, RW-3, and RW-4, respectively.

In this sense, humic and fulvic acids represent up to 80% of natural waters' TOC (as dissolved organics). Humic substances are weak acidic electrolytes with carboxylic and phenolic groups with a micelle-like structure and molecular weights between 500 (fulvic) and 100,000 (humic). Degradation is usually inhibited by the presence of humic acids [12]. The inhibitory effect of humic acids can be attributed to two facts [33,34]: the removal of reactive species by humic acids and the appearance of a competitive reaction between humic acid and NCTs for reactive ·OH species [13].

3.4. Electrochemical Oxidation of a Broad Group of Emerging Pollutants in a WWTP Effluent

This final section investigates the potential of this technique with a broad group of emerging contaminants in the same aqueous matrix (Badajoz-WWTP effluent). The contaminants chosen for this study are divided into three groups: azole pesticides (fluconazole (FLZ), imazalil (IMZ), tebuconazole (TBZ), and penconazole (PNZ)), antibiotics (amoxicillin (AMX), trimethoprim (TMP), and sulfamethoxazole (SMX)), and antidepressants (desvenlafaxine (DVF)). These compounds are included in the substance observation list for monitoring at the European Union, following Directive 2008/105/EC of the European Parliament [35]. All these compounds were added to the Badajoz-WWTP effluent at a concentration of each = 1 μM.

The experimental conditions were the same as those in the previous sections (see experiment EO-4 of Table 1). The conductivity adjustment was carried out by adding Na_2SO_4 until reaching 2.0 $mS \cdot cm^{-1}$. The elimination percentages achieved for azole pesticides at different reaction times (10 and 60 min) are shown in Table 11. As was previously mentioned, no investigations were found about the EO of this group of azole pesticides in real effluents.

Table 11. Azole pesticide removals. Experiment EO-4 (see Table 1). Reaction time (10 and 60 min). Aqueous matrix = Badajoz-WWTP effluent. Initial contaminants concentration of each = 1 μM.

Experiment	$E_{FLZ,10}$ (%)	$E_{IMZ,10}$ (%)	$E_{TBZ,10}$ (%)	$E_{PNZ,10}$ (%)	$E_{FLZ,60}$ (%)	$E_{IMZ,60}$ (%)	$E_{TBZ,60}$ (%)	$E_{PNZ,60}$ (%)
Azole pesticides	23.9	96.3	73.8	77.5	80.6	100	100	100

The removal percentages achieved for antibiotics and antidepressants at different reaction times (5 and 10 min) are shown in Table 12 (experiment EO-4). These results agree with those obtained by Murillo-Sierra et al. [36] for SMX degradation using Na_2SO_4 (0.05 M), a BDD anode, and a carbon-felt cathode. However, these results improve the degradation levels obtained by Brito et al. [37] for AMX oxidation using the same electrolyte (0.1 M) with a TiO_2-modified carbon anode and a steel wire cathode.

Table 12. Antibiotics removal. Experiment EO-4 (see Table 1). Reaction times (5 and 10 min). Aqueous matrix = Badajoz-WWTP effluent. Initial contaminants concentration of each = 1 μM.

Experiment	E_{AMX5} (%)	E_{TMP5} (%)	E_{DVF5} (%)	E_{SMX5} (%)	E_{AMX10} (%)	E_{TMP10} (%)	E_{DVF10} (%)	E_{SMX10} (%)
Antibiotics/ Antidepressants	98.2	57.8	100	98.2	100	88.8	100	100

We can conclude that there is a higher reactivity for antidepressants (antidepressants > antibiotics > azole pesticides > neonicotinoids). This observation supports the assertion that this technique suits NCTs and a large group of emerging contaminants in this effluent type (WWTP effluent) for regeneration purposes.

4. Conclusions

Electrochemical oxidation with boron-doped diamond anodes demonstrated a great potential to remove a broad group of emerging contaminants (antidepressants, antibiotics, azole pesticides, and neonicotinoids) in a WWTP effluent aqueous matrix. While other advanced oxidation techniques achieve similar levels of degradation in similar treatment times, none achieves the mineralization levels achieved through this oxidation system.

Total contaminant removal (100%) of each contaminant and TOC removals between 27–77% were obtained. The energy consumption ranged between $4.60 \cdot 10^{-3}$–$1.44 \cdot 10^{-2}$ $kW \cdot h \cdot g^{-1}$ in this WWTP effluent.

Regarding the influence of operating variables, the applied current density positively affects the contaminant removal, TOC removal, and kinetics but considerably worsens the energy consumption and, therefore, the associated costs. The influence of the conductivity of media was positive (but very soft) on all target variables except for energy consumption, which strongly influences reducing the associated costs by up to 38%.

Concerning the electrolyte type, the best results were obtained by using Na_2SO_4. The aqueous matrix significantly influences the degradation rate of contaminants with the following ranking sequence: Guadiana-river > Badajoz-WWTP effluent > Villar del Rey-reservoir > Almendalejo-WWTP effluent. These results were attributable to anionic species acting as ·OH radical scavengers (such as NO_3^-, HPO_4^{2-}, or HCO_3^-). The process kinetics fit well to a pseudo-first-order pattern, following a reactivity ranking (in WWTP effluent): antidepressants > antibiotics > azole pesticides > neonicotinoids.

Author Contributions: J.R.D.: Supervision, Conceptualization, Writing—original draft preparation, Writing-Reviewing, and Editing; T.G.: Supervision, Conceptualization, Writing—original draft preparation, Methodology, Writing-Reviewing, and Editing; S.E.C.: Laboratory Investigation and Validation; M.M.N.: Laboratory Investigation and Validation. All authors have read and agreed to the published version of the manuscript.

Funding: This research was funded by Ministerio de Ciencia e Innovacion of Spain (Agencia Estatal de Investigación) MCIN/AEI/10.13039/501100011033 under project PID2020-113389RB-I00 as well as the project GR21106 funded by Junta de Extremadura and European Funds for Regional Development (FEDER, EU). APC funded by MDPI.

Data Availability Statement: No new data were created.

Acknowledgments: The authors acknowledge the financial support of this research through the Ministerio de Ciencia e Innovacion of Spain (Agencia Estatal de Investigación) MCIN/AEI/10.13039/501100011033 under project PID2020-113389RB-I00 as well as the project GR21106 funded by Junta de Extremadura and European Funds for Regional Development (FEDER, EU).

Conflicts of Interest: The authors declare no conflict of interest.

References

1. World Health Organization. *Residuos de Plaguicidas en los Alimentos*; World Health Organization: Geneva, Switzerland, 2018.
2. Linhart, C.; Panzacchi, S.; Belpoggi, F.; Clausing, P.; Zaller, J.G.; Hertoge, K. Year-round pesticide contamination of public sites near intensively managed agricultural areas in South Tyrol. *Environ. Sci. Eur.* **2021**, *33*, 1. [CrossRef]
3. Jeschke, P.; Nauen, R.; Schindler, M.; Elbert, A. Overview of the status and global strategy for neonicotinoids. *J. Agric. Food Chem.* **2011**, *59*, 2897–2908. [CrossRef]
4. Selvam, V. Neonicotinoid poisoning and management. *Indian J. Crit. Care Med.* **2019**, *23*, S260–S262. [CrossRef]
5. Bonmatin, J.M.; Giorio, C.; Girolami, V.; Goulson, D.; Kreutzweiser, D.P.; Krupke, C.; Liess, M.; Long, E.; Marzaro, M.; Mitchell, E.A.; et al. Environmental fate and exposure; neonicotinoids and fipronil. *Environ. Sci. Pollut. Res.* **2015**, *22*, 35–67. [CrossRef] [PubMed]
6. Main, A.R.; Michel, N.L.; Headley, J.V.; Peru, K.M.; Morrissey, C.A. Ecological and Landscape Drivers of Neonicotinoid Insecticide Detections and Concentrations in Canada's Prairie Wetlands. *Environ. Sci. Technol.* **2015**, *49*, 8367–8376. [CrossRef] [PubMed]
7. Schaafsma, A.; Limay-Rios, V.; Xue, Y.; Smith, J.; Baute, T. Field-scale examination of neonicotinoid insecticide persistence in soil as a result of seed treatment use in commercial maize (corn) fields in southwestern Ontario. *Environ. Toxicol. Chem.* **2016**, *35*, 295–302. [CrossRef] [PubMed]
8. Zhao, Q.; Ge, Y.; Zuo, P.; Shi, D.; Jia, S. Degradation of Thiamethoxam in aqueous solution by ozonation: Influencing factors, intermediates, degradation mechanism and toxicity assessment. *Chemosphere* **2016**, *146*, 105–112. [CrossRef]
9. Chen, L.; Cai, T.; Cheng, C.; Xiong, Z.; Ding, D. Degradation of acetamiprid in UV/H_2O_2 and UV/persulfate systems: A comparative study. *Chem. Eng. J.* **2018**, *351*, 1137–1146. [CrossRef]
10. Acero, J.L.; Real, F.J.; Javier Benitez, F.; Matamoros, E. Degradation of neonicotinoids by UV irradiation: Kinetics and effect of real water constituents. *Separ. Purif. Technol.* **2019**, *211*, 218–226. [CrossRef]
11. Patil, P.N.; Bote, S.D.; Gogate, P.R. Degradation of imidacloprid using combined advanced oxidation processes based on hydrodynamic cavitation. *Ultrason. Sonochem.* **2014**, *21*, 1770–1777. [CrossRef]
12. Lebik-Elhadi, H.; Frontistis, Z.; Ait-Amar, H.; Amrani, S.; Mantzavinos, D. Electrochemical oxidation of pesticide thiamethoxam on boron doped diamond anode: Role of operating parameters and matrix effect. *Process Saf. Environ. Protect.* **2018**, *116*, 535–541. [CrossRef]
13. Domínguez, J.R.; González, T.; Correia, S. BDD electrochemical oxidation of neonicotinoid pesticides in natural surface waters. Operational, kinetic and energetic aspects. *J. Environ. Manage.* **2021**, *298*, 113538. [CrossRef]
14. Martínez-Huitle, C.A.; Rodrigo, M.A.; Sirés, I.; Scialdone, O. A critical review on latest innovations and future challenges of electrochemical technology for the abatement of organics in water. *Appl. Catal. B Environ.* **2023**, *328*, 122430. [CrossRef]
15. Nidheesh, P.V.; Ganiyu, S.O.; Martínez-Huitle, C.A.; Mousset, E.; Olvera-Vargas, H.; Trellu, C.; Zhou, M.; Mehmet, A.O. Recent advances in electro-Fenton process and its emerging applications. *Crit. Rev. Environ. Sci. Technol.* **2022**, *53*, 887–913. [CrossRef]
16. Ganiyu, S.O.; Martínez-Huitle, C.A.; Oturan, M.A. Electrochemical advanced oxidation processes for wastewater treatment: Advances in formation and detection of reactive species and mechanisms. *Curr. Opin. Electrochem.* **2021**, *27*, 100678. [CrossRef]
17. Palo, P.; Dominguez, J.R.; Sánchez-Martín, J.; González, T. Electrochemical degradation of carbamazepine in aqueous solutions-optimization of kinetic aspects by design of experiments. *Clean-Soil Air Water* **2014**, *42*, 1534–1540. [CrossRef]
18. Rabaaoui, N.; Saad, M.E.K.; Moussaoui, Y.; Allagui, M.S.; Bedoui, A.; Elaloui, E. Anodic oxidation of o-nitrophenol on BDD electrode: Variable effects and mechanisms of degradation. *J. Hazard. Mater.* **2013**, *250*, 447–453. [CrossRef] [PubMed]
19. Zhang, C.; Liu, L.; Wang, J.; Rong, F.; Fu, D. Electrochemical degradation of ethidium bromide using boron-doped diamond electrode. *Sep. Purif. Technol.* **2013**, *107*, 91–101. [CrossRef]
20. Calzadilla, W.; Espinoza, L.C.; Diaz-Cruz, M.S.; Peña-Farfal, C.; Salazar, R. Simultaneous degradation of 30 pharmaceuticals by anodic oxidation: Main intermediaries and by-products. *Chemosphere* **2021**, *269*, 128753. [CrossRef]
21. Yu, B.; Han, Q.; Li, C.; Jin, X.; Dai, Z. Influencing factors of venlafaxine degradation at boron-doped diamond anode. *Arabian J. Chem.* **2022**, *15*, 103463. [CrossRef]
22. Domínguez, J.R.; González, T.; Correia, S.; Domínguez, E.M. Sonochemical degradation of neonicotinoid pesticides in natural surface waters. Influence of operational and environmental conditions. *Environ. Res.* **2021**, *197*, 111021. [CrossRef] [PubMed]

23. Montgomery, D.C. *Design and Analysis of Experiments*, 5th ed.; John Wiley and Sons: New York, NY, USA, 2001.
24. Meijide, J.; Gómez, J.; Pazos, M.; Sanromán, M.A. Degradation of thiamethoxam by the synergetic effect between anodic oxidation and Fenton reactions. *J. Hazard. Mater.* **2016**, *319*, 43–50. [CrossRef] [PubMed]
25. Brahim, M.B.; Ammar, H.B.; Abdelhédi, R. Electrochemical removal of the insecticide imidacloprid from water on a boron-doped diamond and Ta/PbO2 anodes using anodic oxidation process. *Korean J. Chem. Eng.* **2016**, *33*, 2602–2609. [CrossRef]
26. Yang, Y.; Xia, Y.; Wei, F.; Zhang, L.; Yao, Y. Electrochemical oxidation of the pesticide nitenpyram using a Gd-PbO_2 anode: Operation parameter optimization and degradation mechanism. *J. Chem. Technol. Biotechnol.* **2020**, *95*, 2120–2128. [CrossRef]
27. Brillas, E.; Boye, B.; Sirés, I.; Garrido, J.A.; Rodríguez, R.M.; Arias, C.; Cabot, P.L.; Comninellis, C. Electrochemical destruction of chlorophenoxy herbicides by anodic oxidation and electro-Fenton using a boron-doped diamond electrode. *Electrochim. Acta* **2004**, *49*, 4487–4496. [CrossRef]
28. Selcuk, H.; Sene, J.J.; Anderson, M.A. Photoelectrocatalytic humic acid degradation kinetics and effect of pH, applied potential and inorganic ions. *J. Chem. Technol. Biotechnol.* **2003**, *78*, 979–984. [CrossRef]
29. Araújo, K.; dos Santos, E.; Nidheesh, P.V.; Martínez-Huitle, C.A. Fundamentals and advances on the mechanisms of electrochemical generation of persulfate and sulfate radicals in aqueous medium. *Curr. Opin. Chem. Eng.* **2022**, *38*, 100870. [CrossRef]
30. Hoang, N.T.; Nguyen, X.C.; Le, P.C.; Juzsakova, T.; Chang, S.W.; Nguyen, D.D. Electrochemical degradation of pesticide Padan 95SP by boron-doped diamond electrodes: The role of operating parameters. *J. Environ. Chem. Eng.* **2021**, *9*, 105205. [CrossRef]
31. Velappan, K.; Sachio, Y.; Mallaiya, K.; Muthu, M. Anodic oxidation of isothiazolin-3-ones in aqueous medium by using boron-doped diamond electrode. *Diam. Relat. Mat.* **2016**, *69*, 152–159. [CrossRef]
32. Comninellis, C.; Nerini, A. Anodic oxidation of phenol in the presence of NaCl for wastewater treatment. *J. Appl. Electrochem.* **1995**, *25*, 23–28. [CrossRef]
33. Frontistis, Z.; Antonopoulou, M.; Yazirdagi, M.; Kilinc, Z.; Konstantinou, I.; Katsaounis, A.; Mantzavinos, D. Boron-doped diamond electro-oxidation of ethyl paraben: The effect of electrolyte on by-products distribution and mechanisms. *J. Environ. Manag.* **2017**, *195*, 148–156. [CrossRef] [PubMed]
34. Streat, M.; Sweetland, L.A.; Horner, D.J. Removal of pesticides from water using hypercrosslinked polymer phases: Part 3-Mini-column studies and the effect of fulvic and humic substances. *Process Saf. Environ. Protect.* **1998**, *76*, 135–141. [CrossRef]
35. European Commission Decisión de Ejecución (UE). 2020/1161 de la Comisión, de 4 de agosto de 2020, por la que se establece una lista de observación de sustancias a efectos de seguimiento a nivel de la Unión en el ámbito de la política de aguas, de conformidad con la Directiva. In *Diario Oficial de La Unión Europea*; Serie L, 257, 6 de agosto; European Commission Decisión de Ejecución (UE): Maastricht, The Netherlands, 2020; pp. 32–35.
36. Murillo-Sierra, J.C.; Sirés, I.; Brillas, E. Advanced oxidation of real sulfamethoxazole + trimethoprim formulations using different anodes and electrolytes. *Chemosphere* **2018**, *192*, 225–233. [CrossRef] [PubMed]
37. Brito, L.B.; Garcia, L.F.; Caetano, M.P. Electrochemical remediation of amoxicillin: Detoxification and reduction of antimicrobial activity. *Chem. Biol. Interact.* **2018**, *291*, 162–170. [CrossRef] [PubMed]

water

MDPI

Article

UV/Advanced Oxidation Process for Removing Humic Acid from Natural Water: Comparison of Different Methods and Effect of External Factors

Qingchao Shen [1,2], Xiaosan Song [1,2,*], Jishuo Fan [1,2], Cheng Chen [1,2] and Zhuohao Li [1,2]

1 School of Environmental and Municipal Engineering, Lanzhou Jiaotong University, No. 88 Anning West Road, Lanzhou 730070, China; 13964762817@163.com (Q.S.); van1131@163.com (J.F.); 17513188534@163.com (C.C.); 17339901314@163.com (Z.L.)

2 Key Laboratory of Yellow River Water Environment in Gansu Province, Lanzhou Jiaotong University, No. 88 Anning West Road, Lanzhou 730070, China

* Correspondence: songxs@mail.lzjtu.cn

Abstract: Humic acid (HA) is an organic compound naturally present in aquatic environments. It has been found to have detrimental effects on water color, the transport of heavy metals, and the elimination of disinfection by-products (DBPs), thereby exerting an impact on human health. This study introduced four synergistic ultraviolet/advanced oxidation processes (UV/AOPs) systems aimed at eliminating HA from water. The research explored the effect of solution pH, duration of illumination, initial reactant concentration, and oxidant concentration on the degradation of HA. The results indicated that the mineralization rate achieved by individual UV or oxidant systems was less than 15%, which is significantly lower compared to UV/AOPs systems. Among these methods, the UV/peroxymonosulfate (UV/PMS) process demonstrated the highest effectiveness, achieving a mineralization rate of 94.15%. UV/peroxydisulfate (UV/PDS) and UV/sodium percarbonate (SPC) were subsequently implemented, with UV/sulfite (S(IV)) demonstrating the lowest effectiveness at 19.8%. Optimal degradation efficiency was achieved when the initial concentration of HA was 10 mg/L, the concentration of PMS was 3 mmol/L, and the initial pH was set at 5, with an illumination time of 180 min. This experimental setup resulted in high degradation efficiencies for chemical oxygen demand (COD), UV_{254}, and HA, reaching 96.32%, 97.34%, and 92.09%, respectively. The energy efficiency of this process (*EE/O*) was measured at 0.0149 (kWh)/m^3, indicating the capability of the UV/PMS system to efficiently degrade and mineralize HA in water. This offers theoretical guidance for the engineered implementation of a UV/PAM process in the treatment of HA.

Keywords: humic acid; ultraviolet/advanced oxidation processes; techniques; influencing factors

1. Introduction

In China, water resources are significantly contaminated, primarily by organic pollutants, with natural organic matter (NOM) serving as a major pollution source. NOM constitutes a crucial element of aquatic ecosystems and is commonly present in natural water sources, with levels typically varying between 0.1 mg/L and 20 mg/L, demonstrating a progressive escalation [1,2]. Elevated concentrations of NOM impose significant challenges on nearby water treatment plants and ecosystems. In an aqueous environment, the constituents of NOM, specifically humic acid (HA), exhibit a significant ability to chelate heavy metals, leading to the formation of organic–metal complexes. This affects the transportation, bioavailability, and toxicity of heavy metals [3,4]. Although the presence of HA in drinking water does not pose a direct threat to human health, it is responsible for water discoloration and the emission of a strong, unpleasant odor. Common disinfectants utilized in water treatment facilities, such as chlorine or chloramines, undergo a reaction with HA to produce halogenated compounds (trihalomethanes (THMs), haloacetic acids

(HAAs), and halogenated furanones (HFs) [5]), consequently elevating the potential risk of cancer [6].

In recent years, elevated concentrations of aromatic halogenated disinfection by-products (DBPs) have been identified in chlorinated drinking water. These compounds have shown developmental toxicity and growth inhibitory effects that are more pronounced compared to aliphatic halogenated DBPs [7]. Epidemiological studies in humans and toxicological research in animals have established correlations between the consumption of chlorinated drinking water and adverse effects on cancer, reproduction, and development. United States Environmental Protection Agency (EPA) currently establishes the maximum contaminant levels for total THMs and HAAs at 80 ppb and 60 ppb, respectively. In contrast, the United Kingdom adheres to a THM standard of 100 ppb [8]. During the process of water treatment, the interaction of organic substances with metal ions and minerals leads to an increase in the solubility of heavy metals. This phenomenon also necessitates higher chemical dosages, which in turn diminishes treatment effectiveness and results in the production of larger quantities of sludge and DBPs [9]. Furthermore, the existence of humic substances in the water treatment facilities has implications on the efficacy of treatment processes (e.g., coagulation-settling efficiency, coagulant and oxidant dosages, and operational equipment), and fosters the growth of bacteria and the development of biofilms in the water distribution network, thereby giving rise to public health concerns regarding sanitation. Consequently, the management of HA in untreated water has garnered significant interest from the potable water sector [10,11].

The main strategies for eliminating HA encompass a variety of approaches. These include physical methods such as adsorption [12] and filtration [13], chemical techniques such as coagulation [14], electrolysis [15], and oxidation [16,17], as well as biological processes [18]. The advantages and disadvantages of these methods are outlined in Table 1. Advanced oxidation processes (AOPs) have attracted considerable interest in recent years because of their operational simplicity, high efficiency, lack of secondary pollution, and efficacy in decreasing THM formation [19]. AOPs operate through the production of highly oxidative radicals, such as hydroxyl (•OH) and sulfate (SO_4^{-}•) [20], which facilitate the oxidation and decomposition of organic pollutants present in water. However, relying only on AOPs for the degradation of HA frequently proves ineffective in attaining optimal results. Therefore, they are commonly integrated with other technologies, such as ultraviolet/AOPs (UV/AOPs). This integrated method not only efficiently eliminates HA but also minimizes the generation of DBPs, thereby exerting a beneficial effect on the management of organic fouling in water treatment procedures [21].

Table 1. Advantages and disadvantages of different methods for NOM degradation.

Method	Advantages	Disadvantages
Adsorption	① High NOM degradation efficiency ② Simple design and easy operation	① Frequent replacement and regeneration of adsorbents increase costs ② Saturated adsorbents require disposal, causing secondary pollution
Coagulation	Strong adaptability with high NOM degradation efficiency	Causes secondary pollution
Biological	① Can remove biodegradable components of NOM ② Relatively environmentally friendly, no extra chemicals	① Requires additional nutrients ② Poor environmental adaptability
Electrochemical	① No secondary pollution, environmentally friendly ② No need for additional chemicals	High energy consumption
Membrane Filtration	① Simple process, easy to automate, reliable operation ② Low energy consumption	① Severe membrane fouling ② High membrane cost
Advanced Oxidation	① Efficient degradation of organic matter ② Applicable to various water bodies, widely adaptable	① Complex operation, requires monitoring and control of reaction conditions ② Residual oxidants may be toxic

UV-activated AOPs are currently utilized for the elimination of organic compounds from water. However, there is a limited availability of studies assessing their efficacy, particularly for removing HA. Furthermore, there is a scarcity of research on determining the most effective oxidant for the treatment of HA using UV/AOPs. This study examines the efficacy of four oxidants—peroxymonosulfate (PMS), peroxodisulfate (PDS), sodium percarbonate (SPC), and sulfite (S(IV))—when activated by UV light to identify the most efficient AOP for removing HA. This research aims to investigate the effect of initial concentration of HA, oxidant concentration, initial pH, and reaction time on the decontamination of HA. The results of this study are expected to offer insights for the practical implementation of UV/AOP technologies in the treatment of HA.

2. Methods

2.1. Reagents and Equipment

2.1.1. Reagents

HA (fulvic acid, FA $\geq$ 90%) was obtained from Shanghai Macklin Biochemical Co., Ltd. (Shanghai, China); Sodium persulfate ($Na_2S_2O_8$) and anhydrous sodium S(IV) were procured from Shanghai Macklin Biochemical Co., Ltd.; potassium PMS and SPC were acquired from Shanghai Titan Technology Co., Ltd. (Shanghai, China); sulfuric acid (H_2SO_4) and hydrochloric acid (HCl) were obtained from Shanghai National Medicines Reagents Co., Ltd. (Shanghai, China); sodium hydroxide (NaOH) was provided by Sigma-Aldrich Co., Ltd. (Shanghai, China). All chemicals utilized in the study were of analytical grade and did not necessitate additional purification.

2.1.2. Experimental Equipment

To facilitate the development of experiments in this study, a specialized experimental apparatus utilizing UV oxidation was created (Shandong University of Architecture, Jinan, China). The schematic and actual representations of this device are depicted in Figures 1 and 2, respectively. The device is primarily composed of an upper sealing flange, dual-layer acrylic glass tubes, and an innermost glass sleeve. The flange is the location where an inlet for water addition (reagent addition) is situated. The gap between the inner and outer glass tubes functions as a condensation cycling water system, where the water inlet and outlet are strategically positioned at the bottom and top of the outer tube, respectively. The inner glass tube is designed to be removable and includes a drainage outlet at the bottom as well as two sampling ports located at the mid-upper section. This equipment has the capacity to treat a maximum of 4 L of water in a single session.

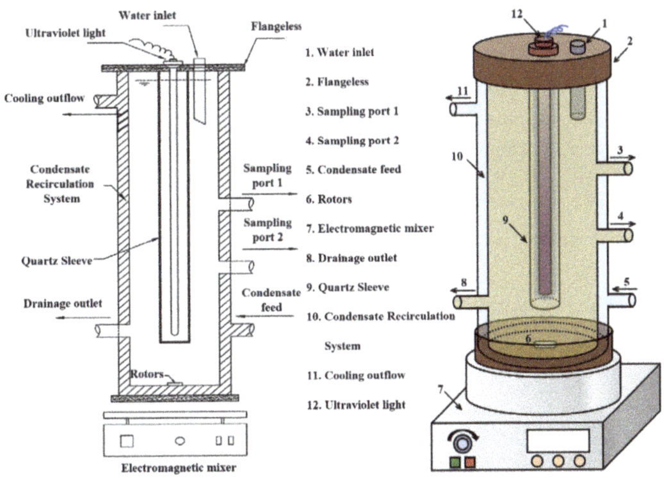

Figure 1. Structure of the advanced oxidation reaction device.

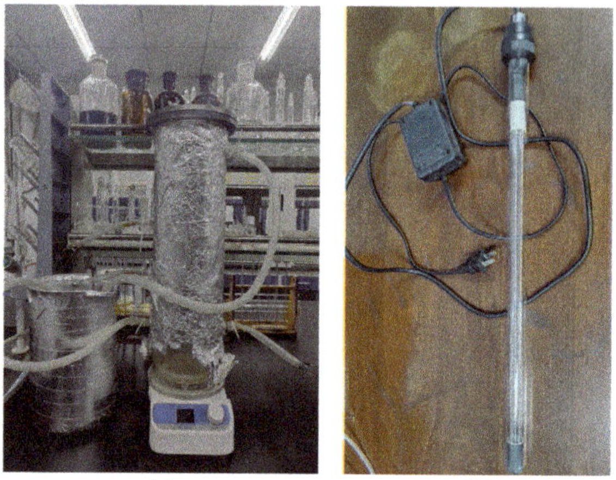

(a) (b)

Figure 2. Diagram of the experimental setup: (**a**) advanced oxidation reaction setup; (**b**) UV lamp.

The design of this experimental apparatus is simple and intuitive for users. The glass tube of the UV lamp can be removed, facilitating the simple substitution with lamps of different specifications and types. Sampling ports are strategically positioned at various heights on the device to facilitate convenient sampling. A supplementary port is situated at the upper part of the device to facilitate the convenient introduction of reagents. The external glass layer is equipped with a condensing water circulation system that helps reduce temperature elevation caused by radiation when the UV lamp is in operation. The full submersible UV lamp used in the test was OSRAM, model HNS 4P SE, with a power of 20 W, a rated operating voltage of 220 V, and an average UV radiation intensity of 3.28 mW/cm^2 as measured by a radiometer. The outer diameter of the UV lamp casing was 25 mm, the diameter at the head was 18 mm, the diameter of the glass tube was 15.5 mm, and the wavelength was 254 nm.

2.2. *Experimental Indicators and Testing Methods*

2.2.1. Routine Indicator Measurement

(1) Physical Indicators

Temperature variations and pH levels in the water samples were observed through the utilization of a thermometer and a pH meter, respectively. During the experiments, the pH range was controlled by utilizing 0.05 mol/L NaOH and 0.05 mol/L H_2SO_4 buffer solutions. Prior to conducting the experiments, the pH meter underwent calibration using standard solutions with pH values of 4.0, 6.86, and 9.18.

(2) Chemical Oxygen Demand (COD)

COD was quantified utilizing the acidic potassium permanganate method, following the guidelines outlined in the standard GB 11892-89 [22]. This approach is applicable for water samples with chloride ion concentrations not exceeding 30 mg/L. When the permanganate index surpasses 10 mg/L, it is advisable to collect smaller volumes of the water sample and dilute it before conducting the test.

2.2.2. Dissolved Organic Carbon (DOC) Measurement

DOC was quantified utilizing a total organic carbon (TOC) analyzer (MULTI N/C 2100, Analytik Jena, Germany, purchased in Beijing, China). Water samples underwent filtration using a 0.45 μm filter membrane prior to analysis to quantify the concentration of dissolved organic carbon. This section of the analysis employed a differential subtraction method to reduce errors associated with the measurement of organic carbon.

2.2.3. UV_{254} Measurement

Temperature variations and pH levels in the water samples were observed through the utilization of a thermometer and a pH meter, respectively. During the experiments, the pH range was controlled by utilizing 0.05 mol/L NaOH and 0.05 mol/L H_2SO_4 buffer solutions. Prior to conducting the experiments, the pH meter underwent calibration using standard solutions with pH values of 4.0, 6.86, and 9.18.

2.2.4. Other Relevant Indicators

(1) Organic Matter Degradation Rate

$$\eta = \frac{C_0 - C_t}{C_0} \times 100\% \quad (1)$$

where η represents the degradation rate of organic matter (%); C_0 represents the initial concentration of organic matter (mg/L); and C_t represents the concentration of organic matter at time t (mg/L).

(2) Specific Electrical Energy per Order (*EE/O*)

$$EE/O = \frac{P \times T}{60 \times V \times \log(C_0/C) \times 1000} \quad (2)$$

where EE/O represents the specific electrical energy per order ((kWh)/m^3); P represents the power of illumination (W); t represents the reaction time (min); V represents the volume of treated water (m^3); and C_0 and C represent the initial and final concentrations of HA (mg/L), respectively.

2.3. Experimental Operation and Procedures

Before initiating the experiment, it is necessary to allow a 20-minute preheating period for the UV lamp. Before initiating the device, it is placed on a magnetic stirrer to guarantee homogeneous mixing and uphold a consistent temperature throughout the reaction. The preheated UV lamp is subsequently inserted into the internal sleeve, and the circulating water system is then attached at the inlet. The reaction solution and associated chemicals are introduced into the glass tube to guarantee uniform exposure of the water sample to UV radiation. The apparatus is enveloped in opaque aluminum foil to reduce external light interference and shield the experimenter's eyes from potential harm caused by UV radiation. Once the UV lamp is activated, in conjunction with the condensation circulation system and the magnetic stirrer, the chemical reaction can commence. The reaction temperature is consistently maintained at 25 ± 3 °C throughout the duration of the experiment. Each experimental group carries out 3 parallel tests. An oxidant with a specific concentration is introduced into the reactor, followed by the activation of the magnetic stirrer at a consistent speed of 630 rpm. Tap water is utilized for condensation purposes to maintain a stable reaction temperature. After the completion of the reaction under different conditions, a specific volume of the reaction solution is gathered, and the reaction is halted for subsequent analysis and measurement. In order to ensure the authenticity and reliability of the data, all the data in this experiment were obtained by taking the mean value from three parallel experiments, and the error bars were added in the plotting process to indicate the range of error.

3. Results and Discussion

3.1. Degradation Efficiency of HA by UV/PMS in Aqueous Solutions

Under the experimental conditions of UV radiation intensity at 3.28 mW/cm^2, initial solution pH at 7, initial concentration of HA at 10 mg/L, and the addition of 3 mmol/L PMS, the solution temperature was controlled at 25 ± 3 °C with a stirring rate of 630 rpm. The reaction was carried out for a duration of 180 min. The degradation effects of HA were examined using three experimental configurations: isolated UV irradiation, isolated PMS treatment, and the combined UV/PMS process.

Figure 3 illustrates the degradation rates when subjected to isolated conditions of UV irradiation and PMS oxidation. For the isolated UV treatment, the degradation rates for COD, TOC, and UV_{254} were 11.01%, 9.84%, and 23.33%, respectively. For the oxidation of isolated PMS, the degradation rates for COD, TOC, and UV_{254} were 10.8%, 19.91%, and 27.7%, respectively. In the isolated UV system, the introduction of UV energy facilitated the cleavage of specific chemical bonds in the pollutants [23], leading to the partial degradation of organic compounds even in the absence of an oxidizing agent. UV photolysis of H_2O, however, produces a minimal quantity of •OH radicals with restricted oxidative potential, leading to decreased degradation rates for HA. In the isolated PMS system, the stability of PMS is relatively high, and its lower redox potential (E^0 = 1.82 V) limits the oxidation and degradation of organic compounds, resulting in incomplete removal of organics [24]. Consequently, both isolated UV and isolated PMS processes demonstrated low degradation efficiencies for COD, TOC, and UV_{254}, indicating their suboptimal performance in removing HA.

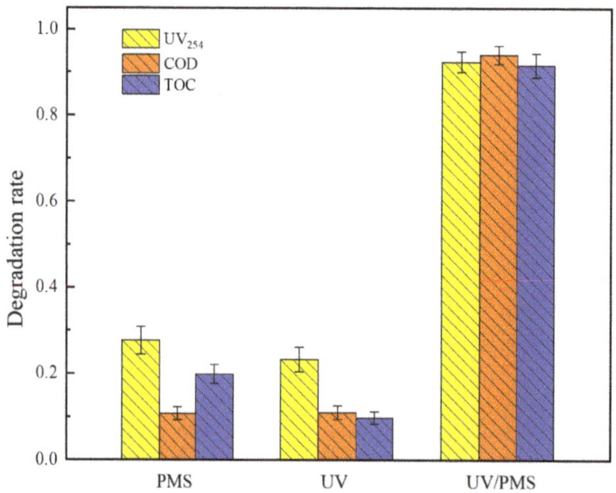

Figure 3. Degradation of HA by isolated UV, isolated PMS, and UV/PMS.

Under the same experimental conditions, the UV/PMS process exhibited significantly higher degradation rates for COD, TOC, and UV_{254} compared to the individual UV or PMS processes, achieving rates of 94.12%, 91.65%, and 92.51%, respectively. In Figure 4, the energy input from UV radiation causes O-O bond in PMS to split. This activation process involves external energy exceeding the bond energy (140~213.3 kJ/mol) [25], leading to the cleavage of the peroxide bond in PMS and the generation of SO_4^-• radicals and •OH. These radicals are potent oxidizing agents that can rapidly degrade various pollutants [26–28]. Therefore, the UV/PMS process is more advantageous for HA degradation compared to the use of UV or PMS alone. Additionally, the UV/PMS process can oxidize organic compounds that are not effectively degraded by PMS alone.

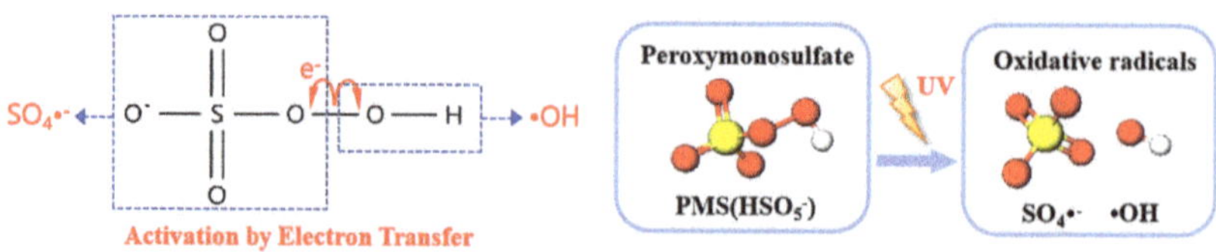

Figure 4. Activation of PMS through electron and energy transfer processes [29].

3.2. Degradation Efficiency of HA by UV/PDS in Aqueous Solutions

Under experimental conditions, a UV radiation intensity of 3.28 mW/cm^2, a solution temperature of 25 ± 3 °C, an initial solution pH of 7, and an initial concentration of 10 mg/L of HA, 3 mmol/L of PDS was introduced. The reaction lasted for 180 min with a stirring rate of 630 rpm. The degradation effects of HA were examined using 3 experimental configurations: isolated UV, isolated PDS, and a combined UV/PDS process. The study aimed to evaluate the effectiveness of UV/PDS AOP in degrading HA.

In Figure 5, when subjected to isolated UV irradiation, the degradation rates for COD, TOC, and UV_{254} were 11.01%, 9.84%, and 23.33% respectively. Conversely, under isolated PDS oxidation, the degradation rates were 24.14% for COD, 16.28% for TOC, and 13.27% for UV_{254}. However, when subjected to identical experimental conditions, the UV/PDS process increased the degradation rates to 89.81% for UV_{254}, 93.60% for COD, and 89.53% for TOC. In comparison to the individual processes of UV and PDS, the combined UV/PDS process significantly enhanced the mineralization rate of HA. In the UV/PDS system, the PDS compound is activated under UV radiation, leading to the generation of $SO_4^{-}\bullet$ radicals possessing a high oxidative potential (Figure 6). These radicals participate in electron transfer, addition, and hydrogen abstraction reactions with organic pollutants. This process breaks down the organic matter into smaller, more degradable molecules, leading to increased degradation rates of organic compounds [30].

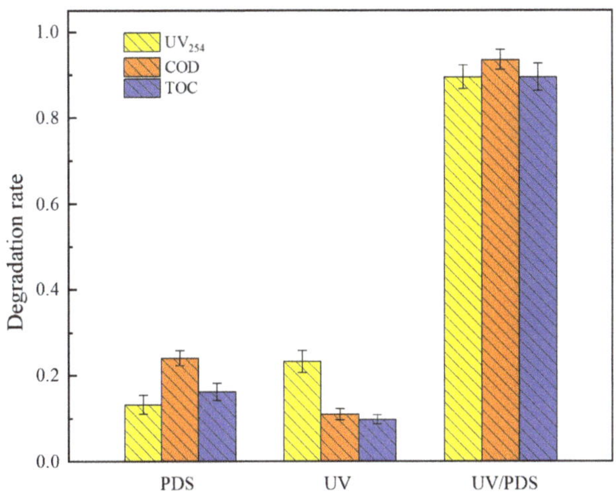

Figure 5. Degradation of HA by isolated UV, isolated PDS, and UV/PDS.

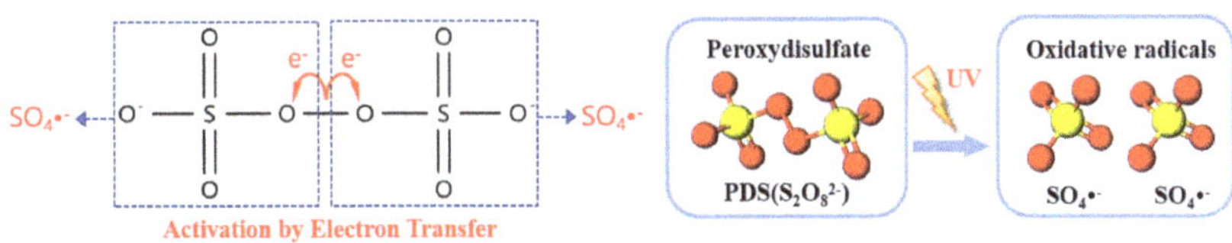

Figure 6. Activation of PDS through electron and energy transfer processes [29].

3.3. Degradation Efficiency of HA by UV/SPC in Aqueous Solutions

The experiment was carried out under conditions with a UV radiation intensity of 3.28 mW/cm^2, an initial solution pH of 7, and an initial concentration of HA at 10 mg/L. SPC was introduced into the solution at a concentration of 3 mmol/L. The solution temperature was controlled at 25 ± 3 °C, while the stirring speed was adjusted to 630 rpm. The duration of the reaction was 180 min. Figure 7 depicts the degradation efficiencies of HA through three processes: isolated UV treatment, isolated SPC treatment, and the combined UV/SPC process.

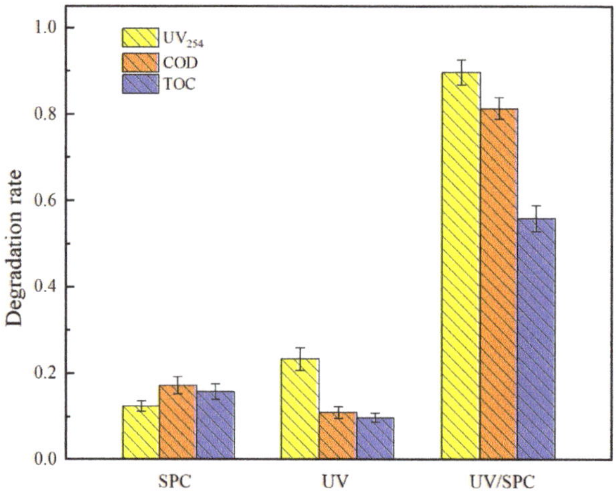

Figure 7. Degradation of organic matter by isolated UV, isolated SPC, and UV/SPC.

In Figure 7, during isolated SPC oxidation, the degradation rates for COD, TOC, and UV_{254} were 17.21%, 15.79%, and 12.48% respectively. Conversely, under isolated UV irradiation, the degradation rates were 11.01% for COD, 9.84% for TOC, and 23.33% for UV_{254}. However, when subjected to identical experimental conditions, the integrated UV/SPC process demonstrated degradation efficiencies of 89.81% for UV_{254}, 81.47% for COD, and 56.00% for TOC. This suggests that the UV/SPC process offers superior degradation efficiencies for organic compounds in comparison to the separate processes of SPC and UV. However, its efficacy is not as pronounced as that of the UV/PMS and UV/PDS systems. The relatively low rate of TOC degradation indicates the breakdown of large molecular organic compounds into smaller molecules, suggesting that HA was not fully mineralized. The decomposition of organic compounds takes place as SPC dissolves in water, leading to the production of hydrogen peroxide (H_2O_2). Upon exposure to UV radiation, H_2O_2 becomes activated and generates highly reactive •OH radicals.

Yuan et al. [31] illustrated in their research on the elimination of HA from water through UV/SPC that H_2O_2 generated from the breakdown of SPC is probably the main supplier of oxidative capability in UV/SPC system. Additionally, the gradual degradation of SPC in water results in the continuous production of H_2O_2, thereby inhibiting the self-decomposition of H_2O_2 and augmenting the oxidative efficiency of UV/SPC system. With an increase in the concentration of SPC, there is a corresponding increase in the generation of highly reactive species such as •OH radicals, thereby enhancing the degradation of HA. However, an overabundance of SPC could potentially scavenge •OH, leading to the formation of hydroperoxy radicals ($HO_2^-\bullet$) (Equation (3)) [32,33]. Considering that $HO_2^-\bullet$ exhibits lower oxidative potency, an excess of SPC may reduce the effectiveness of the system in eliminating HA.

$$\bullet OH + H_2O_2 \rightarrow HO_2^-\bullet + H_2O \quad (3)$$

3.4. Degradation Efficiency of HA by UV/S(IV) in Aqueous Solutions

The experiment was carried out under specific conditions, including a UV radiation intensity of 3.28 mW/cm^2, an initial solution pH of 7, and an initial concentration of HA at 10 mg/L. S(IV) was introduced into the solution at a concentration of 3 mmol/L, while the solution temperature was controlled at 25 ± 3 °C, and the stirring speed was adjusted to 630 rpm. The reaction persisted for a duration of 180 min. The efficiency of organic matter decomposition was examined using three experimental configurations: isolated UV irradiation, isolated S(IV) treatment, and a combined UV/S(IV) process. Sampling and analytical results demonstrating the degradation effects of HA by these three processes are depicted in Figure 8.

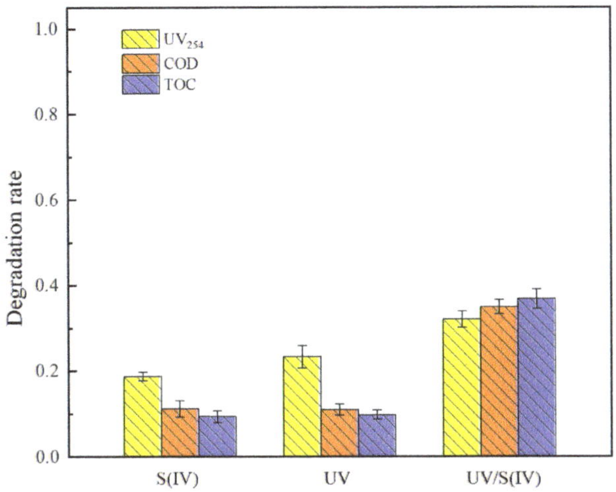

Figure 8. Degradation of organic matter by isolated UV, isolated S(IV), and UV/S(IV).

In Figure 8, during isolated S(IV) oxidation, the degradation rates for COD, UV_{254}, and TOC were 11.22%, 18.76%, and 9.44%, respectively. Conversely, under isolated UV irradiation, the degradation rates were 11.01% for COD, 23.33% for UV_{254}, and 9.84% for TOC. Under identical experimental conditions, the UV/S(IV) process resulted in degradation rates of 32.14% for UV_{254}, 35.06% for COD, and 36.88% for TOC. A comparative analysis indicates that UV/S(IV) process does not substantially improve the degradation efficiencies in comparison to the individual treatments, suggesting suboptimal efficiency in organic degradation. The results indicate that there is minimal degradation of HA within UV/S(IV) system. This is attributed to the low generation of radicals and the intricate, high molecular weight structure of HA, which encompasses numerous functional groups that pose challenges for decomposition. In UV/S(IV) system, the main reactive species are S(IV) radicals ($SO_3^-\bullet$) and hydrated electrons (e^-_{aq}) as denoted in Equation (4). In the presence of oxygen, $SO_3^-\bullet$ species can undergo further transformation into PMS ($SO_5^-\bullet$). The e^-_{aq} is rapidly captured as a result of its high reaction rate constant ($\geq 10^{10}$ $M^{-1}\cdot s^{-1}$) [34], leading to the formation of superoxide radicals ($O_2^-\bullet$). The oxidative potential of $O_2^-\bullet$ is lower than that of $\bullet OH$ and $SO_4^-\bullet$. Consequently, the UV/S(IV) collaborative system exhibits a significantly reduced capacity for organic degradation in comparison to the other collaborative systems previously examined. Furthermore, as demonstrated in Equations (5) to (7), in aerobic environments, the UV/S(IV) system has the potential to produce $SO_4^-\bullet$. Therefore, the reactive species $SO_3^-\bullet/SO_5^-\bullet$, $O_2^-\bullet$, and $SO_4^-\bullet$ have the potential to enhance the degradation of HA [35].

$$SO_3^{2-}(hv) \rightarrow SO_3^-\bullet + e_{aq}^- \quad (4)$$

$$SO_3^-\bullet + O_2 \rightarrow SO_5^-\bullet \quad (5)$$

$$SO_5^-\bullet + {SO_3}^{2-} \rightarrow SO_4^-\bullet + SO_4^{2-} \quad (6)$$

$$2SO_5^-\bullet \rightarrow 2SO_4^-\bullet + O_2 \quad (7)$$

3.5. Comparison of Oxidant Efficacy in HA Degradation

A comparative study was conducted under identical experimental conditions to assess the degradation effectiveness of PMS, PDS, sodium SPC, and S(IV) in oxidative synergy systems for HA. The degradation effects of each synergistic system were examined, and the results are illustrated in Figure 9. In UV/oxidant processes, the degradation of HA by varying concentrations of oxidants exhibited pseudo-first-order kinetics. The specific first-order kinetic constants (kobs) are shown in Table 2.

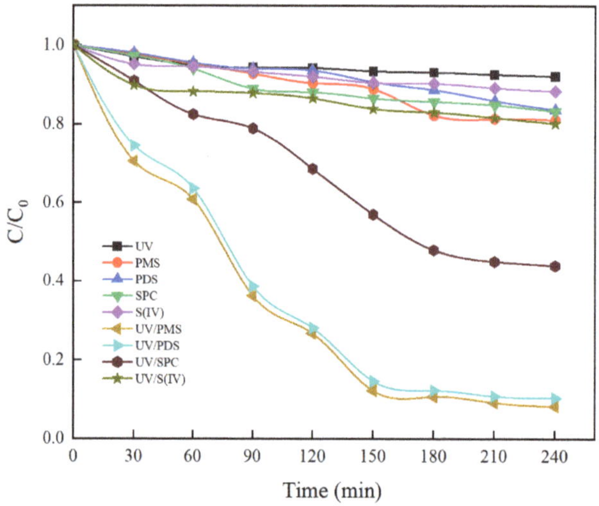

Figure 9. Mineralization effects of different processes on HA.

Table 2. Comparison of rate constants and economic efficiency for different processes.

System	First-Order Kinetic Equation	k_{obs} (min^{-1})	R^2	*EE/O* ((kWh)/m^{-3})
UV/PMS	$Ln(C_0/C) = 0.01034t + 0.1516$	0.01034	0.928	0.0157
UV/PDS	$Ln(C_0/C) = 0.0094t + 0.1355$	0.00940	0.919	0.0204
UV/SPC	$Ln(C_0/C) = 0.00342t + 0.0147$	0.00342	0.975	0.0561
UV/S(IV)	$Ln(C_0/C) = 0.00051t + 0.0077$	0.00051	0.978	0.3750

Under experimental conditions, a UV radiation intensity of 3.28 mW/cm^2, an initial solution pH of 7, an initial HA concentration of 10 mg/L, and the addition of 3 mmol/L AOPs were employed. The reaction was carried out at a solution temperature of 25 ± 3 °C with a stirring speed of 630 rpm for 240 min. In Figure 9, the individual processes (e.g., UV, PMS, PDS, SPC, and S(IV)) employed for HA degradation resulted in minimal mineralization. C/C_0 values for HA were 92.16%, 81.17%, 83.72%, 83.33%, and 88.43% for UV, PMS, PDS, SPC, and S(IV) processes, respectively. Consequently, the mineralization rates were below 15%. In contrast, UV/AOPs synergistic systems such as UV/PMS, UV/PDS, and UV/SPC exhibited enhanced mineralization efficiency, as evidenced by C/C_0 values of 5.85%, 10.47%, and 44.00%, resulting in mineralization rates of 94.15%, 89.53%, and 56%, respectively. Among the synergistic processes, UV/S(IV) exhibited the lowest performance, achieving a C/C_0 value of 80.20% and a mineralization rate of merely 19.8%. A comparative analysis reveals that depending exclusively on UV irradiation or oxidants is inadequate for producing a significant quantity of radicals essential for the efficient mineralization of HA. The activation of oxidants via external energy input is crucial for the generation of highly oxidative radicals. These radicals play a key role in breaking down large organic molecules into inorganic substances. This underscores the synergistic effect of integrating UV/AOPs, which enhances the breakdown of organic substances.

In Figure 10, following a 240-minute reaction period in the oxidation systems, UV_{254} degradation efficiencies for the UV/PMS, UV/PDS, UV/SPC, and UV/S(IV) processes were 95.07%, 89.81%, 87.64%, and 32.14%, respectively. The degradation efficiencies of COD were 96.26%, 93.16%, 81.47%, and 35.06%, respectively. The comparison indicates that the highest UV_{254} and COD degradation efficiencies were observed in the UV/PMS and UV/PDS processes, while the UV/S(IV) process exhibited the lowest efficiency, followed by the UV/SPC process. Analysis of the first-order kinetic equations fitted in Table 1 reveals that k_{obs} for UV/PMS treatment was determined to be 0.01034 min^{-1}, signifying the highest degradation efficiency. The rate constant for the UV/PDS system was determined to be 0.00940 min^{-1}, which was marginally lower compared to the rate constant of the UV/PMS system. The k_{obs} values for the UV/SPC and UV/S(IV) synergistic processes were 0.00342 min^{-1} and 0.00051 min^{-1}, respectively. These values suggest lower rates of organic matter degradation in comparison to the UV/PMS and UV/PDS processes.

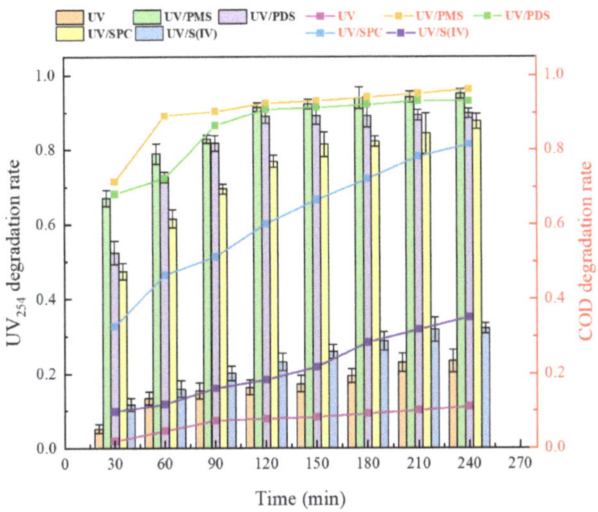

Figure 10. Degradation effects of organic matter by different synergistic processes.

The comparative analysis indicated that UV/PMS process demonstrated superior mineralization and degradation efficiency for HA. PMS exhibits superior oxidizing properties due to its dipole-asymmetric structure and high oxidation potential. Its low molecular orbital energy enhances its electron acceptance capabilities [36], thereby promoting easier activation and the generation of crucial reactive radicals. These radicals efficiently eliminate organic substances from water. While PDS also demonstrates favorable oxidative characteristics, its symmetrical molecular configuration enhances its stability and makes it more challenging to trigger the release of $SO_4^{-}\bullet$. Consequently, a higher amount of UV radiation energy is necessary to produce radicals, as evidenced in Table 1. This elucidates the reason behind the higher *EE/O* for PDS (0.0204 (kWh)/m^3) compared to PMS (0.0157 (kWh)/m^3). Subsequent to PMS and PDS, SPC and S(IV) demonstrate elevated *EE/O* values of 0.0561 (kWh)/m^3 and 0.3750 (kWh)/m^3, respectively.

Upon evaluation of the degradation efficiency of organic matter, mineralization rates, and the economic analysis of specific electrical energy consumption, it can be concluded that the UV/PMS synergistic system represents the optimal option for the elimination of HA. Subsequent to UV/PMS, the UV/PDS synergistic system and UV/SPC synergistic system have demonstrated effectiveness, while the UV/S(IV) synergistic system has shown to be the least effective.

3.6. *Effect of External Conditions on the UV/PMS Process for HA Degradation*

This study examines the effect of the initial solution pH, duration of illumination, concentration of oxidant, and concentration of HA on the efficiency of the UV/PMS process for removing HA. The particular effect mechanisms were examined to ascertain the most favorable operational parameters.

3.6.1. Effect of Initial Solution pH on HA Degradation

The initial pH value of the solution affects the molecular form, solubility of HA, radical generation, and activation of PMS [37,38]. This experiment investigated the degradation of HA under various initial pH conditions (3, 5, 7, 9, 11). Under the specified experimental parameters, including a UV radiation intensity of 3.28 mW/cm^2, an initial concentration of 10 mg/L of HA, the addition of 3 mmol/L of PMS, a solution temperature held at 25 ± 3 °C, and a stirring speed of 630 rpm, the reaction was carried out for 180 min while varying the initial pH values. The results of the sampling and detection are depicted in Figure 11.

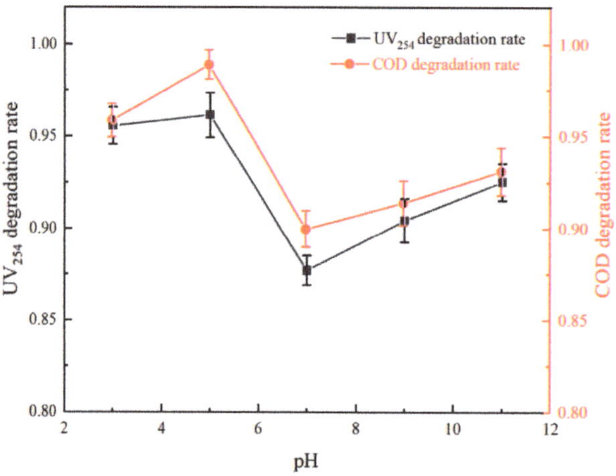

Figure 11. Effect of initial solution pH on degradation of HA in UV/PMS.

In Figure 11, the pH level exerts an impact on the elimination of HA. At a pH of 5, the degradation efficiency of organic matter was maximized, with UV_{254} and COD degradation efficiencies reaching 96.15% and 98.92%, respectively. This resulted in nearly complete mineralization of HA in the solution. The subsequent most significant achievement was observed at a pH of 3, with UV_{254} and COD degradation efficiencies reaching 95.58% and 95.88%, respectively. For pH values within the range of 7 to 11, the rates of UV_{254} and COD degradation were marginally lower compared to those observed in acidic solutions. However, with an increase in pH, the degradation efficiencies exhibited a gradual upward trajectory, peaking at 92.53% and 93.12% at pH 11. The correlation coefficients (R^2) presented in Table 3 demonstrate that the degradation efficiency of HA under various pH conditions adheres to pseudo-first-order reaction kinetics. The first-order kinetic constants indicate that the rate of organic matter degradation was highest at pH = 5, followed by pH = 3, pH = 11, pH = 9, and pH = 7. The calculated results align with the data depicted in Figure 11.

Under conditions of high acidity, molecules of HA remain neutral, thereby augmenting their photochemical activity in comparison to conditions that are neutral or alkaline [39]. An initial acidic pH level enhances light absorption and photochemical reactions, consequently facilitating the efficient decomposition of HA when exposed to UV irradiation. During the alkaline activation of PMS, the main reactive species produced include •OH radicals, singlet oxygen ($^1O_2$), and O_2^-•, which exhibit lower oxidative potentials in comparison to SO_4^-•. Furthermore, in alkaline environments, the reaction between SO_4^-• and

•OH diminishes the oxidation potential of UV-activated persulfates (Equation (8)) [40,41]. This leads to a decrease in the oxidative capacity of UV/PMS at elevated pH values (7~11) in contrast to lower pH values (3~5) [42]. Consequently, slightly acidic conditions are more conducive to the degradation of HA in UV/PMS reaction system, resulting in the highest degradation efficiency for organic matter.

$$SO_4\bullet^- + \bullet OH \rightarrow HSO_5^- \quad k = 1.1 \times 10^{10}\ M^{-1}S^{-1} \tag{8}$$

There was a decrease in pH levels towards the conclusion of this study. This phenomenon may be ascribed to the conversion of OH^- to •OH throughout the reaction and the potential generation of acidic compounds within the system, resulting in a decline in pH.

Table 3. Kinetic fitting of HA degradation at different pH levels.

HA	First-Order Kinetic Equation	k_{obs} (min^{-1})	R^2
3	$Ln(C_0/C) = 0.01467t + 0.0414$	0.01467	0.9868
5	$Ln(C_0/C) = 0.01763t + 0.0585$	0.01763	0.9850
7	$Ln(C_0/C) = 0.00912t + 0.0573$	0.00912	0.9856
9	$Ln(C_0/C) = 0.01249t + 0.0483$	0.01249	0.9907
11	$Ln(C_0/C) = 0.0139t + 0.05940$	0.01390	0.9808

3.6.2. Effect of Illumination Time on HA Degradation

Under the specified experimental parameters, including a UV radiation intensity of 3.28 mW/cm^2, an initial concentration of 10 mg/L of HA, the presence of 3 mmol/L of PMS, a solution temperature held at 25 ± 3 °C, and a stirring speed of 630 rpm, the reaction proceeded for 180 min at the pre-established optimal initial pH. This study aimed to investigate the effect of varying illumination durations on the degradation of HA through the UV/PMS process. The results are illustrated in Figure 12.

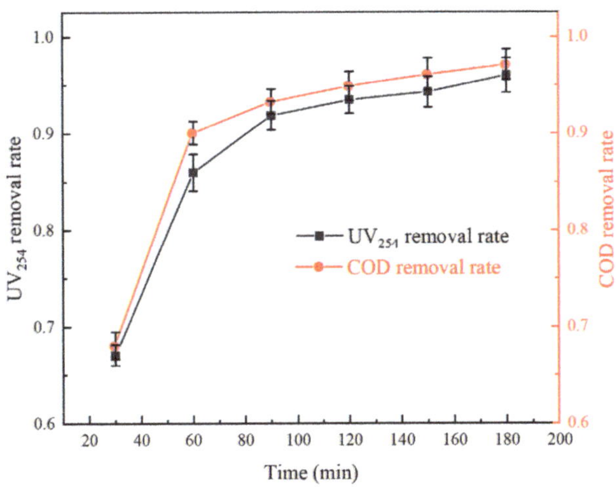

Figure 12. Effect of illumination time on degradation efficiency of organic matter.

In Figure 12, the degradation efficiencies of UV_{254} and COD exhibited a gradual increase with extended illumination time. After 90 min, there was a deceleration in the rate of increase, suggesting a positive correlation between the degradation efficiency of HA in the UV/PMS synergistic process and the duration of illumination. At the conclusion of the experiment, the elimination percentages for UV_{254} and COD stood at 96.02% and 97.12%, respectively, while the presence of HA in the solution led to near-complete mineralization. Figure 13 demonstrates that an extended exposure to light resulted in a transition of the solution's color from dark brown to light yellow. After a duration of 90 min, it was significant that the solution exhibited a nearly transparent appearance. This indicates that prolonged exposure to light results in the generation of additional reactive radicals, thereby augmenting the mineralization rate of HA [43].

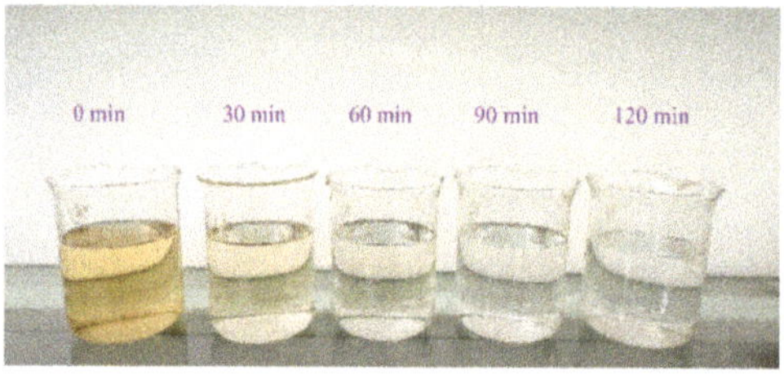

Figure 13. Actual images of HA degradation process solutions from 0 min to 120 min.

3.6.3. Effect of Oxidant Concentration on HA Degradation

The concentration of the oxidant (i.e., PMS) exerts an impact on the degradation efficacy of HA. Higher concentrations of oxidants can lead to an increased generation of oxidative radicals, consequently augmenting the degradation process. This study seeks to examine the true effect of PMS concentration on the degradation of HA. The experimental conditions were established as follows: UV radiation intensity (I_0) was set at 3.28 mW/cm^2, the initial concentration of HA was 10 mg/L, the solution temperature was maintained at 25 ± 3 °C, the stirring speed was set at 630 rpm, and the initial pH was adjusted to 5. The PMS oxidant was introduced at concentrations of 1 mmol/L, 2 mmol/L, 3 mmol/L, 4 mmol/L, 5 mmol/L, and 6 mmol/L. The experiment was carried out for a duration of 180 min to investigate the effect of varying PMS concentrations on the degradation of HA in UV/PMS system. The experimental results are depicted in Figure 14.

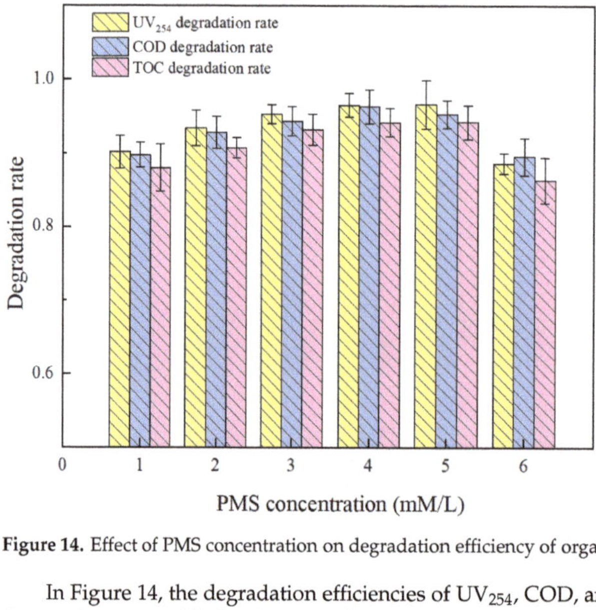

Figure 14. Effect of PMS concentration on degradation efficiency of organic matter.

In Figure 14, the degradation efficiencies of UV_{254}, COD, and TOC exhibited a continuous increase with the rise in oxidant concentration at low levels of PMS (1 mM/L, 2 mM/L, 3 mM/L, 4 mM/L), eventually reaching peak values of 96.47%, 96.29%, and

94.16%, respectively. The efficiency of UV_{254} degradation exceeded that of TOC, suggesting that selective oxidants exhibit a higher reactivity towards UV_{254} or fluorescent additives (e.g., aromatic groups). Higher concentrations of oxidants typically result in increased degradation efficiencies of organic matter [44]. However, upon surpassing a PMS concentration of 4 mM/L, a masking phenomenon was observed [45]. Consequently, the degradation efficiencies of UV_{254}, COD, and TOC decreased to 88.58%, 89.52%, and 86.31%, respectively. This decrease suggests an inhibitory effect of elevated oxidant concentrations on the degradation of HA. The analysis indicated that at elevated concentrations of PMS, there is an increased likelihood of quenching reactions occurring between radicals (Equations (9) and (10)) [46], as well as between excess persulfate and $SO_4^{-}\bullet$ and $\bullet OH$ (Equations (11) and (12)) [47]. This leads to a reduction in the reaction rate between radicals and HA, consequently affecting the degradation efficiency negatively.

$$SO_4^{-}\bullet + H_2O \rightarrow HSO_5^{-} + \bullet OH \tag{9}$$

$$HSO_5^{-} + \bullet OH \rightarrow SO_5^{-}\bullet + H_2O \tag{10}$$

$$SO_4^{-}\bullet + H_2O \rightarrow HSO_5^{-} + \bullet OH \tag{11}$$

$$\bullet OH + \bullet OH \rightarrow H_2O_2 \tag{12}$$

Additionally, the efficiency of degradation is also affected by the technique of oxidant addition. The gradual and continuous addition of the oxidant to the reaction system can help to sustain the radical concentration within an optimal range, thereby enabling the continuous and efficient degradation of HA. This approach proves to be more effective compared to a single-dose addition.

3.6.4. Effect of HA Concentration

Under the specified experimental parameters, including I_0 of 3.28 mW/cm^2, a solution temperature of 25 ± 3 °C, a stirring speed of 630 rpm, an initial pH of 5, and a PMS concentration of 3 mmol/L, HA was synthesized at varying initial concentrations of 5 mg/L, 10 mg/L, 15 mg/L, 20 mg/L, and 25 mg/L. The experiment was carried out over a duration of 180 min to examine the effect of the concentration of HA on the efficacy of degradation in UV/PMS system. The experimental results are depicted in Figure 15.

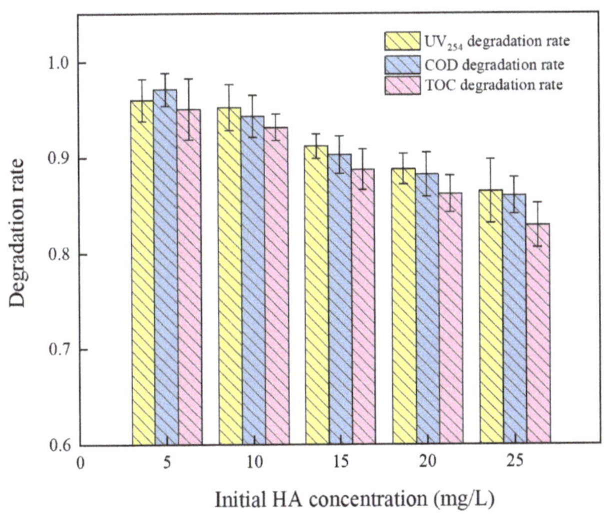

Figure 15. Effect of substrate concentration on degradation efficiency of organic matter.

In Figure 15, larger initial concentrations of HA led to decreased degradation efficiencies, without any discernible optimal concentration. When the initial concentration of HA was raised from 5 mg/L to 25 mg/L, the degradation efficiencies of UV_{254}, COD, and TOC decreased from 96.02%, 97.12%, and 95.05% to 86.44%, 85.98%, and 82.91%, respectively. In comparison to UV_{254}, the degradation efficiency of HA's TOC was found to be lower. This suggests that certain UV-absorbing units or fluorophores underwent partial oxidation to form low molecular weight compounds instead of complete mineralization [48]. Table 4 illustrates that elevated initial concentrations of HA lead to decreased degradation rates of organic matter.

Table 4. Kinetic fitting of HA degradation at different initial substrate concentrations.

HA	First-Order Kinetic Equation	k_{obs} (min^{-1})	R^2
5	$Ln(C_0/C) = 0.0167t + 0.7213$	0.0167	0.9841
10	$Ln(C_0/C) = 0.0149t + 0.6789$	0.0149	0.9812
15	$Ln(C_0/C) = 0.0121t + 0.6591$	0.0121	0.9936
20	$Ln(C_0/C) = 0.011t + 0.6139$	0.0110	0.9868
25	$Ln(C_0/C) = 0.0098t + 0.5631$	0.0098	0.9886

The sluggish elimination of HA can be attributed to several potential factors, including the following: ① A reduction in the quantity of oxidative radicals at a specific persulfate dosage and UV intensity level. As the concentration of organic matter increases, HA and its degradation byproducts compete for $SO_4^-\bullet$ and $\bullet OH$ radicals [49]. ② The augmentation of HA concentration results in a visual darkening of the solution, thereby diminishing its transparency. UV radiation is subsequently obstructed and assimilated by HA molecules and their decomposition intermediates, thereby impeding the activation of PMS [50]. ③ HA functions as a scavenger of $SO_4^-\bullet$ and $\bullet OH$, effectively consuming elevated quantities of reactive radicals [51]. Therefore, in scenarios with ample oxidants, increased concentrations of HA necessitate extended durations to attain equivalent degradation efficiencies.

In summary, within the specified parameters of UV radiation intensity $I_0 = 3.28$ mW/cm^2, solution temperature of 25 ± 3°C, stirring speed of 630 rpm, and initial HA concentration of 10 mg/L, a reaction duration of 180 min, the optimal conditions were identified as an initial reaction pH of 5 and PMS concentration of 3 mmol/L. Under the optimal conditions described, the highest removal efficiencies recorded were a COD degradation efficiency of 96.32%, UV_{254} degradation efficiency of 97.34%, HA mineralization rate of 92.09%, and an *EE/O* of 0.0149 (kWh)/m^3. Table 5 shows the comparison with previous studies.

Table 5. Degradation performance of HA by different UV/AOPs processes.

Processing	Concentration	pH	AOPs	Time	Degradation Rate	Reference
UV/PMS (H_2SO_5)	2 mg·L^{-1}	7	PDS: 0.5 mmol·L^{-1}	180 min	100%	[10]
UV/SPC (Na_2CO_3)	5 mg·L^{-1}	9.9	SPC: 0.5 mmol·L^{-1}	90 min	92.1%	[31]
UV/SPB ($NaBO_3$)	10 mg·L^{-1}	3	SPB: 1 mmol·L^{-1}	60 min	88.8%	[39]
UV/H_2O_2	15 mg·L^{-1}	4	H_2O_2: 3 mmol·L^{-1}	180 min	21.9%	[45]
UV/PDS ($H_2S_2O_8$)		6	PDS: 3 mmol·L^{-1}	120 min	92.9%	[45]
UV/PMS (H_2SO_5)	10 mg·L^{-1}	3	PMS: 3 mmol·L^{-1}	180 min	92.09%	This work

4. Conclusions

This study explored the degradation efficiency of HA through the utilization of UV_{254}, COD, TOC degradation efficiencies, and *EE/O* as economic metrics to evaluate and contrast the effectiveness of different UV/AOPs synergistic processes in comparison to individual processes. The results suggested that both the individual oxidant and UV processes exhibited significantly lower efficacy in treating HA in comparison to the synergistic processes. Among the synergistic processes, UV/PMS exhibited the highest performance, achieving a mineralization rate of up to 94.15%, followed by UV/PDS and UV/SPC. The UV/S(IV) process exhibited the lowest effectiveness, achieving a mineralization rate of only 19.8%. Further exploration of the variables influencing the UV/PMS treatment of HA indicated that acidic environments were more favorable for the degradation of HA, with an optimum pH level of 3. The rate of HA degradation was determined to be directly proportional to the duration of illumination and inversely proportional to the initial concentration of the reactants. The optimal concentration of the oxidant was found to be 3 mmol/L. Under the experimental conditions with an initial concentration of 10 mg/L for HA, 3 mmol/L for PMS, and a starting pH of 5, the reaction was carried out for 180 min. The results showed significant degradation efficiencies: a COD degradation efficiency of 96.32%, a UV_{254} degradation efficiency of 97.34%, HA mineralization rate of 92.09%, and an *EE/O* ratio of 0.0149 (kWh)/m^3. The results illustrate the high efficacy of the UV/PMS synergistic system in the degradation and mineralization of HA in water.

Author Contributions: Conceptualization, Q.S. and X.S.; methodology, Q.S.; software, J.F.; validation, Q.S. and J.F.; formal analysis, Q.S.; investigation, C.C.; resources, Q.S.; data curation, Z.L.; writing—original draft preparation, Q.S.; writing—review and editing, X.S.; visualization, Q.S.; supervision, X.S.; project administration, X.S.; funding acquisition, X.S. All authors have read and agreed to the published version of the manuscript.

Funding: This study was supported by the Scientific Research Program for Higher Educational Institutions in Gansu Province (2020C-038), which is titled "Research on Key Technologies for Water Safety, Health Risk Prevention and Control and Domestic Waste Disposal in the Lanzhou Section of the Yellow River Basin".

Data Availability Statement: All valid data are reflected in the article and authorized to be used.

Conflicts of Interest: The funders had no role in the design of the study; in the collection, analyses, or interpretation of data; in the writing of the manuscript, or in the decision to publish the results.

References

1. Reyes, T.G.; Crisosto, J.M. Characterization of dissolved organic matter in river water by conventional methods and direct sample analysis-time of flight-mass spectrometry. *J. Chem.* **2016**, *11*, 1537370. [CrossRef]
2. Vogt, R.D.; Garmo, Ø.A.; Austnes, K.; Kaste, Ø.; Haaland, S.; Sample, J.E.; Thrane, J.-E.; Skancke, L.B.; Gundersen, C.B.; de Wit, H.A. Factors Governing Site and Charge Density of Dissolved Natural Organic Matter. *Water* **2024**, *16*, 1716. [CrossRef]
3. Ryu, J.H.; Jung, J.H.; Park, K.Y.; Song, W.J.; Choi, B.G.; Kweon, J.H. Humic acid removal and microbial community function in membrane bioreactor. *J. Hazard. Mater.* **2021**, *417*, 126088. [CrossRef] [PubMed]
4. Tang, W.W.; Zeng, G.M.; Gong, J.L.; Liang, J.; Xu, P.; Zhang, C.; Huang, B.B. Impact of humic/fulvic acid on the removal of heavy metals from aqueous solutions using nanomaterials: A review. *Sci. Total Environ.* **2014**, *468*, 1014–1027. [CrossRef] [PubMed]
5. Raj, A.; Dash, S.; Karnena, M.K. A review on techniques used for removal of natural organic matter (NOM) from the water. *IJSREM* **2022**, *6*, 1–10. [CrossRef]
6. Cui, L.; Zhang, Y.Y.; He, K.Y.; Sun, M.M.; Zhang, Z.H. Ti_4O_7 reactive electrochemical membrane for humic acid removal: Insights of electrosorption and electrooxidation. *Sep. Purif. Technol.* **2022**, *293*, 121112. [CrossRef]
7. Bhatnagar, A.; Sillanpää, M. Removal of natural organic matter (NOM) and its constituents from water by adsorption—A review. *Chemosphere* **2017**, *166*, 497–510. [CrossRef] [PubMed]
8. Ruecker, A.; Uzun, H.; Karanfil, T.; Tsui, M.T.K.; Chow, A.T. Disinfection byproduct precursor dynamics and water treatability during an extreme flooding event in a coastal blackwater river in southeastern United States. *Chemosphere* **2017**, *188*, 90–98. [CrossRef]
9. Wang, L.; Wei, S.; Jiang, Z.E. Effects of humic acid on enhanced removal of lead ions by polystyrene-supported nano-Fe (0) nanocomposite. *Sci. Rep.* **2020**, *10*, 19663. [CrossRef]
10. Alayande, A.B.; Hong, S. Ultraviolet light-activated peroxymonosulfate (UV/PMS) system for humic acid mineralization: Effects of ionic matrix and feasible application in seawater reverse osmosis desalination. *Environ. Pollut.* **2022**, *307*, 119513. [CrossRef]
11. Chen, W.; Yu, H.Q. Advances in the characterization and monitoring of natural organic matter using spectroscopic approaches. *Water Res.* **2021**, *190*, 116759. [CrossRef] [PubMed]
12. Li, Q.M.; Li, X.; Zhou, C.Q.; Lu, C.C.; Liu, B.G.; Wang, G.X. Insight into oxidation and adsorption treatment of algae-laden water: Algal organic matter transformation and removal. *J. Chem. Eng.* **2021**, *420*, 129887. [CrossRef]

13. Mulyati, S.; Aprilia, S.; Muchtar, S.; Syamsuddin, Y.; Rosnelly, C.M.; Bilad, M.R.; Samsuri, S.; Ismail, N.M. Fabrication of Polyvinylidene Difluoride Membrane with Enhanced Pore and Filtration Properties by Using Tannic Acid as an Additive. *Polymers* **2022**, *14*, 186. [CrossRef] [PubMed]
14. Zhu, G.C.; Bian, Y.N.; Hursthouse, A.S.; Xu, S.N.; Xiong, N.N.; Wan, P. The role of magnetic MOFs nanoparticles in enhanced iron coagulation of aquatic dissolved organic matter. *Chemosphere* **2020**, *247*, 125921. [CrossRef]
15. Du, T.T.; Zhang, G.; Zou, J. Coupling photocatalytic and electrocatalytic oxidation towards simultaneous removal of humic acid and ammonia−nitrogen in landscape water. *Chemosphere* **2022**, *286*, 131717. [CrossRef] [PubMed]
16. Giannakoudakis, D.A.; Qayyum, A.; Barczak, M.; Colmenares-Quintero, R.F.; Borowski, P.; Triantafyllidis, K.; Colmenares, J.C. Mechanistic and kinetic studies of benzyl alcohol photocatalytic oxidation by nanostructured titanium (hydro)oxides: Do we know the entire story? *Appl. Catal. B Environ.* **2023**, *320*, 121939. [CrossRef]
17. Asria, M.; Naghizadehb, A.; Hasania, A.; Mortazavi-Derazkolab, S.; Javida, A.; Masoudic, F. Sustainable green synthesis of $ZnFe_2O_4$@ZnO nanocomposite using Oleaster tree bark methanolic extract for photocatalytic degradation of aqueous humic acid in the presence of UVc irradiation. *Water Supply Res. Technol.* **2023**, *72*, 1800–1814. [CrossRef]
18. Xu, L.; Zhou, Z.; Graham, N.J.; Liu, M.J.; Yu, W.Z. Enhancing ultrafiltration performance by gravity-driven up-flow slow biofilter pre-treatment to remove natural organic matters and biopolymer foulants. *Water Res.* **2021**, *195*, 117010. [CrossRef] [PubMed]
19. Lado Ribeiro, A.R.; Rodríguez-Chueca, J.J.; Giannakis, S. Urban and industrial wastewater disinfection and decontamination by advanced oxidation processes(AOPs): Current issues and future trends. *Water* **2021**, *13*, 560. [CrossRef]
20. Barisci, S.; Suri, R. Removal of polyfluorinated telomer alcohol by advanced oxidation processes(AOPs) in different water matrices and evaluation of degradation mechanisms. *J. Water Process Eng.* **2020**, *39*, 101745. [CrossRef]
21. Cao, Y.J.; Ren, Y.J.; Zhang, Q.F.; Zhao, M.M.; Bai, C.X.; Wang, T.F. Research Progress of UV-Advanced Oxidation for Treatment of Natural Organic Matters, China. *Chem. Biol. Eng.* **2022**, *39*, 1–5.
22. *GB 11892-891*; Water Quality-Determination of Permanganate Index. National Standard of the People's Republic of China: Beijing, China, 1990.
23. Yang, J.L.; Zhu, M.S.; Dionysiou, D.D. What is the role of light in persulfate-based advanced oxidation for water treatment? *Water Res.* **2021**, *189*, 116627. [CrossRef] [PubMed]
24. Liu, G.Y. Study on the Transformation and Mechanism of Organic Matter in Secondary Effluent in Ultraviolet Persulfate System. Master's Thesis, Beijing University of Chemical Engineering, Beijing, China, 2022.
25. Wang, J.; Wang, S. Activation of persulfate (PS) and peroxymonosulfate (PMS) and application for the degradation of emerging contaminants. *Chem. Eng. J.* **2018**, *334*, 1502–1517. [CrossRef]
26. Liu, B.H.; Ye, M.T.; Ren, Z.X.; Lichtfouse, E.; Chen, Z.B. Towards synergistic combination of biochar/ultrasonic persulfate enhancing removal of natural humic acids from water. *J. Environ. Chem. Eng.* **2022**, *10*, 107809. [CrossRef]
27. Sun, H.Y.; Xing, R.Z.; Ye, X.Y.; Yin, K.K.; Zhang, Y.L.; Chen, Z.; Zhou, S.G. Reactive oxygen species accelerate humification process during iron mineral-amended sludge composting. *Bioresour. Technol.* **2023**, *370*, 128554. [CrossRef] [PubMed]
28. Wang, Q.; Wang, T.; Laila, N.; Huang, K.; Wang, X.W.; Lei, R.; Bai, X.Y.; Xu, Q.Y. Carbon dots/TiO_2 enhanced visible light-assisted photocatalytic of leachate: Simultaneous effects and Mechanism insights. *Water Res.* **2023**, *245*, 120659. [CrossRef] [PubMed]
29. Lee, J.; von Gunten, U.; Kim, J.H. Persulfate-based advanced oxidation: Critical assessment of opportunities and roadblocks. *Environ. Sci. Technol.* **2020**, *54*, 3064–3081. [CrossRef] [PubMed]
30. Sun, X.Y. Removal of Reclaimed Water Disinfection by-Product Precursors Based on Uv Advanced Oxidation Technology. Master's Thesis, Shandong Construction University, Jinan, China, 2020.
31. Yuan, D.; Tang, J.; Nie, Z.; Tang, S. Study on the removal of humic acid from water by ultraviolet activated sodium percarbonate, China. *Yanshan Univ.* **2021**, *45*, 220–226.
32. Bremner, D.H.; Molina, R.; Martínez, F.; Melero, J.A.; Segura, Y. Degradation of phenolic aqueous solutions by high frequency sono-Fenton systems (US-Fe_2O_3/SBA-15-H_2O_2). *Appl. Catal. B Environ.* **2009**, *90*, 380–388. [CrossRef]
33. Li, Y.; Dong, H.; Li, L.; Xiao, J.; Xiao, S.; Jin, Z. Efficient degradation of sulfamethazine via activation of percarbonate by chalcopyrite. *Water Res.* **2021**, *202*, 117451. [CrossRef]
34. Liu, W.K.; Liu, B.; Li, X. UV/Fe(II) synergistically activated S(IV) per-treatment on HA-enhanced Ca^{2+} scaling in NF filtration: Fouling mitigation, mechanisms and correlation analysis of membrane resistance in different filtration stage. *Chemosphere* **2022**, *308*, 136302. [CrossRef] [PubMed]
35. Cao, Y.; Qiu, W.; Li, J.; Zhao, Y.M.; Jiang, J.; Pang, S. Sulfite enhanced transformation of iopamidol by UV photolysis in the presence of oxygen: Role of oxysulfur radicals. *Water Res.* **2021**, *189*, 116625. [CrossRef] [PubMed]
36. Devi, L.G.; Srinivas, M.; Arunakumari, M.L. Heterogeneous advanced photo- Fenton process using peroxymonosulfate and peroxydisulfate in presence of zero valent metallic iron: A comparative study with hydrogen peroxide photo-Fenton process. *J. Water Process Eng.* **2016**, *13*, 117–126. [CrossRef]
37. Wu, P.; Liu, Z.Y.; Stroet, M.; Liao, J.L.; Chai, Z.F.; Mark, A.E.; Ning, L.; Wang, D.Q. Understanding the Effect of pH on the Solubility and Aggregation Extent of Humic Acid in Solution by Combining Simulation and the Experiment. *Environ. Sci. Technol.* **2022**, *56*, 917–927.
38. Wang, W.Y.; Li, R.H.; Bu, F.; Gao, Y.; Gao, B.Y.; Yue, Q.Y.; Yang, M.; Li, Y. Coagulation and membrane fouling mechanism of Al species in removing humic acid: Effect of pH and a dynamics process analysiss. *Sep. Purif. Technol.* **2023**, *309*, 123130. [CrossRef]

39. Yuan, D.L.; Zhai, Z.H.; Zhu, E.Y.; Liu, H.L.; Jiao, T.F.; Tang, S.F. Humic Acid Removal in Water via UV Activated Sodium Perborate Process. *Coatings* **2022**, *12*, 885. [CrossRef]
40. Lominchar, M.A.; Santos, A.; Miguel, E.D.; Romero, A. Remediation of aged diesel contaminated soil by alkaline activated persulfate. *Sci. Total Environ.* **2018**, *622–623*, 41–48. [CrossRef] [PubMed]
41. Lu, Q.; Liu, Y.Z.; Li, B.H.; Feng, L.; Du, Z.W.; Zhang, L.Q. Reaction kinetics of dissolved black carbon with hydroxyl radical, sulfate radical and reactive chlorine radicals. *Sci. Total Environ.* **2022**, *828*, 153984. [CrossRef] [PubMed]
42. Meng, J.Z.; Yuan, S.J.; Wang, W.; Jin, J.L.; Zhan, X.M.; Xiao, L.W.; Hu, Z.H. Photodegradation of roxarsone in the aquatic environment: Influencing factors, mechanisms, and artificial neural network modeling. *Environ. Sci. Pollut. Res.* **2021**, *29*, 7844–7852. [CrossRef]
43. Ji, G.X. Characterization of the Removal of Natural Organic Matter from Source Water by Ultraviolet/Peroxysulfate Advanced Oxidation Technology. Master's Thesis, Shandong Construction University, Jinan, China, 2020.
44. Mengge, F.; Xin, Y.; Qingqing, K.; Lei, Y.; Zhang, X.R.; Aghdam, E.; Yin, R.; Shang, C. Sequential ClO_2-UV/chlorine process for micropollutant removal and disinfection byproduct control. *Sci. Total Environ.* **2022**, *806*, 150354.
45. Tang, S.; Tang, J.; Yuan, D.; Wang, Z.; Zhang, Y.; Rao, Y. Elimination of humic acid in water: Comparison of UV/PDS and UV/PMS. *RSC Adv.* **2020**, *10*, 17627–17634. [CrossRef] [PubMed]
46. Wang, Z.M.; Chen, J.B.; Zhang, L.M.; Li, W.W.; Huang, T.Y. Activated Carbon Supported Co_3O_4 Catalysts to Activate Peroxymonosulfate for Orange, G Degradation. *Huan Jing Ke Xue* **2016**, *37*, 2591–2600.
47. Jiang, F.; Qiu, B.; Sun, D. Advanced degradation of refractory pollutants in incineration leachate by UV/Peroxymonosulfate. *Chem. Eng. J.* **2018**, *349*, 338–346. [CrossRef]
48. Juan, L.; Yang, S.; Jin, J.; Yang, T.; Cao, Y. Oxidative treatment of NOM by selective oxidants in drinking water treatment and its impact on DBP formation in postchlorination. *Sci. Total Environ.* **2022**, *858*, 159908.
49. Xia, G.; Huang, Y.; Li, F.; Wang, L.C.; Pang, J.B.; Li, L.W.; Wang, K. A thermally flexible and multi-site tactile sensor for remote 3D dynamic sensing imaging. *Front. Chem. Sci. Eng.* **2020**, *14*, 1039–1051. [CrossRef]
50. Li, X.; Wu, B.; Zhang, Q.; Xu, D.; Liu, Y.; Ma, F.; Gu, Q.; Li, F. Mechanisms on the impacts of humic acids on persulfate/Fe^{2+}-based groundwater remediation. *Chem. Eng. J.* **2019**, *378*, 122142.
51. Ike, I.A.; Linden, K.G.; Orbell, J.D.; Duke, M. Critical review of the science and sustainability of persulphate advanced oxidation processes. *Chem. Eng. J.* **2018**, *338*, 651–669. [CrossRef]

processes

MDPI

Review

Advances in Ozone Technology for Environmental, Energy, Food and Medical Applications

Kang Zhang [1], Jianzheng Liu [2], Hongkun Lv [1], Xianyang Zeng [3,*], Zhongqian Ling [3], Liwei Ding [1] and Chenyang Jin [3]

[1] State Grid Zhejiang Electric Power Research Institute, Hangzhou 310014, China
[2] Daya Bay Nuclear Power Operations and Management Co., Ltd., Shenzhen 518124, China
[3] College of Energy Environment and Safety Engineering, China Jiliang University, Hangzhou 310018, China
* Correspondence: 06a0204057@cjlu.edu.cn

Abstract: Ozone (O_3), a strong oxidizing agent, has found widespread applications since its structure was confirmed by Schubbe in 1839. It can be produced through ultraviolet radiation, electrochemical methods, or dielectric barrier discharge (DBD), with DBD being the most efficient for large-scale production due to its high stability. Ozone is widely used in environmental management, particularly in water treatment, air pollution control, and soil remediation. In water treatment, ozone effectively removes microorganisms and contaminants without generating secondary pollutants. In air pollution control, it degrades organic compounds in industrial waste and neutralizes toxic gases in automobile exhausts. Ozone also breaks down persistent pollutants like polycyclic aromatic hydrocarbons in soil, improving soil quality. However, challenges remain related to ozone's stability and high production costs. Beyond environmental uses, ozone is critical in industries and medicine. It helps remove pathogens and heavy metals in wastewater treatment, extends shelf life and deactivates mycotoxins in food processing, and shows promise in medical fields like orthopedics and cancer therapy. In the power industry, ozone plays a key role in water treatment and air purification. Overall, ozone technology offers significant potential for both environmental and industrial applications.

Keywords: ozone; dielectric barrier discharge; application

1. Introduction

Ozone (O_3) is an allotrope of oxygen (O_2) composed of three oxygen atoms. It has a distinctive fishy smell and is highly oxidizing [1]. In 1839, German scientist J.D.C. von Schubein (Schonbein) first identified ozone at the Natural Science Congress in Basel, characterizing it as a molecule consisting of one oxygen molecule and one additional oxygen atom. Due to its unstable chemical properties, Schonbein described it as reactive oxygen. In 1840, he formally submitted a report to the Munich Academy of Sciences in Germany, announcing the discovery of ozone. Since then, the properties and functions of ozone have gradually been elucidated through scientific research.

After the efficacy of ozone in disinfection, sterilization, water treatment, and bleaching was recognized, it began to be adopted in industrial applications. In 1868, de Gebeth was the first to apply ozone industrially, using it to oxidize coal tar mixtures to produce products suitable for use in coatings and paints [2]. By 1873, ozone was being used in Europe for sugar refining and linen bleaching [3]. In 1902, the world's first large-scale water treatment facility utilizing ozone was built in Paderborn, Germany. In 1937, the first commercial swimming pool treated with ozone was opened in the United States, and since then, ozone has become the designated water disinfection method for Olympic aquatic competitions. Following World War II, ozone was employed in Europe, the United States, and Japan for preserving fruits and vegetables throughout storage, manufacturing, and transportation [2]. Ozone also found applications in the medical field. During World War II, Japan used ozone for physical therapy, while Russia utilized ozonated air in athletic facilities. Today, ozone has numerous medical applications, including air disinfection in hospital wards and operating theatres, disinfection of medical instruments using ozonated water, and dental treatments for sterilization. Additionally, it is used for gynecological treatments, and ozone microbubble water is employed for its bactericidal activity against pathogens in the mouth and upper respiratory tract, as well as for disinfecting contaminated medical equipment [4]. In the 1960s and 1970s, ozone technology began to be used for treating domestic sewage in the United States, which led to the establishment of an independent ozone technology industry [5]. The International Ozone Association (IOA), founded in 1973 in Canada, has played a key role in advancing ozone technology. The association hosts an international conference every two years to facilitate the exchange of research and advancements. Developed countries have also established regional IOA organizations to foster academic collaboration. In 1982, ozone began to be widely used to sterilize bottled water, and today, it is employed by nearly all manufacturers of mineral and purified water. Ozone applications can be classified into four main categories: water treatment, chemical oxidation, food processing and preservation, and medical treatment. Each of these fields has seen significant advancements in research and equipment development, contributing to the widespread adoption of ozone technology over the past century.

In China, research into and application of ozone technology started relatively late. It was not until the mid-1970s that China began research and development in this field. In the 1990s, the promotion of ozone disinfection technology for mineral water, purified water, and pharmaceutical air sterilization, along with the introduction of small household ozone generators, helped advance China's ozone industry. After 2000, significant breakthroughs were made in the development of large-scale industrial ozone equipment, including the successful production of intermediate frequency ozone generators with capacities ranging from 3 to 120 kg/h, raising China's ozone technology to the international level.

Ozone (O_3) is a pale blue gas with a characteristic fishy odor. It has a higher relative molecular weight than air, is slightly soluble in water, and is more soluble in liquid nitrogen and alkaline solutions. Due to its inherently unstable nature, ozone exists in a transient state, consisting of a V-shaped molecule composed of three oxygen atoms. In its liquid form, ozone decomposes slowly at room temperature and rapidly at elevated temperatures, producing oxygen. It is highly reactive and can explode under impact or friction. The presence of a highly reactive oxygen atom makes ozone an excellent oxidant with a high oxidation potential, making it an ideal oxidizing agent that does not lead to secondary pollution. Ozone's strong oxidizing ability also causes most pigments to fade, which is why it is often used as a bleaching agent.

Ozone is an extremely powerful oxidizing and bactericidal agent, and is one of the strongest oxidants found in nature. In water, its redox potential is second only to that of fluorine, with a value of 2.07 eV. After participating in redox reactions, ozone reverts back to oxygen, making it an efficient oxidant without producing secondary pollution [6]. As a strong oxidant, ozone has the following notable characteristics: (1) it can be used for selective oxidation, resulting in a high yield of the desired product [7]; (2) it has a low oxidation temperature and strong oxidation potential at normal pressure, which is advantageous for the oxidation of sensitive substances [8]; (3) it has a rapid reaction rate and can perform quantitative oxidation [9]; and (4) it is easy to use and manufacture [10].

Ozone is also widely employed as a bleaching agent. In the pulp and paper industry, ozone effectively removes lignin, thereby increasing the whiteness of pulp [11]. In 1976, at the International Pulp Bleaching Conference, Krausler, Kraus, and Reich proposed a mechanism for ozone's reaction with lignin and lignin model compounds. They suggested that when O_3 reacts with lignin, it opens the aromatic ring at C3 and C4. As illustrated in Figure 1, a schematic diagram of the preparation of highly active lignin by ozone oxidation, this results in a highly polar structure that inhibits the chromogenic group's ability to impart color. Ozone can also react with unsaturated double bonds in lignin, producing hydrogen peroxide, which further aids in bleaching. Ozone bleaching is highly efficient and environmentally friendly, indicating a promising future for its use in sustainable pulp bleaching processes.

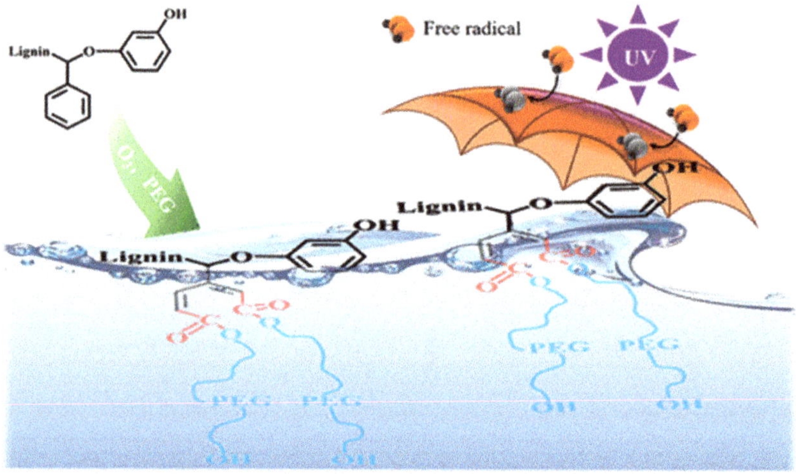

Figure 1. Schematic diagram of preparation of highly active lignin by ozone oxidation [1].

The primary aim of this review is to provide a comprehensive overview of the advancements in ozone technology, focusing on its applications in environmental management, industrial processes, and medical treatment. By synthesizing the latest research, this review not only highlights the versatile applications of ozone in various fields but also critically examines the challenges and limitations associated with its widespread adoption. This paper is novel in its approach to integrating a wide range of applications of ozone, from water and air treatment to its emerging role in medical therapies, which have not been comprehensively addressed in previous literature reviews. The review also offers a discussion on the future directions of ozone technology, particularly in relation to the cost-effectiveness, scalability, and technological advancements needed to improve its practical applications.

2. Method of Ozone Preparation

Due to its physical properties, ozone is highly prone to decomposition, which makes it challenging to store and limits its application and widespread adoption. As a result, ozone is typically generated and used on-site. Currently, there are three primary methods for generating ozone: ultraviolet irradiation, electrolysis, and dielectric barrier discharge. The advantages and disadvantages of different methods have been organized in Table 1.

Table 1. Comparation of ozone generation methods.

Method	Advantages	Disadvantages	Reported Yields	References
Ultraviolet Irradiation	- Simple technology - High ozone yield in small-scale setups	- High energy consumption - Limited scalability for large-scale production	130 g/kWh	[2,3]
Electrochemical Ozone Production	- Suitable for on-site ozone generation - Environmentally friendly (no chemical use)	- Requires high electrical energy - Efficiency drops with increasing water salinity	20 g/kWh	[6]
Dielectric barrier Discharge	- High scalability for large-scale applications - High energy efficiency	- Requires special electrode materials - High voltage operation	200 g/kWh	[11]
Corona Discharge	- Cost-effective for industrial applications - High efficiency for large-scale production	- Requires air or oxygen as input - Potential for high wear and tear on electrodes	150 g/kWh	[12]
Pulsed Power Technology	- High energy efficiency - Precise control over ozone concentration	- Still under development - High cost and complexity	73.94 g/kWh	[13]
Silent Discharge Plasma	- Low-temperature operation - Minimal by-product formation - Eco-friendly	- Requires complex system for precise control - Less widespread in industry	7 g/kWh	[14]

2.1. Ultraviolet Radiation

Ultraviolet light interacts with oxygen molecules, dissociating them into individual oxygen atoms. These oxygen atoms then combine with O_2 molecules to form ozone (O_3). For effective photolysis of O_2 molecules, the radiation energy must be sufficient to dissociate O_2 (i.e., with a wavelength $\lambda < 242$ nm), but must not be high enough to cause ionization ($\lambda > 103$ nm) [2].

$$O_2 + UV \rightarrow O + O \quad (1)$$

$$O + O_2 + M \rightarrow O_3 + M \quad (2)$$

In the stratosphere, under solar radiation, these reactions proceed continuously, resulting in both the continuous formation and destruction of ozone. Researchers have also attempted to produce ozone using UV radiation; however, the UV method has the significant drawback of low production efficiency. If all the UV energy is used to generate ozone, the production efficiency can be as low as 130 g/kWh [2,3]. Due to the low conversion efficiency of electrical energy into optical energy, the actual ozone production efficiency is usually less than 1 g/kWh [4]. The advantages of the UV irradiation method include good reproducibility and low humidity requirements, while the disadvantages include the low concentration of ozone produced, high power consumption, and strict radiation protection requirements. Consequently, the UV method is only suitable for a limited number of low-concentration applications, and its ozone yield is insufficient for large-scale production.

The process of generating ozone using external ultraviolet (UV) radiation involves using a UV light source to split oxygen (O_2) molecules. The high-energy radiation emitted by the UV light source dissociates the oxygen molecules into individual oxygen atoms.

These free oxygen atoms then recombine with other oxygen molecules to form ozone (O_3). This process is typically carried out in specialized reactors to maximize ozone production and increase reaction efficiency, as illustrated in Figure 2.

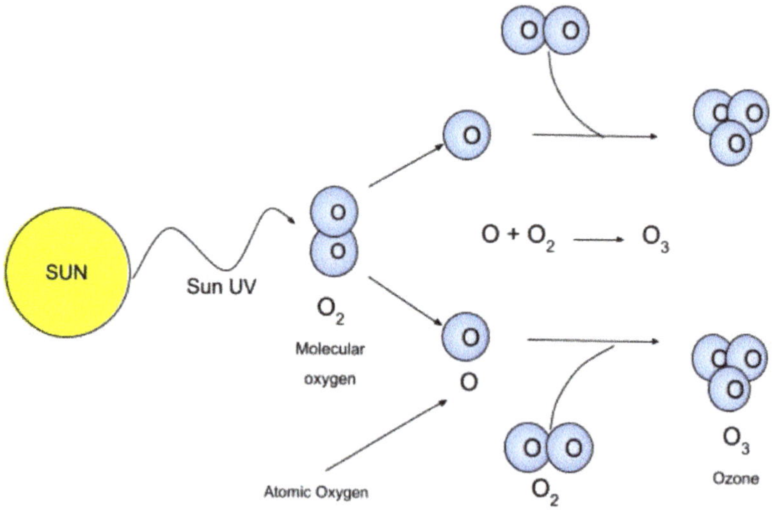

Figure 2. A diagram showing the use of ultraviolet radiation to generate ozone, taken from [5].

2.2. Electrochemical Ozone Production

Electrochemical ozone generation is a highly efficient and environmentally friendly method of producing ozone. This method uses an electric current to drive oxygen molecules in an electrolytic cell to generate ozone. Electrochemical ozone generation allows for precise control of the ozone production process and has significant practical applications across various fields, including water treatment and air purification. The main reaction involved in this process is as follows:

$$3H_2O \rightarrow O_3 + 6H^+ + 6e^- \quad (3)$$

It is known that the electrochemical production of ozone occurs as a result of the oxidation of water on the surface of the anode of an electrochemical cell [6]. In this process, oxygen molecules, under the influence of an electric current, decompose to form ozone. The main factors affecting ozone production include the reaction temperature, anode type and composition, current density, electrolyte composition, and pH. Different anode materials (e.g., platinum, titanium, and electrodes coated with conductive materials) have a significant effect on the efficiency and yield of the electrochemical reaction. The current density determines the rate of ozone production, while the electrolyte composition and pH influence the electrochemical environment and overall reaction efficiency. A significant advantage of the electrochemical method is that it allows for ozone production in a closed system, enabling effective control of the reaction conditions so that external factors such as temperature and humidity have minimal impact on ozone production. The advantages of this method include the long equipment lifespan, high concentration of ozone produced, simplicity in equipment design, and ease of operation and maintenance. Additionally, because the reactions occur in a stable system, the electrochemical method can maintain consistent ozone production and quality over extended periods (Figure 3).

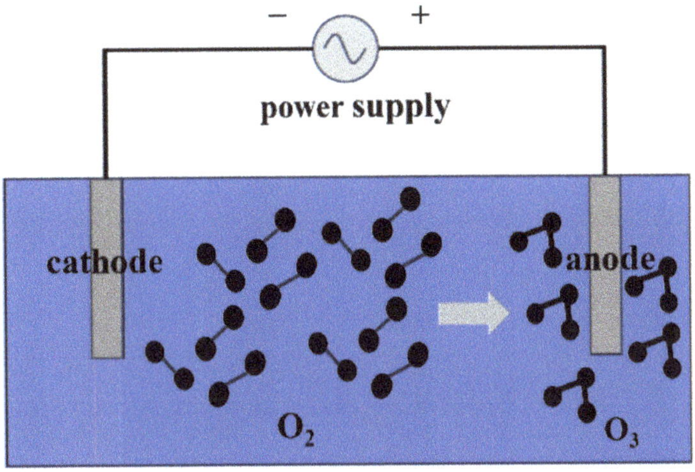

Figure 3. Schematic diagram of electrochemical method for generating ozone.

2.3. Dielectric Barrier Discharge

At present, there are several methods for producing ozone, including the ultraviolet (UV) oxidation method, electrochemical method, and dielectric barrier discharge method. The UV oxidation method involves irradiating oxygen with high-energy UV light to produce ozone. This approach has the advantage of being simple and suitable for small-scale applications. The electrochemical method generates ozone through an electrochemical reaction, with the advantage of producing a high concentration of ozone and working stably in a closed system. However, it has certain drawbacks, such as relatively low ozone production and the need for frequent electrode replacement. The dielectric barrier discharge method offers high ozone generation efficiency, simple equipment, and good stability. This method involves passing a dielectric barrier gas through a high-voltage alternating electric field, which results in corona discharge. The high-energy particles in the corona decompose oxygen molecules into oxygen atoms, which then collide and polymerize to form ozone molecules [7].

$$e + O_2 \rightarrow e + O + O \quad (4)$$

$$O + O_2 + M \rightarrow O_3 + M \quad (5)$$

$$O + O_3 \rightarrow 2O_2 \quad (6)$$

$$e + O_3 \rightarrow e + O_2 + O \quad (7)$$

Among the components involved, M primarily refers to O_2, O_3, and N_2. The oxygen atom in reactions (5) and (6) is generated through the excitation and dissociation of oxygen molecules by high-energy electrons produced during the blocked discharge of the medium in reaction (4).

The key factors influencing dielectric barrier discharge include the applied voltage and frequency [8–10], electrode material [10,11], gas pressure [15], gas composition [16], reactor structure [17,18], and other parameters. Recently, Gou et al. modified the electrode material by using a water flow as the ground electrode, replacing the traditional metal electrode. This approach resulted in a significantly improved ozone generation efficiency compared to that of commercial ozone generators. The ozone concentration reached approximately 13,000 ppm, with efficiency stabilized at around 200 g/kWh during a 400-min stability test [11]. Additionally, Kefeng Shang et al. introduced a volume–surface hybrid dielectric barrier discharge (V-SDBD) by affixing another grounded electrode to the dielectric surface. This configuration demonstrated superior ozone production and benzene decomposition efficiency compared to those of traditional volume dielectric barrier discharge (VDBD) and surface dielectric barrier discharge (SDBD) methods [18]. The dielectric barrier discharge method offers several advantages over UV irradiation and electrolysis, including a high ozone concentration, high yield, and excellent stability. As a result, it has become the focus of extensive research, with more and more studies being conducted on ozone production using this method (Figure 4).

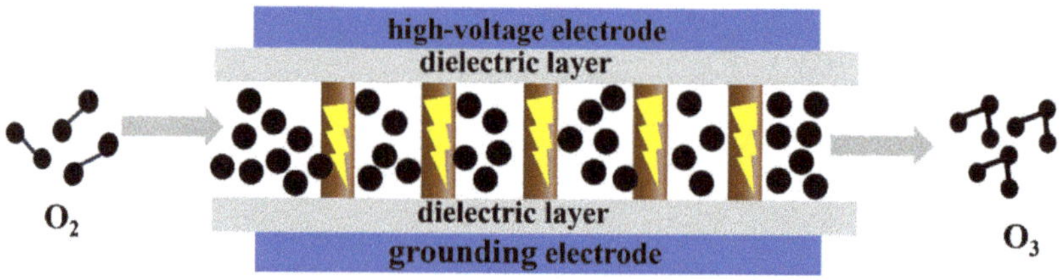

Figure 4. Schematic diagram of ozone generation using the medium barrier discharge method.

2.4. Other Ozone Generation Methods

While ultraviolet irradiation, electrolysis, and dielectric barrier discharge remain the most widely adopted and proven methods for ozone production, several other techniques, including corona discharge, pulsed power technology, and silent discharge plasma, provide promising alternatives or enhancements for specific applications. These methods, while not as widely used as the primary three, offer advantages in particular scenarios, such as improved efficiency, scalability, or temperature sensitivity. They are best suited for specialized uses where the primary methods may face limitations.

2.4.1. Corona Discharge

The corona discharge method is one of the most commonly used techniques for industrial-scale ozone production. It involves applying a high-voltage electrical discharge to oxygen or air, which splits the oxygen molecules into individual atoms. These atoms then recombine with other oxygen molecules to form ozone. This method is highly efficient and cost-effective, especially for large-scale production. It is widely used in applications such as municipal water treatment, air purification, and industrial ozone applications due to its scalability and relatively low operating costs [7].

In recent years, innovations in electrode design and electrical configurations have significantly improved the efficiency and output of corona discharge ozone generators. Advanced dielectric barrier coatings and modified electrode geometries have been explored to enhance the ozone yield while minimizing energy consumption [8]. Jung et al. studied the ozone generation characteristics in a corona discharge system with a glass-fiber layer and found that the addition of the glass-fiber layer significantly enhanced the ozone output (Figure 5) [12].

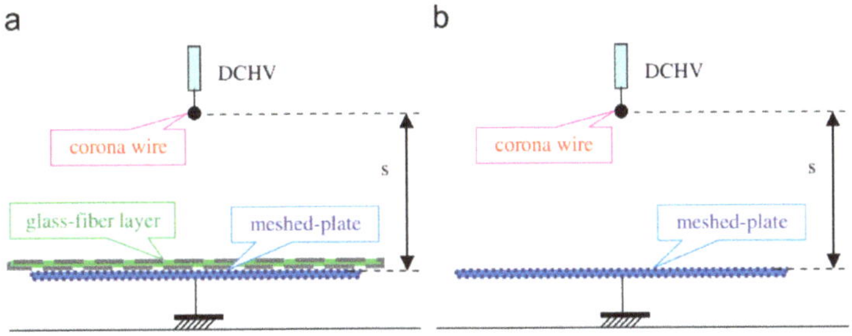

Figure 5. Schematic configuration of the proposed discharge system with glass-fiber layer: (**a**) wire-plate system with glass-fiber layer, (**b**) conventional wire-plate system [12].

2.4.2. Pulsed Power Technology

Pulsed power technology involves delivering high-energy electrical pulses into a gas, typically oxygen or air, to create a plasma state, which leads to ozone formation. This method offers the advantage of high energy efficiency and allows for precise control over ozone generation. Pulsed power technology is particularly beneficial in applications where rapid variation in ozone concentration is required, such as advanced oxidation processes (AOPs) for wastewater treatment or air purification. While still under development, it shows promise for various industrial and environmental applications, especially where flexible, on-demand ozone production is needed [19]. Jin et al. investigated ozone production and nitrogen oxide formation in a micro-hollow surface dielectric barrier discharge reactor driven by nanosecond pulses at atmospheric pressure for the first time (Figure 6) [13].

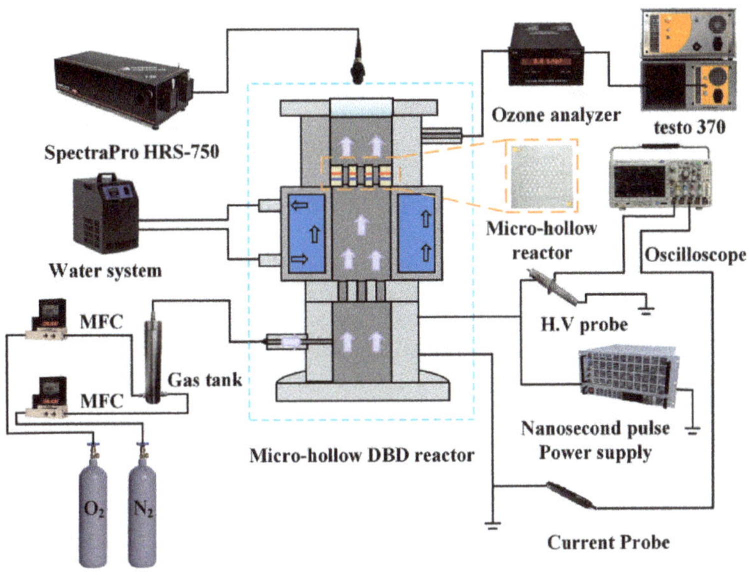

Figure 6. A schematic of pulsed experimental system [13].

2.4.3. Silent Discharge Plasma

Silent discharge plasma, also known as cold plasma, generates ozone through a non-thermal plasma state, without visible sparks or audible noise. The process occurs under low temperatures, which makes this method ideal for applications involving temperature-sensitive materials. Silent discharge plasma is increasingly used in air and water treatment, food processing, and sterilization, as it offers the advantage of ozone production at low temperatures without generating excessive heat. Additionally, it selectively degrades pollutants and minimizes the formation of unwanted by-products, making it suitable for eco-friendly and efficient applications [20]. Ashraf Yehia derived two equations from the experimental setup shown in Figure 7 to predict ozone generation in dry air within a silent discharge reactor [14].

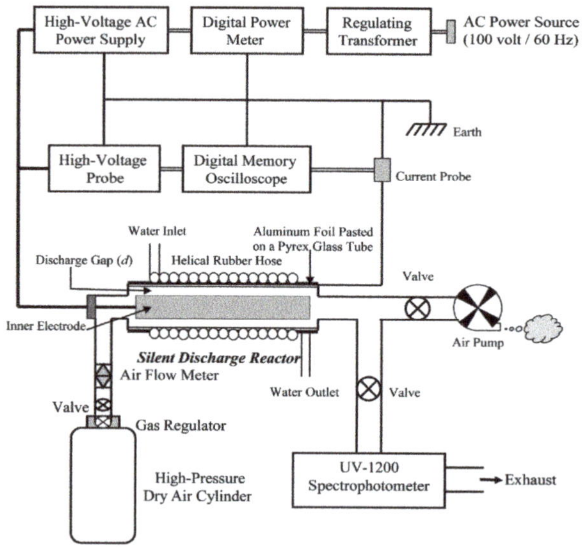

Figure 7. Schematic diagram of the experimental setup [14].

3. Application of Ozone

3.1. Ozone in Environmental Management

Before ozone became widely adopted in environmental management, chlorine was the most commonly used disinfectant. However, due to ozone's superior oxidizing properties and its environmental benefits, it gradually replaced chlorine, which produces harmful by-products detrimental to human health. Additionally, because ozone is relatively easy to generate, it has found broad applications in water treatment, air pollution control, soil remediation, and other pollution control processes (Figure 8).

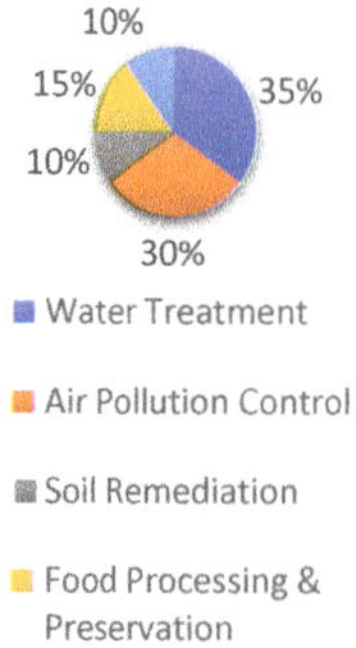

Figure 8. Popularity of ozone applications.

3.1.1. Water Treatment

The strong oxidizing properties of ozone, its effective purifying ability, and the absence of secondary contamination allow it to play a significant role in water treatment. The use of ozone in water treatment was first initiated in France [21], and, today, it is widely employed for the disinfection of drinking water as well as in wastewater treatment. In addition to its disinfection capabilities, ozone is also effective in controlling the color and taste of water [22], making it a popular choice in municipal wastewater treatment.

Ozone has demonstrated strong efficacy in disinfecting and removing fungi and bacteria present in water. Studies have shown that a concentration of 1.5 mg/L of ozone can eliminate 99% of Candida albicans, while a dose of 60 mg/L can remove 78% of Aspergillus flavus [23]. Moreover, ozone effectively removes chlorine-resistant bacteria by damaging both their cellular structure and genetic material [24]. For example, after ozone treatment, the DNA content of Bacillus cereus spores sharply decreases, although some target gene fragments are retained. Additionally, the spore structure undergoes significant changes, leading to the release of intracellular substances.

The efficiency of ozone in wastewater treatment is also notable: it disinfects more rapidly than chlorine and does not produce carcinogenic by-products. Pharmaceuticals are consumed in large quantities worldwide, and these pharmaceutical compounds ultimately reach wastewater treatment facilities after being excreted from the human body. Several studies have demonstrated that ozonation can effectively remove most pharmaceutical and personal care products (PPCPs) from secondary effluents within 10–15 min. Further research is required to optimize the ozonation process, particularly to minimize the ozone dosage while ensuring the simultaneous degradation of PPCPs [25]. Hollender et al. investigated the removal of PPCPs from secondary effluents using ozone, successfully removing approximately 55 micropollutants with various functional groups from municipal wastewater. Compounds with activated aromatic components, amine groups, or double bonds, such as sulfamethizole and carbamazepine, exhibited high second-order reaction rate constants with ozone ($>10^4$ $M^{-1}s^{-1}$) and were found to have concentrations below the detection limit of the O_3/DOC (dissolved organic carbon) ratio, which was only 0.47. In contrast, other compounds, such as the antidepressant venlafaxine (amine), had an O_3/DOC ratio of 0.62, indicating effective elimination [26]. Figure 9 shows the ozone treatment process of urban sewage.

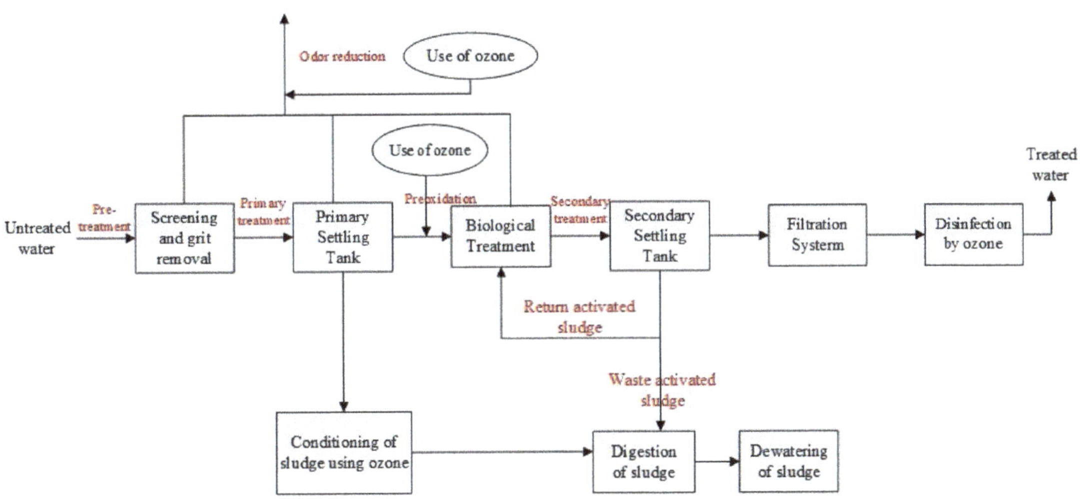

Figure 9. Schematic diagram of ozone treatment of urban sewage [27].

Furthermore, the use of ozone oxidation for textile wastewater purification offers promising potential for reuse, providing both direct environmental and economic benefits. Research conducted by Tecnotessile showed that an ozone dosage of 30 g/m^3 is sufficient to achieve the effective decolorization of textile wastewater, with a contact time of approximately 60 min. Increasing the dosage beyond this level did not yield additional improvements in decolorization. However, when the contact time is reduced to 30 min, an optimal dosage of 40 g/m^3 is required [28]. Ferrero [29] also reported that the removal of chemical oxygen demand (COD) and detergents became effective when the ozone dosage exceeded 50 mg/L.

Overall, the application of ozone in water treatment has vast potential and promising prospects. With ongoing technological advancements and reductions in cost, ozone is expected to be utilized in more fields, playing an increasingly important role in the protection and sustainable use of water resources. At the same time, it is crucial to continue exploring and researching innovative water treatment technologies to address the escalating issue of water pollution and safeguard our water resources and ecological environment.

3.1.2. Air Pollution Control

First and foremost, the application of ozone in atmospheric pollution control is primarily focused on the treatment of industrial waste gases. Industrial emissions often contain significant amounts of organic compounds and pollutants. If these substances are released directly into the atmosphere, they can cause substantial environmental damage. Ozone treatment technology offers an effective solution by oxidizing and decomposing these pollutants, transforming them into harmless substances, thus purifying the waste gases. Given that ozone oxidation of industrial gases generates non-toxic products such as oxygen, the following process steps can be implemented to render the emissions harmless: First, the industrial waste gases are captured and passed through a water filter. Next, the sulfuric and nitrous acids produced by the ozone treatment are completely and quantitatively converted into sulfuric and nitric acids. Finally, the resulting acids are neutralized into non-harmful products [30]. Ozone oxidation has the capability to simultaneously remove multiple pollutants, including SO_2, NO_x, organic pollutants, and mercury. A schematic diagram of the technical system is shown in Figure 10. Typically, after passing through the air preheater and dust control device, the flue gas temperature can be reduced to 200 °C, or in most cases, even below 170 °C. At these lower temperatures, ozone exhibits a high oxidation potential, which is favorable for the oxidation reactions. Additionally, the relatively clean conditions of the flue gas help to alleviate end-of-pipe treatment challenges, such as dust clogging and catalyst deactivation. Studies have shown that the optimal oxidation temperatures for NO and organic pollutants are below 130 °C. To ensure proper oxidation temperatures for odor removal, excess heat can be exchanged through a heat exchanger, and the recovered heat can be used for on-site heating via heat recovery technology. The ozone generated by medium barrier discharge can be effectively injected into an oxidation reactor, where it undergoes advanced oxidation with a small amount of ozone, aided by a catalyst. Under various ozone injection and reaction conditions, pollutants such as NO, organic compounds, and Hg_0 are oxidized into NO_2, N_2O_5, CO_2, H_2O, Cl_2, HCl, Hg^{2+}, and other substances. These highly soluble oxidized pollutants are then directed to the absorption section, typically a wet scrubber, where they are removed along with SO_2. In summary, the ozone oxidation–absorption process has been well established and is a promising method for industrial gas purification [20].

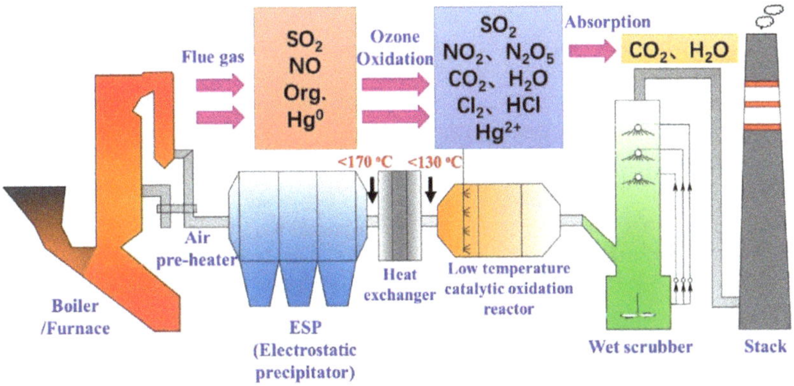

Figure 10. Schematic diagram of ozone removing pollutants, cited from [20].

Secondly, ozone also plays a significant role in the treatment of vehicle exhaust. Vehicle emissions contain harmful gases such as nitrogen oxides (NO_x) and sulfur dioxide (SO_2), which are major contributors to air pollution. Ozone treatment technology reacts ozone with carbon monoxide (CO), nitrogen oxides (NO_x), and unburned hydrocarbons (HC) in the exhaust, converting them into harmless carbon dioxide (CO_2), nitrogen (N_2), and water vapor (H_2O) before they are released into the atmosphere. This process effectively reduces the atmospheric pollution caused by vehicle exhaust. Compared to the direct use of plasma technology, the addition of ozone leads to a higher conversion efficiency of NO_x into NO_2 under the same specific input energy (SIE) [31].

However, despite its significant advantages in atmospheric pollution control, the application of ozone faces certain challenges and limitations. For example, the concentration of ozone and treatment duration must be precisely controlled to prevent any unnecessary harm to the environment and human health. Additionally, the capital investment and operational costs associated with ozone treatment systems are important factors that must be considered.

3.1.3. Soil Remediation and Pollution Control

Polycyclic aromatic hydrocarbons (PAHs) are ubiquitous organic compounds primarily originating from the incomplete combustion of petroleum products and fossil fuels. Due to their persistence and significant environmental and health risks, PAHs are classified as priority pollutants in many countries. Given the persistence of PAHs in soil and their potential hazards, effective remediation methods are essential. Among various remediation technologies, ozone soil remediation has gained considerable attention due to its unique advantages. Ozone's strong oxidizing properties allow it to effectively degrade PAHs, particularly those pollutants that are resistant to biodegradation. This ozone-based remediation method involves directly injecting ozone into the contaminated soil, ensuring targeted and efficient treatment. Consequently, ozonation has emerged as an attractive option for remediating PAH-contaminated soil, offering effective solutions for environmental matrices contaminated with recalcitrant pollutants [32]. Ozone soil remediation technology is an innovative approach that utilizes the strong oxidizing power of ozone to effectively treat contaminated soils, removing organic pollutants, heavy metals, and other harmful substances. By injecting ozone directly into the contaminated area, this method allows for quick reactions with refractory organic pollutants, significantly improving the soil quality [33]. Numerous studies have demonstrated the successful application of ozone and advanced oxidation processes in treating various forms of soil contamination [34].

In recent years, ozone soil remediation technology has seen further development and application. Among chemical methods, the ozone oxidation process has gained increasing attention due to its ability to rapidly degrade pollutants. Liu et al. [35] explored a coupled process of soil washing and ozone oxidation to remediate artificially contaminated soil. This combined approach not only enhanced remediation effectiveness but also expanded the range of applications for ozone soil remediation technology.

Ozone offers broad potential for soil remediation. Ozone oxidation can break down organic pollutants and toxic compounds in the soil, purify the soil environment, and even improve the soil structure, thereby promoting plant growth and supporting ecosystem restoration. However, when applying ozone for soil remediation, factors such as its environmental stability, by-product generation, and operational costs must be carefully considered. Therefore, combining ozone technology with other remediation methods, such as bioremediation and chemical remediation, can enhance efficiency and reduce costs. The integrated use of diverse technologies allows for a more comprehensive and effective approach to soil remediation (Figure 11).

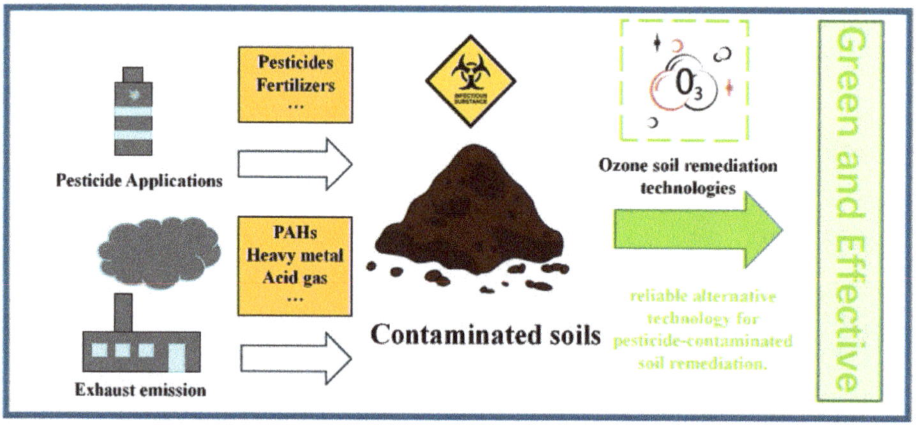

Figure 11. Ozone remediation of soil contaminants.

3.2. *Ozone in Manufacturing*

3.2.1. Industrial Wastewater Treatment

With the rapid pace of industrialization, wastewater treatment has become an increasingly critical issue, particularly for wastewater containing complex pollutants and hazardous substances, such as cyanide-containing effluents, coking wastewater, printing and dyeing wastewater, and municipal wastewater. These types of wastewater not only pose a significant environmental threat but can also cause long-term damage to human health. In this context, ozone treatment technology has garnered widespread attention due to its unique advantages. Ozone is widely utilized in wastewater treatment, primarily due to its excellent reliability and reactivity. As a broad-spectrum disinfectant and a strong oxidant, ozone possesses powerful oxidative properties that allow it to effectively remove a wide range of pollutants. It can efficiently degrade harmful substances such as pathogens, persistent organic pollutants, pesticides, and heavy metals found in wastewater. The application of ozone in treating industrial wastewater—such as cyanide-containing effluents, coking wastewater, printing and dyeing wastewater, as well as municipal wastewater—deserves further exploration, particularly in the context of drinking water disinfection and pre- and post-treatment processes [33]. Ozone's strong oxidizing ability allows it to act as both a disinfectant and an advanced oxidant in wastewater treatment. As illustrated in

Figure 12, an advanced oxidation process (AOP), which combines aerobic biodegradation and ozone treatment through a sequential batch reactor (SBR), has been shown to achieve a pollutant removal rate of 50% when applied to industrial wastewater with high organic loads (TOC > 3 g/L, COD > 12 g/L, BOD_5 > 2 g/L) [36].

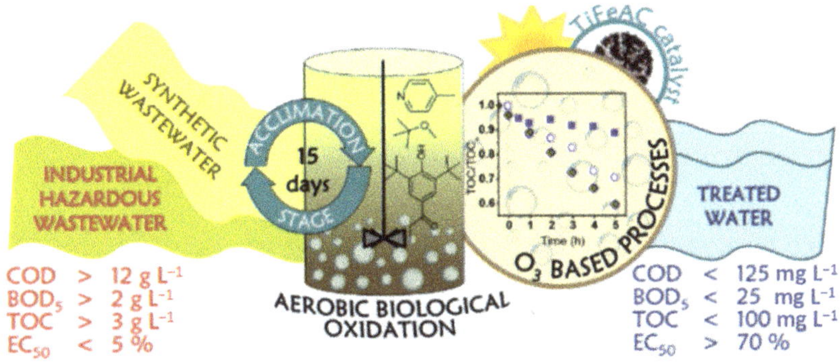

Figure 12. Schematic diagram of wastewater treatment [36].

Every day, large volumes of wastewater from various industries and facilities worldwide continue to contain harmful substances such as pathogens, persistent pollutants, pesticides, and heavy metals like arsenic, chromium, copper, boron, and nickel. These pollutants pose significant risks to both human health and the environment. A typical example is the molasses brewing industry, which generates wastewater with high concentrations of degradable organic matter and dissolved salts. For heavily polluting industries such as molasses brewing, ozone treatment technology has demonstrated considerable potential. P. Asaithambi and colleagues conducted a comparative study on the pollutant removal efficiency of three different treatment methods: ozone oxidation, electrocoagulation, and ozone-assisted electrocoagulation. They found that ozone-assisted electrocoagulation was the most effective process for removing pollutants [37]. In addition to this, A.M. Chávez et al. proposed a combined process of aerobic biological degradation (SBR) and ozone-based advanced oxidation processes (AOPs). This process uses SBR to treat industrial and municipal wastewater (e.g., MIW wastewater) by biodegrading the water with activated sludge. By combining biodegradation with ozone oxidation, this method more effectively removes harmful substances and achieves superior wastewater treatment. This combined approach has shown great promise as an efficient treatment solution [36].

As technology continues to advance, future developments in ozone treatment will focus on enhancing efficiency, safety, and environmental sustainability. Ozone treatment is expected to become increasingly widespread and popular in the field of industrial wastewater treatment.

3.2.2. Food Processing and Preservation

With the improvement of living standards and growing awareness of health among consumers, food processing and preservation technologies are receiving increasing attention. Ozone, as a highly effective oxidant, holds significant potential in the field of food processing and preservation. This paper provides a comprehensive review of the application of ozone in food processing, focusing on its role in inactivating mycotoxins and preserving fruits and vegetables. The aim is to offer insights that can guide the further development of ozone technology in this area.

Mycotoxins are toxic metabolites produced by fungi, which pose serious health risks. As shown in Figure 13, these toxins are present in various foods worldwide [38] and are commonly found in food and feed products. The genera Aspergillus, Fusarium, and Penicillium are the primary producers of mycotoxins. Aspergillus, in particular, is known for producing nephrotoxins (e.g., ochratoxin A, OTA) and carcinogens (e.g., aflatoxins, AFs), and is prevalent in many food products. Studies have demonstrated that ozone gas can effectively inactivate Fusarium and Aspergillus, making ozone treatment a safe and environmentally friendly technology for food preservation and contamination control [39]. Fruits and vegetables, while essential for a healthy diet, are highly perishable and prone to spoilage after harvest, compromising both their quality and safety. Research by Elodie Sarron et al. has shown that ozone treatment can prevent and control microbial growth on vegetables, preserving their appearance, sensory qualities, and nutritional properties. Ozone can be applied in both the liquid and gas phases: in the liquid phase, it can disinfect processed water and vegetables, while in the gas phase, it can help disinfect and preserve vegetables during storage [40]. The versatility of ozone makes it a promising food processing agent. Its rapid decomposition and low residual effect make it an attractive alternative to traditional preservatives used in food storage. Ozone technology is gradually replacing conventional hygiene and fumigation methods, such as chlorine, steam or hot water treatments, and insecticides like phosphine, aluminum phosphide, and methyl bromide (fumigation) [41]. This shift reflects ozone's growing appeal as a green, safe, and effective solution in the food preservation industry.

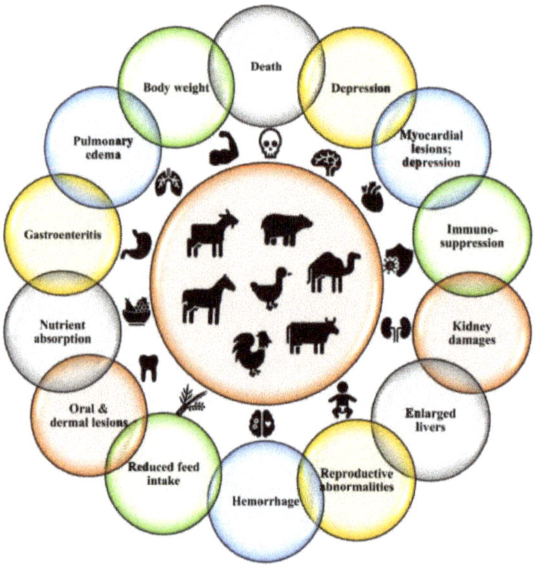

Figure 13. Effects of mycotoxins on animal health [38].

Although ozone offers promising applications in food processing and preservation, several challenges remain. First, the generation and utilization of ozone require specialized equipment and technical expertise, placing significant demands on both the technological capabilities and management skills of the enterprise. Second, the concentration and exposure time of ozone must be carefully controlled to prevent any adverse effects on food quality and safety.

In conclusion, ozone holds substantial potential in the field of food processing and preservation. With ongoing research and technological advancements, ozone technology is expected to provide safer and more effective preservation solutions, aligning with consumer demand for healthy, high-quality food products.

3.3. Ozone in Medical Treatment

Ozone, a gas with unique chemical properties, has gained widespread application in the medical field in recent years. Its remarkable bactericidal, anti-inflammatory, antioxidant, analgesic, and immunomodulatory effects have made it a valuable therapeutic agent in various medical areas, including orthopedics, pain management, and cancer treatment.

In orthopedics and pain medicine, ozone is particularly effective due to its anti-inflammatory and analgesic properties. For chronic pain conditions such as neck, shoulder, back, and leg pain, ozone therapy has been shown to significantly reduce patient discomfort. Additionally, ozone has demonstrated effectiveness in the acute and recovery stages of cerebral hemorrhage, improving cerebral oxygenation and promoting patient recovery through multiple mechanisms [42]. Minimally invasive oxygen–ozone (O_2-O_3) therapy, which leverages the biochemical effects of O_2-O_3 mixtures, is commonly employed to treat musculoskeletal pain. Current data suggest that minimally invasive O_2-O_3 therapy for musculoskeletal neuropathic pain may be both beneficial and relatively safe [43]. Ozone therapy has long been used for its ability to inactivate a wide range of viruses and tumors, and it is increasingly being utilized in the treatment of musculoskeletal disorders, including rheumatoid arthritis, lumbar facet joint syndrome, subacromial bursitis, and carpal tunnel syndrome [42].

Cancer, one of the leading causes of death globally, is typically treated with radiotherapy and chemotherapy. However, these treatments can induce oxidative stress and chemotherapy-induced peripheral neuropathy (CIPN), damaging healthy tissue. While options for preventing or managing these side effects remain limited, ozone therapy has shown promise by inducing controlled oxidative stress, which triggers adaptive antioxidant responses in healthy tissues, potentially mitigating some of the damaging effects of cancer treatments [44,45].

Recent advancements have also highlighted ozone's potential in cancer therapy. Studies have demonstrated that medical ozone can inhibit the growth of more than 90% of lung, breast, and uterine tumor cells. Furthermore, ozone can induce tumor cell death through the rapid generation of reactive oxygen species, laying the groundwork for its potential use in immune checkpoint blockade therapy. Bernardino Clavo and colleagues have reviewed the most significant studies on ozone as an adjuvant in cancer therapy, finding that ozone improves hemoglobin dissociation curves, increases 2,3-diphosphoglycerate levels, enhances local blood flow, and alleviates tumor hypoxia, all of which support its potential benefits in cancer treatment [46]. Ozone therapy has demonstrated a wide range of therapeutic effects, from pathogen disinfection to cancer treatment and pain management. In clinical practice, ozone is typically used adjunctively, often in combination with other treatments to enhance or complement their therapeutic mechanisms. Although its use as a standalone treatment remains controversial, ozone's effectiveness when combined with other therapies is widely recognized [47].

In conclusion, the application of ozone in medicine holds vast potential. With continued research into its properties and therapeutic efficacy, it is expected that ozone will play an increasingly important role in various medical fields, contributing significantly to advancements in human health (Table 2).

Table 2. Key findings on ozone applications.

Application Area	Key Findings	References
Water Treatment	- Ozone removes turbidity, organic contaminants, and chlorine-resistant bacteria. - Efficient for wastewater disinfection and removing pharmaceuticals.	[23–25]
Air Pollution Control	- Ozone reduces oxidizable substances in industrial emissions. - Effectively treats NO_x, organic pollutants, and mercury. - Combined with plasma/adsorbent for NO_x treatment.	[20,30,31]
Soil Remediation	- Ozone helps degrade organic pollutants in soil. - Effective for remediating polluted soils in an eco-friendly manner.	[33–35]
Food Processing and Preservation	- Ozone can sterilize food and extend shelf life. - Non-toxic and leaves no harmful residues on food surfaces.	[38–40]
Medical Treatment	- Ozone used for sterilization of medical equipment and wound treatment. - Improves immune response and speeds up recovery in certain cases.	[42–45]

4. Ozone in the Power Industry

Ozone (O_3), a potent oxidizing agent, has demonstrated significant potential in the power industry, particularly in areas such as water treatment, air purification, and equipment maintenance. Its unique chemical properties enable ozone to play a crucial role in enhancing the power production efficiency, ensuring the smooth operation of equipment, and contributing to environmental protection.

4.1. Ozone in Water Treatment

In the power industry, particularly in thermal and nuclear power plants, water treatment plays a crucial role in ensuring the stable operation of power generation. Given the significant volume of water required in the power production process, wastewater treatment and cooling water management are of paramount importance. While wastewater treatment is addressed in Section 3.2.1, the focus here shifts to the ozone treatment of cooling water.

Cooling water treatment is a key application of ozone technology in the power sector, as cooling systems often encounter issues with algae and bacterial growth. Chlorination has traditionally been used to prevent biological fouling in cooling water systems. However, chlorination has notable drawbacks, including health risks, acute toxicity, and the potential to form harmful chlorinated organic compounds [48]. As a result, there is increasing interest in alternative methods for cooling water treatment. Ozone has shown significant promise as an effective solution for controlling water quality in cooling systems. It offers several advantages, including (1) providing effective corrosion control for most alloys, (2) removing existing scale and preventing its recurrence, and (3) damaging or inactivating microorganisms that may cause biocorrosion or biopollution [49]. Furthermore, with ongoing advancements in this technology, a novel cooling water treatment approach, the Integrated Ozone Treatment Cooling System (IOTCS), has been proposed. This system combines pinch analysis with mathematical programming to optimize heat exchanger configurations, maximizing water and energy savings while minimizing the overall costs [50].

4.2. Effect of Ozone Air Purification

Maintaining good air quality during power generation is essential, particularly in the context of plant maintenance and servicing. The combustion of coal and other fossil fuels in conventional thermal power plants results in a range of emissions, including carbon dioxide, sulfur oxides, nitrogen oxides, particulate matter, and heavy metals. These emissions not only contribute to environmental pollution but also pose significant risks to human health.

Today, the efficiency of exhaust gas purification has been enhanced through the use of specialized ozone-saturated solutions [51]. Ozone can effectively improve the working environment by eliminating odors, volatile organic compounds (VOCs), and microorganisms from the air. This is especially beneficial in enclosed or semi-enclosed workspaces, where ozone's bactericidal properties can help reduce the transmission risk of pathogenic microorganisms, thereby protecting worker health.

4.3. Application of Ozone in Equipment Maintenance and Protection

The use of ozone in plant maintenance should not be overlooked. Over extended periods of operation, equipment in the power industry can be significantly affected by various pollutants, leading to a decline in performance. Currently, oxidants such as potassium permanganate, nitric acid, and hydrogen peroxide, along with complexing agents like oxalic acid, are used to decontaminate primary circuit equipment in nuclear power plants. However, the high concentrations of reagents, the multi-stage nature of the process, and the need for multiple treatment cycles to achieve the desired effectiveness with conventional techniques result in large volumes of waste. Ershov et al. have demonstrated that concentrated ozone is an effective and environmentally friendly technology for decontaminating nuclear power plant equipment [52].

Ultraviolet (UV) ozone surface cleaning methods are also well established for treating surfaces to remove contaminants. This process involves photo-oxidative decomposition, where contaminants are excited or dissociated by short-wavelength UV light. UV light at 245.4 nm decomposes oxygen, producing oxygen atoms and ozone. Ozone then absorbs longer-wavelength radiation, breaking down into oxygen atoms as well. The excited pollutant molecules and free radicals generated from pollutant dissociation react with atomic oxygen to form simpler, volatile molecules, which are subsequently removed. UV ozone is also used for cleaning alumina substrates during the processing of thin-film hybrid circuits [53]. The schematic diagram is shown in Figure 14, as quoted from [53].

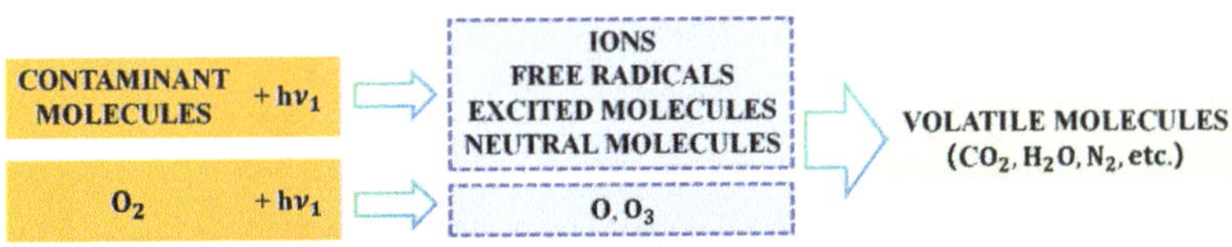

Figure 14. Simplified schematic representation of UV/ozone cleaning process cited by [53].

This highlights that ozone can serve as an effective cleaning agent to remove oil, dust, and other pollutants from equipment surfaces, playing a crucial role in maintaining equipment cleanliness and hygiene. Additionally, ozone treatment of insulating materials is particularly valuable. It has been shown that the resistance and service life of insulating materials treated with ozone can be significantly improved, thereby reducing equipment failures and downtime, while enhancing the overall reliability of power production.

5. Conclusions and Outlooks

The origin of ozone (O_3) can be traced back to 1839, when Schube first confirmed that it is formed through the combination of oxygen molecules (O_2) and oxygen atoms (O). Ozone is widely utilized across various industries and applications, including water treatment, bleaching, food preservation, and medicine, primarily due to its strong oxidizing and sterilizing properties. Ozone can be produced through three main methods: ultraviolet radiation, electrochemistry, and dielectric barrier discharge. The ultraviolet method is less efficient and is typically used for small-scale production. The electrochemical method, on the other hand, generates high and stable ozone concentrations in a closed system, though the output is generally low.

In the realm of environmental management, ozone has found broad application in several key areas, including water treatment, air pollution control, and soil remediation. In water treatment, ozone's powerful oxidizing properties and its ability to avoid secondary pollution make it highly effective at removing harmful microorganisms and pollutants, thereby improving water quality. In air pollution control, ozone plays an important role in decomposing organic matter and pollutants found in industrial waste gases. It can also convert harmful gases in automobile exhaust into harmless substances. Finally, ozone has proven effective in soil remediation, where its strong oxidizing properties degrade refractory pollutants, such as polycyclic aromatic hydrocarbons (PAHs), improving the soil environment. Despite its wide-ranging potential, ozone technology faces challenges related to stability and cost.

Beyond environmental applications, ozone has significant uses in industry and medicine. In wastewater treatment, ozone serves as a potent oxidant, efficiently removing pathogens, persistent pollutants, and heavy metals. It is commonly employed in processes such as the sequential batch activated sludge process and ozonated advanced oxidation processes, particularly in the treatment of wastewater containing cyanide or coking residues. In food processing, ozone is used to preserve food by eliminating contaminants and extending the shelf life. In the medical field, ozone has shown considerable promise, particularly in orthopedics, pain management, and cancer treatment. Its anti-inflammatory and antioxidant effects have contributed to improved treatment outcomes, with particularly encouraging results in adjuvant therapy.

Despite its advantages as a powerful oxidizing agent, several limitations must be considered for its widespread adoption and further development. One major challenge is the technical limitations associated with ozone production methods. The efficiency of ozone generation, particularly using ultraviolet radiation, remains low, and the high energy consumption involved in some production techniques makes them less cost-effective. Additionally, the storage and transportation of ozone present significant difficulties due to its unstable nature. From an economic standpoint, the high cost of ozone generation equipment and the need for regular maintenance contribute to the overall expense of ozone-based applications. While ozone has proven effective in small-scale operations, the scalability of its use in large industrial systems remains a barrier. Furthermore, regulatory challenges surrounding the safe use of ozone, particularly in air and water treatment, are often complicated by safety concerns and varying regulations across different regions. These factors may hinder the broader implementation of ozone technology in certain sectors.

Given these challenges, there are promising future directions for ozone technology. Future research could focus on advancing production methods to improve efficiency and reduce energy consumption. Developing more sustainable and cost-effective ozone generators could make large-scale applications more feasible. Additionally, exploring the potential of hybrid technologies, which combine ozone with other treatment methods, may increase its effectiveness while reducing costs. The role of ozone in emerging fields, such as cancer therapy and advanced medical treatments, shows great promise and warrants further exploration. Additionally, there is a need for comprehensive studies on the environmental impact and potential by-products of ozone-based processes to ensure their sustainability in the long term. Overall, further research is crucial to overcome the existing limitations and unlock the full potential of ozone technology, especially in large-scale and economically viable applications.

Author Contributions: Conceptualization, K.Z. and J.L.; methodology, H.L. and L.D.; software, K.Z.; validation, J.L. and H.L.; formal analysis, X.Z.; investigation, Z.L. and L.D.; resources, X.Z.; data curation, X.Z.; writing—original draft preparation, C.J.; writing—review and editing, X.Z.; visualization, Z.L.; supervision, K.Z.; project administration, J.L.; funding acquisition, L.D. All authors have read and agreed to the published version of the manuscript.

Funding: This work is supported by the Science and Technology Project of State Grid Corporation of China (5400-202419199A-1-1-ZN).

Data Availability Statement: No new data were created or analyzed in this study.

Conflicts of Interest: Authors Kang Zhang, Hongkun Lv and Liwei Ding were employed by State Grid Zhejiang Electric Power Research Institute. Author Jianzheng Liu was employed by Daya Bay Nuclear Power Operations and Management Co., Ltd. The remaining authors declare that the research was conducted in the absence of any commercial or financial relationships that could be construed as a potential conflict of interest.

References

1. Shi, C.; Zhang, S.; Wang, W.; Linhardt, R.J.; Ragauskas, A.J. Preparation of highly reactive lignin by ozone oxidation: Application as surfactants with antioxidant and anti-UV properties. *ACS Sustain. Chem. Eng.* **2019**, *8*, 22–28.
2. Eliasson, B.; Kogelschatz, U. Ozone Generation with Narrow–Band UV Radiation. *Ozone Sci. Eng.* **1991**, *13*, 365–373. [CrossRef]
3. Claus, H. Ozone generation by ultraviolet lamps. *Photochem. Photobiol.* **2021**, *97*, 471–476.
4. Peng, Z.; Day, D.A.; Symonds, G.A.; Jenks, O.J.; Stark, H.; Handschy, A.V.; de Gouw, J.A.; Jimenez, J.L. Significant Production of Ozone from Germicidal UV Lights at 222 nm. *Environ. Sci. Technol. Lett.* **2023**, *10*, 668–674. [CrossRef]
5. Meher, P.; Deshmukh, N.; Mashalkar, A.; Kumar, D. Ozone (O_3) generation and its applications: A review. *AIP Conf. Proc.* **2023**, *2764*, 070011.
6. Thanos, J.C.; Wabner, D.W. Elektrochemische abscheidung von sauerstoff und ozon an bleidioxid und platin-anoden in wässrigen elektrolyten mit ^{18}O-markiertem wasser. *Electrochim. Acta* **1985**, *30*, 753–756.
7. Kogelschatz, U.; Eliasson, B.; Hirth, M. Ozone Generation from Oxygen and Air: Discharge Physics and Reaction Mechanisms. *Ozone Sci. Eng.* **1988**, *10*, 367–377. [CrossRef]
8. Gadkari, S.; Gu, S. Numerical investigation of co-axial DBD: Influence of relative permittivity of the dielectric barrier, applied voltage amplitude, and frequency. *Phys. Plasmas* **2017**, *24*, 053517.
9. Valdivia-Barrientos, R.; Pacheco-Sotelo, J.; Pacheco-Pacheco, M.; Benítez-Read, J.S.; López-Callejas, R. Analysis and electrical modelling of a cylindrical DBD configuration at different operating frequencies. *Plasma Sources Sci. Technol.* **2006**, *15*, 237.
10. Jahanmiri, A.; Rahimpour, M.; Shirazi, M.M.; Hooshmand, N.; Taghvaei, H. Naphtha cracking through a pulsed DBD plasma reactor: Effect of applied voltage, pulse repetition frequency and electrode material. *Chem. Eng. J.* **2012**, *191*, 416–425.
11. Gou, X.; Yuan, D.; Wang, L.; Xie, L.; Wei, L.; Zhang, G. Enhancing ozone production in dielectric barrier discharge utilizing water as electrode. *Vacuum* **2023**, *212*, 112047.
12. Jung, J.-S.; Moon, J.-D. Corona discharge and ozone generation characteristics of a wire-plate discharge system with a glass-fiber layer. *J. Electrost.* **2008**, *66*, 335–341.
13. Jin, C.; Lin, F.; Peng, B.; Wei, L.; Ling, Z.; Zeng, X.; Yuan, D.J.V. Nanosecond Pulsed Multi-hollow Surface Dielectric Barrier Discharge for Ozone Production. *Vacuum* **2025**, *238*, 114252.
14. Yehia, A. Assessment of ozone generation in dry air fed silent discharge reactors. *Phys. Plasmas* **2012**, *19*, 023503.
15. Yuan, D.; Wang, Z.; Ding, C.; He, Y.; Whiddon, R.; Cen, K. Ozone production in parallel multichannel dielectric barrier discharge from oxygen and air: The influence of gas pressure. *J. Phys. D Appl. Phys.* **2016**, *49*, 455203.
16. Wei, L.; Yuan, D.; Zhang, Y.; Hu, Z.; Tan, Z.; Dong, G.; Tao, S. An analysis of the effect of inert gases on ozone generation using dielectric barrier discharge in oxygen. *Eur. Phys. J. D* **2014**, *68*, 17.
17. Liang Chen, H.; Ming Lee, H.; Been Chang, M. Enhancement of energy yield for ozone production via packed-bed reactors. *Ozone Sci. Eng.* **2006**, *28*, 111–118.
18. Shang, K.; Wang, M.; Peng, B.; Li, J.; Lu, N.; Jiang, N.; Wu, Y. Characterization of a novel volume-surface DBD reactor: Discharge characteristics, ozone production and benzene degradation. *J. Phys. D Appl. Phys.* **2019**, *53*, 065201.
19. Banaschik, R.; Lukes, P.; Jablonowski, H.; Hammer, M.U.; Weltmann, K.-D.; Kolb, J.F. Potential of pulsed corona discharges generated in water for the degradation of persistent pharmaceutical residues. *Water Res.* **2015**, *84*, 127–135.
20. Lin, F.; Wang, Z.; Zhang, Z.; He, Y.; Zhu, Y.; Shao, J.; Yuan, D.; Chen, G.; Cen, K. Flue gas treatment with ozone oxidation: An overview on NOx, organic pollutants, and mercury. *Chem. Eng. J.* **2020**, *382*, 123030.
21. Glaze, W.H. Drinking-water treatment with ozone. *Environ. Sci. Technol.* **1987**, *21*, 224–230.

22. Rahman, M.; Jasim, S.; Yanful, E.; Ndiongue, S.; Borikar, D. Advanced oxidation treatment of drinking water: Part II. Turbidity, particles and organics removal from Lake Huron water. *Ozone Sci. Eng.* **2010**, *32*, 295–304.
23. Rojas-Valencia, M. Research on ozone application as disinfectant and action mechanisms on wastewater microorganisms. *Virus* **2011**, *3*, 263–271.
24. Ding, W.; Jin, W.; Cao, S.; Zhou, X.; Wang, C.; Jiang, Q.; Huang, H.; Tu, R.; Han, S.-F.; Wang, Q. Ozone disinfection of chlorine-resistant bacteria in drinking water. *Water Res.* **2019**, *160*, 339–349.
25. Paucar, N.E.; Kim, I.; Tanaka, H.; Sato, C. Ozone treatment process for the removal of pharmaceuticals and personal care products in wastewater. *Ozone Sci. Eng.* **2019**, *41*, 3–16.
26. Hollender, J.; Zimmermann, S.G.; Koepke, S.; Krauss, M.; McArdell, C.S.; Ort, C.; Singer, H.; Von Gunten, U.; Siegrist, H. Elimination of organic micropollutants in a municipal wastewater treatment plant upgraded with a full-scale post-ozonation followed by sand filtration. *Environ. Sci. Technol.* **2009**, *43*, 7862–7869.
27. Tripathi, S.; Hussain, T. Water and wastewater treatment through ozone-based technologies. In *Development in Wastewater Treatment Research and Processes*; Elsevier: Amsterdam, The Netherlands, 2022; pp. 139–172.
28. Ciardelli, G.; Ranieri, N. The treatment and reuse of wastewater in the textile industry by means of ozonation and electroflocculation. *Water Res.* **2001**, *35*, 567–572.
29. Ferrero, F.; Nano, A. L'ozono in tintoria ci può dare una mano Ozone can help in dyeing. *Riv. Tecnol. Tessili* **1995**, *8*, 67–72.
30. Parisheva, Z.; Demirev, A. The effect of ozone on harmful, oxidizable substances in industrial waste gases. *Environ. Prot. Eng.* **1995**, *20*, 137–144.
31. Apeksha, M.; Rajanikanth, B. Plasma/adsorbent system for NO_x treatment in diesel exhaust: A case study on solid industrial wastes. *Int. J. Environ. Sci. Technol.* **2019**, *16*, 2973–2988.
32. Russo, L.; Rizzo, L.; Belgiorno, V. PAHs contaminated soils remediation by ozone oxidation. *Desalination Water Treat.* **2010**, *23*, 161–172.
33. Wang, T.C.; Qu, G.; Li, J.; Lu, N. Transport characteristics of gas phase ozone in soil during soil remediation by pulsed discharge plasma. *Vacuum* **2014**, *101*, 86–91.
34. Pawłat, J.; Stryczewska, H.D.; Ebihara, K. Sterilization techniques for soil remediation and agriculture based on ozone and AOP. *J. Adv. Oxid. Technol.* **2010**, *13*, 138–145.
35. Liu, J. Soil remediation using soil washing followed by ozone oxidation. *J. Ind. Eng. Chem.* **2018**, *65*, 31–34.
36. Chávez, A.; Gimeno, O.; Rey, A.; Pliego, G.; Oropesa, A.; Álvarez, P.; Beltrán, F. Treatment of highly polluted industrial wastewater by means of sequential aerobic biological oxidation-ozone based AOPs. *Chem. Eng. J.* **2019**, *361*, 89–98.
37. Asaithambi, P.; Aziz, A.R.A.; Daud, W.M.A.B.W. Integrated ozone—Electrocoagulation process for the removal of pollutant from industrial effluent: Optimization through response surface methodology. *Chem. Eng. Process. Process Intensif.* **2016**, *105*, 92–102.
38. Sujayasree, O.; Chaitanya, A.; Bhoite, R.; Pandiselvam, R.; Kothakota, A.; Gavahian, M.; Mousavi Khaneghah, A. Ozone: An advanced oxidation technology to enhance sustainable food consumption through mycotoxin degradation. *Ozone Sci. Eng.* **2022**, *44*, 17–37.
39. Afsah-Hejri, L.; Hajeb, P.; Ehsani, R.J. Application of ozone for degradation of mycotoxins in food: A review. *Compr. Rev. Food Sci. Food Saf.* **2020**, *19*, 1777–1808.
40. Sarron, E.; Gadonna-Widehem, P.; Aussenac, T. Ozone treatments for preserving fresh vegetables quality: A critical review. *Foods* **2021**, *10*, 605. [CrossRef]
41. Pandiselvam, R.; Subhashini, S.; Banuu Priya, E.; Kothakota, A.; Ramesh, S.; Shahir, S. Ozone based food preservation: A promising green technology for enhanced food safety. *Ozone Sci. Eng.* **2019**, *41*, 17–34.
42. Seyam, O.; Smith, N.L.; Reid, I.; Gandhi, J.; Jiang, W.; Khan, S.A. Clinical utility of ozone therapy for musculoskeletal disorders. *Med. Gas Res.* **2018**, *8*, 103–110. [PubMed]
43. Jandura, J.; Vajda, M.; Cech, M.; Ryska, P. Oxygen–Ozone Therapy of Musculoskeletal Neck Pain: A Review. *J. Pers. Med.* **2024**, *14*, 326. [CrossRef]
44. Clavo, B.; Martínez-Sánchez, G.; Rodríguez-Esparragón, F.; Rodríguez-Abreu, D.; Galván, S.; Aguiar-Bujanda, D.; Díaz-Garrido, J.A.; Cañas, S.; Torres-Mata, L.B.; Fabelo, H. Modulation by ozone therapy of oxidative stress in chemotherapy-induced peripheral neuropathy: The background for a randomized clinical trial. *Int. J. Mol. Sci.* **2021**, *22*, 2802. [CrossRef] [PubMed]
45. Clavo, B.; Rodríguez-Esparragón, F.; Rodríguez-Abreu, D.; Martínez-Sánchez, G.; Llontop, P.; Aguiar-Bujanda, D.; Fernández-Pérez, L.; Santana-Rodríguez, N. Modulation of oxidative stress by ozone therapy in the prevention and treatment of chemotherapy-induced toxicity: Review and prospects. *Antioxidants* **2019**, *8*, 588. [CrossRef] [PubMed]
46. Clavo, B.; Santana-Rodriguez, N.; Llontop, P.; Gutierrez, D.; Suárez, G.; Lopez, L.; Rovira, G.; Martinez-Sanchez, G.; Gonzalez, E.; Jorge, I.J. Ozone therapy as adjuvant for cancer treatment: Is further research warranted? *Evid. Based Complement. Altern. Med.* **2018**, *2018*, 7931849.

47. Smith, A.J.; Oertle, J.; Warren, D.; Prato, D. Ozone therapy: A critical physiological and diverse clinical evaluation with regard to immune modulation, anti-infectious properties, anti-cancer potential, and impact on anti-oxidant enzymes. *Open J. Mol. Integr. Physiol.* **2015**, *5*, 37–48.
48. Wellauer, R.; Oldani, M. Cooling water treatment with ozone. *Ozone Sci. Eng.* **1990**, *12*, 243–253.
49. You, S.H.; Tseng, D.H.; Guo, G.L.; Lee, S.Y. Mechanism and effects of ozone treatment for cooling water system. *J. Environ. Sci. Health Part A* **2000**, *35*, 87–107.
50. Ataei, A.; Gharaie, M.; Parand, R.; Panjeshahi, E. Application of ozone treatment and pinch technology in cooling water systems design for water and energy conservation. *Int. J. Energy Res.* **2010**, *34*, 494–506.
51. Sydykova, G.; Umbetova, S.; Baimakhanova, Z.; Abieva, G.; Kurmanbayev, G. Modern Applications of Ozone Technology. *Evergreen* **2023**, *10*, 2308–2316.
52. Ershov, B.; Seliverstov, A.; Basiev, A.; Basiev, A.; Korchagin, Y.P. Application of concentrated ozone for decontamination of equipment in a nuclear power plant. *At. Energy* **2009**, *107*, 89–94.
53. Vig, J.R. UV/ozone cleaning of surfaces. *J. Vac. Sci. Technol. A Vac. Surf. Film.* **1985**, *3*, 1027–1034.

water

MDPI

Article

Synergistic Coupling of In Situ Oxygenation and Advanced Oxidation Processes Using a Novel Lime-Based Composite for Water Quality Management in *Litopenaeus vannamei* Ponds

Muhammad Irfan Afif [1,2], Hanifah Widi Astuti [1], Niken Tunjung Murti Pratiwi [1,*], Bambang Widigdo [1], Mohammad Khotib [2], Nia Rosiana [4] and Muhammad Faisal [5]

1 Department of Aquatic Resources Management, Faculty of Fisheries and Marine Sciences, IPB University, Bogor 16680, Indonesia; irfanafif@apps.ipb.ac.id (M.I.A.)
2 Integrated Laboratory and Advanced Research, IPB University, Bogor 16680, Indonesia
3 Department of Chemistry, Faculty of Mathematics and Natural Sciences, IPB University, Bogor 16680, Indonesia
4 Department of Agribusiness, Faculty of Economics and Management, IPB University, Bogor 16680, Indonesia
5 Department of Physics, Faculty of Mathematics and Natural Sciences, Brawijaya University, Malang 65145, Indonesia
* Correspondence: niken_tmpratiwi@apps.ipb.ac.id

Abstract

Effective management of water quality is critical for *Litopenaeus vannamei* aquaculture, yet it remains a significant technological hurdle for traditional farmers facing benthic anaerobiosis and toxic metabolite accumulation. This study introduces a novel approach by synergistically integrating calcium peroxide (CaO_2), titanium dioxide (TiO_2), and peracetic acid (PAA) encapsulated within Fe–alginate granules. Unlike conventional methods that treat oxygen depletion and toxicity separately, this composite is designed to simultaneously facilitate in situ oxygenation and advanced oxidation processes (AOPs) directly at the sediment–water interface. The physicochemical properties and radical generation mechanisms of the synthesized composites were characterized using FTIR, XRD, SEM, and ESR. In laboratory simulations of pond conditions, the synergistic efficacy of these composites was evaluated against critical parameters, including dissolved oxygen (DO), ammonia, and sulfide. Experimental results revealed that the application of 5 mg/L CP-T-PAA product to the sediment with an AOP system exhibited superior performance, generating the highest intensity of hydroxyl (•OH) and superoxide ($•O_2^-$) radicals. This optimized treatment effectively maintained DO levels above ~2 mg/L at the sediment–water interface for 21 days (3 weeks) and achieved removal efficiencies of 94% for ammonia, 89% for sulfide, and 93% for turbidity. Multi-criteria decision analysis (TOPSIS) validated this formulation as the ideal solution. Consequently, this novel composite presents a sustainable, user-friendly strategy for enhancing environmental stability in traditional shrimp farming.

Keywords: *Litopenaeus vannamei*; advanced oxidation processes; in situ oxygenation; Fe–alginate encapsulation; water quality management

1. Introduction

Water quality management in aquaculture, particularly in Pacific white shrimp (*Litopenaeus vannamei*) ponds, is a fundamental and evolving challenge addressed through various treatments. Water quality in these ponds can fluctuate rapidly due to factors such as overfeeding, meteorological conditions, unregulated influent water from rivers, and organismal respiration. Critical water quality parameters include dissolved oxygen (DO) and ammonia,

https://doi.org/10.3390/w18030296

which necessitate rigorous monitoring [1]. The deterioration of water quality, driven by fluctuations in these parameters, is a significant determinant of cultured shrimp health [2]. Indeed, recent cases of diminished aquacultural productivity have been attributed to the difficulty of controlling pond water quality to maintain shrimp health [3].

Although numerous disease control strategies centered on water quality management have been explored, such as biofloc technology [4] and recirculating aquaculture system [5], significant limitations persist in technological adoption among farmers. Several studies highlight gaps in current practices, such as inconsistent monitoring, difficulty understanding advanced methods, and various socioeconomic barriers [6]. The consequences of these gaps are particularly evident for traditional shrimp farmers, such as those in Indonesia, who still account for a substantial proportion—approximately 90%—of national shrimp production [7]. Consequently, there is a significant and unmet demand for user-friendly technologies that farmers can readily implement in their shrimp ponds.

Self-supplying oxygen-releasing materials are recognized for their ability to release oxygen over a sustained period. Calcium peroxide (CaO_2), for instance, have been explored due to their controlled oxygen release kinetics [8], which have potential to maintain DO levels in shrimp ponds, ensuring that both aquatic organisms and aerobic bacteria have sufficient oxygen for respiration and the decomposition of toxic contaminants [9]. The efficiency of these oxygen-releasing materials can be enhanced by coupling them for synergistic effect with reactive oxygen generators involved in advanced oxidation processes (AOPs) [10]. AOPs are water treatment technologies that utilize physicochemical procedures to generate highly reactive species, most notably hydroxyl radicals (OH•), which can degrade pollutants and disinfect pathogenic bacteria [11]. This reaction can be initiated with strong oxidants and ultraviolet photocatalysis. Pathogen disinfection is achieved through a cascade of free radical formation initiated by the AOP, which involves the production of reactive oxygen species (ROS) to cycle oxygen utilization from the self-supplying material through to the generation of the superoxide radical anion, O_2^{-}•. Superoxide is then rapidly converted to hydrogen peroxide (H_2O_2) by superoxide dismutase. These free radicals can destroy microorganisms or other foreign bodies within the biota through the activation of NADPH oxidase (NOX) in the cells [12,13]. Furthermore, O_2^{-}• and H_2O_2 react to produce OH•, which can simultaneously and directly cleave the bonds of organic matter in the water via primary, propagation, and termination reactions [14]. The reduction in toxicants from anaerobic organic matter decomposition through AOP treatment can occur as an abstraction reaction in which the hydroxyl radical attacks a covalent bond, resulting in the formation of water [15].

This study investigated the synergistic effects of a self-supplying oxygen-releasing material combined with an advanced oxidation process generator on seawater samples designed to simulate shrimp aquaculture conditions. The specific objectives were to elucidate the physicochemical properties and radical generation mechanisms (•OH and O_2•$^{-}$) of the composite using characterization techniques, assess its synergistic efficacy in sustaining dissolved oxygen levels and degrading critical pollutants (ammonia and sulfide) under simulated aquaculture conditions via coupled in situ oxygenation and an advanced oxidation process (AOP), and determine the optimal formulation for practical application to address technological gaps in traditional *Litopenaeus vannamei* shrimp farming.

2. Methodology

2.1. Experiments

This research was completed over a period of 6 months from May to November 2024 at the Advanced Research and Integrated Laboratory of IPB University. While these laboratory-scale simulations utilize static aquariums—which differ from the dynamic hy-

https://doi.org/10.3390/w18030296

draulic and biological complexity of commercial shrimp ponds—the experimental setup was designed to rigorously evaluate the physicochemical efficacy of the composite. The use of authentic alluvial soil from traditional ponds and standardized artificial seawater ensures that the sediment–water interface conditions closely mimic the chemical environment faced by benthic organisms in actual farming scenarios. This study was conducted experimentally and comprised three stages: product preparation, characterization, and laboratory-scale testing.

The product preparation stage involved the preparation of various products for subsequent study. A self-supplying oxygen material was synthesized using pro-analytical grade $Ca(OH)_2$ (ACS reagent, ≥95.0%, Sigma-Aldrich, St. Louis, MO, USA), H_2O_2 (30% w/w, MilliporeSigma, Darmstadt, Germany), TiO_2 nanopowder (21 nm primary particle size (TEM), ≥99.5%, Merck KGaA, Darmstadt, Germany), and CH_3CO_3H (38–40 wt.% in acetic acid, Merck KGaA, Darmstadt, Germany). The manufacture of CaO_2 followed the method of Dong et al. [16]. There were three additional target products. First, CaO_2 (hereafter referred to as CP) was composited with CH_3CO_3H (hereafter referred to as PAA) at a 3:1 ratio to create CP-PAA. CP was then composited with TiO_2 (hereafter referred to as T) at a 3:3 ratio to form CP-T. Finally, CP was composited with T and PAA at a 3:3:1 ratio to form CP-T-PAA. A total of 1 kg of each product was prepared. Subsequently, a portion of each product underwent dry granulation, as detailed by Zhang et al. [17], and was formulated with Fe–alginate 5% in the proportion process to form 2 mm tablets. The synthesized products proceeded to the characterization stage.

The characterization stage aimed to examine the crystal structure, chemical composition, and physical properties of the products, which were subsequently monitored for quality and evaluated for performance. At this stage, characterization included a surface morphology study using a Thermo Scientific Prisma E Scanning Electron Microscope (SEM, Eindhoven, The Netherlands), crystal phase analysis using a Malvern Panalytical Aeris X-ray Diffractometer (XRD, Malvern Panalytical B.V., Almelo, The Netherlands), functional group analysis using a Shimadzu IRPrestige-21 Fourier Transform Infrared (FTIR) Spectroscope (Kyoto, Japan), and an estimation of radical production using a Tektronix TDS1001B (Tektronix, Inc., Shanghai, China) for electron spin resonance (ESR) analysis. The reference methods for the surface morphology study, FTIR analysis, and XRD analysis were adapted from Piyarat et al. [18], while the electron spin resonance analysis followed the procedure described by Faisal et al. [19], with calculations to estimate the free radicals based on Equations (1) and (2). The characterized target product was subsequently tested artificially on a laboratory scale.

$$g = \frac{hf}{\mu_B B} \quad (1)$$

where

g = g-factor;
μ_B = Bohr magneton ($\mu_B = 9.274078 \times 10^{-24}$ Am^2);
h = Planck's constant ($h = 6.625 \times 10^{-34}$ W s^2);
f = Resonant frequency (Hz);
B = External magnetic field (T).

$$B = \mu_0 \left(\frac{4}{5}\right)^{3/2} \frac{n}{r} I \quad (2)$$

where

B = External magnetic field (T);
μ_0 = 1.2566×10^{-6} V s/A m;
n = Number of Helmholtz ($n = 320$);

https://doi.org/10.3390/w18030296

r = Helmholtz coil radius ($r = 6.8$ cm);
I = Current in Helmholtz coil (A).

The purpose of the laboratory-scale testing stage was to test various target products as precursors to validate their ability to produce dissolved oxygen and minimize the toxicants produced by anaerobic organic matter decomposition. The experiments were organized into four sets as follows:

- Set 1 involved a control treatment (no product applied) and evaluations of CP, CP-PAA, CP-T, and CP-T-PAA powders without the application of an advanced oxidation process (non-AOP).
- Set 2 included the same control and powdered materials as Set 1, but all were subjected to an advanced oxidation process (AOP).
- Set 3 consisted of a control treatment and evaluations of the materials in granular form—CP, CP-PAA, CP-T, and CP-T-PAA granules—without an advanced oxidation process (non-AOP).
- Set 4 set included the same control and granulated materials as Set 3, but all were subjected to an advanced oxidation process (AOP).

The experimental setup consisted of glass aquariums (45 cm × 30 cm × 15 cm). To strictly control the sediment–water ratio, the bottom of each aquarium was lined with 3 cm of alluvial soil, and the system was filled with exactly 5 L of artificial seawater. The artificial seawater was made following Alkhadra et al.'s method [20]. The treatment dosage was set at 5 mg/L (w/v) relative to the total water volume (i.e., 25 mg of product per 5 L aquarium). This dosage was selected based on safety thresholds for aquaculture, which suggest maintaining CaO_2 concentrations below 0.1% [21]. The products pre-mixed with alluvial soil before seawater filling. A Philips UV-C Hg low pressure 4 W lamp (Signify, Pila, Poland) was used during the test and installed inside the cover as an AOP treatment (Figure 1). Several measurements were performed by carefully sampling and measuring the water at the surface of the substrate weekly (for 3 weeks in total), as shown in Table 1.

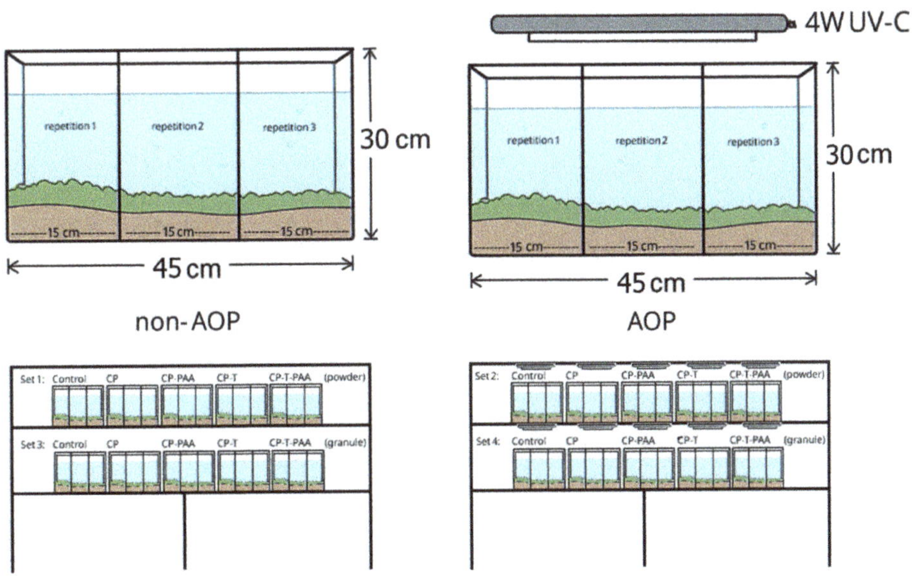

Figure 1. Illustration of non-UV treatment with UV treatment at laboratory-scale test stage.

https://doi.org/10.3390/w18030296

Table 1. Parameters measured at the laboratory test stage.

No. Parameters	Units	Methods/Instruments
Water quality in situ *parameter*		
1. pH	-	Calibrated Instruments Hanna HI2002-02 (Hanna Instruments, Inc., Smithfield, RI, USA)
2. Dissolved oxygen (DO).	mg/L	Calibrated Instruments Lutron DO-5510 (Lutron Electronic Enterprise Co., Ltd., Taipei, Taiwan)
3. Oxidation Reduction Potential (ORP)	mV	Calibrated Instruments Hanna HI2002-02 (Hanna Instruments, Inc., Nușfalău, Romania)
4. Turbidity	NTU	Calibrated Instruments HACH 2100q (Hach Company, Loveland, CO, USA)
Water quality ex situ *parameter*		
5. Ammonia	mg/L	Phenate-Spectrophotometers, Bridgewater [22]
6. Sulfide	mg/L	Methylene Blue-Titrimetry, Bridgewater [22]

Physicochemical parameters, including dissolved oxygen (DO), pH, oxidation reduction potential (ORP), and turbidity, were measured in situ using calibrated portable water, quality meters. All measurements were conducted in triplicate to minimize experimental error. Ammonia analysis was performed using the phenate method on 25 mL samples. In this method, ammonia reacts with hypochlorite and phenol in the presence of a sodium nitroprusside catalyst to form an intense indophenol blue compound. The absorbance of the resulting complex was measured spectrophotometrically using a Hach DR 1900 (Hach Company, CO, USA) at a wavelength of 640 nm. Sulfide concentrations were determined using the methylene blue method. A sample of 7.5 mL was used for sulfide analysis. This analysis relies on the reaction of sulfide with N,N-dimethyl-p-phenylenediamine in the presence of ferric chloride to produce methylene blue dye. The intensity of the blue color, which is proportional to the sulfide concentration, was quantified using a Hach DR 1900 spectrophotometer at a wavelength of 665 nm.

2.2. Data Analysis

Statistical analysis for each treatment was conducted separately using ANOVA to determine the correlation between sampling results. The fingerprinting method was employed to determine whether the experimental factors within the given treatments induced any changes. If the fingerprinting results led to the rejection of the null hypothesis, further analysis was performed. This subsequent analysis was necessary to identify the specific factors that significantly contributed to the research treatment. Tukey's Test was used post hoc. Statistical data processing was carried out using IBM SPSS 6.

To elucidate the underlying structure and relationships within the multivariate water quality dataset, Principal Component Analysis (PCA) was performed using R software 4.5.0. This analysis was performed to reduce the dimensionality of the data, which included all measured parameters (pH, DO, ORP, turbidity, ammonia, and sulfide). The primary objective was to transform the correlated variables into a set of uncorrelated principal components (PCs) that captured the maximum variance [23]. The results were visualized using score plots to identify clustering patterns among the different treatments and loading plots to determine the influence and contribution of each original water quality parameter to the observed separation along the principal components. This allowed for a comprehensive assessment of how the treatments grouped based on their overall impact on water quality.

Multi-criteria decision analysis (MCDA) was performed using the Technique for Order Preference by Similarity to Ideal Solution (TOPSIS), following Uzun et al.'s modified

https://doi.org/10.3390/w18030296

approach [24] to integrate all measured water quality parameters into a single performance index for each treatment. The parameters included dissolved oxygen (DO), oxidation reduction potential (ORP), pH, ammonia (NH_3), hydrogen sulfide (H_2S), and turbidity. Prior to analysis, the mean values of each parameter per treatment were computed from the experimental replicates. The results were visualized as a horizontal bar chart, where each bar represented the TOPSIS score (C_i) for a given treatment. This graphical representation facilitated a clear comparison of the overall effectiveness of each treatment in improving wastewater quality. Treatments with consistently high TOPSIS scores were interpreted as exhibiting superior multi-parameter performance and considered optimal candidates for practical wastewater management applications.

3. Results and Discussion

3.1. Product Characterization

The experimental phase successfully yielded powder and granulated versions of four distinct products: CP, CP-PAA, CP-T, and CP-T-PAA. These materials were subsequently advanced to the characterization stage. The products were characterized using Fourier Transform Infrared (FTIR) Spectroscopy, Scanning Electron Microscopy (SEM), X-ray Diffraction (XRD), and reactive oxygen species analysis via electron spin resonance (ESR). The FTIR spectroscopic analysis was conducted on eight distinct CaO_2-based composite materials, which included pure CaO_2 powder (CP), binary composites with TiO_2 (CP-T) and peracetic acid (CP-PAA), ternary composites (CP-T-PAA), and a granulated form with Fe–alginate. The spectral data revealed the characteristic functional groups and molecular interactions within the composite matrices.

The FTIR spectra of all products are shown in Figure 2. The pure CaO_2 powder exhibited several characteristic absorption bands, indicating the presence of surface hydroxyl groups, peroxide functionalities, and a degree of carbonation, which is typical for CaO_2 materials exposed to atmospheric conditions. The addition of TiO_2 to CaO_2 introduced new spectral features. In accordance with Subbotina and Barsukov [25], TiO_2 (anatase) displayed characteristic peroxo absorptions at approximately 852 and 912 cm^{-1}, along with a broad surface OH band in the 3400–3650 cm^{-1} region. The bands observed at 3694.81 and 3640.80 cm^{-1} were consistent with this assignment, confirming the incorporation of TiO_2 and its surface hydroxylation.

The incorporation of peracetic acid also significantly altered the spectral profile. The spectrum clearly demonstrated the successful integration of peracetic acid, evidenced by its characteristic carbonyl (C=O) stretching vibration around 1660–1670 cm^{-1} and C-O stretching modes in the 1000–1150 cm^{-1} region. Furthermore, the inclusion of Fe–alginate introduced biopolymer characteristics to the spectrum. As reported by Mollah et al. [26], Huamani-Palomino et al. [27], and Yu et al. [28], alginate exhibits distinctive carboxylate absorptions in the 1080–1400 cm^{-1} range, pyranose ring vibrations at 1200–1000 cm^{-1}, and fingerprint features at 820–860 cm^{-1}. The granulated system with Fe–alginate demonstrated the successful incorporation of all components while retaining the identity of the individual functional groups. This indicated successful encapsulation of the active components to provide controlled release properties, as evidenced by the characteristic carboxylate (1400–1600 cm^{-1}) and glycosidic (1000–1200 cm^{-1}) bands, consistent with the findings of Elhoudi et al. [29].

https://doi.org/10.3390/w18030296

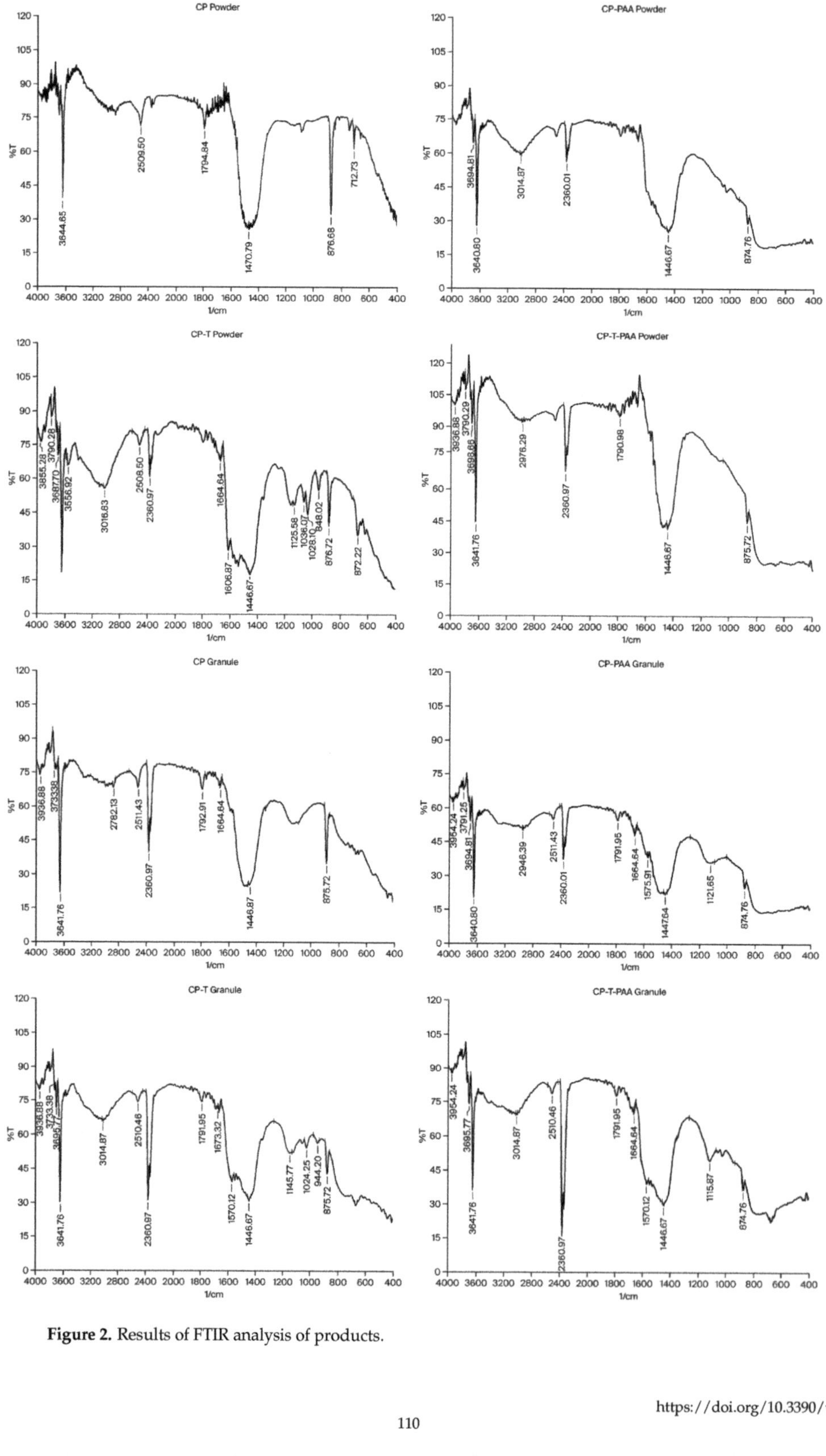

Figure 2. Results of FTIR analysis of products.

https://doi.org/10.3390/w18030296

X-ray diffraction (XRD) analysis results, depicted in Figure 3, revealed that the characteristics of calcium peroxide were consistent with its tetragonal crystal structure. The primary peaks observed at 18.1° and 34.1° corresponded to the tetragonal CaO_2 phase, in agreement with the Joint Committee on Powder Diffraction Standards (JCPDS)'s pattern. Additional peaks at 47.1–48.1° and 50.8° further confirmed the presence of calcium peroxide [30]. This crystallinity directly correlated with the coarse crystalline surface morphology observed via scanning electron microscopy (SEM), as depicted in Figure 4, which displayed irregular aggregates (0.5–3.0 μm) with discernible porosity [31]. The granulation of CP demonstrated how the Fe–alginate coating influenced its structure and morphology. The XRD pattern showed a slight decrease in peak intensity while the tetragonal structure was retained, indicating that the coating preserved the crystalline core while creating a protective layer. SEM analysis confirmed this relationship through a morphological transformation into smooth, spherical clusters (1.0–5.0 μm) with reduced porosity [32]. The crystalline core remained intact beneath the alginate matrix, as evidenced by the preserved XRD peak positions with only minor changes in intensity.

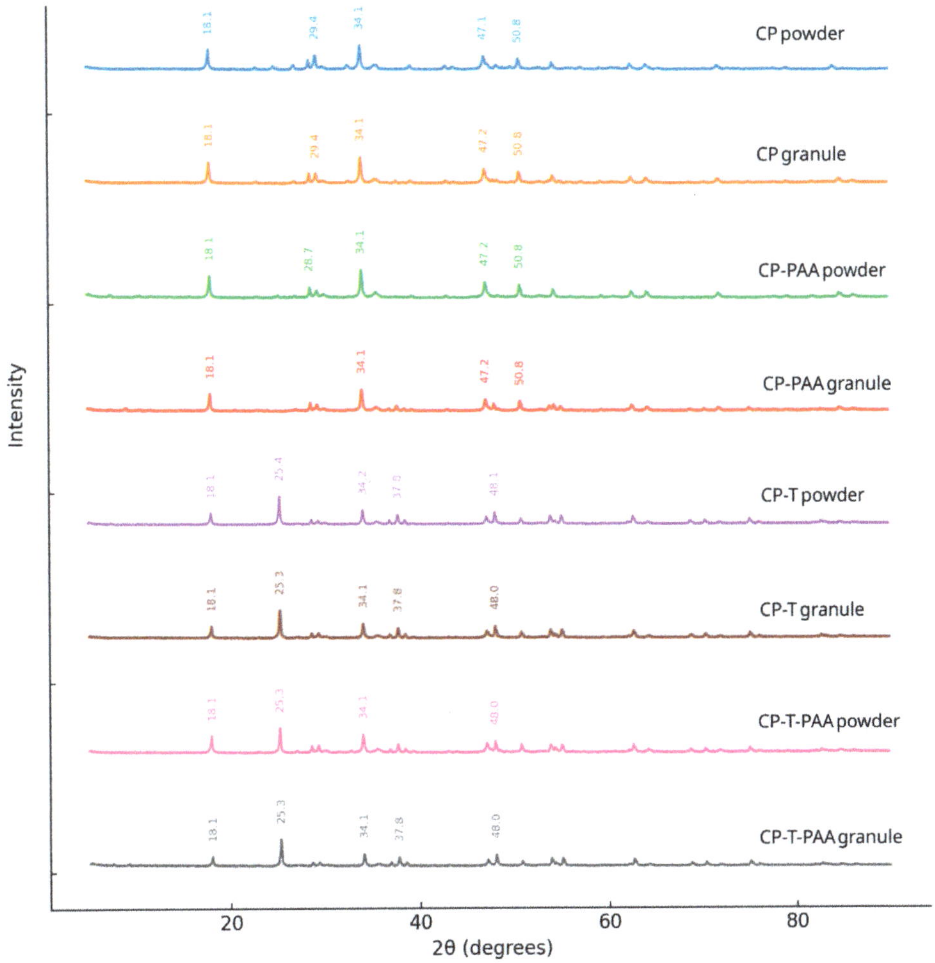

Figure 3. Results of XRD analysis of products.

https://doi.org/10.3390/w18030296

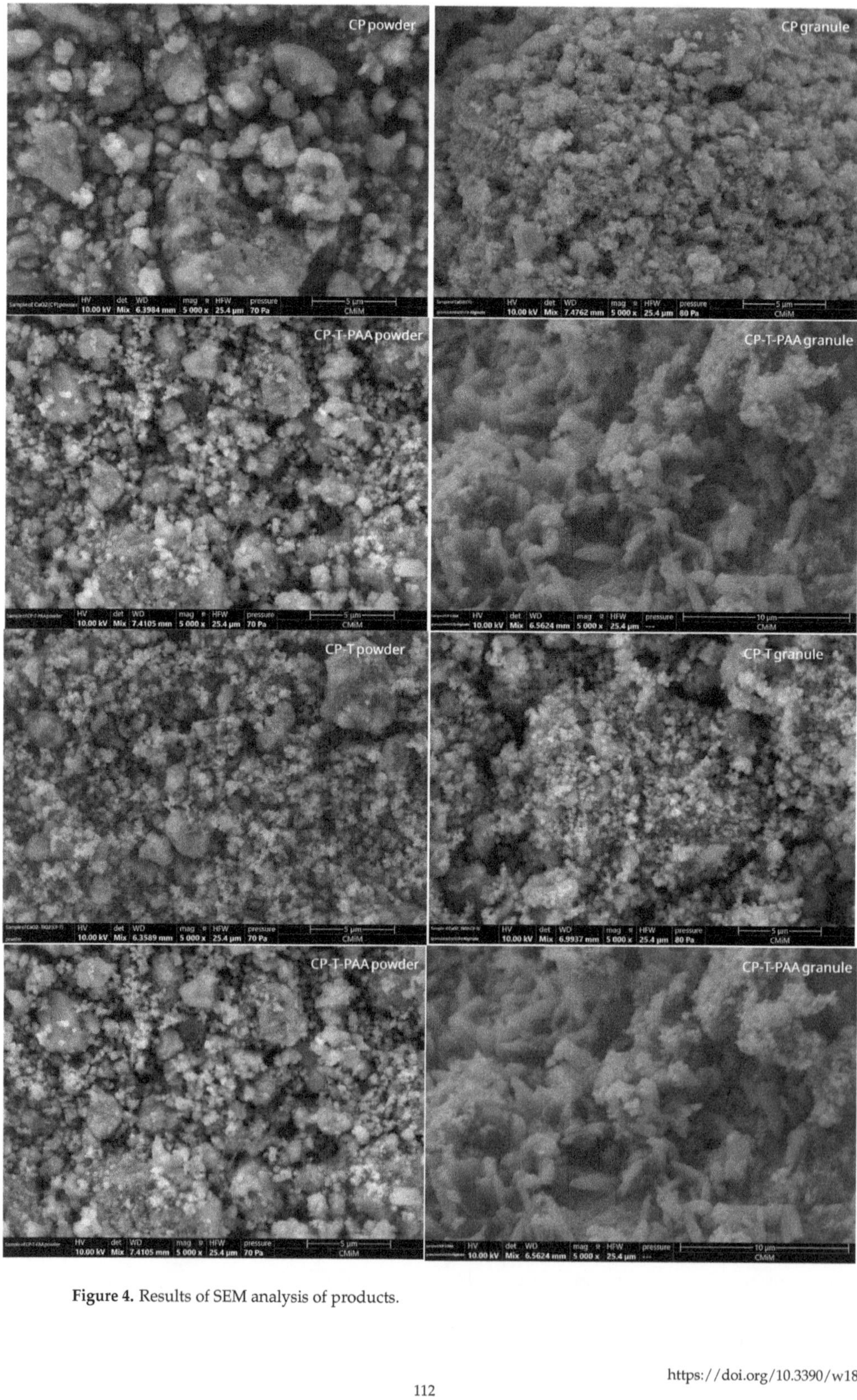

Figure 4. Results of SEM analysis of products.

https://doi.org/10.3390/w18030296

The CP-PAA products, in both powder and granular forms, exhibited only a difference in intensity compared to the unmodified CP. This suggested a structural disruption of the regular tetragonal CaO_2 lattice due to the addition of peracetic acid. This structural modification was directly correlated with the SEM observations of smaller, more uniform aggregates (0.3–2.5 μm in powder form) with a slightly coarse surface. The structure–function relationship in CP-PAA was evident: the modified crystal structure resulted in enhanced stability and improved compatibility with the alginate coating matrix [30]. SEM imaging showed that the CP-PAA granules achieved remarkable uniformity (2.0–8.0 μm) with a smooth surface and a 3.2-fold increase in size. This superior coating efficiency was a direct outcome of the structural modifications that enhanced surface–coating interactions, as confirmed by the retained XRD patterns with consistent peak positions but altered intensities.

XRD analysis results for the binary CP-T composite showed CaO_2 peaks identical to those of anatase at 25.3°, indicating a partial structural modification resulting from the incorporation of TiO_2 [33,34]. The SEM morphology directly reflected this structural complexity through a heterogeneous surface texture and a mixed-phase appearance (0.4–2.8 μm). The correlation between the phase mixing observed in XRD and the morphological heterogeneity in SEM demonstrated how structural diversity manifested at the microscopic level. The CP-T granules (1.5–6.0 μm) exhibited a uniform coating that successfully encapsulated the heterogeneous structure beneath, creating a smooth outer surface while maintaining the functionality of the dual-phase core.

The CP-T-PAA composite represented the most sophisticated structure–morphology relationship. XRD analysis revealed a complex diffraction pattern that combined the effects of both TiO_2 and peracetic acid modification, resulting in moderate overall crystallinity. The fine structure observed in SEM, characterized by particles of 0.3–2.0 μm with a very smooth texture, correlated directly with this structural complexity. The synergistic effect of the dual modification created optimal conditions for the alginate coating. Consequently, the CP-T-PAA granules achieved exceptional uniformity (3.0–10.0 μm), with the highest size increase factor of 5.0. This performance stemmed from the combined structural modifications, which created optimal surface chemistry for alginate interaction, as evidenced by the preserved structural integrity observed in the XRD results of the coated matrix [30].

Subsequent product characterization focused on radical formation. Figure 5 illustrates the mean g-factor values (blue bars) and radical intensities (red/orange bars). The observed g-factor values, which ranged from 1.6 to 2.0, were characteristic of oxygen-centered radicals, specifically hydroxyl radical (•OH) and superoxide radical (O_2^{-}•) [35,36]. These species were identified as dominant in this advanced oxidation process.

The fundamental mechanism was initiated by the dissolution of calcium peroxide, which yielded hydrogen peroxide (Equation (3)). This hydrogen peroxide served as a precursor for hydroxyl radical formation through various pathways, including Fenton-like reactions in the presence of iron (Equation (4)). Concurrently, calcium peroxide was capable of direct oxygen release (Equation (5)), from which superoxide (Equations (6)–(8)) radicals can form under suitable electron-accepting conditions [35].

$$CaO_2 + 2H_2O \rightarrow Ca(OH)_2 + H_2O_2 \quad (3)$$

$$Fe^{2+} + H_2O_2 \rightarrow Fe^{3+} + OH^- + {}^{\bullet}OH \quad (4)$$

$$2H_2O_2 \xrightarrow{\text{auto-decomposition due to base of } Ca(OH)_2} 2H_2O + O_2 \quad (5)$$

$$Fe^{2+} + O_2 \rightarrow Fe^{3+} + O_2^{\bullet-} \quad (6)$$

$$H_2O_2 + {}^{\bullet}OH \rightarrow H_2O + HO_2^{\bullet}, \textit{propagation} \quad (7)$$

https://doi.org/10.3390/w18030296

$$HO_2^{\bullet} \rightleftharpoons H^+ + O_2^{\bullet -}, \textit{propagation} \quad (8)$$

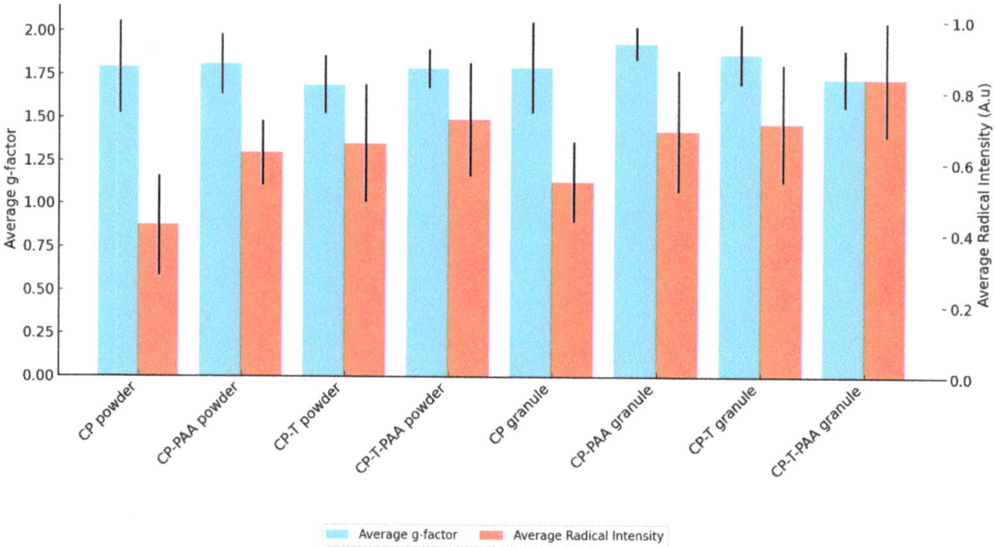

Figure 5. Characterization of free radicals by electron spin resonance (ESR).

The incorporation of peracetic acid into the CP-PAA system enhanced radical generation. Peracetic acid acted as both an independent oxidant and a source of organic peroxy radicals, particularly acetyl peroxy radical. More significantly, the co-present hydrogen peroxide from calcium peroxide dissolution had a synergistic effect [37] that enriched the formation pathways and diversified the types of reactive species generated. This synergistic interaction was particularly evident in the iron-containing systems, where PAA facilitated Fe(III)/Fe(II) cycling (Equations (9) and (10)), dramatically amplifying hydroxyl radical production through enhanced Fenton chemistry.

$$Fe^{3+} + CH_3C(O)OOH \rightarrow Fe^{2+} + CH_3C(O)OO^{\bullet} + H^+ \quad (9)$$

$$Fe^{2+} + H_2O_2 \rightarrow Fe^{3+} + OH^- + {}^{\bullet}OH \quad (10)$$

The addition of titanium dioxide to the CP-T system introduced a photocatalytic enhancement that altered the radical formation profile. Under UV light activation, which provided photon energy (hv), TiO_2 generated electron–hole pairs (e_{cb}^- and h_{vb}^+, Equation (11)) that participated in distinct radical formation reactions: electrons reduced molecular oxygen to form superoxide radicals (Equation (12)), while holes oxidized water molecules to produce hydroxyl radicals (Equation (13)). Furthermore, the photocatalytic process accelerated the decomposition of hydrogen peroxide derived from calcium peroxide, creating an additional pathway for hydroxyl radical formation, as shown in Equations (14)–(16) [38]. The ternary combination system, CP-T-PAA, exhibited the highest radical intensity due to multi-pathway synergy that integrated all individual mechanisms into a comprehensive oxidative system. This formulation concurrently generated hydroxyl, superoxide, and organic peroxide radicals through the photocatalytic activation of both hydrogen peroxide and peracetic acid. The titanium dioxide facilitated electron transfer processes that not only enhanced individual radical formation pathways but also created novel reaction routes through the interaction of a diverse range of radical species.

$$TiO_2 + hv \rightarrow e^-_{cb} + h^+_{vb} \quad (11)$$

$$O_2 + e^-_{cb} \rightarrow O_2^{\bullet -} \quad (12)$$

$$H_2O + h^+_{vb} \rightarrow {}^{\bullet}OH_2 + H^+ \quad (13)$$

$$H_2O_2 + e^-_{cb} \rightarrow {}^{\bullet}OH + OH^- \quad (14)$$

$$H_2O_2 + O_2^{\bullet -} \rightarrow {}^{\bullet}OH + OH^- + O_2 \quad (15)$$

$$OH^- + h^+_{vb} \rightarrow {}^{\bullet}OH \quad (16)$$

A crucial observation was that the granular formulations consistently demonstrated higher radical intensities compared to the powder formulations across all systems (Figure 5). This enhancement is attributed to the Fe–alginate encapsulation, which provided diffusion-controlled release of active components, thereby maintaining optimal reactant concentrations over an extended period. The iron component within the Fe–alginate coating served as a Fenton catalyst, promoting additional hydroxyl radical formation via the catalytic cycle shown in Equation (4). Moreover, the encapsulation matrix afforded protection against radical scavenging by environmental components, prevented premature degradation, and sustained the radical-generating capacity for a longer duration [39]. A more detailed discussion is provided in the next section.

3.2. The Laboratory-Scale Testing Stage

The laboratory-scale water quality testing results indicated that each treatment had a significant effect on key parameters (DO and ORP), as illustrated in Figure 6. The dissolved oxygen (DO) showed a highly significant difference ($p < 0.001$) among treatments (detailed in Supplementary Materials). Formulations utilizing AOPs consistently demonstrated superior performance. The CP-T-PAA Powder AOP and CP-T Granule AOP treatments successfully achieved the highest mean DO concentrations. The ORP values also exhibited a significant increase following AOP treatment ($p < 0.001$) compared to the control and non-AOP treatments (details are provided in the Supplementary Materials). This increase in ORP indicates more oxidative environmental conditions, which strongly support the degradation of organic matter and the detoxification of harmful compounds in the water [37]. The AOP mechanism, which generates reactive oxygen species (ROS), particularly hydroxyl radicals (OH) with a high oxidation potential, was crucial to effectively degrading organic pollutants and toxic compounds. Other parameters, such as pH, turbidity, ammonia, and H_2S, revealed that the composite lime granule treatment with an AOP significantly improved the aquatic environmental conditions. For instance, a trend towards pH stability was observed with the AOP-treated lime granule. In terms of clarity, the CP-T Granule AOP treatment showed the best performance, with a turbidity removal efficiency reaching 92–93%. This treatment was also highly effective in reducing toxic compounds. The ammonia (NH_3-N) concentration was successfully lowered by up to 94% through an enhanced nitrification process supported by the dissolved oxygen supply, while hydrogen sulfide (H_2S) was reduced by 89%. The removal of ammonia and sulfide is directly driven by the oxidative capability of the generated radical species. Hydroxyl radicals (•OH) attack ammonia molecules typically via hydrogen abstraction, forming amide radicals (•NH_2) which are subsequently oxidized through a series of reactions to form nitrite and ultimately stable nitrate (NO_3^-) [40]. Similarly, sulfide species (H_2S and HS^-) undergo electrophilic attack by •OH and superoxide radicals (•O_2^-), leading to their sequential oxidation into

https://doi.org/10.3390/w18030296

elemental sulfur (S^0) and finally to sulfate (SO_4^{2-}) [41]. This radical-mediated oxidation rapidly transforms toxic reduced metabolites into their less harmful oxidized forms, thereby mitigating toxicity in the water column.

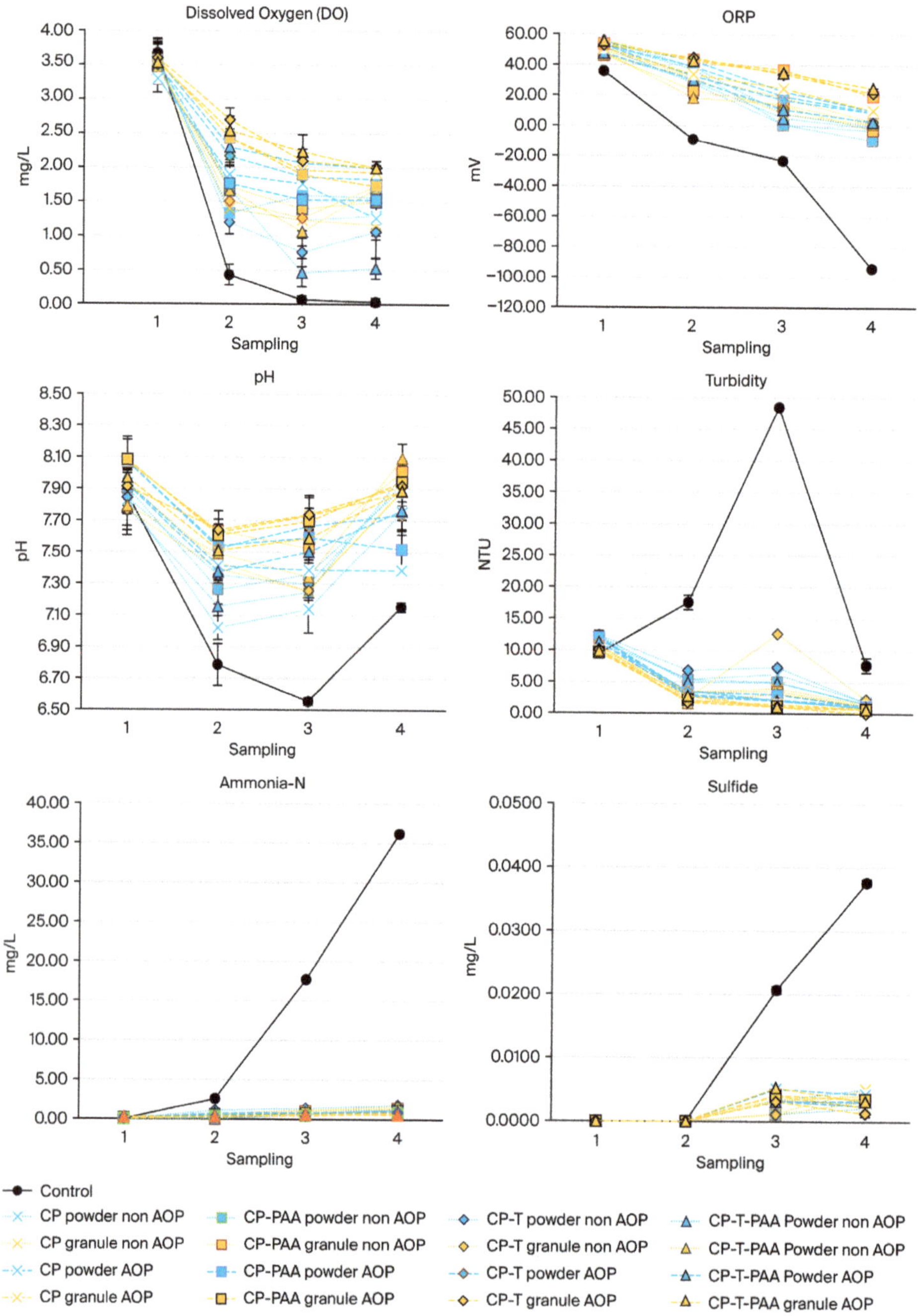

Figure 6. Water quality measurement following each treatment (4 sampling times).

https://doi.org/10.3390/w18030296

Based on Figure 7A, the granule formulations consistently outperformed the powders and clustered among the top AOP treatments. The TOPSIS score integrating all six parameters confirmed that triple synergy achieved the most balanced improvement in water quality improvement. The combination of CP-T-PAA granules and an AOP system emerged as the optimal treatment (Figure 7B) due to its triple synergy, combining (1) passive O_2/H_2O_2 release from CaO_2, (2) TiO_2 photocatalysis, and (3) PAA activation. The order of chemical reactions was briefly mentioned in Equations (4)–(16).

Empirical evidence of the effectiveness of this composite has been discussed in several previous studies, though further research is needed. Acetylperoxyl ($CH_3COOO\bullet$) and acetyloxyl ($CH_3COO\bullet$) radicals exhibit distinct reactivity, showing enhanced selectivity toward electron-rich organics and superior near-neutral pH performance [42]. Recent studies demonstrated that an PAA-based AOP achieved 96.2% pharmaceutical removal in 15 min ($k = 0.241\ min^{-1}$), with $\bullet OH$ contributing ~86.8% oxidative activity when iron catalysts were present [35].

Synergistic interactions are critical. PAA-CaO_2 synergy provides temporal complementarity, which immediate high-intensity oxidation from PAA and sustained H_2O_2 generation from CaO_2, PAA-TiO_2's synergy enhances charge carrier separation and prevents active site blocking [43], and PAA-UV synergy creates a radical cocktail ($\bullet OH$, $CH_3COO\bullet$, $CH_3COOO\bullet$, $O_2\bullet^-$) with complementary reactivity patterns, reducing incomplete oxidation.

Granules encapsulated within Fe–alginate provided controlled release, which is fundamentally different from the immediate dispersion of the powder formulations. Alginate hydrogels exhibit pH-responsive swelling and diffusion-controlled release [39]. Upon immersion, gradual hydration creates tortuous diffusion pathways moderating oxidant release, as described by Fick's law (Equation (17)):

$$J = -D(\frac{dC}{dx}),\ \text{where}\ \frac{dC}{dx} = \frac{C_{out} - C_{in}}{dx} \tag{17}$$

where J represents the diffusive flux, D represents the diffusion coefficient of the product, and dC/dx represents the concentration gradient. Theoretical estimates based on Fick's law suggest that the Fe–alginate matrix reduces the effective diffusion coefficient to the order of $10^{-12}\ m^2/s$, which is consistent with the observed sustained release time of over 24 h compared to the rapid dissolution (D approx. $10^{-9}\ m^2/s$) typically seen with non-encapsulated powders. This offers three advantages: (1) sustained availability over 24 h versus burst release, satisfying continuous oxygen demand; (2) localized hot spots with elevated oxidant concentrations, enhancing local kinetics while maintaining moderate bulk concentrations; and (3) improved utilization efficiency by matching supply with demand, reducing non-productive consumption.

The Fe–alginate layer is an integral catalytic component and not merely passive carrier. Iron ionically cross-linked with alginate carboxylates creates heterogeneous catalysts in which Fe centers are immobilized yet accessible to diffusing H_2O_2 [44]. As H_2O_2 transits the Fe–alginate shell, it encounters immobilized Fe sites, triggering Fenton reactions (Equations (18) and (19)):

$$\equiv\text{Alg-COO-Fe}^{2+} + H_2O_2 \rightarrow \equiv\text{Alg-COO-Fe}^{3+} + \bullet OH + OH^- \tag{18}$$

$$\equiv\text{Alg-COO-Fe}^{3+} + H_2O_2 \rightarrow \equiv\text{Alg-COO-Fe}^{2+} + HO_2\bullet + H^+ \tag{19}$$

This built-in Fenton system ensures that every H_2O_2 molecule participates in radical generation before exiting, dramatically improving radical yield [45]. Fe–alginate also catalyzes PAA decomposition, generating Fe(IV) species with 4.2–10.8 higher degradation rates [46]. Unlike homogeneous systems, immobilized iron cycles repeatedly without

https://doi.org/10.3390/w18030296

loss, improving economic viability. Alginate carboxylates provide pH buffering, enabling effective Fenton catalysis at the neutral pH (7–8) typical of *Litopenaeus vannamei* culture.

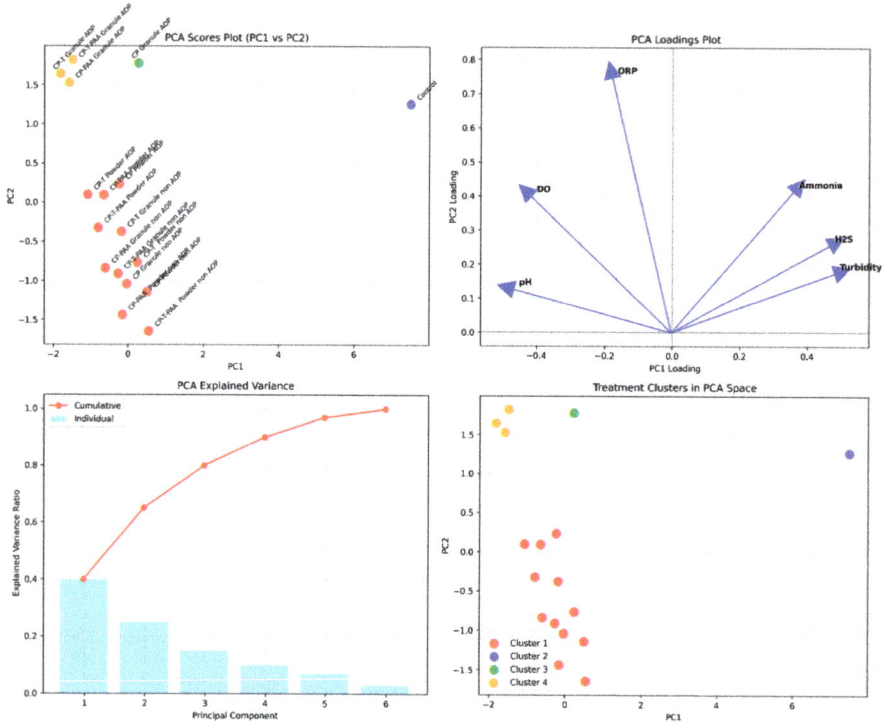

(A)

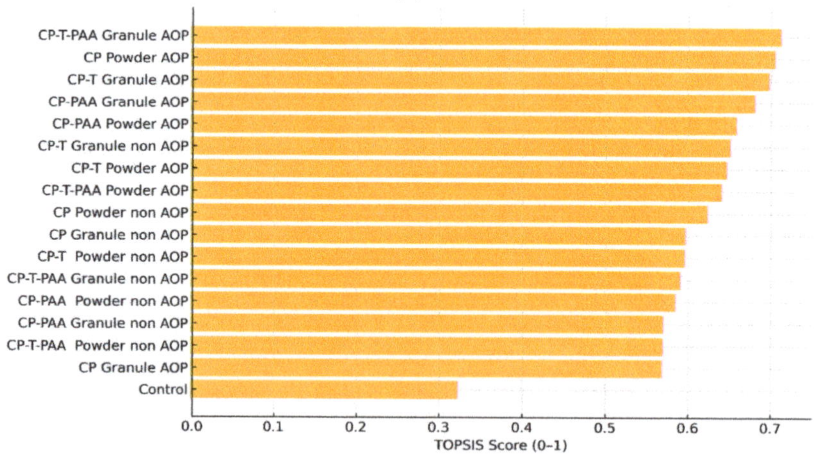

(B)

Figure 7. (**A**) Principal Component Analysis (PCA) of the water quality measurement; (**B**) TOPSIS score ranking for all treatments based on multi-criteria water quality parameters (DO, pH, ORP, Ammonia, Sulfide, Turbidity). The TOPSIS score (*Ci*) ranges from 0 to 1, where a higher score indicates a closer proximity to the ideal solution—representing the optimal balance between high oxygenation efficacy and low toxic metabolite accumulation. The CP-T-PAA Granule AOP treatment achieved the highest score, validating it as the most effective formulation.

https://doi.org/10.3390/w18030296

3.3. Practical Implication

The CP-T-PAA granules address critical gaps in aquaculture water treatment by providing simultaneous multi-parameter improvement through integrated AOP mechanisms. As outlined in the Introduction, a critical challenge in aquaculture—particularly for traditional farmers—is the gap between available technologies and practical implementation. The CP-T-PAA Granule AOP formulation addresses this gap through several user-friendly features. First, unlike complex aeration systems, chemical dosing pumps, or biofloc management protocols that require technical expertise and continuous monitoring, granule application involves straightforward broad-casting into ponds, similar to the conventional liming practices already familiar to farmers. Second, the formulation simultaneously addresses multiple water quality challenges (low DO, high organic matter, ammonia, H_2S, and turbidity) with a single treatment, eliminating the need for multiple separate interventions and their associated complexity. Third, the sustained-release nature of granules provides an extended treatment duration (demonstrated in this study to be over 24 h; likely longer under field conditions), reducing the frequency of application and monitoring compared to short-acting interventions. Fourth, unlike pure oxygen systems (explosion risk), ozone generators (toxicity concerns), or strong acids/bases (handling hazards), the encapsulated formulation presents minimal safety risks during transport, storage, and application, increasing accessibility for small-scale farmers.

In traditional aquaculture systems lacking mechanical aeration, the sediment–water interface frequently exhibits anoxic conditions. This environment inhibits bacterial nitrification, shifting the process toward sulfate reduction and resulting in ammonia accumulation through ammonification. However, the administration of 5 mg/L of the CP-T-PAA granule with an AOP system demonstrated the ability to maintain dissolved oxygen (DO) levels of approximately 2 mg/L at the substrate surface, thereby facilitating the decomposition of organic matter by benthic bacteria.

While it is widely established that the optimal DO level for *Litopenaeus vannamei* survival exceeds 4 mg/L, this standard primarily applies to the water column and is often unattainable at the bottom of the pond due to strong anoxic tendencies. Maintaining a DO level of 2 mg/L within the substrate establishes a habitable resting zone. Although this concentration is below the saturation required for high metabolic activity, it meets the basal metabolic requirements for resting phases and effectively mitigates sulfide toxicity. This allows the shrimp to maintain their natural benthic orientation, thereby maximizing the volumetric utilization of the culture system and minimizing density-dependent stress.

Throughout the 21 days of experimental period, a preliminary safety assessment was conducted by monitoring specific biological endpoints in the test aquariums. Daily observations showed no acute mortality and no behavioral abnormalities (e.g., lethargy or loss of appetite) in the test organisms exposed to the 5 mg/L dosage. This implies that the residual by-products of the AOP reaction (primarily water and oxygen) and the stable Fe-alginate carrier are chemically benign at this concentration.

A primary concern regarding the application of AOP-based materials in aquaculture is the potential ecotoxicity of residual oxidants and reaction by-products on the cultured species. In this study, the safety of the CP-T-PAA composite is ensured through two key mechanisms: chemical compatibility and release kinetics. Chemically, the decomposition products of composite components are environmentally benign. Calcium peroxide and peracetic acid dissociate into oxygen rapidly [47,48]; moreover, the products used in this study were limited to the substrate, and peroxide residues rapidly decomposed with the AOP system in the water column. In recent years, titanium dioxide has emerged as a multifunctional agent in aquaculture, where it is utilized both for water quality remediation and the improvement of aquatic organism health [49]. Regarding dosage safety, the applied concentration of 5 mg/L is substantially below the toxicity thresholds reported in the literature. Previous toxicological assessments have indicated that calcium peroxide concentrations of up to 1000 mg/L (0.1%) are safe for sensitive aquatic organisms [21]. Furthermore, the Fe–alginate encapsulation plays a critical role in mitigating oxidative stress due to kinetical aspects. Unlike free powder application, which causes a rapid surge in hydrogen peroxide, the granule form facilitates a controlled, zero-order release profile. This prevents acute exposure shocks to the shrimp, ensuring that radical generation remains localized to the granule surface and sediment interface where benthic remediation is most needed, rather than dispersing aggressively into the water column. However, it is important to distinguish these acute observations from chronic impacts. Future studies should incorporate histopathological analysis of shrimp gills and hepatopancreas to rule out potential microscopic tissue damage from long-term exposure to reactive radical species.

Economically, the synthesis of CP-T-PAA granules entails higher initial raw material costs compared to conventional products. To provide a rational economic justification, a cost-efficiency analysis was modeled based on a standard $1000 m^3 aquaculture pond over monthly operational cycle (Table 2). The conventional approach typically requires frequent application of agricultural lime (e.g., dolomite) to buffer pH, combined with commercial probiotics and oxygen tablets. While the raw material cost of the synthesized CP-T-PAA composite is estimated to be significantly higher than lime due to the precursors (TiO_2, PAA, and coated with Fe-Alginate), the dosage-to-efficacy ratio offers a competitive advantage. However, the economic justification lies in its dual functionality and operational efficiency. The granules' controlled-release mechanism enables them to significantly outperform conventional peroxide treatments, which are often limited by rapid decomposition rates. Furthermore, the enhanced generation of reactive radicals by the AOP system suppresses toxic metabolites detrimental to the cultured biota. Consequently, when evaluated on a cost-per-unit-efficiency basis, this composite offers a feasible, user-friendly alternative for maintaining optimal water quality over extended periods, particularly in traditional aquaculture systems constrained by limited resources and technical expertise.

Table 2. Estimated operational cost comparison between Conventional Treatment and CP-T-PAA Composite for a 1000 m^3 pond over monthly cycle.

Cost Component	Conventional Treatment (Lime + Probiotics)	CP-T-PAA Composite with AOP System
1. Material Inputs		
Primary Agent	Agricultural Lime (dolomite)	CP-T-PAA Composite
Application Frequency	Once a week	Once a month
Dosage per Application	20 mg/L (2 kg)	5 mg/L (5 kg)
Total Quantity Required	80 kg	5 kg
Est. Unit Price *	0.5 USD/kg	12 USD/kg (synthesized estimate)
Subtotal Material Cost	40 USD	60 USD
2. Additional		
Secondary Material	Probiotics and Oxygen Tablets	UV installation and electricity costs/month
Total Quantity Required	Each 3 L/week and 2 kg/month	Each 1 package and 16.2 kWh
Est. Unit Price *	Each 2.5 USD/L and 8.8 USD/kg	Each 18.5 USD/package and 0.080 USD/kWh
Subtotal Additive Cost	47.6 USD	19.8 USD
Total Estimated Cost	87.6 USD	79.8 USD

Note: * Prices are based on average price in Indonesia markets.

4. Conclusions

This study describes the successful synthesis and evaluation of a novel multifunctional lime-based composite designed to address critical water quality challenges in *Litopenaeus vannamei* aquaculture. The combination of 5 mg/L of CP-T-PAA product added to the sediment with an AOP system demonstrated superior performance, characterized by the highest intensity hydroxyl (•OH) and superoxide (•O_2^-) radical generation due to the synergistic coupling of photocatalysis and chemical oxidation, which was also validated

https://doi.org/10.3390/w18030296

through TOPSIS analysis. This composite effectively maintained dissolved oxygen levels at ~2 mg/L at the sediment–water interface for 21 days while significantly elevating the oxidation reduction potential (ORP) and water clarity, and achieving high removal efficiencies for ammonia (94%) and sulfide (89%). Furthermore, the Fe–alginate encapsulation successfully addressed slow-release material challenges. Consequently, this novel composite offers a promising, user-friendly, and sustainable strategy for traditional shrimp farmers to enhance pond productivity and stability without the need for complex infrastructure, thereby contributing to the advancement of the blue economy.

However, this study is subject to certain limitations. The experiments were conducted in a controlled laboratory environment which does not fully capture the complex hydrodynamic fluctuations, biological interactions, and variable nutrient loads typical of open shrimp ponds. Therefore, the next steps for this research should focus on conducting pilot-scale field trials to validate the composite's efficacy under dynamic pond conditions. Additionally, a comprehensive cost–benefit analysis is recommended to assess the economic feasibility of mass-producing this composite for widespread adoption by traditional shrimp farmers.

Supplementary Materials: The following supporting information can be downloaded at: https://www.mdpi.com/article/10.3390/w18030296/s1, Table S1. Temporal variation of Dissolved Oxygen (mg/L) across different treatments over 21 days; Table S2. Temporal variation of pH across different treatments over 21 days; Table S3. Temporal variation of Oxidation Reduction Potential (mV) across different treatments over 21 days; Table S4. Temporal variation of Turbidity (NTU) across different treatments over 21 days; Table S5. Temporal variation of Ammonia (mg/L) across different treatments over 21 days; Table S6. Temporal variation of Sulfide (mg/L) across different treatments over 21 days.

Author Contributions: M.I.A.: conceptualization, methodology, formal analysis, writing—original draft and editing. N.T.M.P.: supervision, validation, and writing—review. B.W.: supervision and conceptualization. M.K.: methodology and data interpretation. N.R.: validation. M.F.: data interpretation. H.W.A.: research assistant and draft editing. All authors have read and agreed to the published version of the manuscript.

Funding: The authors gratefully acknowledge financial support from the Korea–Indonesia MTCRC Joint Research Initiative 2024 [Contract Number: 10/MTCRC/VII/2024]. The APC was funded by the authors.

Data Availability Statement: The original contributions presented in this study are included in the article/Supplementary Materials. Further inquiries can be directed to the corresponding author.

Acknowledgments: The authors would like to thank the Advanced Research and Integrated Laboratory of IPB University for facilitating the experiments and providing the necessary instrumentation.

Conflicts of Interest: The authors declare no conflict of interest.

Abbreviations

The following abbreviations are used in this manuscript:

AOP(s)	Advanced Oxidation Processes
ANOVA	Analysis of Variance
CP	Calcium Peroxide
CP-T	Composited Calcium Peroxide and Titanium Dioxide
CP-PAA	Composited Calcium Peroxide and Peracetic Acid
CP-T-PAA	Composited Calcium Peroxide, Titanium Dioxide, and Peracetic Acid
DO	Dissolved Oxygen
ESR	Electron Spin Resonance
FTIR	Fourier Transform Infrared Spectroscopy

JCPDS	Joint Committee on Powder Diffraction Standards
MCDA	Multi-Criteria Decision Analysis
NADPH	Nicotinamide Adenine Dinucleotide Phosphate Hydrogen
NOX	NADPH Oxidase
NTU	Nephelometric Turbidity Unit
ORP	Oxidation Reduction Potential
PAA	Peracetic Acid
PCA	Principal Component Analysis
ROS	Reactive Oxygen Species
SEM	Scanning Electron Microscopy
TEM	Transmission Electron Microscope
TOPSIS	Technique for Order Preference by Similarity to Ideal Solution
UV	Ultraviolet
XRD	X-ray Diffraction

References

1. Boyd, C.E. General Relationship between Water Quality and Aquaculture Performance in Ponds. In *Fish Diseases*; Elsevier: Amsterdam, The Netherlands, 2017; pp. 147–166.
2. Zheng, M.; Gao, B.; Zhang, J.; El-Din, M.G.; Snyder, S.A.; Wu, M.; Tang, L. In-Situ Chemical Attenuation of Pharmaceutically Active Compounds Using CaO_2: Influencing Factors, Mechanistic Modeling, and Cooperative Inactivation of Water-Borne Microbial Pathogens. *Environ. Res.* **2022**, *212*, 113531. [CrossRef]
3. Seethalakshmi, P.; Rajeev, R.; Kiran, G.S.; Selvin, J. Shrimp Disease Management for Sustainable Aquaculture: Innovations from Nanotechnology and Biotechnology. *Aquac. Int.* **2021**, *29*, 1591–1620. [CrossRef]
4. Lara, G.; Krummenauer, D.; Abreu, P.C.; Poersch, L.H.; Wasielesky, W. The Use of Different Aerators on *Litopenaeus vannamei* Biofloc Culture System: Effects on Water Quality, Shrimp Growth and Biofloc Composition. *Aquac. Int.* **2017**, *25*, 147–162. [CrossRef]
5. Luan, Y.; Wang, Y.; Liu, C.; Lv, L.; Xu, A.; Song, Z. Effects of Potassium Monopersulfate on Nitrification Activity and Bacterial Community Structure of Sponge Biocarrier Biofilm in *Litopenaeus vannamei* Aquaculture System. *Environ. Technol.* **2024**, *45*, 3354–3366. [CrossRef]
6. Betanzo-Torres, E.A.; MdlÁ, P.-Á.; Sandoval-Herazo, L.C.; Molina-Navarro, A.; Rodríguez-Montoro, I.; González-Moreno, R.H. Factors That Limit the Adoption of Biofloc Technology in Aquaculture Production in Mexico. *Water* **2020**, *12*, 2775. [CrossRef]
7. Deni, A. The development of shrimp culture in Indonesia. In Proceedings of the Korean Society of Fisheries and Aquaculture Sciences Aquaculture Division Academic Conference, Jeju Island, Republic of Korea, 3–4 November 2022.
8. Cao, Y.; Gu, D.; Li, G.; Huang, M.; He, W. A Review on the Application of Slow-Release Oxygen Materials in the Remediation of Polluted Rivers and Lakes. *J. East China Norm. Univ. Nat. Sci.* **2024**, *2024*, 9.
9. Ma, Z.; Ge, Z.; Liu, K.; Wang, C.; Wu, T.; Zhang, J. Application of Calcium Peroxide for Efficient Treatment of Surface Water Turbidity: Mechanisms and Microbial Community Responses. *J. Environ. Chem. Eng.* **2023**, *11*, 110905. [CrossRef]
10. Hou, Z.; Wang, W.; Dong, N.; Chen, P.; Ge, L.; Tan, F.; Wong, P.K. A Dual-Oxidant Advanced Oxidation Process System Containing CaO_2 and Peroxymonosulfate for Organic Pollutant Degradation: High Adaptability and Synergistic Effect. *Sep. Purif. Technol.* **2023**, *308*, 122909. [CrossRef]
11. Zulkarnaini, Z.; Gumelar, G.; Zainuddin, E. Anaerobic Ammonium Oxidation Performance in Shrimp Pond Wastewater Treatment. *Andalasian Int. J. Appl. Sci.* **2022**, *2*, 51–56. [CrossRef]
12. Checa, J.; Aran, J.M. Reactive Oxygen Species: Drivers of Physiological and Pathological Processes. *J. Inflamm. Res.* **2020**, *13*, 1057–1073. [CrossRef]
13. Vermot, A.; Petit-Härtlein, I.; Smith, S.M.E.; Fieschi, F. NADPH Oxidases (NOX): An Overview from Discovery, Molecular Mechanisms to Physiology and Pathology. *Antioxidants* **2021**, *10*, 890. [CrossRef]
14. Stefan, I. *Advanced Oxidation Processes for Water Treatment Fundamentals and Applications*; IWA Publishing: London, UK, 2018.
15. Kuntari, C. Uji Aktivitas Penangkapan Radikal Hidroksil Oleh Ekstrak Etanol the Hijau Dan the Hitam Dengan Metode Deoksiribosa. Master's Thesis, Universitas Sanata Dharma, Yogyakarta, Indonesia, 2007.
16. Dong, G.; Zhang, L.; Hua, X. Calcium Peroxide Powder and Its Making Method. CN1104996A, 12 July 1995.
17. Zhang, Q.; Wei, Y.; Zhang, T.; Han, B.; Liu, K.; Chen, B. Preparation of CaO Granules Using the Granulation Method. *Adv. Appl. Ceram.* **2018**, *117*, 334–339. [CrossRef]

https://doi.org/10.3390/w18030296

18. Piyarat, V.; Tunlawit, S.; Chanat, C.; Chalor, J.; Chainarong, S.; Ann, K.; Rattana, B. Remediating Oxytetracycline-Contaminated Aquaculture Water Using Nano Calcium Peroxide (nCaO_2) Produced from Flue Gas Desulfurization (FGD) Gypsum. *Environ. Technol. Innov.* **2021**, *24*, 101861.
19. Faisal, M.; Juswono, U.P.; Santoso, D.R.; Widodo, C.S. The Effectiveness of Herbal Medicine Mangosteen Peel Extract (Garcinia Mangostana) to Prevent Free Radicals Occurrence and Decrease in Hemoglobin Levels in the Blood Caused by Diabetes Mellitus. *Trends Sci.* **2025**, *22*, 9250. [CrossRef]
20. Alkhadra, M.A.; Gao, T.; Conforti, K.M.; Tian, H.; Bazant, M.Z. Small-Scale Desalination of Seawater by Shock Electrodialysis. *Desalination* **2020**, *476*, 114219. [CrossRef]
21. Wang, C.; Qi, C.; Li, Z. Evaluation of Calcium Peroxide as a New Water Purifying and Oxygen Releasing Agent in Aquaculture. *Life Sci. Res.* **2012**, *16*, 345–349.
22. Bridgewater, L.L. *Standard Methods for the Examination of Water and Wastewater*; American Public Health Association: Washington, DC, USA, 2017.
23. Greenacre, M.; Groenen, P.J.; Hastie, T.; d'Enza, A.I.; Markos, A.; Tuzhilina, E. Principal Component Analysis. *Nat. Rev. Methods Primer* **2022**, *2*, 100.
24. Uzun, B.; Taiwo, M.; Syidanova, A.; Uzun Ozsahin, D. The Technique For Order of Preference by Similarity to Ideal Solution (TOPSIS). In *Application of Multi-Criteria Decision Analysis in Environmental and Civil Engineering; Professional Practice in Earth Sciences*; Uzun Ozsahin, D., Gökçekuş, H., Uzun, B., LaMoreaux, J., Eds.; Springer: Cham, Switzerland, 2021.
25. Subbotina, I.R.; Barsukov, D.V. Direct Evidence of the Key Role of UV-Formed Peroxide Species in Photocatalytic Gas-Solid Oxidation in Air on Anatase TiO_2 Particles. *Phys. Chem. Chem. Phys.* **2020**, *22*, 2200–2211. [CrossRef] [PubMed]
26. Mollah, M.; Faruque, M.R.I.; Bradley, D.A.; Khandaker, M.U.; Al-Assaf, S. FTIR and Rheology Study of Alginate Samples: Effect of Radiation. *Radiat. Phys. Chem.* **2022**, *202*, 110500. [CrossRef]
27. Huamani-Palomino, R.G. Functionalization of an Alginate-Based Material by Oxidation and Reductive Amination. *Polymers* **2021**, *13*, 255. [CrossRef]
28. Yu, Z.; Zhou, Z.; Huang, G. Two-Dimensional FTIR Spectroscopic Characterization of Functional Groups of NaOCl-Exposed Alginate. *ACS Appl. Bio Mater.* **2018**, *1*, 593–603. [CrossRef] [PubMed]
29. Elhoudi, M. Comparison of Green Bio-Based Cerium/Alginate vs. Copper/Alginate Beads: A Study of Vibrational and Thermal Properties Using Experimental and Theoretical Methods. *J. Mol. Model.* **2022**, *28*, 37. [CrossRef]
30. Bîrcă, A.C.; Gherasim, O.; Niculescu, A.G.; Grumezescu, A.M.; Vasile, B.Ș.; Mihaiescu, D.E.; Neacșu, I.A.; Andronescu, E.; Trușcă, R.; Holban, A.M.; et al. Infection-Free and Enhanced Wound Healing Potential of Alginate Gels Incorporating Silver and Tannylated Calcium Peroxide Nanoparticles. *Int. J. Mol. Sci.* **2024**, *25*, 5196. [CrossRef] [PubMed]
31. Wu, X.; Han, X.; Guo, Y.; Liu, Q.; Sun, R.; Wen, Z.; Dai, C. Application Prospect of Calcium Peroxide Nanoparticles in Biomedical Field. *Rev. Adv. Mater. Sci.* **2023**, *62*, 20220308. [CrossRef]
32. Machida-Sano, I.; Ogawa, S.; Hirakawa, M.; Namiki, H. Evaluation of Three-Dimensional Porous Iron-Cross-Linked Alginate as a Scaffold for Cell Culture. *Int. Sch. Res. Not.* **2014**, *2014*, 375758. [CrossRef]
33. Nemr, O.T.; Abdel-wahab, M.S.; Hamza, Z.S.; Ahmed, S.A.; El-Bassuony, A.A.; Abdel-Gawad, O.F.; Mohamed, H.S. Investigating the Anticancer and Antioxidant Potentials of a Polymer-Grafted Sodium Alginate Composite Embedded with CuO and TiO_2 Nanoparticles. *J. Polym. Environ.* **2024**, *32*, 2713–2728. [CrossRef]
34. Naveed, A.B.; Javaid, A.; Zia, A.; Ishaq, M.T.; Amin, M.; Farooqi, Z.U.R.; Mahmood, A. TiO_2/g-C_3N_4 Binary Composite as an Efficient Photocatalyst for Biodiesel Production from Jatropha Oil and Dye Degradation. *ACS Omega* **2022**, *8*, 2173–2182. [CrossRef]
35. Xue, Y.; Sui, Q.; Brusseau, M.L.; Zhang, X.; Qiu, Z.; Lyu, S. Insight on the Generation of Reactive Oxygen Species in the CaO_2/Fe(II) Fenton System and the Hydroxyl Radical Advancing Strategy. *Chem. Eng. J.* **2018**, *353*, 657–665. [CrossRef]
36. Samoilova, R.I.; Dikanov, S.A. Superoxide Radical Formed on the TiO_2 Surface Produced from $Ti(OiPr)_4$ Exposed to H_2O_2/KOH. *Inorganics* **2023**, *11*, 274. [CrossRef]
37. Li, S.; Zou, J.; Wu, J.; Sun, B.; Zhao, M.; Liu, D.; Cheng, Q.; Tan, H.; Ma, J. New Insights into Natural Polyphenol-Enhanced Fe (III)/Peracetic Acid System under Acidic pH Conditions: The Overlooked Role of Coexisting Hydrogen Peroxide. *Environ. Sci. Technol.* **2025**, *59*, 10608–10619.
38. Bizirtsakis, P.A.; Anagnostopoulou, K.; Sarasidis, V.C.; Petsi, P.; Moschona, A.; Plakas, K.V.; Lambropoulou, D.A. A Comparative Study of Advanced Oxidation Processes for the Removal of the Antibiotic Sulfadoxine from Water—Transformation Products and Toxicity. *Appl. Sci.* **2025**, *15*, 793. [CrossRef]
39. Pedrali, D.; Scarafoni, A.; Giorgi, A.; Lavelli, V. Binary alginate-whey protein hydrogels for antioxidant encapsulation. *Antioxidants* **2023**, *12*, 1192. [CrossRef]
40. Yang, X.; Tao, Y.; Murphy, J.G. Kinetics of the Oxidation of Ammonia and Amines with Hydroxyl Radicals in the Aqueous Phase. *Environ. Sci. Process. Impacts* **2021**, *23*, 1906–1913. [CrossRef]
41. Olson, K.R. Are Reactive Sulfur Species the New Reactive Oxygen Species? *Antioxid. Redox Signal.* **2020**, *33*, 1125–1142.

https://doi.org/10.3390/w18030296

42. Zhan, H.; Liu, X.; Huang, J.; Wang, Y.; Zhou, Y.; Chen, W.; Tang, J. Iron Electrocoagulation Activated Peracetic Acid for Efficient Degradation of Sulfamethoxazole. *Chem. Eng. Res. Des.* **2024**, *201*, 182–194. [CrossRef]
43. Zheng, F.; Cheng, Y.; Dong, H.; Meng, Q.; Cai, J.; Gao, Y.; Zhang, T. Insights into the Novel Oxidation Process of Ozone/Peracetic Acid: Kinetics Evaluation, Degradation Pathways, and Toxicity Assessment. *Chem. Eng. J.* **2023**, *473*, 145964. [CrossRef]
44. Dong, Z.; Li, Z.; Zhang, J.; Sun, Y.; Zhao, S.; Yang, Y.; Wang, L. EDTA-Modified Zero-Valent Iron Activated Peracetic Acid for Sulfamethazine Removal: Performance and Mechanism. *Sep. Purif. Technol.* **2024**, *330*, 125574. [CrossRef]
45. Lu, X.; Chen, Y.; Li, R.; Shao, B.; Zhang, X.; Gao, J.; He, Q. Insight into the Activation of Peracetic Acid by Cobalt-Nitrogen-Doped Porous Carbon for Efficient Norfloxacin Degradation: Performance and Mechanism. *Sep. Purif. Technol.* **2024**, *338*, 126572. [CrossRef]
46. Garrido-Ramírez, E.G.; Theng, B.K.G.; Mora, M.L. Clays and Oxide Minerals as Catalysts and Nanocatalysts in Fenton-like Reactions—A Review. *Appl. Clay Sci.* **2010**, *47*, 182–192. [CrossRef]
47. Das, A.; Sun, Y.; Sarkar, D.J.; Kumar, V.S.; Das, B.K. Biopolymer-Encapsulated Calcium Peroxide Tablets for Slow Sustained Release of Dissolved Oxygen in Fish Tank. *Aquac. Eng.* **2025**, *110*, 102524. [CrossRef]
48. Liu, D.; Straus, D.L.; Pedersen, L.F.; Good, C.; Lazado, C.C.; Meinelt, T. Towards Sustainable Water Disinfection with Peracetic Acid in Aquaculture: A Review. *Rev. Aquac.* **2024**, *16*, 1621–1646. [CrossRef]
49. Lin, Y.L.; Zheng, N.Y.; Chen, Y.S.; Chang, C.C. Electro-Forward Osmosis through a Titanium-Dioxide-Modified Membrane to Enhance Aquaculture Wastewater Recovery. *Desalination* **2024**, *570*, 117078. [CrossRef]

https://doi.org/10.3390/w18030296

water

MDPI

Article

Deep Learning-Based Rolling Forecasting of Dissolved Oxygen in Shandong Peninsula Coastal Waters

Yanjun Wang [1,2,3], Jinming Song [1,2,*], Xuegang Li [1,2] and Guorong Zhong [2]

1 University of Chinese Academy of Sciences, Beijing 100049, China; yjwang@qdio.ac.cn (Y.W.); lixuegang@qdio.ac.cn (X.L.)
2 Key Lab of Marine Ecology & Environment, Institute of Oceanology, Chinese Academy of Sciences, Qingdao 266071, China; zhongguorong@qdio.ac.cn
3 Department of Marine Science Data Center, Institute of Oceanology, Chinese Academy of Sciences, Qingdao 266071, China
* Correspondence: jmsong@qdio.ac.cn

Abstract: Changes in nearshore water quality directly influence ecosystem stability and the sustainability of aquaculture production. Among these factors, rapid fluctuations in dissolved oxygen (DO) can compromise the physiological functions of aquatic organisms, often leading to mass mortality events and significant economic losses. To enhance the predictive capability of DO in marine ranching areas, this study evaluates multiple forecasting approaches, including AutoARIMA, XGBoost, BlockRNN-LSTM, BlockRNN-GRU, TCN, Transformer, and an ensemble model that integrates these methods. Using hourly DO observations from coastal buoys, we performed multi-step rolling forecasts and systematically assessed model performance across multiple evaluation metrics (MAPE, RMSE, and R^2), complemented by residual and error distribution analyses. The results show that the ensemble model, based on deep learning techniques, consistently outperforms individual models, achieving higher forecast robustness and more effective variance control, with MAPE values maintained below 4% across all three buoys. Building upon these findings, we further developed and deployed a DO forecasting and early-warning system centered on the ensemble framework. This system enables end-to-end functionality, including automatic data acquisition, real-time prediction, hypoxia risk identification, and alert dissemination. It has already been applied in marine ranching operations, providing 1–3 day forecasts of DO dynamics, facilitating the early detection of hypoxia risks, and significantly improving the scientific support and responsiveness of aquaculture management.

Keywords: dissolved oxygen; coastal waters; deep learning; rolling forecasting; time series modeling; marine ranching

1. Introduction

Dissolved oxygen is a fundamental indicator of water quality and ecosystem stability. In nearshore marine ranching areas, abrupt declines in DO can induce stress responses in fish and shellfish, suppress feeding and growth, and even cause large-scale asphyxiation and mortality, leading to severe ecological and economic losses [1]. In recent years, DO levels in nearshore waters have exhibited a general declining trend, with hypoxic events occurring more frequently and posing direct threats to both ecosystems and cultured organisms. Strengthening the rapid and accurate forecasting of DO in marine ranching areas is therefore essential for the timely detection of potential hypoxia risks and the development of effective management strategies [2–4].

For the prediction and early warning of DO in nearshore aquaculture areas, early research primarily relied on physical models and statistical approaches, such as multiple linear regression (MLR), Autoregressive Integrated Moving Average (ARIMA), and Automatic Autoregressive Integrated Moving Average (AutoARIMA) [5,6], Although these methods are simple in structure and easy to interpret, they are limited in their ability to capture the nonlinear dynamics of DO. In recent years, researchers have increasingly applied machine learning approaches, such as support vector machines (SVM) [7], random forests (RF) [8], and extreme gradient boosting (XGBoost) [9], which have significantly improved the accuracy of single-step predictions. Some studies have further incorporated feature selection methods to enhance modeling efficiency [10].

To further enhance predictive performance, neural network-based deep learning methods have been extensively applied in DO forecasting, including multilayer perceptrons (MLP) [11], generalized regression neural networks (GRNN) [12], temporal models such as long short-term memory (LSTM) and gated recurrent units (GRU) [13,14], convolutional neural networks (CNN) [15], hybrid CNN-LSTM models [16], and, more recently, Transformer architectures [17]. Owing to their strong nonlinear representation and temporal memory capabilities, these models are particularly well suited to capturing the complex relationships between DO and factors such as temperature, salinity, and chlorophyll. They have already demonstrated promising results in DO prediction across diverse environments, including rivers, lakes, bays, and estuaries [18–21].

Several early-warning systems for dissolved oxygen (DO) monitoring have been developed in recent years. For instance, Xue et al. [22] designed a real-time DO prediction and warning system for carp aquaculture using neural-network and decision-tree models, enabling 10–60 min forecasts. Fakhrudin et al. [23] established an online stratification-based early-warning platform for Lake Maninjau, Indonesia, which continuously monitors temperature and DO profiles and issues SMS alerts before mass fish mortality events. More recently, Shaghaghi et al. [24] developed *DOxy*, an IoT- and machine-learning-based low-cost DO monitoring device capable of real-time sensing and threshold-based alerting, although it does not perform time-series forecasting. Anupama et al. [25] further combined random forest prediction with IoT sensors for river ecosystem management to enhance DO prediction accuracy. These studies provide valuable references for DO monitoring and risk management.

Although substantial progress has been made in DO prediction modeling, several key limitations remain. First, most existing studies rely on single models whose predictive accuracy is inherently limited when applied to complex and highly variable marine environments. Second, the capability for multi-step forecasting remains insufficient. Many models can only predict the next time point, offering very limited lead time for management actions. In real-world marine environmental regulation and aquaculture operations, it is crucial to forecast several hours or even days ahead to allow timely adjustment, water quality intervention, and disaster prevention. Third, although recent studies have begun to explore early-warning frameworks for hypoxia and water quality monitoring, most approaches remain model-centric, emphasizing prediction accuracy over the automated integration of real-time observations and early-warning mechanisms. With the growing availability of high-frequency buoy data, developing intelligent systems that combine real-time forecasting with dynamic alert generation has become increasingly important for effective marine environmental management.

To overcome these limitations, this study developed a multi-step DO forecasting framework based on nearshore buoy observations in the Shandong Peninsula. Unlike conventional single-model approaches, the proposed framework integrates multiple deep learning architectures within a unified structure to enhance predictive stability and accuracy in complex coastal environments. The model enables reliable 1–3 day DO forecasts, effectively addressing the limited lead time of traditional one-step prediction models. Furthermore, the optimized forecasting model was embedded into a near-real-time early-warning system, enabling automatic assimilation of buoy observations and dynamic alerts for potential hypoxia events, thereby providing proactive technical support for ecological protection and marine ranching management.

To provide a clear overview of the study design, Figure 1 presents the overall workflow of this research, including data acquisition, data preprocessing, model construction, forecasting, performance evaluation, and system construction.

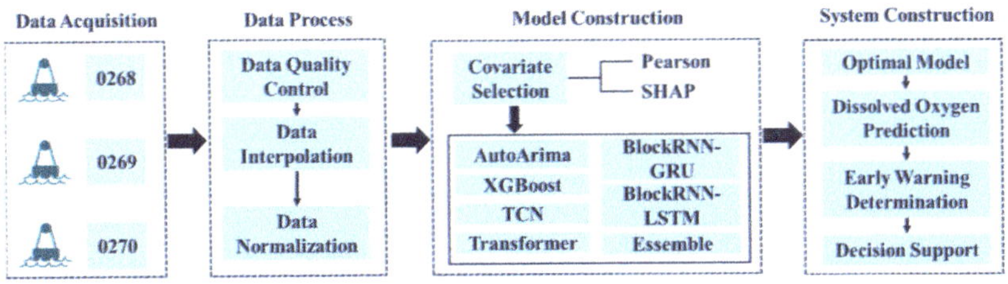

Figure 1. Overall workflow and framework of the dissolved oxygen forecasting study.

2. Dataset Description and Preprocessing

2.1. Data Source

The marine environmental monitoring data used in this study were obtained from three coastal sites in the Shandong Peninsula, China—Laizhou Bay, Changdao, and Sanggou Bay—where buoys 0268, 0269, and 0270 were deployed, respectively. The geographical locations of these sites are shown in Figure 2, and the observed parameters, sampling frequency, observation depth, and regional information are summarized in Table 1. Due to deployment schedules and intermittent maintenance, the data coverage periods differed across buoys: buoy 0268 provided valid records from 10 November 2024 to 17 April 2025, buoy 0269 from 5 September 2024 to 12 May 2025, and buoy 0270 from 4 September 2024 to 30 April 2025.

Table 1. Observation parameters, sampling frequency, and depth of each buoy.

Buoy ID	Area	Parameter	Unit	Frequency (min)	Depth (m)
0268	Laizhou Bay	Sea Temperature	°C	15	−3, −6
		DO	μmol/kg	30	−1
		Salinity	‰	15	−3, −6
		NN	mg/L	60	−1
		DOC	μmol/kg	60	−1
		Turbidity	NTU	30	−1
		Chl-a	RFU	30	−1
		CV	m/s	15	−2, −4, −6
		AP	hPa	15	2
		WS	m/s	15	2
		WH	m	15	−1

Note(s): DO—Dissolved Oxygen; Chl-a—Chlorophyll-a; DOC—Dissolved Organic Carbon; NN—Nitrate Nitrogen; CV—Current Velocity; AP—Air Pressure; WS—Wind Speed; WH—Wave Height.

Measurement depth: Positive values indicate sensor height *above* the sea surface (e.g., AP, WS), and negative values indicate depth *below* the sea surface (e.g., DO, CV, Chl-a).

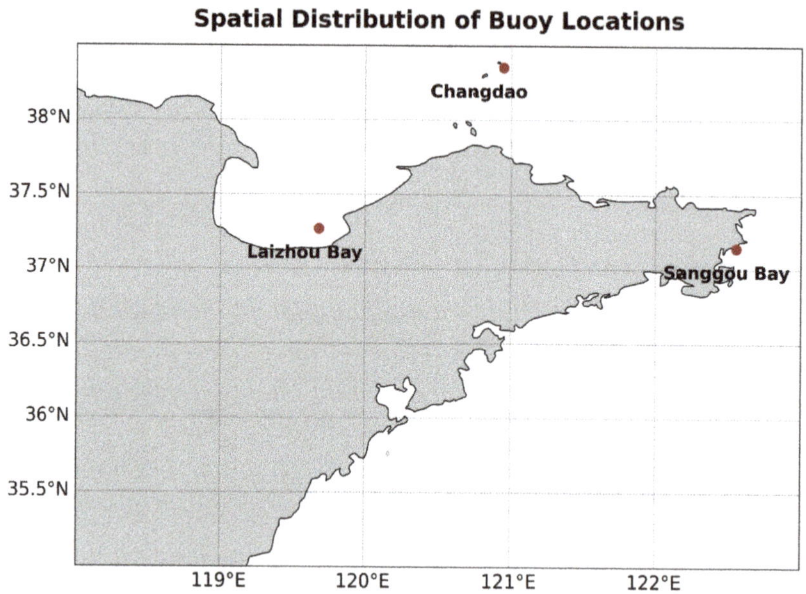

Figure 2. Spatial distribution of buoy locations.

2.2. Data Quality Control and Preprocessing

Prior to model training, the observational data from the three buoys were subjected to preprocessing and quality control to ensure the accuracy and physical consistency of the model inputs, thereby reducing the impact of sensor errors and anomalous fluctuations on the predictions.

2.2.1. Quality Control of Buoy Data

Since raw monitoring data often contain missing values, outliers, or sensor drift, directly using them for model training and prediction may impede model convergence and generalization, or even introduce significant biases. To address this, we designed a two-step quality control (QC) strategy: threshold-based QC and spike detection QC. In the threshold-based step, reasonable ranges were defined according to typical nearshore conditions (e.g., temperature 0–35 °C, salinity 15–40 PSU, dissolved oxygen 150–500 μmol/kg, chlorophyll 0–100 μg/L, nitrate nitrogen 0–5 mg/L, DOC 0–20 mg/L, current velocity 0–3 m/s, air pressure 950–1100 hPa, wind speed 0–25 m/s, wave height 0–5 m), thereby removing values that were clearly unrealistic or affected by sensor noise. On this basis, a spike detection method based on the 3σ (three-sigma) principle was applied [26], which identifies local anomalies by considering the differences between each observation and its neighboring values. The local rate of change is defined as:

$$\Delta t = max(\mid x_t - x_{t-1} \mid, \mid x_t - x_{t+1} \mid) \quad (1)$$

Here, $\mid x_t - x_{t-1} \mid$ and $\mid x_t - x_{t+1} \mid$ represent the differences between the current observation and its preceding and succeeding values, respectively. To establish the threshold for spike detection, this study defined it based on the statistical characteristics of the differenced series:

$$\theta = \mu_d + k \times \sigma_d \quad (2)$$

Here, μ_d and σ_d denote the mean and standard deviation of the differenced series, respectively, and k is an empirical coefficient (set to 3 in this study). When $\Delta_t > \theta$, the point is identified as a spike anomaly and removed. The quality-controlled data from each buoy are shown in Figure 3.

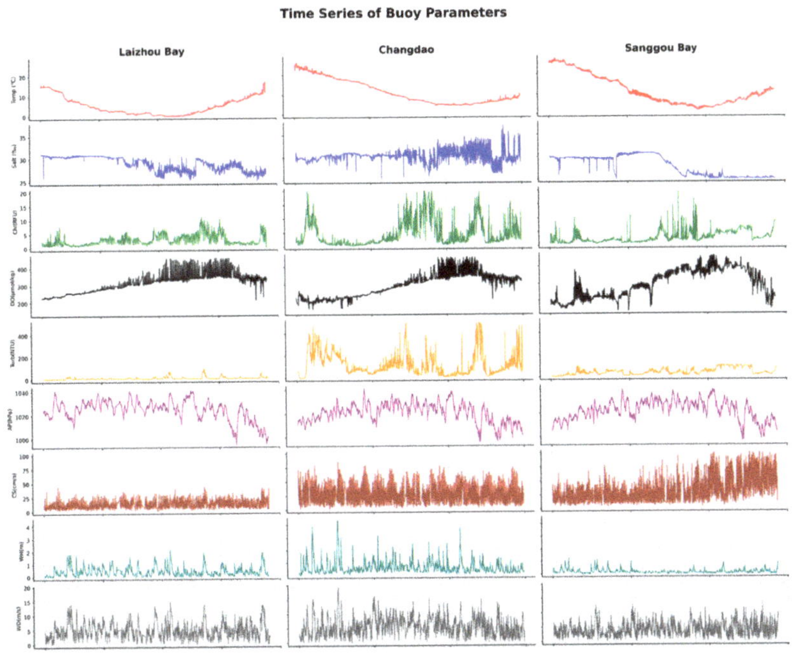

Figure 3. Time series of key environmental parameters at each buoy station after quality control Colored lines represent different variables: red line for temperature, blue line for salinity, green line for chlorophyll, black line for dissolved oxygen, yellow line for turbidity, purple line for air pressure, dark red line for current velocity, cyan-green line for wave height, and gray line for wind speed.

2.2.2. Data Preprocessing of Buoy Data

To ensure continuity in deep learning model predictions, missing values in the monitoring data were filled using linear interpolation for the target variable (dissolved oxygen) and its main covariates (temperature, salinity, and chlorophyll). This procedure removed temporal discontinuities caused by data gaps, thereby ensuring that the models received complete and continuous input sequences during training and forecasting. Furthermore, to harmonize the temporal resolution of different buoys and parameters and to facilitate subsequent sliding-window sample construction, all variables were resampled at 1 h intervals.

Since the parameters differ substantially in magnitude and units (e.g., temperature: 0–30 °C, salinity: 25–35, chlorophyll: 0–10 μg/L), directly feeding them into a neural network may lead to imbalanced gradient updates and hinder model convergence. To mitigate the effects of differing scales and value ranges, and to enhance the numerical stability and convergence speed of neural network training, this study applied min–max normalization to linearly rescale all variables into the [0, 1] range. The standard formula is:

$$X\prime = \frac{X - X_{min}}{X_{max} - X_{min}} \tag{3}$$

Here, X denotes the original variable value, X' represents the normalized value within the range [0, 1], and X_{min} and X_{max} are the minimum and maximum values of the variable in the training samples, respectively.

For sample partitioning, the data from each buoy were divided strictly in chronological order, with the first 70% used as the training set for parameter fitting and feature learning, and the remaining 30% reserved as the test set for validating rolling multi-step forecasts. During model training, a sliding-window strategy was employed to generate multi-step forecasting samples (Figure 4). Specifically, consecutive historical observations were segmented into fixed-length input windows, which were paired with the corresponding DO values over a future horizon to construct a large number of input–output pairs for model learning. This approach not only effectively captures the temporal dynamics of DO driven by multiple variables (e.g., temperature, salinity, chlorophyll), but also systematically augments the training dataset and enhances the model's generalization capability across different temporal patterns.

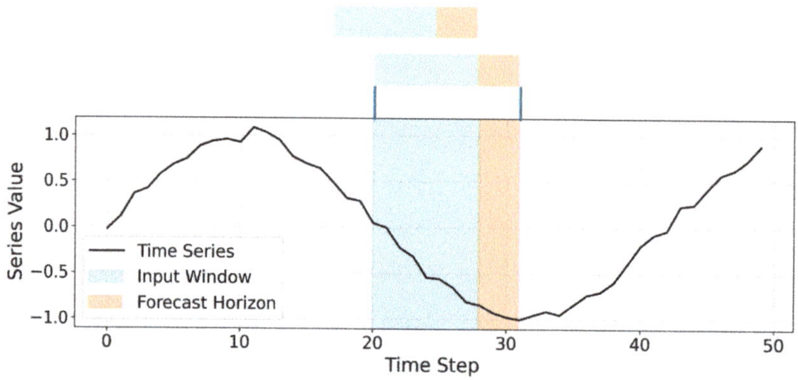

Figure 4. Illustration of the Sliding Window Strategy.

In the testing phase, rolling forecasts were conducted on the reserved test sequences, simulating real-world applications in which future predictions are continuously generated from observed historical data. This design enabled a comprehensive evaluation of model stability and generalization performance across different forecasting horizons.

3. Model Construction

3.1. Covariate Selection for DO Forecasting

A comparative analysis of the Pearson correlation coefficients and the Shapley Additive Explanations (SHAP) results based on the Random Forest (RF) model for buoys 0268, 0269, and 0270 (Figures 5–7) indicates that temperature consistently acts as the dominant controlling factor of DO. Across all three sites, temperature showed a strong negative correlation with DO (Pearson coefficients of approximately −0.8 to −0.9, with Spearman and MI indices showing similar patterns), confirming the robustness of this regulatory effect across regions. SHAP analysis further supported this finding, as multiple lagged temperature features (e.g., tempt-25, tempt-45) consistently ranked among the most influential predictors. These results demonstrate that temperature variations not only directly affect DO but also impose significant lagged effects, consistent with the physical mechanism by which elevated water temperature reduces oxygen solubility and gradually leads to DO depletion over time.

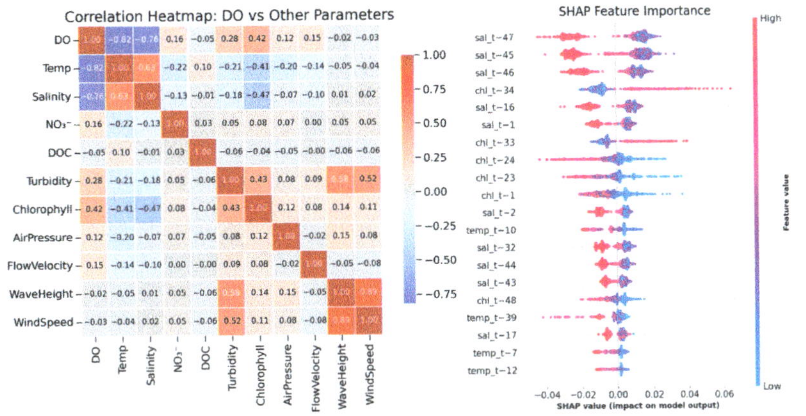

Figure 5. Multivariate Correlation and SHAP Analysis—Buoy 0268.

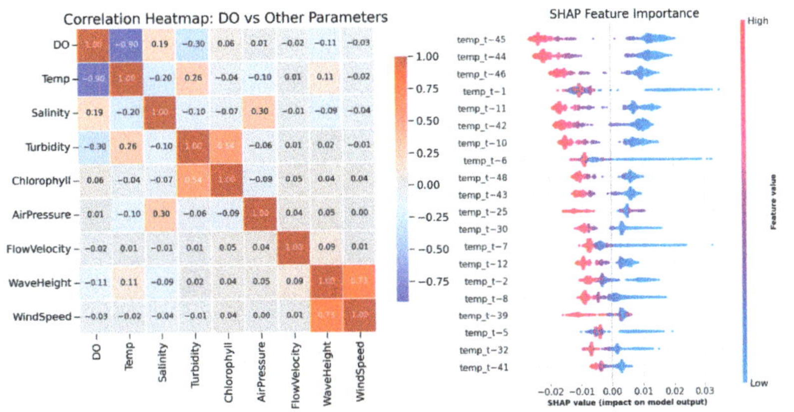

Figure 6. Multivariate Correlation and SHAP Analysis—Buoy 0269.

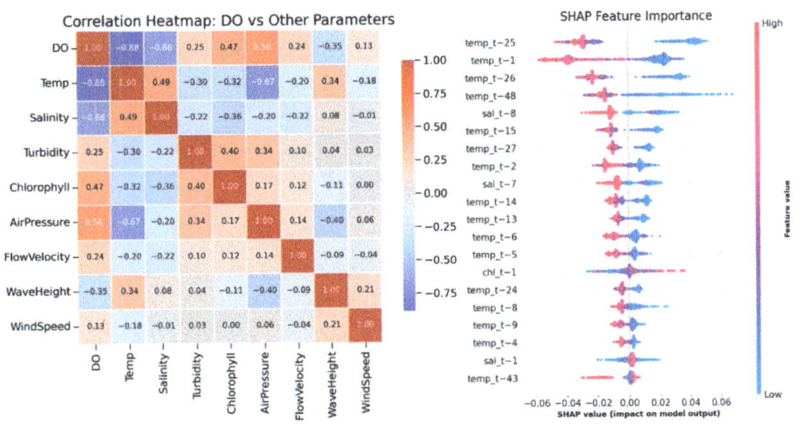

Figure 7. Multivariate Correlation and SHAP Analysis—Buoy 0270.

Salinity exhibited more heterogeneous effects across the three buoys. At buoys 0268 and 0270, salinity was moderately to strongly negatively correlated with DO (Pearson coefficients ranging from −0.66 to −0.76), with several lagged features contributing substantially in the SHAP analysis. This indicates that salinity variations in these regions play a non-negligible role in regulating DO, likely through indirect mechanisms associated with water mass exchange or mixing processes. By contrast, at buoy 0269, although salinity showed some statistical correlation with DO, its contribution to model predictions was negligible. This suggests that in this region, salinity may primarily represent long-term background variability rather than short-term dynamics.

Chlorophyll primarily reflected signals associated with biological processes. At buoys 0268 and 0270, chlorophyll exhibited a moderate positive correlation with DO (Pearson ≈ 0.4–0.5) and frequently appeared in the SHAP analysis as short-lag features (e.g., chl_{t-1}). This suggests that algal photosynthesis contributed to elevated DO concentrations, with effects typically manifested on short timescales. In contrast, at buoy 0269, chlorophyll displayed weak correlations and minimal predictive importance, likely due to stronger water exchange in this region, which may obscure biological signals.

Other environmental factors, including wind speed, current velocity, wave height, and air pressure, exhibited weak correlations with DO across all three buoys and contributed minimally in the SHAP analysis. This suggests that their direct influence on short-term DO variability is limited and may only become significant through indirect mechanisms or under extreme conditions.

Overall, the results demonstrate that temperature, salinity, and chlorophyll are the principal environmental drivers of DO variability in nearshore waters. Among them, temperature consistently showed strong dominance and pronounced lagged effects across all sites, making it the most stable controlling factor; salinity exerted a significant regulatory influence in certain regions, largely associated with hydrodynamic processes; and chlorophyll captured biological response signals on short timescales. Collectively, these physical (temperature, salinity) and biological (chlorophyll) drivers represent the primary mechanisms governing DO variability and were therefore identified as the key input factors for subsequent modeling.

3.2. Forecasting Model Architectures

In this study, seven representative time-series forecasting models were employed to perform 24-step multi-horizon predictions of surface DO concentrations based on buoy observations, and their performances were systematically compared. These models were selected to represent three major categories of forecasting approaches. The AutoARIMA model served as a classical statistical baseline for capturing linear temporal dependencies. XGBoost represented a machine-learning regression method capable of modeling nonlinear relationships between DO and environmental factors. The deep-learning architectures—BlockRNN-LSTM, BlockRNN-GRU, Temporal Convolutional Network (TCN), and Transformer—were employed to learn complex temporal dynamics through recurrent, convolutional, and attention mechanisms. Furthermore, a deep-learning ensemble model was developed by integrating the predictions of the four deep architectures to combine their complementary strengths and reduce the bias and variance inherent in individual models. The core structures and key hyperparameters of all models are summarized in Table 2. Detailed explanations of the key hyperparameters listed in Table 2 are provided in Table S1.

Among the deep learning models, TCN and Transformer are particularly representative. The former leverages dilated convolutions and residual structures to efficiently capture local and multi-scale temporal features, while the latter exploits self-attention mechanisms to model global dependencies and flexibly handle multivariate inputs. These two approaches thus represent two cutting-edge paradigms: "convolution-based local pattern modeling" and "attention-based global dependency modeling." To illustrate their modeling logic, schematic diagrams of the two network structures are provided in Figures 8 and 9. Detailed descriptions of the deep learning architectures (BlockRNN–LSTM, BlockRNN–GRU, and TCN) are provided in the Appendix A.

Table 2. Summary of the seven predictive models with core structures and key hyperparameters.

Model Category	Model Name	Core Structural Characteristics	Key Hyperparameters
Statistical	AutoARIMA	ARIMA with automatic order/seasonality selection	P = 5, q = 5, P = 2, Q = 2, m = 24, d = 1, D = 1
Machine Learning	XGBoost	Gradient-boosted decision trees	n_estimators = 100, max_depth = 6, learning_rate = 0.3, subsample = 0.8, colsample_bytree = 0.8, min_child_weight = 5
Deep Learning	BlockRNN-LSTM	Recurrent network with LSTM blocks (block-wise sequence modeling)	input_length = 144, output_length = 24, hidden_size = 32, n_layers = 3, dropout = 0.2, batch_size = 16
Deep Learning	BlockRNN-GRU	Recurrent network with GRU blocks (block-wise sequence modeling)	input_length = 144, output_length = 24, hidden_size = 64, n_layers = 2, dropout = 0.2, batch_size = 16
Deep Learning	TCN	Dilated causal 1D convolutions with residual/skip connections	input_length = 144, output_length = 24, kernel_size = 5, num_filters = 5, dilation = 2, dropout = 0.1
Deep Learning	Transformer	Self-attention encoder–decoder with causal masking	input_length = 96, output_length = 24, d_model = 16, n_heads = 4, n_layers = 2, ff_dim = 64, dropout = 0.1, batch_size = 16
Deep Learning	Ensemble (LSTM + GRU + TCN + Transformer)	Fusion of four deep nets (weighted averaging/stacking)	models = [GRUmodel, LSTMmodel, TCNmodel, Transmodel], fusion_strategy = NaiveEnsembleModel, weights = [0.25,0.25,0.25,0.25]

To enhance forecasting stability and accuracy, a deep-learning ensemble model was developed by integrating the predictions of four independently trained architectures: BlockRNN-LSTM, BlockRNN-GRU, TCN, and Transformer. These models capture complementary temporal characteristics—recurrent architectures (LSTM and GRU) are effective in modeling short- and medium-term dependencies, while convolutional (TCN) and attention-based (Transformer) networks better represent long-range temporal patterns. After individual training with optimized hyperparameters, their 24-step forecasts were aggregated using an equal-weight averaging scheme, which effectively reduces the bias and variance of individual models and enhances the robustness of multi-step dissolved oxygen forecasting under dynamic marine conditions.

Each model was trained and evaluated using hourly buoy observations. The input variables included DO, temperature, salinity, and chlorophyll. Among them, the AutoARIMA model performed univariate forecasting using only the DO time series (seasonal period m = 24), while all other models (XGBoost, BlockRNN-LSTM, BlockRNN-GRU, TCN, Transformer, and the ensemble) adopted a multivariate framework that combined DO with environmental covariates as inputs. The details are summarized in Table 3.

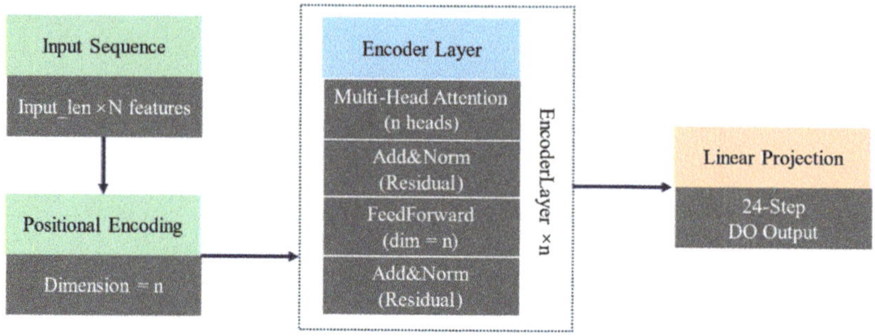

Figure 8. Schematic diagram of the Transformer model architecture.

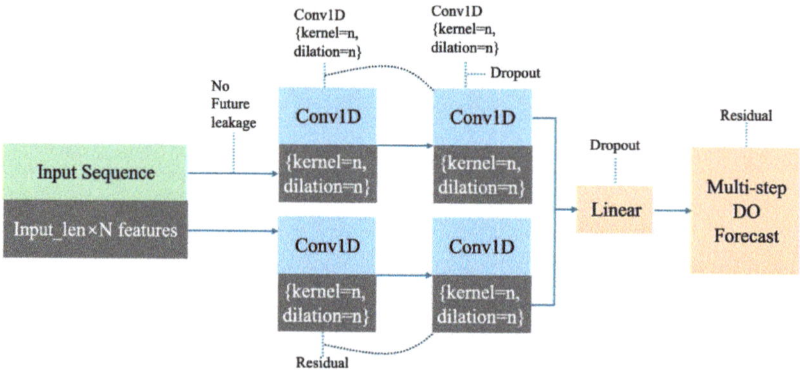

Figure 9. Schematic diagram of the TCN model architecture.

Table 3. Input variables and lag configurations used in the forecasting models.

Model	Target Variable	Input Variables	Lag Range (hours)
AutoARIMA	DO	Time, DO	t-1~t-24
XGBoost	DO	Time, DO, Temp, Sal, Chl	t-1~t-72
BlockRNN-LSTM	DO	Time, DO, Temp, Sal, Chl	t-1~t-144
BlockRNN-GRU	DO	Time, DO, Temp, Sal, Chl	t-1~t-144
TCN	DO	Time, DO, Temp, Sal, Chl	t-1~t-144
Transformer	DO	Time, DO, Temp, Sal, Chl	t-1~t-144
EnsembleModel	DO	Time, DO, Temp, Sal, Chl	t-1~t-144

To ensure a fair comparison, all models were optimized and tested within a unified sliding-window backtesting framework. For XGBoost, key hyperparameters (n_estimators, max_depth, learning_rate) were tuned using the Optuna Bayesian optimization algorithm, which adaptively searches the parameter space based on previous evaluation results to efficiently find the best configuration. For the deep-learning models, major hyperparameters such as input_chunk_length, hidden_dim, batch_size, dropout, and n_epochs were optimized through grid search, a systematic trial of predefined parameter combinations to identify the one yielding the lowest validation error.

4. Results

We compared the forecasting accuracy of each model at the three nearshore buoy stations (0268, 0269, and 0270), with the results summarized in Table 3. The evaluation metrics included Mean Absolute Percentage Error (MAPE), Root Mean Squared Error (RMSE), and the coefficient of determination (R^2), defined as follows:

$$\mathrm{MAPE} = \frac{100\%}{n}\sum_{t=1}^{n}\left|\frac{y_t - \hat{y}_t}{y_t}\right| \tag{4}$$

$$\mathrm{RMSE} = \sqrt{\frac{1}{n}\sum_{t=1}^{n}(y_t - \hat{y}_t)^2} \tag{5}$$

$$\mathrm{R}^2 = 1 - \frac{\sum_{t=1}^{n}(y_t - \hat{y}_t)^2}{\sum_{t=1}^{n}(y_t - \overline{y})^2} \tag{6}$$

Here, y_t denotes the observed value, $\hat{y}_t$ the predicted value, $\overline{y}$ the mean of observations, and n the sample size. MAPE reflects the relative error level of the model, RMSE measures the absolute magnitude of prediction bias, and R^2 characterizes the model's ability to explain the variance in the observations.

As shown in Table 4, the deep learning models (Transformer, LSTM, GRU, TCN) consistently outperformed both the statistical model (AutoARIMA) and the machine learning model (XGBoost). AutoARIMA exhibited persistently larger errors across stations (higher RMSE and lower R^2), highlighting its limited capacity to capture the nonlinear dynamics of DO. By contrast, the deep learning models demonstrated stronger temporal modeling and fitting capabilities at all three sites. Overall, the ensemble forecasting model (Ensemble) achieved the highest predictive accuracy across stations, effectively improving accuracy while mitigating the instability observed in individual models.

Table 4. Comparison of rolling prediction errors for different models at multiple sites.

Buoy ID	Model	Train			Test		
		Mape	RMSE (μmol/kg)	R^2	Mape	RMSE (μmol/kg)	R^2
0268	AutoArima	0.97%	6.171	0.98	6.02%	27.89	0.39
	XGBoost	2.21%	12.76	0.93	5.43%	28.05	0.39
	LSTM	1.37%	6.64	0.96	3.1%	16.28	0.79
	GRU	1.47%	5.97	0.97	3.09%	15.97	0.8
	Transformer	2.40%	10.66	0.95	2.53%	12.33	0.88
	TCN	1.4%	6.28	0.98	2.59%	13.59	0.86
	Essemble	1.01%	5.02	0.98	2.11%	11.01	0.9
0269	AutoArima	1.22%	5.66	0.98	5.48%	26.57	0.36
	XGBoost	3.34%	13.82	0.94	4.45%	21.88	0.57
	LSTM	2.71%	10.22	0.97	3.15%	14.87	0.8
	GRU	2.57	9.55	0.97	2.85%	13.44	0.83
	Transformer	2.86%	11.06	0.96	2.32%	10.83	0.89
	TCN	1.96%	7.49	0.98	3.03%	14.61	0.8
	Essemble	1.52%	5.81	0.98	2.06%	10.23	0.91
0270	AutoArima	2.06%	8.28	0.98	5.59%	23.11	0.89
	XGBoost	5.01%	19.89	0.93	6.65%	27.65	0.84
	LSTM	3.52%	12.89	0.97	4.35%	18.6	0.93
	GRU	3.64%	13.19	0.97	4.22%	17.9	0.93
	Transformer	4.74%	17.13	0.94	4.7%	19.9	0.92
	TCN	2.55%	9.55	0.98	4.14%	17.37	0.94
	Essemble	1.79%	6.48	0.98	3.7%	15.84	0.95

To further examine whether the forecasting errors of different models were statistically different, a non-parametric Friedman test was applied to the absolute residuals derived from the rolling 24 h-ahead predictions on the test datasets for the three buoy stations (0268, 0269, and 0270). The Friedman test compares multiple related samples by ranking their errors and yields a chi-square (χ^2) statistic and a corresponding p-value to assess the overall significance. The results revealed significant differences among models at all stations (χ^2 = 578.99–1745.71, $p < 0.001$), indicating that the forecasting errors were not drawn from the same distribution. Subsequently, pairwise Wilcoxon signed-rank tests with Holm correction for multiple comparisons were conducted to identify which models exhibited significantly lower forecasting errors. The post hoc analysis showed that the deep learning-based models (Transformer, TCN, BlockRNN-GRU, and BlockRNN-LSTM) and the ensemble model achieved significantly smaller errors than the traditional statistical (AutoARIMA) and machine-learning (XGBoost) models across all stations (adjusted $p < 0.05$).

In addition, the time series plots of observed and predicted dissolved oxygen for all buoys and models on the testing dataset are presented in Figure 10. These visual comparisons further confirm the quantitative findings in Table 4, showing that the deep learning and ensemble models closely follow the temporal variations of measured DO, whereas the statistical and traditional machine learning models exhibit noticeable deviations during abrupt changes.

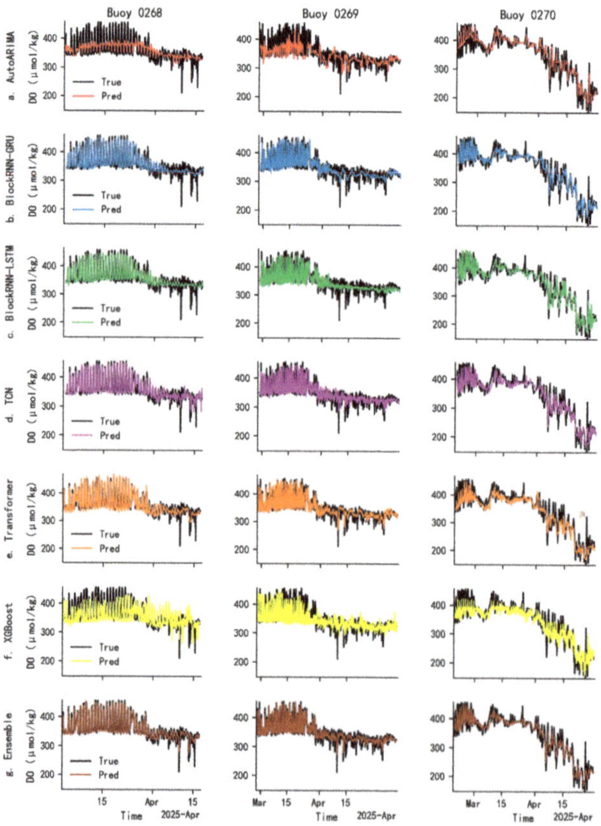

Figure 10. Time series comparison between observed and predicted dissolved oxygen concentrations on the testing dataset at all buoy stations using different models: (a) AutoARIMA, (b) BlockRNN-GRU, (c) BlockRNN-LSTM, (d) TCN, (e) Transformer, (f) XGBoost, and (g) Ensemble.

5. Discussion

5.1. Model Residual Analysis

Figure 11 shows the residual distributions of different models at the three buoy stations. Overall, the ensemble forecasting model exhibited the most stable residual characteristics across all sites, with a median close to zero and the smallest dispersion, indicating strong robustness and unbiased performance. The deep learning models outperformed the statistical and machine learning methods, displaying smaller residual magnitudes and more concentrated distributions. By contrast, AutoARIMA and XGBoost exhibited wider residual fluctuations and more extreme values, highlighting their limited stability in prediction.

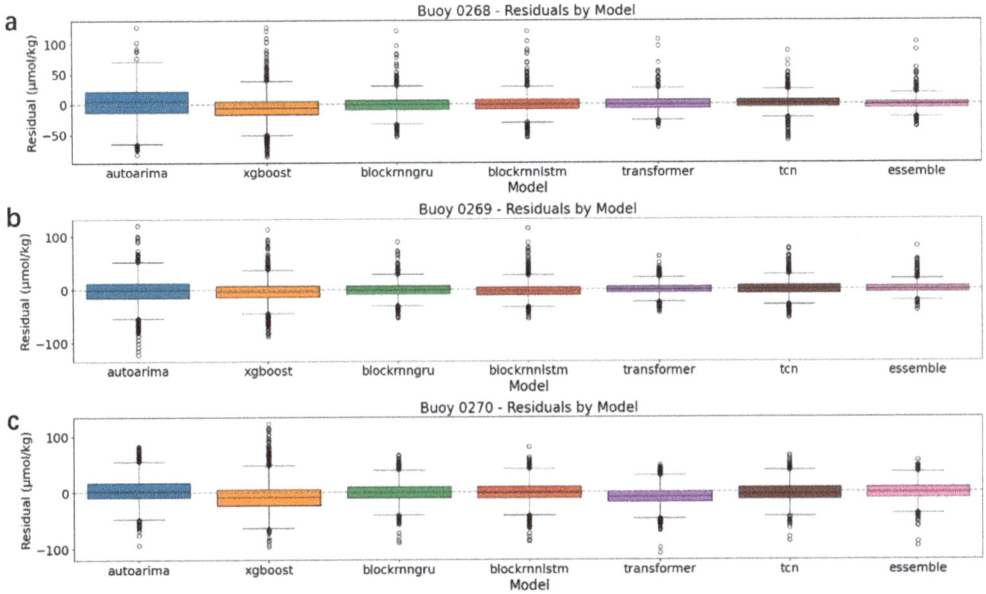

Figure 11. Residual distributions of seven models at three buoy stations: (**a**) Buoy 0268, (**b**) Buoy 0269, and (**c**) Buoy 0270. Boxplots display the median (center line), interquartile range (box), and extreme values (whiskers and outliers).

5.2. Evaluation of Ensemble Forecasting Models

To further evaluate the performance of the ensemble forecasting model in multi-site DO prediction, Figure 12 presents its results at three representative buoys (0268, 0269, and 0270). For each buoy, the left panel displays a time-series comparison between observed and predicted DO values, while the right panel shows the histogram of prediction residuals (observation minus prediction). The time-series results demonstrate that the ensemble model accurately reproduces DO variation patterns at all three sites, effectively capturing both diurnal oscillations and abrupt changes. The residual distributions further reveal that prediction errors are largely concentrated within −20 to +20 μmol/kg, approximately following a normal distribution with mean values close to zero. This indicates that the model predictions are essentially unbiased and highly stable. Notably, despite the distinct geographical settings of the three buoys, the model consistently delivered stable and accurate forecasts across these spatially heterogeneous regions, highlighting its strong robustness.

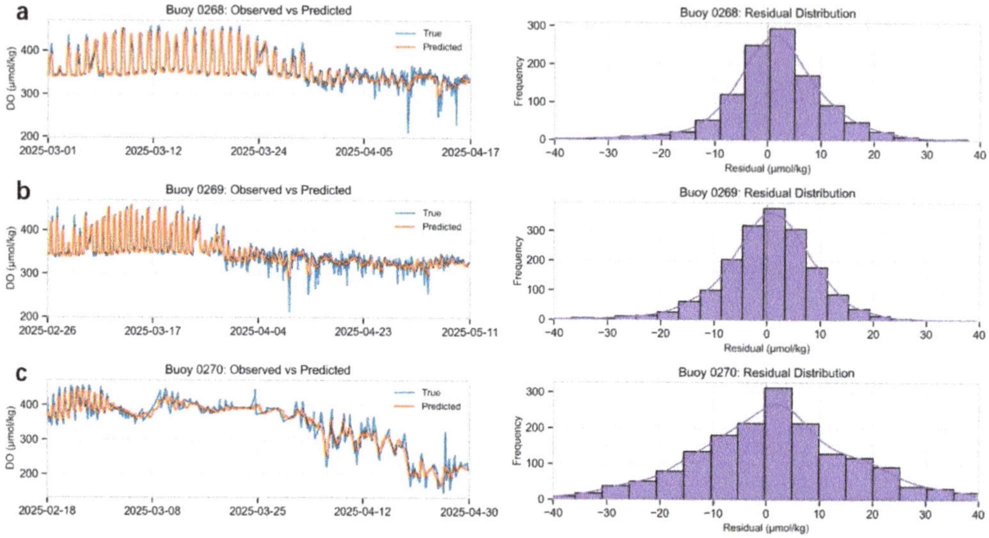

Figure 12. Ensemble model results at three buoy stations: (**a**) Forecast curves and residual distributions for Buoy 0268, (**b**) Buoy 0269, and (**c**) Buoy 0270.

Furthermore, the predictive uncertainty of the ensemble model was evaluated by calculating the standard deviation among the predicted values of its four submodels (GRU, LSTM, TCN, and Transformer) at each time step during the testing period, reflecting the inter-model spread rather than the residual variance. The mean inter-model standard deviations were 5.912 μmol/kg, 6.182 μmol/kg, and 7.536 μmol/kg for buoys 0268, 0269, and 0270, respectively, indicating generally low uncertainty and high stability of the ensemble forecasts across different sites.

Within the rolling forecasting framework, we evaluated the ensemble forecasting model using prediction horizons of 24, 48, and 72 h (Table 5). The results show that the error levels under the three strategies are generally comparable and increase only slightly with longer horizons. R^2 remained stable across different horizons and stations, showing only minor declines as the forecast lengthened. This indicates that the model maintains stable and reproducible error characteristics within the 1–3 day forecasting range.

Table 5. Ensemble Model Error Across Forecast Horizons and Buoys (24/48/72 h).

Buoy ID	Forecast Horizon	MAPE	RMSE (μmol/kg)	R^2
0268	24	2.11%	11.01	0.9
	48	2.43%	12.9	0.87
	72	2.83%	13.96	0.84
0269	24	2.06%	10.23	0.91
	48	2.47%	11.91	0.87
	72	2.71%	12.94	0.84
0270	24	3.7%	15.84	0.95
	48	3.85%	16.01	0.94
	72	4.17%	17.2	0.93

5.3. Comparison of Model Accuracy and Computational Efficiency for Each Buoy

For comparison, the statistical model (AutoARIMA) was executed on a CPU, while all other models were trained and tested on an NVIDIA RTX 4070Ti GPU. Figure 13 compares the three buoys in terms of forecasting accuracy (SMAPE, %) and computational cost (seconds). The results show that the ensemble forecasting model achieved the lowest SMAPE (approximately 2–3%) across all stations, underscoring its clear advantage in accuracy, albeit with higher computational demand. This makes it more suitable for accuracy-oriented applications, such as environmental monitoring and hypoxia risk early warning in nearshore marine ranching. In contrast, AutoARIMA was both less accurate (SMAPE ≈ 5–6%) and relatively time-consuming, providing limited practical benefits. XGBoost, also CPU-based, offered faster computation but produced larger errors (SMAPE ≈ 5–6.5%), suggesting its value primarily as a rapid baseline. By comparison, the deep learning models executed on a GPU outperformed the traditional approaches overall. Among them, TCN stood out by maintaining relatively low SMAPE while achieving the shortest computation time, demonstrating excellent timeliness and making it particularly suitable for applications with stringent real-time requirements, such as factory-based recirculating aquaculture systems requiring immediate regulation.

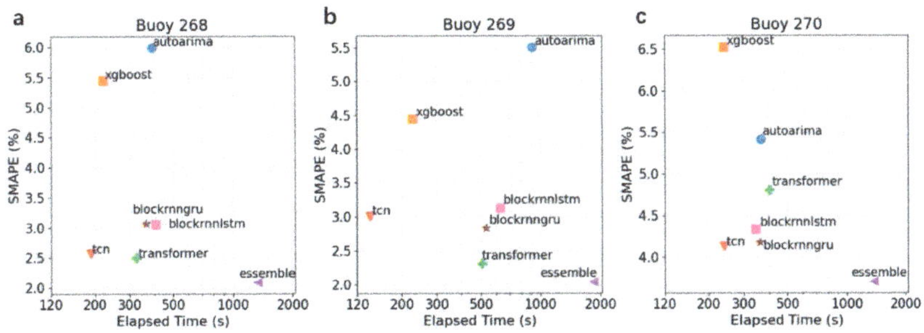

Figure 13. Trade-off between prediction accuracy and computational efficiency for seven models at three buoy stations: (**a**) Buoy 0268, (**b**) Buoy 0269, and (**c**) Buoy 0270. The x-axis denotes the elapsed training and forecasting time (s), while the y-axis shows the Symmetric Mean Absolute Percentage Error (SMAPE, %).

5.4. Low-Oxygen Early-Warning System for Marine Ranching

Traditional environmental early-warning systems for marine ranching have mostly relied on numerical models to simulate hydrodynamic and ecological processes in order to anticipate potential hypoxia events. However, numerical models are often constrained by long computation cycles, complex deployment and maintenance, and limited capacity for real-time applications, which restrict their widespread use in nearshore aquaculture zones—particularly when responding to sudden hypoxic events.

To address these limitations, this study developed a hypoxia early-warning system tailored for marine ranching, based on buoy observations deployed in aquaculture waters. The system uses the Ensemble Regression model—identified in this study as the best-performing predictor—as its core, with key environmental factors such as temperature, salinity, and chlorophyll as input variables, to generate hourly forecasts of DO concentration up to 72 h in advance. Model execution supports GPU acceleration, ensuring high prediction accuracy while significantly reducing computational costs.

For effective early warning, two fixed ecological thresholds were incorporated into the system:

(1) Ecological warning line (5 mg/L or 152 μmol/kg): Indicates the onset of mild hypoxia, where sensitive organisms may exhibit stress responses such as reduced feeding

and metabolic activity. Enhanced monitoring and moderate adjustments in farming operations are recommended.

(2) Hypoxia alert line (3 mg/L or 93 μmol/kg): Represents severe hypoxia levels, posing significant survival risks to cultured organisms. Immediate emergency interventions, such as oxygenation or water exchange, are advised.

By applying these thresholds, the system automatically evaluates 72 h DO forecasts and cross-references predicted values below the alert line against an expert knowledge base to generate decision-support recommendations. The operational performance of the early-warning module was also examined. No false negatives were observed during the monitoring period, and a few false positives were mainly attributed to sensor drift or fouling, which caused abnormally low DO readings and led the model to generate underestimated forecasts. Figure 14 provides a schematic illustration of the decision-support early-warning system developed for Laizhou Bay.

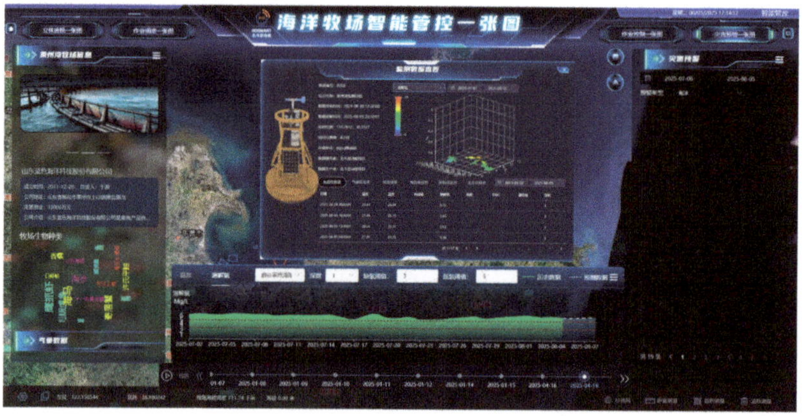

Figure 14. Prototype of the dissolved oxygen (DO) forecasting and early-warning system developed in this study. The left panel shows the basic introduction of the marine ranching area; the central part displays the buoy observation data, with the lower section showing the observation line, prediction line, and warning line of the early-warning system; the right panel illustrates the types of potential disasters.

6. Conclusions

This study systematically compared six single-model time-series forecasting methods—AutoARIMA, XGBoost, BlockRNN-LSTM, BlockRNN-GRU, TCN, and Transformer—for predicting dissolved oxygen (DO) from nearshore buoy observations.

A unified 24 h rolling forecasting framework was implemented across three buoy stations (0268, 0269, and 0270), and model performance was evaluated using MAPE, RMSE, and R^2 metrics. The comparison results show that deep learning models consistently outperform the traditional AutoARIMA and XGBoost methods. Among the single models, the Transformer and TCN architectures exhibited the most stable and accurate performance (MAPE $\approx$ 2.7%, RMSE $\approx$ 13–14 μmol kg^{-1}, $R^2 \approx$ 0.87–0.90), while the LSTM and GRU models demonstrated complementary temporal learning capabilities.

Based on these comparative findings and the structural complementarity among different deep learning models, this study further developed a multi-model ensemble forecasting framework that integrates the predictions of LSTM, GRU, TCN, and Transformer—representing the final proposed model of this work. This ensemble model further enhanced forecasting accuracy, achieving a mean MAPE of 2.6%, RMSE of 12.4 μmol kg^{-1}, and

$R^2 \approx 0.92$ across all sites—corresponding to an improvement of about 20–30% over the best single model and more than 50% over AutoARIMA.

Building on this framework, we deployed a near-real-time DO forecasting and early-warning system that provides a complete workflow from buoy data acquisition and real-time prediction to hypoxia risk identification and alert dissemination. The system has been successfully applied in marine ranching operations, providing reliable 1–3 day forecasts and issuing timely warnings before potential hypoxia events, thereby strengthening both scientific decision-making and emergency-response capability in aquaculture management.

Supplementary Materials: The following supporting information can be downloaded at: https://www.mdpi.com/article/10.3390/w17213102/s1. Table S1: Descriptions of key hyperparameters used in this study.

Author Contributions: Conceptualization, Y.W. and J.S.; Methodology, Y.W.; Software, Y.W. and G.Z.; Validation, Y.W., J.S. and G.Z.; Writing—original draft preparation, Y.W.; Writing—review and editing, J.S. and X.L.; Supervision, J.S. and X.L.; Funding acquisition, J.S. All authors have read and agreed to the published version of the manuscript.

Funding: This research was funded by the National Key Research and Development Program of China (Grant No. 2022YFC3104305), the National Natural Science Foundation of China (Grant No. 42176200), and the Strategic Priority Research Program of the Chinese Academy of Sciences (Grant No. XDB42000000). The APC was funded by the Institute of Oceanology, Chinese Academy of Sciences.

Data Availability Statement: The original data presented in the study are openly available in http://dx.doi.org/10.12157/IOCAS.20251002.001.

Conflicts of Interest: The authors declare no conflict of interest.

Appendix A

Detailed descriptions of machine learning and deep learning models used in this study

BlockRNN–LSTM

The BlockRNN–LSTM model is a recurrent neural network that incorporates Long Short-Term Memory (LSTM) units to learn nonlinear temporal dependencies. Each LSTM cell contains input, forget, and output gates that regulate the information flow through time, enabling the model to capture long-range temporal correlations while avoiding vanishing-gradient problems. In this study, the BlockRNN implementation in Darts was used with multiple stacked layers (input_chunk_length = 144 h, output_chunk_length = 24 h), allowing sequence-to-sequence forecasting of dissolved oxygen variations.

BlockRNN–GRU

The BlockRNN–GRU model replaces LSTM cells with Gated Recurrent Units (GRUs), which merge the input and forget gates into an update gate to reduce parameter count and computational cost. GRUs maintain strong temporal modeling ability while being faster to train. Similar to the LSTM configuration, the GRU model processes 144 h input windows to predict the next 24 h, providing an efficient alternative for short-term dissolved-oxygen forecasting.

Temporal Convolutional Network (TCN)

The TCN model applies one-dimensional dilated causal convolutions with residual and skip connections to model long-term dependencies. By increasing the dilation factor, the receptive field expands exponentially without loss of resolution, enabling the network to capture both short- and long-term temporal patterns. TCNs allow full parallelization during training and often outperform RNNs when handling long sequences. In this work, the TCN model was configured with kernel_size = 5, num_filters = 5, and dilation = 2.

References

1. Laffoley, D.; Baxter, J.M. *Ocean Deoxygenation: Everyone's Problem*; IUCN: Gland, Switzerland, 2019; ISBN 978-2-8317-2014-2.
2. Gachloo, M.; Liu, Q.; Song, Y.; Wang, G.; Zhang, S.; Hall, N. Using Machine Learning Models for Short-Term Prediction of Dissolved Oxygen in a Microtidal Estuary. *Water* **2024**, *16*, 1998. [CrossRef]
3. Ahmed, A.A.M.; Jui, S.J.J.; Chowdhury, M.A.I.; Ahmed, O.; Sutradha, A. The Development of Dissolved Oxygen Forecast Model Using Hybrid Machine Learning Algorithm with Hydro-Meteorological Variables. *Environ. Sci. Pollut. Res.* **2023**, *30*, 7851–7873. [CrossRef]
4. Liang, X.; Jian, Z.; Tan, Z.; Dai, R.; Wang, H.; Wang, J.; Qiu, G.; Chang, M.; Li, T. Dissolved Oxygen Concentration Prediction in the Pearl River Estuary with Deep Learning for Driving Factors Identification: Temperature, pH, Conductivity, and Ammonia Nitrogen. *Water* **2024**, *16*, 3090. [CrossRef]
5. Moon, J.; Lee, J.; Lee, S.; Yun, H. Urban River Dissolved Oxygen Prediction Model Using Machine Learning. *Water* **2022**, *14*, 1899. [CrossRef]
6. Chen, C.-C.; Gong, G.-C.; Chou, W.-C.; Shiah, F.-K. Hypoxia in Autumn of the East China Sea. *Mar. Pollut. Bull.* **2020**, *152*, 110875. [CrossRef]
7. Garabaghi, F.H.; Benzer, S.; Benzer, R. Modeling Dissolved Oxygen Concentration Using Machine Learning Techniques with Dimensionality Reduction Approach. *Environ. Monit. Assess.* **2023**, *195*, 879. [CrossRef]
8. Abba, S.I.; Linh, N.T.T.; Abdullahi, J.; Ali, S.I.A.; Pham, Q.B.; Abdulkadir, R.A.; Costache, R.; Nam, V.T.; Anh, D.T. Hybrid Machine Learning Ensemble Techniques for Modeling Dissolved Oxygen Concentration. *IEEE Access* **2020**, *8*, 157218–157237. [CrossRef]
9. Granata, F.; Zhu, S.; Nunno, F.D. Dissolved Oxygen Forecasting in the Mississippi River: Advanced Ensemble Machine Learning Models. *Environ. Sci. Adv.* **2024**, *3*, 1537–1551. [CrossRef]
10. Li, W.; Fang, H.; Qin, G.; Tan, X.; Huang, Z.; Zeng, F.; Du, H.; Li, S. Concentration Estimation of Dissolved Oxygen in Pearl River Basin Using Input Variable Selection and Machine Learning Techniques. *Sci. Total Environ.* **2020**, *731*, 139099. [CrossRef] [PubMed]
11. Yang, J. Predicting Water Quality through Daily Concentration of Dissolved Oxygen Using Improved Artificial Intelligence. *Sci. Rep.* **2023**, *13*, 20370. [CrossRef]
12. Olyaie, E.; Zare Abyaneh, H.; Danandeh Mehr, A. A Comparative Analysis among Computational Intelligence Techniques for Dissolved Oxygen Prediction in Delaware River. *Geosci. Front.* **2017**, *8*, 517–527. [CrossRef]
13. Heddam, S. Intelligent Data Analytics Approaches for Predicting Dissolved Oxygen Concentration in River: Extremely Randomized Tree Versus Random Forest, MLPNN and MLR. In *Intelligent Data Analytics for Decision-Support Systems in Hazard Mitigation: Theory and Practice of Hazard Mitigation*; Deo, R.C., Samui, P., Kisi, O., Yaseen, Z.M., Eds.; Springer: Singapore, 2021; pp. 89–107, ISBN 978-981-15-5772-9.
14. Hu, Y.; Liu, C.; Wollheim, W.M. Prediction of Riverine Daily Minimum Dissolved Oxygen Concentrations Using Hybrid Deep Learning and Routine Hydrometeorological Data. *Sci. Total Environ.* **2024**, *918*, 170383. [CrossRef]
15. Wei, L.; Guan, L.; Qu, L. Prediction of Sea Surface Temperature in the South China Sea by Artificial Neural Networks. *IEEE Geosci. Remote Sens. Lett.* **2020**, *17*, 558–562. [CrossRef]
16. Liang, W.; Liu, T.; Wang, Y.; Jiao, J.J.; Gan, J.; He, D. Spatiotemporal-Aware Machine Learning Approaches for Dissolved Oxygen Prediction in Coastal Waters. *Sci. Total Environ.* **2023**, *905*, 167138. [CrossRef]
17. Chang, W.; Li, X.; Dong, H.; Wang, C.; Zhao, Z.; Wang, Y. Real-Time Prediction of Ocean Observation Data Based on Transformer Model. In Proceedings of the 2021 ACM International Conference on Intelligent Computing and Its Emerging Applications, Jinan, China, 28–29 December 2021; Association for Computing Machinery: New York, NY, USA, 2022; pp. 83–88.
18. Barzegar, R.; Aalami, M.T.; Adamowski, J. Short-Term Water Quality Variable Prediction Using a Hybrid CNN–LSTM Deep Learning Model. *Stoch. Environ. Res. Risk Assess.* **2020**, *34*, 415–433. [CrossRef]
19. Ayesha Jasmin, S.; Ramesh, P.; Tanveer, M. An Intelligent Framework for Prediction and Forecasting of Dissolved Oxygen Level and Biofloc Amount in a Shrimp Culture System Using Machine Learning Techniques. *Expert Syst. Appl.* **2022**, *199*, 117160. [CrossRef]
20. Ziyad Sami, B.F.; Latif, S.D.; Ahmed, A.N.; Chow, M.F.; Murti, M.A.; Suhendi, A.; Ziyad Sami, B.H.; Wong, J.K.; Birima, A.H.; El-Shafie, A. Machine Learning Algorithm as a Sustainable Tool for Dissolved Oxygen Prediction: A Case Study of Feitsui Reservoir, Taiwan. *Sci. Rep.* **2022**, *12*, 3649. [CrossRef]
21. Chen, X.; Zhao, C.; Chen, J.; Jiang, H.; Li, D.; Zhang, J.; Han, B.; Chen, S.; Wang, C. Water Quality Parameters-Based Prediction of Dissolved Oxygen in Estuaries Using Advanced Explainable Ensemble Machine Learning. *J. Environ. Manag.* **2025**, *380*, 125146. [CrossRef]
22. Xue, H.; Wang, L.; Li, D. Design and Development of Dissolved Oxygen Real-Time Prediction and Early Warning System for Brocaded Carp Aquaculture. In *Proceedings of the Computer and Computing Technologies in Agriculture VI*; Li, D., Chen, Y., Eds.; Springer: Berlin/Heidelberg, Germany, 2013; pp. 35–42.

23. Fakhrudin, M.; Subehi, L.; Jasalesmana, T.; Dianto, A. Dissolved Oxygen and Temperature Stratification Analysis for Early Warning System Development in Preventing Mass Mortality of Fish in Lake Maninjau, West Sumatera-Indonesia. *IOP Conf. Ser. Earth Environ. Sci.* **2019**, *380*, 012002. [CrossRef]
24. Shaghaghi, N.; Fazlollahi, F.; Shrivastav, T.; Graham, A.; Mayer, J.; Liu, B.; Jiang, G.; Govindaraju, N.; Garg, S.; Dunigan, K.; et al. DOxy: A Dissolved Oxygen Monitoring System. *Sensors* **2024**, *24*, 3253. [CrossRef]
25. Anupama, P.; Kumar, E.V.; Ajanth, S.; Anugna, K.; Venkatesh, J. ML-Based Predicting of Dissolved Oxygen Levels for Sustainable River Ecosystem Management. *J. Sci. Eng. Technol. Manag. Sci.* **2025**, *2*, 590–601. [CrossRef]
26. Li, S.; Wang, B.; Deng, Z.; Wu, B.; Zhu, X.; Chen, Z. Data Quality Control Method of a New Drifting Observation Technology Named Drifting Air-Sea Interface Buoy. *J. Ocean Univ. China* **2024**, *23*, 11–22. [CrossRef]

processes

MDPI

Article

Evaluation of the Efficiency of Using an Oxidizer in the Leaching Process of Gold-Containing Concentrate

Bagdaulet Kenzhaliyevich Kenzhaliyev, Nessipbay Kyandykovich Tussupbayev, Gulnar Zhanuzakovna Abdykirova, Aigul Kairgeldyevna Koizhanova, Dametken Yedilovna Fischer, Zhazira Amangeldiyevna Baltabekova and Nazira Orakkyzy Samenova *

Institute of Metallurgy and Ore Beneficiation JSC, Satbayev University, Shevchenko Str., 29/133, Almaty 050010, Kazakhstan; bagdaulet_k@satbayev.university (B.K.K.); n.tussupbayev@satbayev.university (N.K.T.); abdgul@mail.ru (G.Z.A.); a.koizhanova@satbayev.university (A.K.K.); d.fischer@satbayev.university (D.Y.F.); zh.baltabekova@satbayev.university (Z.A.B.)

* Correspondence: nazira.orakkyzy@gmail.com; Tel.: +7-(707)-5333629

Abstract: This article presents the results of cyanide leaching of gold-containing concentrate using the trichlorocyanuric acid (TCCA) oxidizer. Gold-containing concentrate was obtained from a gold tailings sample from a gold recovery factory (GRF) in one of the deposits of Kazakhstan that have not previously been studied for concentrability. According to X-ray phase analysis and energy dispersive spectrometry (DSM) data, the main compounds in the tailings sample under study are pyrite FeS_2, quartz SiO_2, calcite $CaCO_3$, albite $NaAlSi_3O_8$, muscovite $KAl_2Si_3AlO_{10}(OH)_8$, dolomite $CaMg(CO_3)_2$, and oxidized iron compounds. Microscopic studies of the concentrate have established the presence of ultrafine gold with sizes from Au 0.9 to 10.2 μm in pyrite. Obtaining the gold-containing concentrate with a gold content of 15.95 g/t is possible according to the enrichment scheme, which includes centrifugal separation, classification according to the fineness class −0.05 mm, additional grinding of hydrocyclone sands to a fineness of 90.0–95.0% of the class finer than 0.050 mm, and control centrifugal separation. Since pyrite in technogenic raw materials is the main gold-containing mineral, this paper presents studies on the oxidizability of pyrite with the TCCA oxidizer. The results of studies on the oxidation of pyrite using the TCCA oxidizer show the products of its hydrolysis oxidize pyrite with the formation of various iron compounds on its surface. Pretreatment of gold-containing concentrate with oxidizer TCCA for 3 h before the cyanidation process (20 h) allows for an increase in the recovery of gold in the solution by 5.8%.

Keywords: stale tailings of a processing factory; grinding; centrifugal separation; pyrite; gold; redox potential; thermodynamic analysis; extraction

1. Introduction

Over the past decades, there has been a significant depletion of rich ore reserves. As a result, it has become necessary to search for and introduce new methods of producing metals from non-traditional sources of raw materials. Stale tailings of processing plants, dumps of off-balance sheets, and substandard ores are a source of expansion of the mineral resource base. In the industrially developed countries of the world, the level of use of industrial waste reaches 70–80%. For Kazakhstan, which produces a significant share of mineral products and has a strong mining potential, the problem of industrial waste disposal is of paramount importance. The low-level use of man-made raw materials in the republic is explained by the lack of technology and equipment for processing many types of waste. An important circumstance is that the cost of commercial products from industrial waste is usually lower than from ores of mineral deposits extracted by traditional methods. The advantage of man-made dumps is the readiness of the product directly for processing (ores have already been lifted from the subsurface, washed, and disintegrated). Another equally important aspect of the "thin gold" problem is that a huge number of man-made dumps accumulated over many decades are becoming profitable due to new technological opportunities and rising gold prices. Therefore, the development of technologies for processing gold-containing technogenic raw materials is an urgent task for the gold mining industry. The progress in improving methods for extracting useful components allows us to consider man-made dumps as a very attractive source of raw materials [1–3]. Man-made dumps can often compete in terms of content and reserves with newly discovered deposits today. Involvement in the processing of these wastes will not only allow obtaining additional products but also reduce environmental damage to the environment.

In [4], the possibility of obtaining gold and iron concentrate from gold-containing tailings by performing successive operations such as reduction roasting, mechanical activation, leaching, and magnetic separation is shown.

The effect of short-term mechanical activation of gold extraction mill tailings on the sulfide flotoability was studied [5,6]. Flotation of finely ground tailings under the optimal reagent regime allowed the increase in the recovery of gold in concentrate from 29.0 to 45.4% with the residual metal content in the waste at the level of 0.2–0.3 g/t.

The authors of [7] present the results of tests on the concentrability of gold-containing tailings of the Mazove mine (Zimbabwe) with a gold content of 1.1 g/t. The processing technology includes the processes of flotation and grinding of flotation concentrate to a fineness of less than 25 microns, which ensures the opening of gold and subsequent sorption cyanidation.

Gravity enrichment has become widespread due to its advantages over other methods of processing mineral raw materials, which include its cheapness, environmental safety, separation of minerals without changing their properties, and a wide range of fineness of separated mineral particles. In the practice of processing gold-containing ores, centrifugal separators are widely used, in which the separation of minerals occurs under the action of centrifugal accelerations that are tens and hundreds of times greater than the acceleration of gravity. The use of centrifugal separators made it possible to significantly reduce the size limit of the separated minerals to 0.02 mm [8].

Positive results of using centrifugal separators have been obtained in the processing of gold-containing ores from placer and indigenous deposits, current and stale tailings from processing plants, tantalum-niobium, hematite, chromium ores, ilmenite-zircon sands, and coal slurries [9–14].

A significant part of the gold in the concentrate is finely interspersed and associated with pyrite and arsenopyrite, which makes it difficult to directly cyanide the enrichment products. Processing of persistent gold-containing raw materials is carried out according to technologies based on the use of pre-oxidative roasting, autoclave and bacterial oxidation, and ultrafine grinding with subsequent cyanidation [15–19]. The most common method of opening fine gold associated with pyrite and arsenopyrite and implemented in the practice of processing resistant gold-containing raw materials is oxidative roasting [20,21]. In the pre-oxidation process, a porous structure of mineral complexes is formed, which promotes the penetration of cyanide solutions. Technologies for processing resistant gold-containing ores under the "roasting-cyanidation" scheme are implemented at enterprises in Canada, South Africa, the USA, Australia, and other countries [15]. The method of oxidative roasting is most widely used in the processing of refractory ores, but it has the following main disadvantages: high production costs and serious environmental pollution with a large amount of sulfur and arsenic oxides.

The process of bacterial leaching in relation to gold-containing raw materials has become widespread in world practice in the form of a chemical bio-oxidation of resistant gold-containing concentrates. The preliminary bacterial treatment of gold-containing raw materials ensures the opening of sulfides and improves the recovery of gold into solution during cyanidation [22–26].

Currently, there are about 20 plants successfully operating in the world for processing persistent gold-containing concentrates in Australia, South Africa, Peru, Ghana, China, Kazakhstan, Uzbekistan, Russia, and other countries [27].

Biotechnologies can be applied to high arsenic gold-containing concentrates. Bacterial oxidative leaching is an inexpensive and environmentally friendly process for releasing gold from the sulfide matrix. Gold recovery during cyanidation of concentrate ground to a fineness of −30 microns was 55.3% after 48 h of cyanidation. The use of pre-biooxidation of gold-containing concentrate for 2 days allowed us to dissolve 90% of the gold [13]. The disadvantages of the process are the long oxidation cycle and high requirements for the technological equipment used in the leaching process.

The autoclave method of oxidative decomposition of sulfide minerals is known and implemented in the practice of processing persistent gold-containing ores. Water pulp containing sulfides is heated in an autoclave to a temperature of 180–280 °C at an oxygen pressure exceeding the vapor pressure. Gold and silver remain an insoluble residue from which they can be extracted by cyanidation or other hydrometallurgical methods. The technology of autoclave oxidation–cyanidation makes it possible to extract up to 97% of gold from concentrates [28].

Processing of polymetallic gold-containing concentrates by autoclave oxidation makes it possible to simultaneously extract non-ferrous metals into marketable products [28–30].

The use of oxidative leaching at atmospheric pressure can significantly reduce capital costs in contrast to technologies such as oxidative roasting, autoclave, or bacterial leaching. The oxidizer of sulfide minerals is oxygen. Oxygen is supplied using supersonic ejector devices that provide a high rate of mass transfer of oxygen in the reactor. When sulfides are oxidized, a large amount of heat is released, so the operating temperature is close to the boiling point of the pulp (90–95 °C). At such operating temperatures, according to theoretical data, leaching occurs in two stages. In the first step, the sulfide mineral (SM) is oxidized to soluble sulfate and elemental sulfur.

There are many studies on the chemical oxidation of gold-containing pyrite and arsenopyrite sulfides using oxidizing agents [31].

There is little information in the literature about the use of organic chlorides for opening gold from iron sulfides. Trichlorocyanuric acid (TCCA) is an organic molecule of chlorinated isocyanate with the chemical formula: $C_3N_3O_3Cl_3$.

Based on extensive research, trichlorocyanuric acid (TCCA), a cyclic organic chloride containing three chlorines [32,33], can make up for the lack of inorganic chlorides. TCCA is hydrolyzed to form HClO, HClO dissociates to form ClO−, Cl_2, and O_2 are also formed as a result of subsequent reactions, as shown in the Equations (2)–(5) [34–38]. All four types are oxidizing agents, among which HClO is the most active.

$$C_3N_3O_3Cl_3 + 3H_2O = C_3N_3O_3H_3 + 3HClO \quad (1)$$

$$3ClO = 2Cl^- + ClO_3^- \quad (2)$$

$$2HClO = 2HCl + O_2 \quad (3)$$

$$5Cl^- + ClO_3^- + 6H^+ = 3Cl_2 + 3H_2O \quad (4)$$

$$7Cl^- + 3ClO_3^- + 10H^+ = 4Cl_2 + 2ClO_2 + 5H_2O \quad (5)$$

$$HClO \leftrightarrow H^+ + ClO^- \quad Kp = 7 \times 10^{-9} \quad (6)$$

$$Cl_2 + H_2O \leftrightarrow HClO + H^+ + Cl^- \quad Kp = 3.94 \times 10^{-4} \quad (7)$$

In accordance with Equations (6) and (7) [17], the distribution of the main hydrolysis products from TCCA in an aqueous solution at various pH values was revealed. As can be seen from Figure 1, when the pH value is greater than 7.5, the predominant hydrolysis products are ClO^-; when the pH value is from 3.5 to 7.5, the main type is HClO; and when the pH value is less than 3.5, Cl_2 acts as the main oxidizing agent. Among them, HClO has the highest redox potential and the strongest oxidizing capacity.

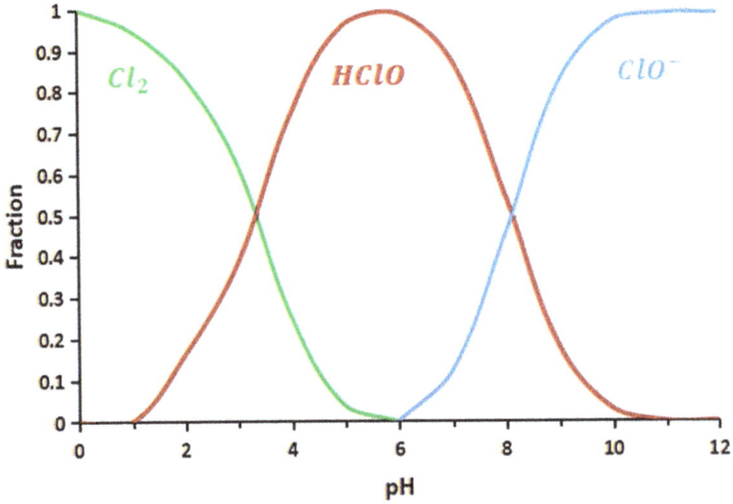

Figure 1. Distribution of the main types of hydrolysis products from TCCA at different pH values.

The aim of this work is to develop an effective method for pre-opening gold by oxidizing the sulfide part of the concentrate with trichlorocyanuric acid, followed by cyanidation. Since pyrite in a gold-containing concentrate is the main gold-containing mineral, this paper presents studies on the oxidation of pyrite with trichlorocyanuric acid.

2. Materials and Methods

Our studies were performed to develop technological solutions for the recovery of gold from mature tailings at one of the gold recovery factories (GRF) in Kazakhstan. Mature flotation tailings are a product with a gold content of up to 1.23 g/t. Studies on the oxidation of pyrite using trichloroisocyanuric acid were carried out. Research has been carried out on the oxidation of pyrite using trichloroisocyanuric acid. The following methods were used during our studies: X-ray fluorescent elemental analysis (wave-dispersive combined spectrometer Axios "PANalyical" (Eindhoven, Holland)); X-ray diffraction analysis (diffractometer "D8-ADVANCE" Bruker Elemental GmbH (Berlin, Germany)); electron microscopic analysis (microprobe analyzer JEOL "JEOLJXA-8230" (Tokyo, Japan)); and fire assay with AAS finish (NSAM 497-XC method). The spectra of solutions were obtained on an "Avatar IR-Fourier spectrometer 370" in the spectral range of 4000–500 cm^{-1} from capillary layers in KRS-5 windows.

For research, an average sample for studying physical and chemical properties and samples for technological research were selected from the sample of the initial dump tailings. To conduct research, a medium sample was selected from a sample of the original dump tailings to study the physicochemical properties and a sample for technological re-search.

Experiments on gravity enrichment were performed on the Knelson "KS-MD3" laboratory centrifugal separator (Savona, Canada). Technological parameters of raw material enrichment on a centrifugal separator: weight of the suspension—500 g; the size of the initial material—90–95% of the class −0.05 + 0 mm; and the flow rate of diluent water—4.0 L/min; acceleration of the centrifugal field—90 m/s^2.

Oxidation of pyrite monomineral with a solution of trichloroisocyanuric acid depending on the mixing time and TCCA concentration was carried out according to the functional scheme shown in Figure 2.

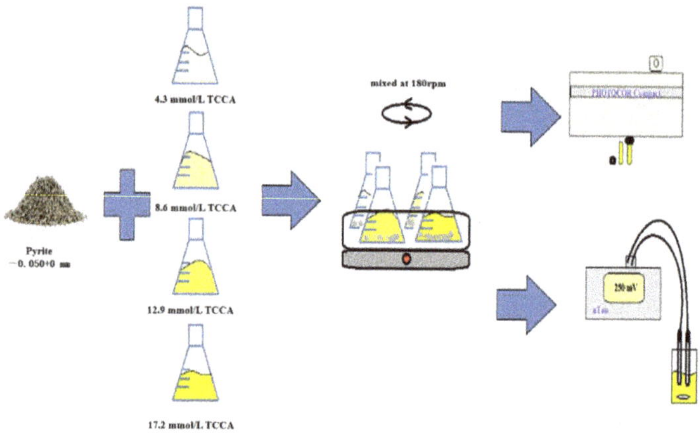

Figure 2. Measurement of the zeta potential and redox potential.

The zeta potentials of a pyrite monomineral with a size of −0.050 + 0 mm before and after interaction with TCCA were determined using Photocor Compact zeta potential and particle size—PhotocorAnalyzer. A total of 1 g of pyrite was added to 50 mL of an aqueous solution with concentrations of 4.3; 8.6; 12.9; and 17.2 mmol/L TCCA. Samples of a 50 mL mineral pulp solution were filtered through a filter paper using yellow tape. To control the pH, a solution with a concentration of 0.05 M NaOH or 0.05 M H_2SO_4 was used. With constant mixing of the samples for 180 min, the kinetics of the zeta potential change was measured as a function of the TCCA concentration at 20 °C.

The ζ-potential of the system was measured at 20 °C using a Photocor analyzer "COMPACT" (Moscow, Russia). The device was equipped with a laser with a wavelength of 657 nm/36 MW, and the measurements were carried out in round vials with an internal diameter of 14.8 mm. The correlation function for each sample was obtained by averaging 10 curves, each of which was obtained over 30 s.

The redox potential (ROP) of a −0.050 + 0 mm pyrite system with different TCCA concentrations was controlled using a combined Pt/Ag-AgCl ROP electrode in an ETHANE pH/ionomer. The ROP kinetics of the samples was measured every 10 min for 3 h at 20 °C.

It is known that due to the formation of different chlorine compounds during the hydrolysis of trichlorocyanuric acids, the oxidation of the process at different pH differs. So, at a pH closer to 1, atomic chlorine is released, which is a strong oxidizer, and at a pH of 5–7, the release of free chlorine is insignificant and requires a long oxidation time. Oxidation was carried out for 5 h, until the complete consumption of the chlorine compound (with sampling to determine the potential sampling time: 3 to 5 h), since the remaining chlorine in the pulp will interfere with the process of further cyanide leaching.

3. Results and Discussion

The material composition of the ore was studied. Studies on the concentrability of gold-containing tailings using a centrifugal separator Knelson were carried out.

To determine the phase composition of the flotation tailings sample, X-ray phase analysis (XRD) was performed in Figure 3. According to the X-ray diffraction analysis, the following minerals were determined in the sample: quartz, sericite, chlorite, feldspar, muscovite, and sulfides (Table 1).

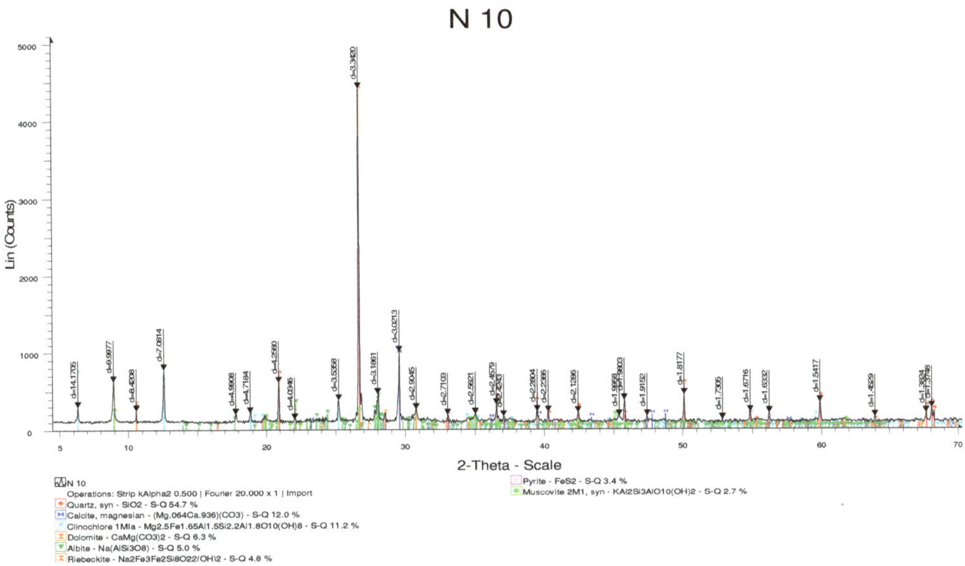

Figure 3. Results of XRD of the initial ore.

Table 1. X-ray diffraction analysis of the initial ore.

Compound Name	Formula	Content, %
Quartz, syn	SiO_2	54.7
Calcite, magnesian	$(Mg_{0.064}Ca_{0.936})(CO_3)$	12.0
Clinochlore 1MIa	$Mg_{2.5}Fe_{1.65}Al_{1.5}Si_{2.2}Al_{1.8}O_{10}(OH)_8$	11.2
Dolomite	$CaMg(CO_3)_2$	6.3
Albite	$Na(AlSi_3O_8)$	5.0
Riebeckite	$Na_2Fe_3Fe_2Si_8O_{22}(OH)_2$	4.8
Pyrite	FeS_2	3.4
Muscovite 2M1, syn	$KAl_2Si_3AlO_{10}(OH)_2$	2.7

To determine the phase composition of the flotation tailings sample, X-ray phase analysis (XRP) was performed. According to the X-ray phase analysis, the following minerals were determined in the sample: quartz, sericite, chlorite, feldspar, muscovite, and sulfides (Table 1).

The results of the X-ray fluorescence analysis of stale GRF tails, shown in Table 2, were obtained using an Axios X-ray fluorescence wave dispersion spectrometer manufactured by Panalytical (Eindhoven, Holland). The spectrograms were processed using Super Q software (Omnian 37).

Table 2. Results of the X-ray fluorescence analysis of gold recovery plant tailings.

Chemical Element	Content, %	Chemical Element	Content, %
O	47.195	Cr	0.037
Na	1.976	Mn	0.091
Mg	2.131	Fe	5.293
Al	8.022	Co	0.013
Si	28.273	Ni	0.013
P	0.055	Cu	0.004
S	0.527	Zn	0.013
Cl	0.064	Sr	0.014
K	0.993	Zr	0.005
Ca	4.908	Pb	0.018
Ti	0.355		

Analysis of the distribution of gold by size class indicates that the main gold is distributed by size class +0.2; −0.2 + 0.1; −0.1 + 0.07; −0.07 + 0.05 mm. For example, in the +0.2 mm fineness class, the gold content was 4.0 g/t, with a yield of 9.4%, and up to 30.57% of gold is concentrated in it. In size classes −0.2 + 0.1; 0.1 + 0.07; −0.07 + 0.05 mm, the gold content is 1.3 g/t, 1.25 g/t, and 1.32 g/t, respectively. In the class of −0.05 + 0 mm, 21.27% of gold is concentrated, while the output is 44.36% with a content of 0.59 g/t.

The products of sieve analysis of the stale tailings sample were studied on a JEOL "JEOLJXA-8230" (Tokyo, Japan)). Samples were placed on a double-sided adhesive electrically conductive carbon tape from NISSHIN EM Co., Ltd. (Tokyo, Japan). The results of energy dispersive spectrometry (DPS analysis) "from an area" of the fineness class −0.071 + 0.05 mm (with an increase of ×100) are shown in Figure 4, which allows us to estimate the concentration of elements on the surface, Au was 18.58 ms% or 3.71 mol%. Most of the SEM images were taken in the backscattered electron mode (COMRO), which minimizes resolution degradation and provides better images of such powders compared to the secondary image observation mode (SEI). During the DSP analysis, a beam current of about 10 nA was selected, which corresponds to a sufficient data accumulation rate.

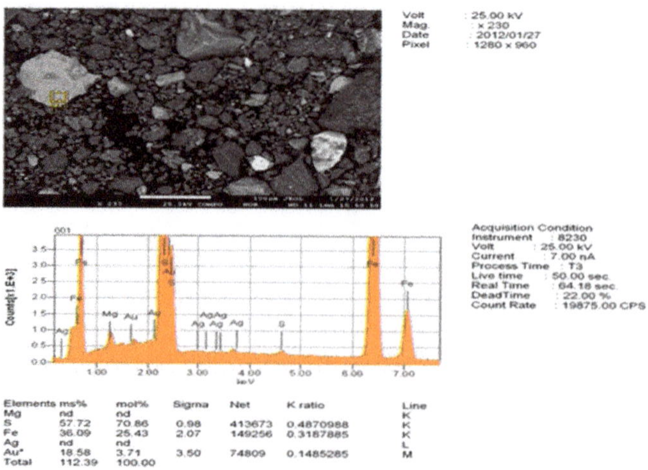

Figure 4. Results of DSP analysis of pyrite.

Microscopic studies on the surface (m = 8–10 g, d = 25 mm) revealed the presence of free-form gold grains, ranging in size from Au 0.9 to 0.2 μm Au-ultrafine and fine gold (Figure 5). The shape of gold particles is diverse: elongated, isometric, ellipsoid, spongy, spherical, scaly with a developed surface, and lamellar with uneven contours. The surface of the particles is clean, smooth, rough, or bumpy.

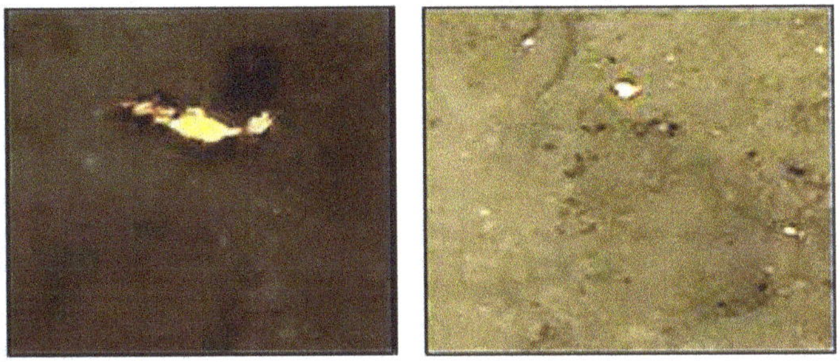

Au 0.9 × 1.6 μm   Au 0.8 × 1.0 μm

Figure 5. Free gold particles in polystyrene.

The presence of oxidized iron compounds in the studied sample of mature tailings of a gold extraction plant indicates that the sulfide minerals (pyrite and chalcopyrite) present in the tailings were oxidized to form iron oxides, hydroxides, sulfates, and carbonates as a result of prolonged exposure to climatic conditions.

Oxidation of pyrite. To find out the possibility of gold-containing pyrite disclosure using an organic chlorine-containing reagent TCCA, depending on the time of the process and its concentration, we conducted preliminary studies of its interaction with monomineral pyrite. The zeta potential in the shear plane provides important information necessary for analyzing electrostatic interactions between particles, suspension stability, and particle adsorption on mineral surfaces.

To assess the state of the surface of sulfide minerals and the electrostatic component of the interaction forces between particles, the electrokinetic potential was measured. Figure 6 shows the zeta potential of pyrite as a function of pH.

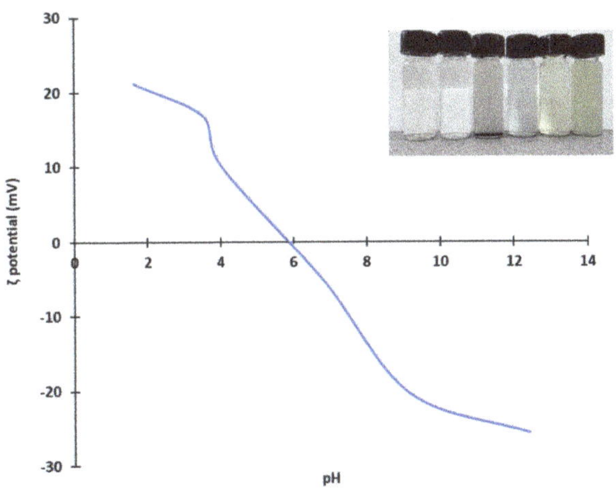

Figure 6. ζ—potential of pyrite as a function of pH.

With increasing pH in neutral and alkaline media, pyrite has a negative electrokinetic potential, varying from zero to −25 mV (Figure 5). Pyrite has a high negative charge under alkaline conditions and becomes positively charged at pH < 6. With increasing pH values, the absolute value of the zeta potential gradually increased. This is consistent with experimental data in the literature [39].

The histogram (Figure 7) shows the effect of TCCA concentration on the pyrite zeta potential. The concentration of TCCA has a significant effect on the zeta potential. As the concentration of trichloroisocyanuric acid increases in the solution, a large number of iron compound ions are formed and, accordingly, the zeta potential value becomes positive. This means that the reaction of pyrite and trichloroisocyanuric acid produces Fe^{2+}, FeO^{+}, and $[Fe(H_2O)_6]^{3+}$, which are adsorbed on the surface of the mineral pyrite. On the other hand, as mentioned above, films consisting of goethite and hematite can form on the surface of pyrite, which also charge the surface of pyrite in a positive charge. However, these films can be dissolved in a solution of one of the products of TCCA hydrolysis, namely in HCI solution by the following Reactions (8) and (9):

$$FeOOH + 3HCl = FeCl_3 + 2H_2O \quad (8)$$

$$Fe_2O_3 + 6HCl = 2FeCl_3 + 3H_2O \quad (9)$$

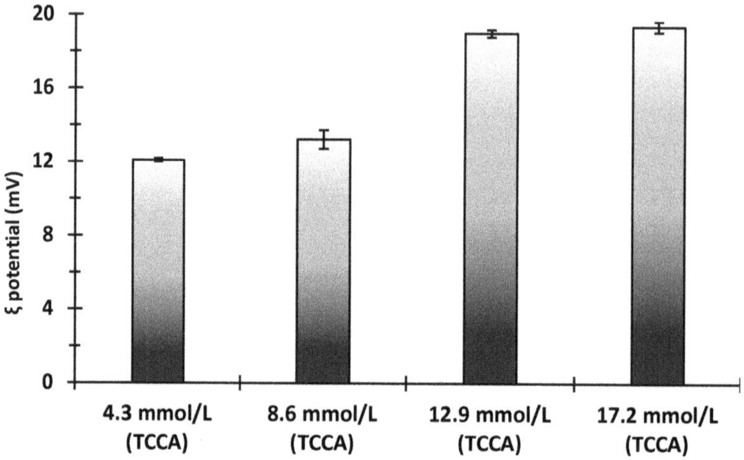

Figure 7. Influence of TCCA concentration on the zeta potential of pyrite.

Figure 8 shows changes in the electrokinetic potential depending on the concentration of the TCCA solution, where it is shown that with an increase in the concentration of TCCA, the value of the ξ-potential increases in the positive direction. This is due to the oxidation reaction of pyrite with the products of hydrolysis of TCCA, namely hypochlorous acid (HClO), which is more formed when TCCA is decomposed by water (see Reactions (1)–(5)). Consequently, as mentioned above, a large amount of iron (II, III) ions is formed.

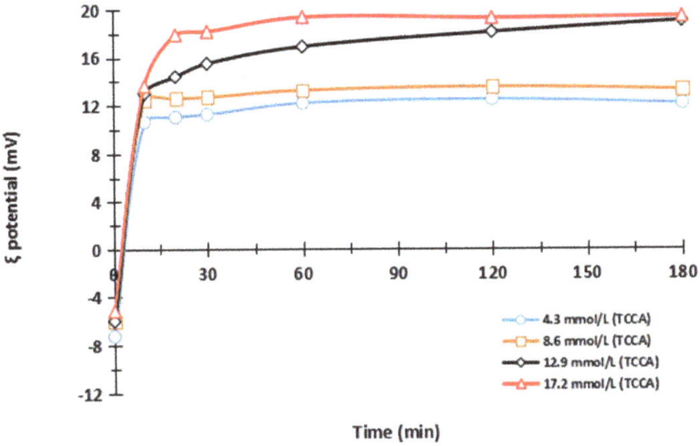

Figure 8. Kinetics of zeta potential change as a function of TCCA concentration.

Thermodynamic analysis. It is known that when a dry TCCA powder is added to an aqueous solution, the hydrolysis reaction proceeds according to Equation (1). Then various chlorine compounds are formed as a result of redox disproportionation reactions (see Equations (2)–(5)). As is known (5)–(7), hypochlorous acid (HClO) is mainly formed—concentration of 2–2.5 g/L at pH 6 for 3–5 h, the following reactions can occur without air purging:

$$FeS_2 + 4HClO = FeSO_4 + S + 4HCl \qquad \Delta G = -1024.0 \text{ kJ} \tag{10}$$

$$FeS_2 + 2HClO = FeCl_2 + 2S + H_2O + 0.5O_2 \qquad \Delta G = -371.4 \text{ kJ} \tag{11}$$

According to the Gibbs energy value calculated using a computer program HSC Chemisty 8, it can be judged that the Reaction (10) is mainly taking place. At the same time, hydrochloric acid reacting with iron oxides (hematite, goethite) can form iron (II, III) cations, increasing the ξ—potential in the positive direction, as indicated above.

Measurements were carried out using IR spectroscopy to determine the potential mechanism by which TCCA is adsorbed on mineral surfaces (Figure 9). To investigate the mechanism of TCCA with pyrite, the IR spectra of a pure pyrite sample and a pyrite–TCCA sample were determined to understand the nature of the interaction.

In the TCCA IR spectrum, the absorption peak at 3346 cm^{-1} was attributed to −OH. The absorption peaks at 1641 and 1323 cm^{-1} were assigned to the carboxylic carbonyl group, respectively. The absorption peaks at 1623 and 1440 cm^{-1} were attributed to the aromatic ring with a double bond. Absorption peaks between 1100 and 1000 cm^{-1} were attributed to C-O deformation. The results of IR spectroscopy are consistent with previous results of TCCA characterization [34]. The spectrum shows automatic correction of the baseline and automatic smoothing in the range of 1000–950 cm^{-1}. The information obtained indicates that TCCA molecules contain a large number of OH^-, C-O, which can bind to mineral surfaces and enhance the hydrophilicity of mineral particles. The presence of a band in the spectrum corresponding to the oscillation of the sulfate ion at a wavenumber of 916 cm^{-1} indicates the coordination of the metal sulfate ion. In the IR spectrum of pyrite, the band at 1085 cm^{-1} was attributed to the vibration of stretching of single bonds.

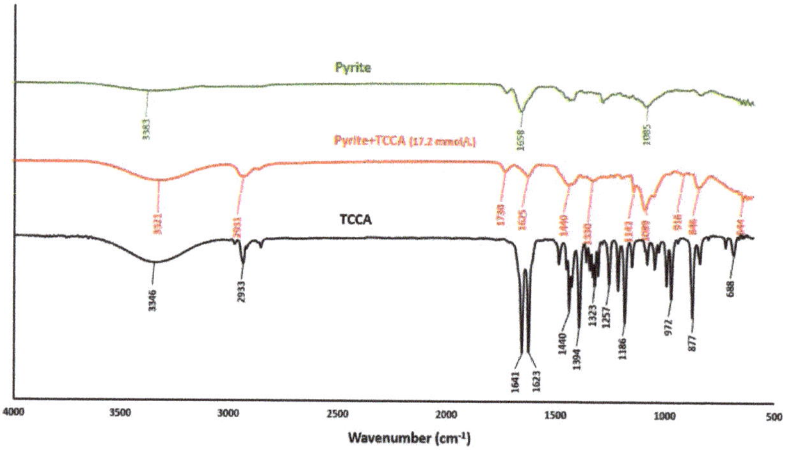

Figure 9. IR spectra of pyrite before and after TCCA treatment.

To determine which of the above reactions are more likely to occur, we performed thermodynamic calculations using a well-known computer program HSC Chemisty 8, which showed the following results: when pyrite is oxidized using HClO and air oxygen, reactions occur very easily (12), (13) and (17), (18). These calculated reactions are confirmed by IR spectroscopic data.

$$2FeS_2 + HClO + 6.5O_2 = Fe_2O_3 + 4SO_2 + HClO_3 \quad \Delta G = -1560.2\ kJ \tag{12}$$

$$2FeS_2 + HClO + 6O_2 = Fe_2O_3 + 4SO_2 + HClO_2 \quad \Delta G = -1546.4\ kJ \tag{13}$$

$$FeS_2 + HClO + 4.5O_2 = FeSO_4 + SO_2 + HClO_4 \quad \Delta G = -896.5\ kJ \tag{14}$$

$$FeS_2 + 2HClO + 5O_2 = FeSO_4 + S + 2HClO_4 \quad \Delta G = -525.1\ kJ \tag{15}$$

$$FeS_2 + 2HClO + 1.5O_2 = FeCl_2 + 2SO_2 + H_2O \quad \Delta G = -829.4\ kJ \tag{16}$$

$$FeS_2 + 4HClO + 5.5O_2 + H_2O = FeCl_2 + 2H_2SO_4 + 2HClO_4 \quad \Delta G = -1104.3\ kJ \tag{17}$$

$$FeS_2 + 2HClO + 6.5O_2 + H_2O = FeSO_4 + H_2SO_4 + 2HClO_4 \quad \Delta G = -1032.5\ kJ \tag{18}$$

Pyrite oxidation is known as an electrochemical process. The histogram (Figure 10) shows the effect of TCCA concentration on the pyrite redox potential. However, pyrite is inert, and an aqueous solution of pyrite has a low ROP of about 100–130 mV. In the oxidation process, it can be detected only at ROP above 200 mV [4]. The redox potential mainly depends on the activity of iron ions, which means that pyrite will oxidize faster if there is a higher percentage of iron ions in the solution.

The redox potential also changes in the same way as the electrokinetic potential changes, which are shown in Figure 11.

With an increase in the concentration of the TCCA solution, the ROP of the system increases accordingly, leading to greater oxidation of pyrite. The optimal oxidation time of pyrite is 60 min.

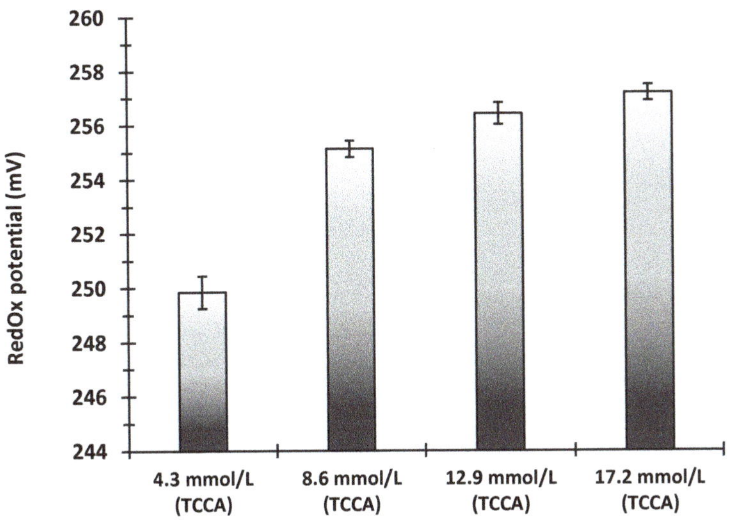

Figure 10. Effect of TCCA concentration on the redox potential of pyrite.

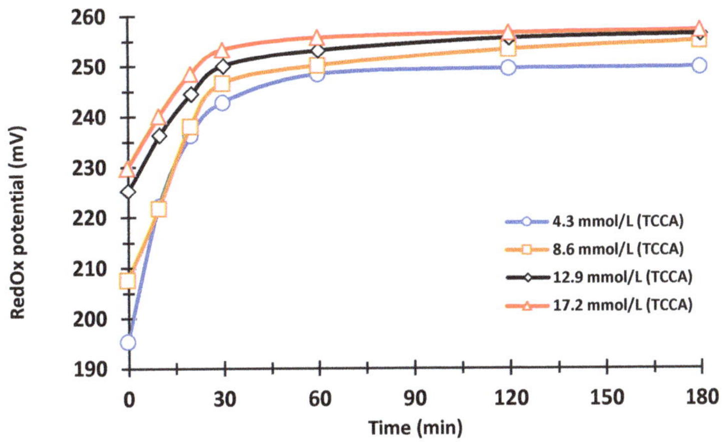

Figure 11. Kinetics of changes in ROP as a function of TCCA concentration.

Thus, the results of studies on the oxidation of pyrite using the TCCA oxidizer show that the products of its hydrolysis oxidize pyrite to produce various iron compounds.

Large-scale laboratory tests on the enrichment of initial gold-containing tailings in a centrifugal separator were carried out according to the scheme shown in Figure 12. The first stage of centrifugal separation was carried out at the initial fineness, then the tailings of the first centrifugal separation were further ground to a fineness of 90–95% less than −0.05 + 0 mm (Figure 13).

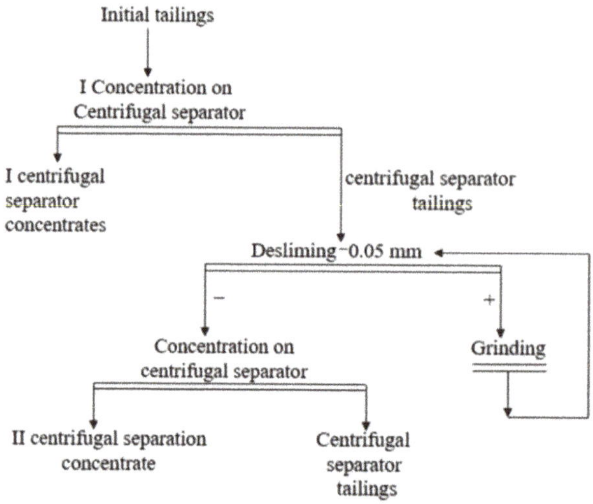

Figure 12. Scheme of enrichment of stale mill tailings using a centrifugal separator.

Figure 13. Knelson KS-MD 3 centrifugal concentrator and the gravitational enrichment process.

Centrifugal separation was carried out at a cone rotation speed of 750 min^{-1} and a turbulizing water flow rate of 6.0 L/min, acceleration of the gravitational fall of 90 G.

The results of stage enrichment of stale tailings on a centrifugal separator Knelson are presented in Table 3.

Table 3. Results of stage enrichment of stale tailings in a centrifugal separator.

Products	Yield, %	Gold Content, g/t	Gold Recovery, %
I centrifugal separator concentrates	3.22	17.1	43.33
II centrifugal separation concentrate	3.19	14.8	37.39
Combined ash concentrate	6.41	15.95	80.72
Centrifugal separator tailings	93.61	0.26	19.28
Initial tailings	100.0	1.263	100.0

The results of the experiments show that the enrichment of stale tailings of GRE in a centrifugal separator makes it possible to obtain a combined gold-containing concentrate with a gold content of 15.95 g/t, with a yield of 6.41%. Gold losses with flotation tailings are 19.28%.

Obtaining dump tailings with a gold content of 0.264 g/t is possible according to the enrichment scheme, which includes centrifugal separation, classification according to the fineness class −0.05 mm, additional grinding of hydrocyclone sands to a fineness of 90.0–95.0% of the class finer than −0.05 mm, and control centrifugal separation. The resulting gold-containing concentrate with a gold content of 15.95 g/t is suitable for further processing by the hydrometallurgical method.

Cyanidation of the obtained gold-containing concentrate was preceded by pre-oxidation of sulfides using TCCA for 3 h at a concentration of 2 g/L. The results of leaching the gold-containing concentrate are shown in Figure 14 as a function of the cyanidation time.

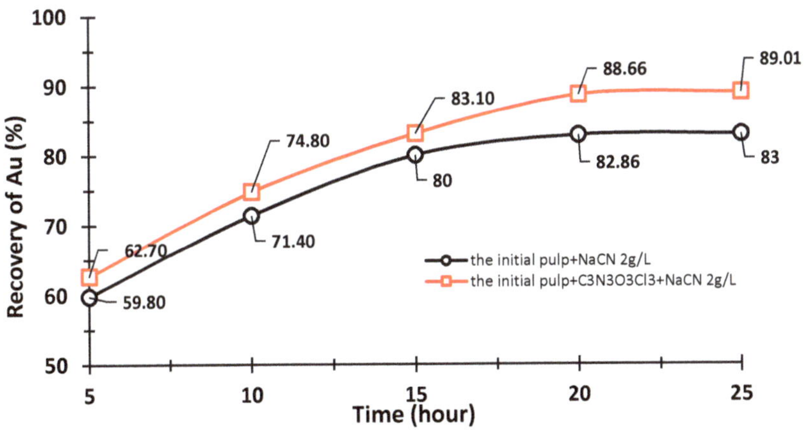

Figure 14. Dependence of gold extraction into solution on cyanidation time.

From the results obtained, it follows that pretreatment of gold-containing concentrate with an oxidizer TCCA for 3 h before the cyanidation process (20 h) allows for an increase in the recovery of gold in the solution by 5.8%.

In this paper, the oxidation of pyrite in TCCA solution is studied by the redox potential and zeta potential and thermodynamic analysis of the reactions. The results of studies on the oxidation of pyrite using the TCCA oxidizer show that the products of its hydrolysis oxidize pyrite produce various iron compounds and thereby contribute to the intensification of the cyanidation process of gold-containing concentrate.

Sulfate ions in the solution were analyzed by complex titration. A total of 1 g of monomineral was mixed with TCCA (17.2 mmol/L), and then an aliquot was taken and titrated with EDTA. The amount of sulfate ions was 3.22 mmol/L at the initial TCCA. After interaction with monomineral, its amount increased by 16.12 mmol/L, that is, the presence of 12.90 mmol/L sulfate ions in the total solution is explained by the oxidation of the monomineral surface.

4. Conclusions

The conclusions of this study are as follows:

- Chemical oxidation of pyrite occurs mainly in an acidic and slightly alkaline environment. Pyrite has a high negative charge under alkaline conditions and becomes positively charged at pH < 6. With an increase in pH in neutral and alkaline media, pyrite has a negative electrokinetic potential, varying from zero to −25 mV.
- The results of studies on the oxidation of pyrite using the TCCA oxidizer show that the products of its hydrolysis oxidize pyrite with the formation of various iron compounds on its surface.
- The results of the experiments show that the enrichment of stale tailings of GRF in a centrifugal separator allows you to get a combined gold-containing concentrate with a gold content of 15.95 g/t, with a yield of 6.39%, which, not being conditioned, allows you to cyanide a relatively small mass of it, which as a result reduces the operating costs for processing gold-containing concentrate. Gold recovery in Knelson's concentrate was 80.72%.
- It was found that pretreatment of gold-containing concentrate with TCCA and subsequent leaching in cyanide solutions can increase the recovery of gold in solution by 5.8%.

Author Contributions: Conceptualization, B.K.K., N.K.T., and G.Z.A.; methodology, G.Z.A. and N.O.S.; software, N.O.S.; validation, A.K.K., D.Y.F., and Z.A.B.; formal analysis, N.K.T. and G.Z.A.; investigation, D.Y.F. and A.K.K.; resources, N.K.T.; data curation, N.O.S. and Z.A.B.; writing—original draft preparation, N.K.T. and G.Z.A.; writing—review and editing, N.K.T. and N.O.S.; visualization, D.Y.F. and Z.A.B.; supervision, B.K.K.; project administration, B.K.K.; funding acquisition, B.K.K. All authors have read and agreed to the published version of the manuscript.

Funding: This research has been funded by the Committee of Science of the Ministry of Science and Higher Education of the Republic of Kazakhstan (Grant No. BR21882140).

Data Availability Statement: Some or all of the data or code supporting the results of this study are available from the corresponding authors upon request.

Conflicts of Interest: The authors declare no conflicts of interest.

References

1. Master Plan for the Development of the Mining and Metallurgical Industry of the Republic of Kazakhstan Until 2030. Available online: https://kapital.kz/economic/4765/v-rk-razrabotayut-master-plan-razvitiya-gorno-metallurgicheskogo-kompleksa.html (accessed on 4 December 2023).
2. Kenzhaliyev, B.; Surkova, T.; Yessimova, D.; Baltabekova, Z.; Abikak, Y.; Abdikerim, B.; Dosymbayeva, Z. Extraction of noble metals from pyrite cinders. *Chemengineering* **2023**, *7*, 14. [CrossRef]
3. Toktar, G.; Magomedov, D.R.; Koizhanova, A.K.; Abdyldaev, N.N.; Bakraeva, A.N. Extraction of gold from low-sulfide gold-containing ores by beneficiating method using a pressure generator for pulp microaeration. *Kompleks. Ispol'zovanie Miner. Syr'â/Complex. Use Miner. Resour./Miner. Shikisattardy Keshendi Paid.* **2023**, *325*, 62–71. [CrossRef]
4. Zhang, L.; Jiang, T.; Guo, X.-Y.; Tian, Q.-H.; Zhong, S.-P.; Dong, L.; Qin, H.; Liu, Z.-W.; Makuza, B. Sustainable processing of gold cyanide tailings: Reduction roasting, mechanical activation, non-cyanide leaching, and magnetic separation. *Hydrometallurgy* **2023**, *217*, 106028. [CrossRef]
5. Bragin, V.I.; Burdakova, E.A.; Kondrateva, A.A.; Plotnikova, A.A.; Baksheeva, I.I. Dressability of old gold-containing tailings by flotation. *J. Min. Sci.* **2019**, *54*, 663–670. [CrossRef]
6. Chang, C.S.; Yusoff, A.H.; Mohamed, C.A.R.; Liu, S.F.; Shoparwe, N.F.; Husain, N.A.; Azlan, M.N. Geochemistry of Rare Earth Elements in Pahang River Sediment, Malaysia. *Kompleks. Ispol'zovanie Miner. Syr'â/Complex. Use Miner. Resour./Miner. Shikisattardy Keshendi Paid.* **2024**, *331*, 42–50. [CrossRef]
7. Bantshi, A.M.; Makuvise, P. Extraction of gold from sands and slimes tailings dump from Mazowe mine, Zimbabwe. In *Proceedings of the 3rd Pan American Materials Congress*; Springer: Berlin/Heidelberg, Germany, 2017; pp. 507–517. [CrossRef]
8. Chen, Q.; Yang, H.-Y.; Tong, L.-L.; Niu, H.-Q.; Zhang, F.-S.; Chen, G.-M. Research and application of a Knelson concentrator: A review. *Miner. Eng.* **2020**, *152*, 106339. [CrossRef]

9. Guney, A.; Önal, G.; Atmaca, T. New aspect of chromite gravity tailings re-processing. *Miner. Eng.* **2001**, *14*, 1527–1530. [CrossRef]
10. Sen, S. Gold recovery by KC from grinding circuit of Bergama CIP plant. *Rem. Rev. Esc. Minas* **2010**, *63*, 539–545. [CrossRef]
11. Uslu, T.; Sahinoglu, E.; Yavuz, M. Desulphurization and deashing of oxidized fine coal by Knelson concentrator. *Fuel Process. Technol.* **2012**, *101*, 94–100. [CrossRef]
12. Kökkılıç, O.; Langlois, R.; Waters, K.E. A design of experiments investigation into dry separation using a Knelson concentrator. *Miner. Eng.* **2015**, *72*, 73–86. [CrossRef]
13. Abbruzzese, S.; Ubaldini, F.; Veglio, L.; Toro, L. Preparatory bioleaching to the conventional cyanidation of arsenical gold ores. *Miner. Eng.* **1994**, *7*, 49–60. [CrossRef]
14. Kenzhaliyev, B.K. Innovative Technologies Providing Enhancement of Non-Ferrous, Precious, Rare and Rare Earth Metals Extraction. *Kompleks. Ispol'zovanie Miner. Syr'â/Complex. Use Miner. Resour./Miner. Shikisattardy Keshendi Paid.* **2019**, *310*, 64–75. [CrossRef]
15. Lodeyshchikov, V.V. *Technology for Extracting Gold and Silver from Refractory Ores*; OJSC "Irgiredmet": Irkutsk, Russia, 1999; p. 452.
16. Hapid, A.; Zullaikah, S.; Kawigraha, A.; Sudiyanto, Y.; Nareswari, R.B.; Quitain, A.T. Oxidation of sulfide mineral and metal extraction analysis in the microwave-assisted roasting pretreatment of refractory gold ore. *Arab. J. Chem.* **2024**, *17*, 105447. [CrossRef]
17. Watling, H. Microbiological Advances in Biohydrometallurgy. *Minerals* **2016**, *6*, 49. [CrossRef]
18. Fomchenko, N.V.; Muravyov, M.I.; Kondrateva, T.F. Two-stage bacterial–chemical oxidation of refractory gold-containing sulfidic concentrates. *Hydrometallurgy* **2010**, *101*, 28–34. [CrossRef]
19. Koizhanova, A.K.; Toktar, G.; Banks Craig, E.; Magomedov, D.R.; Kubaizhanov, A.A. Research of hydrometallurgical method of leaching gold from flotation tails with using bio-oxidation. *Kompleks. Ispol'zovanie Miner. Syr'â/Complex. Use Miner. Resour. /Miner. Shikisattardy Keshendi Paid.* **2020**, *314*, 28–39. [CrossRef]
20. Amaya, D.; Bernal, S.; Garnica, M.; Reslen, R.; Correa, R. Improved roasting of some colombian gold ores. *Rev. Dyna* **2013**, *80*, 70–77.
21. Karimova, L.M.; Oleinikova, T.O.; Mansurov, B.E.; Saganbek, S. Oxidizing roasting and cyanidation for the processing of refractory gold concentrates. *Obogashchenie Rud.* **2023**, *3*, 10–15. [CrossRef]
22. Boduen, A.; Zalesov, M.; Melamud, V.; Grigorieva, V.; Bulaev, A. Combined Bacterial and Pressure Oxidation for Processing High-Sulfur Refractory Gold Concentrate. *Processes* **2023**, *11*, 3062. [CrossRef]
23. Johnson, D.B. The Evolution, Current Status, and Future Prospects of Using Biotechnologies in the Mineral Extraction and Metal Recovery Sectors. *Minerals* **2018**, *8*, 343. [CrossRef]
24. Nestor, D.; Valdivia, U.; Chaves, A.P. Mechanisms of bioleaching of a refractory mineral of gold with Thiobacillus ferrooxidans. *Int. J. Miner. Process.* **2001**, *62*, 187–198. [CrossRef]
25. Van Aswegen, P.C.; Van Niekerk, J.; Olivier, W. The BIOX process for the treatment of refractory gold concentrate. In *Biomining*; Rawlings, D.E., Johnson, B.D., Eds.; Springer: Berlin/Heidelberg, Germany, 2007; pp. 1–35. [CrossRef]
26. Mahmoud, A.; Cezac, P.; Hoadley, A.F.A.; Contaminea, F.; D'Hugues, P. A review of sulfide minerals microbially assisted leaching in stirred tank reactors. *Int. Biodeterior. Biodegrad.* **2017**, *119*, 118–146. [CrossRef]
27. Sedelnikova, G.V. Comparison of autoclave and bacterial leaching. *Gold Technol.* **2014**, *2*, 110–115.
28. Soto-Uribe, J.C.; Valenzuela-Garcia, J.L.; Salazar-Campoy, M.M.; Parga-Torres, J.R.; Tiburcio-Munive, G.; Encinas-Romero, M.A.; Vazquez-Vazquez, V.M. Gold extraction from a refractory sulfide concentrate by simultaneous pressure leaching/oxidation. *Minerals* **2023**, *13*, 116. [CrossRef]
29. Adewuyi, S.O.; Ahmed, H.A.M.; Ahmed, H.M.A. Methods of ore pretreatment for comminution energy reduction. *Minerals* **2020**, *10*, 423. [CrossRef]
30. Valenzuela, A.; Valenzuela, J.L.; Parga, J.R. Effect of pretreatment of sulfide refractory concentrate with sodium hypochlorite, followed by extraction of gold by pressure cyanidation, on gold removal. *Adv. Chem. Eng. Sci.* **2013**, *3*, 7. [CrossRef]
31. Feng, F.; Sun, Y.X.; Rui, J.Y.; Yu, L.; Liu, J.M.; Zhang, N.; Zhao, M.X.; Wei, L.W.; Lu, C.S.; Zhao, J.; et al. Study of the "Oxidation-complexation" coordination composite ionic liquid system for dissolving precious metals. *Appl. Sci.* **2020**, *10*, 3625. [CrossRef]
32. Puvvada, G.V.K.; Murthy, D.S.R. Selective precious metals leaching from a chalcopyrite concentrate using chloride/hypochlorite media. *Hydrometallurgy* **2000**, *58*, 185–191. [CrossRef]
33. Basu, N.; Maity, S.K.; Chaudhury, A.; Ghosh, R. Trichloroisocyanuric acid (TCCA):an efficient green reagent for activation of thioglycosides toward hydrolysis. *Carbohydr. Res.* **2013**, *369*, 10–13. [CrossRef]
34. Samusev, A.L.; Tomskaya, E.S. Modern methods for intensifying the process of leaching gold from refractory mineral raw materials. *Min. Inf. Anal. Bull.* **2015**, *8*, 100–105.
35. Teut, A.O.; Kuimov, D.V.; Kosyanov, E.A. Extraction of gold from refractory sulfide ores using the electrochlorination method. In Proceedings of the New Technologies for Enrichment and Complex Processing of Difficult-to-Enrich Natural and Technogenic Mineral Raw Materials, Upper Pyshma, Russia, 10 October 2011.
36. Li, S.K.; Gu, G.H.; Qiu, G.Z.; Chen, Z.X. Flotation and electrochemical behaviors of chalcopyrite and pyrite in the presence of N-propyl-N0—Ethoxycarbonyl thiourea. *Trans. Nonferrous Met. Soc. China.* **2018**, *28*, 1241–1247. [CrossRef]
37. Feng, B.; Feng, Q.; Lu, Y. The effect of lizardite surface characteristics on pyrite flotation. *App. Surf. Sci.* **2012**, *259*, 153–158. [CrossRef]

38. Bicak, O.; Ekmekci, Z.; Bradshaw, D.J.; Harris, P.J. Adsorption of guar gum and CMC on pyrite. *Miner. Eng.* **2007**, *20*, 996–1002. [CrossRef]
39. Cheng, W.; Deng, Z.; Tong, X.; Lu, T. Hydrophobic Agglomeration of Fine Pyrite Particles Induced by Flotation Reagents. *Minerals* **2020**, *10*, 801. [CrossRef]

processes

MDPI

Article

The Effect of Optimizing the Stripping and Drying Parameters During Industrial Extraction on the Physicochemical Properties of Soybean Oil

Toktam Mohammadi-Moghaddam [1,2], Hamid Bakhshabadi [3], Abolfazl Bojmehrani [4], Marcos Eduardo Valdes [5] and Afsaneh Morshedi [5,*]

1 Workplace Health Research Center, Neyshabur University of Medical Sciences, Neyshabur 141473474-14139, Iran; mohammadit1@nums.ac.ir
2 Department of Food Science and Technology, Neyshabur University of Medical Sciences, Neyshabur 141473474-14139, Iran
3 Department of Agriculture, Minab Higher Education Center, University of Hormozgan, Bandar Abbas 7916193145, Iran; h.bakhsabadi@hormozgan.ac.ir
4 Khorasan Cotton and Oilseeds Company, Neyshabur 9331143317, Iran; a.bojmehrani@yahoo.com
5 Facultad de Ciencias Gastrnomicas y Turismo, Universidad UTE, Quito 170147, Ecuador; marcos.valdes@ute.edu.ec
* Correspondence: afsaneh.morshedi@ute.edu.ec

Abstract: Soybean oil is the second most consumed vegetable oil worldwide and is recognized as a source of heart-healthy polyunsaturated fatty acids. Optimizing the extraction process in the oil industry is essential for both economic and environmental sustainability. This research aimed to determine the optimal conditions for various extraction parameters—stripper temperature (110–140 °C), stripper pressure (150–210 mbar), and dryer pressure (60–120 mbar)—and their effects on the physicochemical properties of soybean oil. These properties include oil-insoluble fine substances, acidity, the color index, peroxide value, oxidative stability, and moisture content. The results indicated that the stripper temperature significantly influenced oil-insoluble fine substances, acidity, the color index, and peroxide value ($p < 0.05$). The optimal conditions for oil extraction were found to be a stripper temperature of 110 °C, a stripper pressure of 150 mbar, and a dryer pressure of 120 mbar. Under these conditions, the oil-insoluble fine substances, acidity, the color index, peroxide value, oxidative stability, and moisture content of soybean oil were in the ranges of 0.2–0.58%, 0.63–1.15%, 4.3–5.5, 0.67–1.23 meqO_2/kg, 3–5.5, and 0.05–0.11%, respectively. These findings provide valuable insight for optimizing soybean oil extraction processes to enhance quality and efficiency. Future advancements in industrial oil extraction are expected to focus on integrating efficient, eco-friendly technologies and enhancing precision through automation and data analytics to optimize yield and minimize waste.

Keywords: soybean; oil extraction; stripper; dryer; optimization

1. Introduction

Plant oils are an important source of essential nutrients in the human diet. The usage forms are different: raw form, creams, mayonnaise, ice cream, or other food products. In food products, oils are mixed with emulsifying agents, such as proteins, phospholipids, and surfactants, and then homogenized to create a stable oil-in-water emulsion [1]. Soybean (*Glycine max*) is an important food crop known for its rich content of oil and plant proteins [2]. As one of the most widely consumed cooking oils, soybean oil ranks as the second most consumed vegetable oil globally, accounting for approximately 50% of the edible vegetable oil supply and 30% of all fats and oils produced worldwide [3]. Given its critical role in global food security, soybean cultivation is essential for meeting the nutritional needs of a growing population, as it contributes significantly to both caloric intake and protein supply [4]. This economically significant oilseed crop contains around~35–40% protein, ~20% lipids, ~9% dietary fiber, and ~8.5% moisture content [2,5]. Additionally, soybean oil is characterized by its rich biochemical composition, including high levels of linoleic and α-linolenic acids, along with various phospholipids, triglycerides, and minor components, such as isoflavones and saponins. The biochemical composition of plants with essential oils can significantly vary depending on the location and climatic conditions in which they are cultivated [5–7].

In 2021, global soybean production exceeded 388 million tons, with 34.8% produced in Brazil, 31.1% in the USA, and 11.9% in Argentina, according to the FAO [8]. Soybean oil is particularly valued for its commercial importance and nutritional benefits, such as being rich in polyunsaturated fatty acids, namely linoleic acid (about 51%) and α-linolenic acid (around 7–10%) [9]. It has been recognized as a source of heart-healthy polyunsaturated fatty acids and vitamin E, which possesses antioxidant properties [10].

The soybean is the most produced oilseed crop in the world [11]. Oil extraction is one of the most critical steps in seed oil processing because it determines the quality and quantity of the oil extracted [12]. The two primary industrial methods for oil production are mechanical processing and solvent extraction, with solvent extraction being the most widely used method for lipid extraction and the method can affect the physicochemical properties of the oil [13,14]. In solvent extraction, organic solvents like hexane are commonly used owing to their ability to break down plant cell walls or disrupt the interaction between lipids and the tissue matrix, allowing for effective oil extraction costs and the ability to produce a defatted meal with an acceptable odor and low residual oil content. However, various parameters, including temperature and pressure, can significantly influence the quality and quantity of the oil and meal obtained from oilseeds [14]. While much research has been conducted on optimizing the quantity and quality of oil during extraction, there is limited research focused on industrial-scale extraction parameters, including temperature (110–125 and 140 °C), stripper pressure (150, 180, and 210 mbar), and the pressure of the oil dryer (60, 90, and 120 mbar), on the physicochemical properties of soybean oil. These properties include oil-insoluble fine substances, acidity, the color index, peroxide value, oxidative stability, and moisture content. We used response surface methodology and central composite rotatable design to optimize these parameters, ultimately identifying the optimal conditions for soybean extraction. Hexane is the main solvent used in industry for oil extraction due to its high efficiency and practicality [15]. Oil extraction with hexane provides high oil recovery with low production costs. This method has additional advantages, such as producing a defatted meal with an acceptable odor and low residual oil content [16,17]. Various parameters can influence the quality and quantity of the oil and meal obtained from oilseeds, making it crucial to determine the optimal conditions for oil extraction [9,13,15,16,18–22]. Researchers have extensively studied the quantity and quality of oils during extraction [9,13,15,16,18–22]. The purpose of this study was to optimize part of the process of oil extraction (separating hexane from miscella) in order to produce higher quality soybean oil.

2. Materials and Methods

2.1. Raw Materials

Soybeans (*Gorgan variety*) were sourced from Gorgan, Golestan province, Iran, and transported to the Khorasan Cotton and Oilseeds Company in Neyshabur, Khorasan Razavi, Iran, for the production of oil and flour.

2.2. Oil Extraction

Upon arrival at the factory, the soybeans were stored in beehive-shaped silos and were purified to remove impurities. The seeds were then fed into a cracker (Buhler, Alzenau, Germany, capacity of 500 tons per day) and broken down into smaller particles. Next, they were transferred to a cooking pot (Andreotti, Calenzano, Italy, capacity of 500 tons per day), where the temperature and moisture content were adjusted to 60 °C and 12%, respectively. The seeds remained in this stage for approximately 40 min. The effect of sampling time before entering the line on some properties of soybeans is mentioned in Table 1.

Table 1. The effect of sampling time before entering the line on some properties of soybeans *.

Characteristics	Sampling Time (Hour)								
	8	10	12	14	16	18	20	22	24
Acidity (% oleic acid)	0.45 ± 0.01 [a]	0.45 ± 0.02 [a]	0.46 ± 0.01 [a]	0.45 ± 0.02 [a]	0.47 ± 0.02 [a]	0.45 ± 0.01 [a]	0.45 ± 0.01 [a]	0.45 ± 0.02 [a]	0.46 ± 0.01 [a]
Peroxide value ($meqO_2/kg$)	0.53 ± 0.02 [a]	0.52 ± 0.03 [a]	0.52 ± 0.01 [a]	0.53 ± 0.02 [a]	0.52 ± 0.03 [a]	0.52 ± 0.01 [a]	0.50 ± 0.03 [a]	0.52 ± 0.01 [a]	0.51 ± 0.02 [a]

* Data are the mean of three replications at three different work times; Data with the same letters show the lack of significance at the 5% level.

The heated soybeans were then processed in a flicker (Buhler, Germany, capacity of 250 tons per day) to create flakes. Soybean oil was extracted from the flakes using hexane solvent in an extractor (operating at 50 °C for 7 h), producing a miscella (a mixture of hexane and oil) containing about 30% oil. After passing through a strainer, the miscella entered the economizer, where its oil content increased to about 70%. It then proceeded to the evaporator, where the oil content in the miscella reached approximately 90–95%. In the next stage, the miscella entered the stripper, which was operated at three different levels of pressure (150, 180, and 210 mbar) and three levels of temperature (110, 125, and 140 °C). Afterward, the miscella was transferred to the dryer, which was also operated at three different levels of pressure (60, 90, and 120 mbar) and a temperature of 120 °C to completely separate and recover the solvent from the oil. Finally, the oil was cooled and stored in oil tanks. The stripper and dryer in the production line of the Khorasan Cotton and Oilseeds Company were manufactured by Andreotti, Italy, with the capacity of approximately 80 tons per day. On average, the oil remained in these devices for about 2.5 h. Valves on these devices allow for sampling, which was conducted every two hours. The data used in this study represent the average of at least 50 samples. Table 2 shows the treatments studied in this research, which included 20 treatments with 6 replications at the central point. It is important to note that to ensure uniformity of the oil and to prevent other processes from influencing the measured characteristics, the conditions of the subsequent stages were kept constant across all treatments. In the stripper, both direct and indirect steam were used, while in the dryer, only direct steam was applied, with the pressure controlled accordingly. The Khorasan Cotton and Oilseeds factory utilizes DeSmet extractors, a type of horizontal extractor with uneven solvent and sample flow. Valves installed along the processing route were used for sampling.

Table 2. Treatments used in this study.

No	Stripper Temperature	Stripper Pressure	Dryer Pressure
1	110	150	60
2	140	150	60
3	110	210	60
4	140	210	60
5	110	150	120
6	140	150	120
7	110	210	120
8	140	210	120
9	110	180	90
10	140	180	90
11	125	150	90
12	125	210	90
13	125	180	60
14	125	180	120
15	125	180	90
16	125	180	90
17	125	180	90
18	125	180	90
19	125	180	90
20	125	180	90

2.3. Oil-Insoluble Fine Substances

To measure the amount of oil-insoluble fine substances, 10 mL of soybean oil was poured into centrifuge tubes (Thermo, Tokyo, Japan) and centrifuged at 4000 rpm for 10 min. The percentage of oil-insoluble fine substances was determined by multiplying the mass of the material deposited inside the tube by 10 [23].

2.4. Determination of Color Index

A UV–Visible spectrophotometer (Shimadzu, Kyoto, Japan) and the AOCS Cd 13-92 [24] method were used to measure the color index. So, the optical density of the oil was measured at wavelengths of 460, 550, 620, and 670 nm, then the color index was determined according to the yellow color of Leviband (Equation (1)), as follows:

$$\text{Color index} = 1.29A_{460} + 69.7A_{550} + 41.2A_{620} - 56.4A_{670} \quad (1)$$

This formula was used to calculate the color index, which is typically used to measure the color of a substance based on how it absorbs light.

A_{460}, A_{550}, A_{620}, A_{670}: these are absorbance values of the material at specific wavelengths of light (460 nm, 550 nm, 620 nm, and 670 nm). The result of the formula gives a numerical value that presents the color of the substance. This can be used to identify the material or analyze its properties.

2.5. Acidity

The acidity of the soybeans and soybean oil was measured following the AOCS 3-63 method [24]. First, 5 g of sample was mixed with 20–30 mL of ethanol. Then, a few drops of phenolphthalein were added, and the mixture was titrated with 0.1 N NaOH solution until a pink color appeared. Acidity was then calculated using Equation (2):

$$A = \frac{2.82 \times V}{W} \quad (2)$$

where V is the volume of titrant (NaOH) used to neutralize the acid in the sample, W is the weight of the sample being analyzed, and A represents the free fatty acids, expressed as oleic acid in 100 g of sample. The constant 2.82 was used to adjust the calculation for the specific acid (oleic acid).

2.6. Peroxide Value

The peroxide value is important in food science because it indicates the extent of oxidation, which can be lead to rancidity in oils. The peroxide value of the soybeans and soybean oil was measured following the AOCS 8-53 method [24]. Approximately 5 g of sample was mixed with 300 mL of acetic acid-chloroform solvent (in a 3:2 v/v). After stirring, 0.5 mL of saturated potassium iodide solution was added and the mixture was left in the dark for 1 min. Next, 30 mL of distilled water was added to the solution, which was then slowly titrated with 0.1 M sodium thiosulfate until the yellow color disappeared. Afterward, 0.5 mL of starch reagent was added and the titration was continued until the blue color disappeared. The peroxide value was then calculated using Equation (3). This formula was used to calculate the peroxide value (P), which is a measure of the amount of peroxides in fats or oils:

$$P = \frac{S \times M \times 100}{W} \tag{3}$$

where S is the volume of titrant (usually sodium thiosulfate in mL), M is the molarity of the titrant (sodium thiosulfate solution), W is the weight of the sample being tested in grams, and P is the peroxide, expressed in milliequivalents of oxygen per kilogram of each sample. Additionally, 100 is a constant factor used to scale the result for expression in standard units.

2.7. Oxidative Stability Measurement

The stability of the soybean oil was determined using a Rancimat (Ohm Meter, Liestal, Switzerland) and the AOCS Cd 12b-92 method [24].

2.8. Moisture Content

The moisture content was measured according to the AOAC 44-15 method [25]. About 2 g of sample was weighed in a container that had previously been dried to a constant weight in a laboratory oven (Memmert, Schwabach, Germany). The sample was then dried in an oven at 100 °C for 3–5 h. After cooling in a desiccator, the moisture content was calculated based on the difference in weight.

2.9. Statistical Analysis

Response surface methodology (RSM) features include the design of experiments to efficiently explore the input space, fitting of polynomial models to approximate the true response surface, and the use of contour plots and other visualization techniques to understand response behavior. It is widely used in optimization to find the best operating conditions for a system or process, particularly when the response is influenced by multiple variables and their interactions. This makes RSM particularly valuable in fields like engineering, manufacturing, and product development, where it helps in identifying optimal conditions and enhancing performance. RSM was used to evaluate the effects of fixed parameters (stripper temperature (X_1), stripper pressure (X_2), and dryer pressure (X_3)) on variable parameters (moisture content, acidity, peroxide value, color parameter, oxidative stability, and oil-insoluble fine substances) using a central composite rotatable design. The primary focus of this study was to investigate the interaction of these factors and identify the optimal conditions for the oil extraction process from soybeans. Therefore,

RSM was selected for this analysis. To assess the response surface, a quadratic polynomial equation was fitted for each independent variable (Equation (4)), as follows:

$$y = \beta_0 + \sum_{i=1}^{3} \beta_i X_i + \sum_{i=1}^{3} \beta_{ii} X_{ii}^2 + \sum_{i=1}^{2} \sum_{j=i+1}^{3} \beta_{ij} X_i X_j \tag{4}$$

where Y represents the estimated response (moisture content, acidity, peroxide value, color parameter, oxidative stability, and oil-insoluble fine substances), β_{ii}, β_i, β_0, and β_{ij} are constant coefficients, and x_j and x_i denote encoded independent variables. The quality and accuracy of the regression model, as well as the appropriateness of the fit, were assessed using analysis parameters, fitting weakness, and the coefficient of determination. Statistical analysis was performed using Design Expert software (version 6.0.2). To compare certain characteristics of the input soybeans at different times, a completely randomized design and SAS software (version 7) were used, with Duncan's multiple range test applied to compare means at the 95% confidence level.

3. Results and Discussion

3.1. Some Properties of Soybeans Before Entering the Line

Table 3 presents the average data from three work shifts. The time at which the soybeans entered the production line had no significant effect on the acidity and peroxide value of the sample ($p > 0.05$), indicating the uniformity and homogeneity of the soybeans entering the line. It is worth noting that the Khorasan Cotton and Oilseeds Company operates three production shifts. Due to the lack of significant differences at the 5% level among the samples taken at different times and shifts, it could be concluded that the influence of the sampler was neutralized. The acidity and peroxide value of the samples ranged from 0.45% to 0.47% and 0.50 to 0.53 meqO_2/kg, respectively.

Table 3. Model selection for dependent variables.

	Oil-Insoluble Fine Particle Content		Oil Acidity		Color		Peroxide Value		Oxidative Stability		Moisture Content	
Models	**Sum of Squares**	**Pb > F**	**Sum of Squares**	**Pb > F**	**Sum of Squares**	**Pb > F**	**Sum of Squares**	**Pb > F**	**Sum of Squares**	**Pb > F**	**Sum of Squares**	**Pb > F**
Intercept	3.42	-	14.79	-	418.52	-	16.89	-	461.23	-	0.106	-
Linear	0.0979	<0.001	0.0901	0.009	3.30	0.002	0.104	0.009	0.771	0.003	0.003	0.0009
2FI	0.0058	0.1134	0.0543	0.005	0.865	0.082	0.065	0.004	0.1651	0.212	0.002	0.601
Quadratic	0.0025	0.4149	0.0005	0.983	0.329	0.398	0.0008	0.975	0.0433	0.765	0.0005	0.253
Cubic	0.006	0.0531	0.0337	<0.01	0.979	<0.01	0.039	0.001	0.341	0.002	0.0002	0.787
Residual	0.0019	-	0.0002	-	0.0295	-	0.0001	-	0.032	-	0.0008	-
Total	3.53	-	14.97	-	424.03	-	17.10	-	462.58	-	0.1109	-

3.2. Oil-Insoluble Fine Substances

During the extraction process, the extracted oil contains some fine solids that are insoluble in the oil and must be separated. This separation occurs in a decanter or separator, where fine materials are collected as insoluble substances at the end of the tank, and the oil is then filtered [15]. Increasing the temperature and pressure during the process can lead to chemical reactions that cause some soluble compounds to become insoluble, thereby increasing the amount of fine substances in the oil.

Table 3 indicates that the best model for the effect of operating parameters on the oil-insoluble fine substances was the linear model. Table 4 demonstrates that variations in stripper temperature, stripper pressure, and dryer pressure significantly affected the oil-insoluble fine substances ($p < 0.001$). As shown in Figure 1a–c, increases in stripper temperature, stripper pressure, and dryer pressure reduced the amount of oil-insoluble fine substances. The best model results suggested that the effect of stripper temperature on the oil-insoluble fine substances was more significant than that of other parameters

(Table 5). The concentration of oil-insoluble fine substances of soybean oil ranged from 0.2% to 0.58%. Bakhshabadi et al. (2017) investigated the effects of operating parameters on oil extraction from sunflowers and reported that increased processing temperature raised the level of insoluble fine matter, which aligned with the findings of this study [26]. Farzaneh et al. (2017) observed similar results in oil extraction from rapeseed [23]. Abad and Shahidi (2020) developed a robust stripping method for removing minor components from edible oils and reported that this method was much better than column chromatography [20].

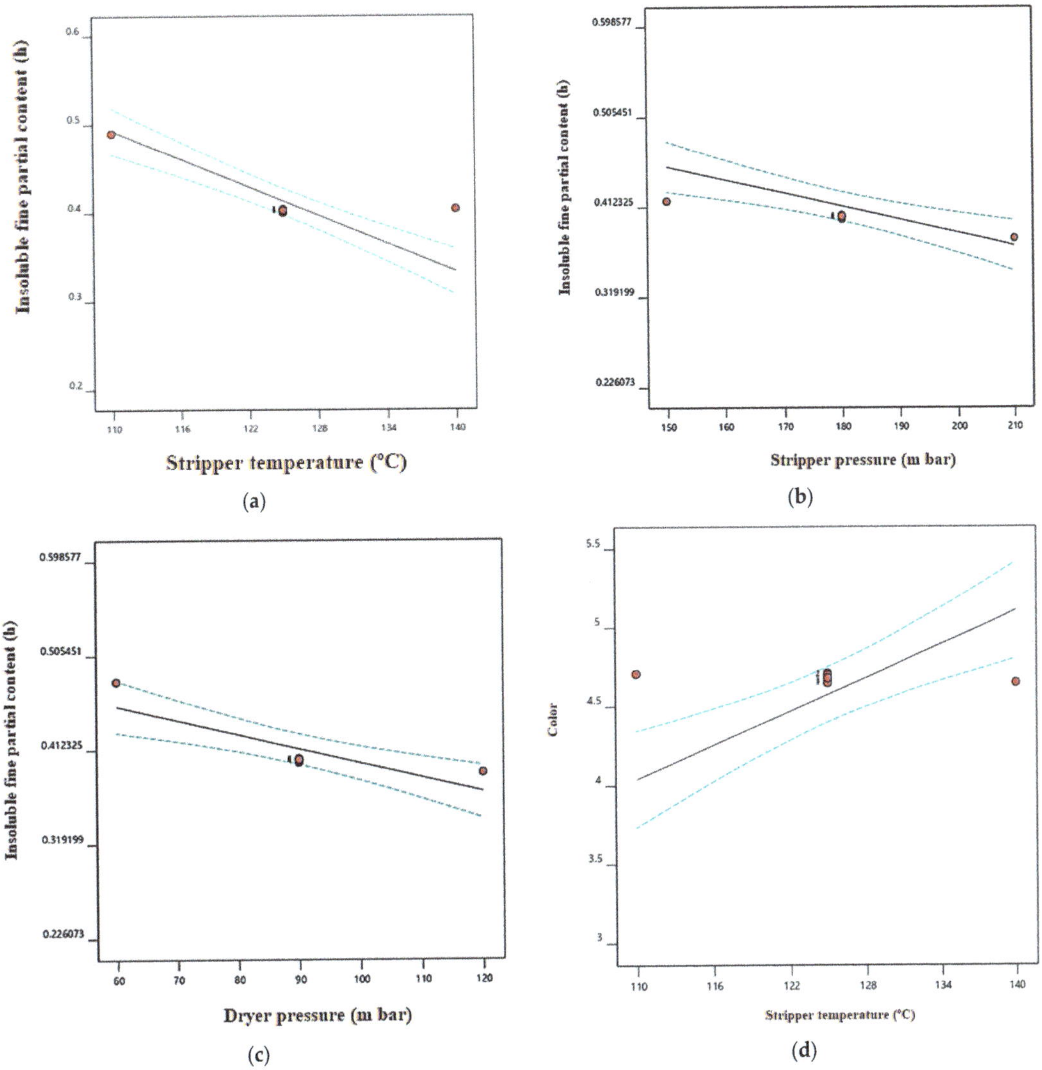

Figure 1. The effects of (**a**) stripper temperature, (**b**) stripper pressure, and (**c**) dryer pressure on the oil-insoluble fine substances and (**d**) stripper temperature on the color index of soybean oil. Solid line: design point, Dashed line: 95% Cl bands, Number: Repetition in the central points of the design.

Table 4. Analysis of variance for determined parameters.

Source	Oil-Insoluble Fine Particle Content		Oil Acidity		Color		Peroxide Value		Oxidative Stability		Moisture Content	
	Sum of Squares	Pb > F	Sum of Squares	Pb > F	Sum of Squares	Pb > F	Sum of Squares	Pb > F	Sum of Squares	Pb > F	Sum of Squares	Pb > F
Model	0.098	<0.001	0.144	0.0005	3.30	0.002	0.169	0.0005	0.771	0.003	0.003	0.0009
X_1	0.063	<0.001	0.085	<0.001	2.85	0.0003	0.097	<0.01	0.676	0.0005	0.001	0.006
X_2	0.017	0.0009	0.003	0.343	0.441	0.092	0.004	0.284	0.090	0.135	0.001	0.078
X_3	0.018	0.0007	0.003	0.315	0.008	0.814	0.003	0.308	0.004	0.732	0.0004	0.074
X_1^2	-	-	-	-	-	-		-	-	-	-	-
X_2^2	-	-	-	-	-	-		-	-	-	-	-
X_3^2	-	-	-	-	-	-		-	-	-	-	-
X_1X_2	-	-	0.034	0.003	-	-	0.041	0.003	-	-	-	-
X_1X_3	-	-	0.015	0.036	-	-	0.016	0.041	-	-	-	-
X_2X_3	-	-	0.006	0.154	-	-	0.007	0.141	-	-	-	-
Residual	0.016	-	0.034	-	2.20		0.039		0.582	-	0.002	
Lack of Fit	0.016	-	0.034	-	2.20	-	0.039	-	0.581	-	0.002	-
Pure Error	0.000005	-	0.000	-	0.003		0.000		0.0006	-	0.000006	-
Cor Total	0.114	-	0.178	-	5.50		0.209		1.35	-	0.004	-

X_1 = stripper temperature, X_2 = stripper pressure, and X_3 = dryer pressure.

Table 5. Designed equation models for dependent variables.

Number	Dependent Variable	Equation	R^2	R^2-Adj	cv	Predicted Data	Real Data
1	Oil-insoluble fine particle content (%)	$y = +0.413 - 0.0798\ X_1 - 0.041\ X_2 - 0.042\ X_3$	0.858	0.832	7.68	0.49	0.47
2	Oil acidity (% oleic acid)	$y = +0.860 + 0.092\ X_1 + 0.016\ X_2 - 0.017\ X_3 - 0.065\ X_1X_2 - 0.042\ X_1X_3 - 0.0275\ X_2X_3$	0.801	0.712	5.98	0.69	0.69
3	Color	$y = +4.57 + 0.534\ X_1 + 0.210\ X_2 + 0.028\ X_3$	0.699	0.624	8.11	3.80	3.50
4	Peroxide value (meq O_2/kg oil)	$y = +0.919 + 0.097\ X_1 + 0.019\ X_2 - 0.018\ X_3 - 0.072\ X_1X_2 - 0.044\ X_1X_3 + 0.031\ X_2X_3$	0.810	0.722	6.01	0.72	0.73
5	Oxidative stability (h)	$y = +4.80 - 0.260\ X_1 - 0.095\ X_2 - 0.021\ X_3$	0.669	0.589	3.97	5.20	5.30
6	Moisture content (%)	$y = +0.073 - 0.010\ X_1 - 0.012\ X_2 - 0.006\ X_3$	0.732	0.662	14.33	0.09	0.08

3.3. Color Index

Color is a crucial quality characteristic of food that significantly impacts its acceptability. If a food product does not have the right color, it will face a severe decrease in supply value. Other quality characteristics, such as aroma, taste, and texture, are evaluated after consumption and sometimes only after initial purchase and use [27]. Lee et al. (2004) reported that the formation of brown substances in heat-processed compounds results from non-enzymatic browning reactions, including Millard reactions, caramelization, and phospholipid degradation. This explains the increase in the color index with higher processing temperature [28]. Table 3 illustrates that the linear model provided a better fit for the color index of soybean oil compared to other models. The analysis results also indicated that only the linear parameter of stripper temperature significantly affected the color index of the oil ($p < 0.01$) (Table 4). As depicted in Figure 1d, increasing the stripper temperature elevated the color index of soybean oil samples. Table 5 highlights that among all of the operational parameters studied, stripper temperature had the most significant effect on the color index. The color index of soybean oil ranged from 4.3 to 5.5. Bakhshabadi et al. (2018) found that increasing the temperature during the extraction of oil from Nigella sativa seeds led to phospholipid degradation and a corresponding increase in oil color [29]. Mitra et al. (2009), using supercritical carbon dioxide extraction and RSM for pumpkin seed oil, reported Hunter L, a, b coordinates of a (1.51 ± 0.52), b (19.10 ± 1.19), and L (4.15 ± 1.72), indicating a green to yellowish color for pumpkin oil [30]. Similarly, Ma et al. (2019) reported that pepper seed oil had a yellowish color [31].

3.4. Acidity

Acidity and acid value are critical quality characteristics of oils, serving as standards of purity. While refined oils are typically free of free fatty acids, significant amounts of these compounds are present in crude oils [32]. Increased acidity is associated with the chemical decomposition of triglycerides and the breaking of ester bonds between fatty acids, leading to higher levels of free fatty acids [33]. Table 3 shows the results of the fitting data for soybean oil acidity. The 2FI model was identified as the best fit for the acidity data ($p = 0.0543$). Statistical analysis indicated that the linear parameter of stripper temperature, as well as the interactions between stripper temperature and pressure and stripper temperature and dryer pressure, significantly affected oil acidity ($p < 0.05$) (Table 4). Figure 2a illustrates how stripper temperature and pressure impact soybean oil acidity. Increasing the stripper temperature continuously raised the acidity of soybean oil. At lower temperatures, the acidity increased with stripper pressure, but at higher stripper temperatures, it decreased with increasing pressure. Additionally, the acidity increased with higher dryer pressure at lower stripper temperatures but decreased with increasing dryer pressure at higher stripper temperature (Figure 2c). As shown in Table 4, the effect of stripper and dryer pressure on oil acidity was insignificant compared to stripper temperature. Aligning with the results in this section, Sesti Osseo et al. (2004) [34] also showed that at low temperatures, with increasing pressure, the oil acidity and peroxide value increased, but at higher temperatures with increasing pressure, these characteristics decreased. This is probably because with the increase in pressure there is the need for higher temperature; as a result, the increase in pressure reduces the effect of temperature to some extent, and it is also possible that some of the antioxidant compounds that are transferred into the oil are less damaged at higher pressures, so they prevent further increase in acidity.

Table 4 shows that the linear parameter of stripper temperature had the greatest effect on the acidity of soybean oil. The acidity of soybean oil was in the range of 0.63–1.15%. Bakhshabadi et al. (2017) reported similar findings when studying the impact of microwaves on the physicochemical properties of Nigella sativa seed oil. They observed that high process temperature and triglyceride breakdown into free fatty acids led to increased acidity [35]. Ma et al. (2019) compared pressure-assisted extraction (PAE), ultrasound-assisted extraction (UAE), and conventional solvent extraction (CSE) via RSM to optimize pressure parameters in pepper seed oil extraction. They found that PAE resulted in the lowest acid value of 93.89 mg KOH/g) [31].

According to Codex standards, for refined vegetable oils, including soybean oil, the maximum acid values are typically ≤0.6 mg KOH/g for refined oils and ≤4.0 mg KOH/g for crude (unrefined) oils [36].

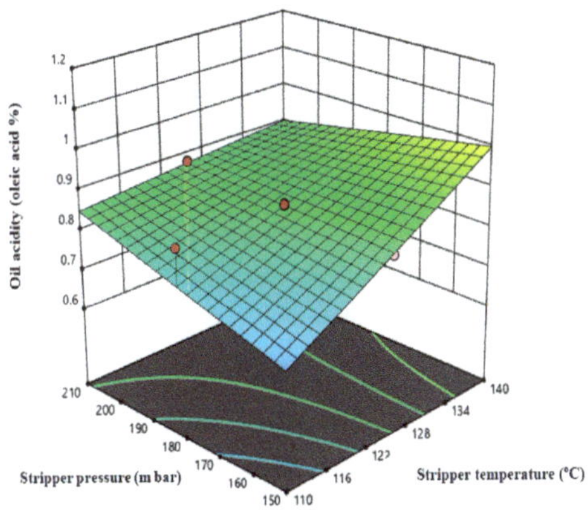

(a)

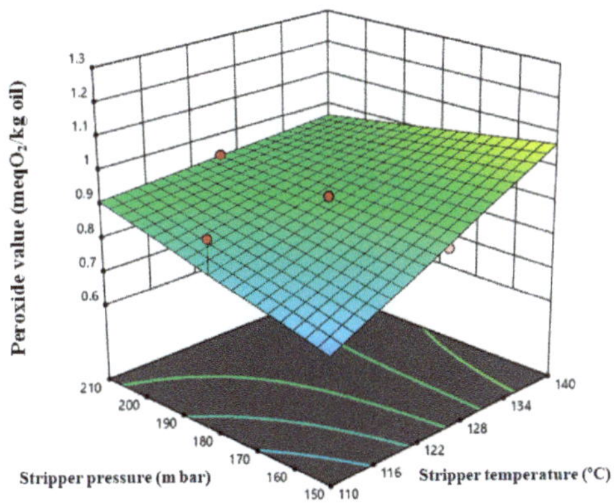

(b)

Figure 2. *Cont.*

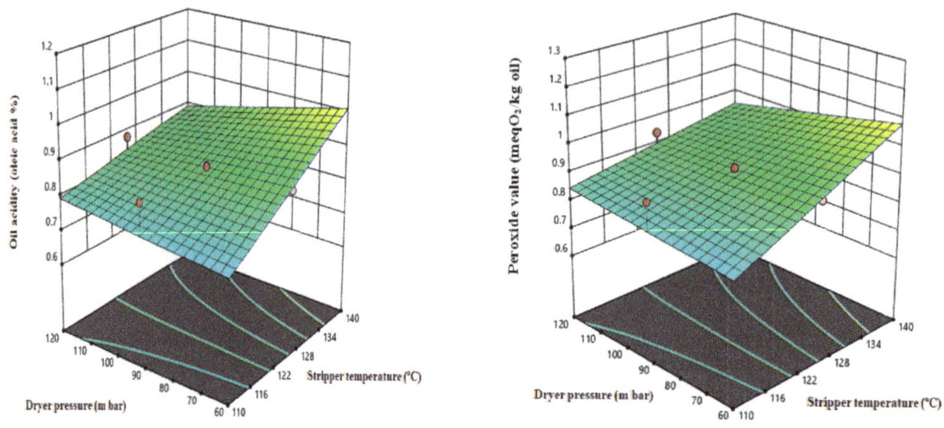

Figure 2. The effect of (**a**,**b**) temperature and pressure of stripper and (**c**,**d**) stripper temperature and pressure dryer on the acidity and peroxide value of soybean oil. Bold circle symbol: above surface and Faint circle symbol: below surface.

3.5. Peroxide Value

Peroxide value is a primary indicator of fatty substances. Generally, oils with a higher degree of unsaturation are more prone to oxidation. As peroxide levels increase, they lead to the formation of aldehydes and ketones, which contribute to undesirable smells and tastes in fatty substances [23]. Peroxide value is also a good indicator of freshness; for instance, in refined soybean oil, a peroxide value of 1 or less suggests product freshness [37]. An increase in peroxide value can often be attributed to higher processing temperature, which accelerates oxidation. Heat enhances the rate of free radical formation, which in turn promotes the oxidation of unsaturated fatty acids [38]. Lipid peroxidation has been shown to be exponentially dependent on temperature. The magnitude of the temperature effect on each of the kinetic parameters and rate constants can be investigated through the temperature coefficient, which is calculated by semi-logarithmic regression of the parameters on temperature [39]. Table 3 shows that the best model for fitting the peroxide value was the 2FI model (p = 0.004). It can also be seen in Table 3 that the effect of the linear parameter of stripper temperature and the interaction between temperature and stripper pressure as well as stripper temperature and dryer pressure on the peroxide value of soybean oil was significant ($p < 0.05$). As the stripper temperature increased, the peroxide value of the oil increased, but with the increase in stripper pressure, the peroxide value increased at low temperatures and decreased at high temperatures (Figure 2b). In addition, it can be seen in Figure 2d that the peroxide value was reduced with the increase in dryer pressure. According to the results of Table 4, the linear parameter of the stripper temperature had the greatest effect on the peroxide value of soybean oil. In this study, the peroxide value of soybean oil was from 0.67 to 1.23 meqO_2/kg. The peroxide value of crude soybean oil should be less than 15 meqO_2/kg, and it was very low in this study. Mitra et al. (2009) and Ma et al. (2019) reported peroxide values of 3.46 $\pm$ 0.42 meqO_2/kg for pumpkin seed oil and 1.47 m mol/kg for pepper seed oil, respectively [30,31]. Emmons et al. (1999) highlighted that the conditions and type of operation applied during oilseed processing significantly affected peroxide levels. Their research indicated that the oxidation of phospholipids, besides photo-oxidation, also contribute to higher peroxide values in oil extraction [40]. The international standards for peroxide value in oils, such as those provided by the Codex Alimentarius or ISO standards, specify acceptable limits to ensure oil quality and safety for consumption. For refined soybean oil, the peroxide value is typically set at a maximum of 10 meqO_2/kg (milliequivalents of active oxygen per kilogram of oil).

3.6. Oxidative Stability of Soybean Oil

Oxidative stability refers to the duration it takes for an oil to reach a point where oxidation indicators, such as peroxide value or carbonyl number, sharply increase, resulting in the production of unpleasant tastes and odors. Oxidation leads to spoilage, which degrades food quality and causes off-flavors and smells. Evaluating oxidative stability is crucial for understanding the chemical, physical, and nutritional changes that occur in oils during thermal processes. One of the key indicators of oxidative stability is the oxidation stability index [41]. However, measuring the oxidative stability index alone does not fully evaluate oil quality, but it provides insight into the initial state of the oil sample [42]. Table 3 indicates that the linear model was the most effective for fitting the oxidative stability data of soybean oil ($p = 0.003$). Table 4 indicates that the linear parameter of the stripper temperature significantly impacted the oxidative stability of soybean oil ($p < 0.05$). The results demonstrated that an increase in stripper temperature decreased the oxidative stability of the oil (Figure 3a and Table 5). This decrease in oxidative stability with higher stripper temperature can be attributed to reductions in tocopherol and antioxidant compounds due to increased heat, as well as the increase in free fatty acids at higher stripper temperature [43–45]. The oxidative stability of soybean oil in this study ranged from 3 to 5.5. Samaram et al. (2014) found that the extraction method affected the oxidative stability of papaya seed oil, with ultrasound-assisted extraction showing higher oxidative stability compared to Soxhlet and solvent extraction methods [46].

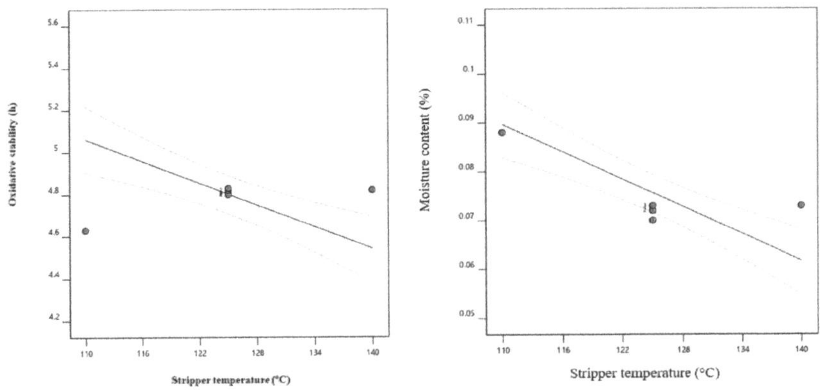

(a) (b)

Figure 3. The effect of (**a**,**b**) stripper temperature on the oxidative stability and moisture content of soybean oil. Solid line: design point, Dashed line: 95% Cl bands, Number: Repetition in the central points of the design.

The peroxide value of refined vegetable oils (including soybean oil) is ≤10 meqO_2/kg according to Codex standards [36]. While, according to the European Union, the maximum peroxide value is 10 meqO_2/kg for refined oils and 15–20 meqO_2/kg for cold-pressed or unrefined oils [47].

3.7. Moisture Content

The linear model was identified as the best fit for the moisture content data ($p = 0.0009$) (Table 3). The data analysis indicated that both the linear parameters of temperature and stripper pressure significantly affected the moisture content of the oil ($p < 0.05$) (Table 4).

The results showed that increasing the temperature of the stripper led to a decrease in the moisture content of the oil (Table 5 and Figure 3b). The reduction in moisture content with higher process temperature was more pronounced than the effect of pressure, as the increased temperature facilitated greater evaporation of moisture. The moisture content of soybean oil ranged from 0.05 to 0.11%. Laoretani et al. (2014) reported that higher process temperature result in decreased oil moisture [48]. Rostami et al. (2014) and Bakhshabadi et al. (2017) observed a decrease in moisture content with increasing process temperature, consistent with the findings of this research [15,26].

3.8. Optimizing Soybean Oil Extraction on an Industrial Scale

Considering that the oil extraction of soybean on an industrial scale was conducted under specific conditions (stripper temperature 110–140 °C, stripper pressure 150 to 210 mbar, and dryer pressure 60 to 120 mbar), the optimal conditions for achieving minimal oil-insoluble fine materials, acidity, peroxide value, moisture content, and color index while maximizing oxidative stability were determined. The results indicated that the best conditions for soybean oil extraction were a stripper temperature of 110 °C, stripper pressure of 150 mbar, and dryer pressure of 120 mbar ($R^2 = 0.763$). To validate the model predicted by the software, the data obtained under these optimal conditions were compared with the same characteristics under real conditions (Table 4). Except for the color index, there were no significant differences between the real and predicted values. Subroto et al. (2015) reported the optimal conditions for extracting oil from *Jatropha curcas* L. kernels as 19 MPa pressure, 90 °C pressing temperature, and 3.8% (w.b) moisture content, yielding an oil extraction rate of 87.8% [49]. Rezzoug et al. (2005) used RSM to evaluate various conditions for extracting essential oil from rosemary leaves. The optimal conditions they identified were a pressure level of 410 KPa, a moisture content of 0.40 g H_2O/g of dry material, and a processing time of 15.8 min, resulting in a predicted essential oil yield of 96% using a polynomial equation. Their results highlighted the significant effects of processing temperature and time on the extraction of essential oil from rosemary leaves [50]. Mitra et al. (2009) studied oil extraction from pumpkin seeds using supercritical carbon dioxide and reported a maximum yield of 37% under the optimal conditions of 32,140 KPa pressure and 68.1 °C for 94.6 min [30].

4. Conclusions

Extraction is the most prevalent method used in the industry for oil production. To achieve high-quality and high-quantity oil, designing an effective process in crucial. This research examined various parameters of soybean oil extraction, including stripper temperature (110–140 °C), stripper pressure (150–210 mbar), and dryer pressure (60 to 120 mbar), and optimized the extraction process on an industrial scale. Increasing the stripper temperature was found to decrease the oil-insoluble fine substances, oxidative stability, and moisture content, while increasing acidity, the color index, and peroxide value. An increase in stripper pressure reduced the oil-insoluble fine substances and moisture content. Additionally, higher dryer pressure decreased the oil-insoluble fine substances and peroxide value. The analysis indicated that the stripper temperature had a more significant impact on oil-insoluble fine substances, acidity, the color index, and peroxide value compared to other parameters. The optimal conditions of soybean oil extraction were identified as a stripper temperature of 110 °C, stripper pressure of 150 mbar, and dryer pressure of 120 mbar. The findings of this research provide valuable insight for the oil industry, helping to determine the best conditions for soybean oil extraction. The future of industrial oil extraction methods is likely to see significant advancements with the integration of more efficient and environmentally friendly technologies, such as supercritical fluid extraction and enzyme-assisted processes. Innovations in automation and data analytics will also enhance the precision and scalability of extraction methods, optimizing yield and reducing waste during the process.

Author Contributions: T.M.-M.: conceptualization, writing—original draft, review and editing: H.B.: methodology, supervision, project administration: A.M.: writing—review and editing, visualization: M.E.V. and A.B.: writing—original draft, data curating. All authors have read and agreed to the published version of the manuscript.

Funding: This research received no external funding.

Data Availability Statement: The original contributions presented in the study are included in the article; further inquiries can be directed to the corresponding author.

Conflicts of Interest: Author Abolfazl Bojmehrani was employed by the Khorasan Cotton and Oilseeds Company. The remaining authors declare that the research was conducted in the absence of any commercial or financial relationships that could be construed as a potential conflict of interest.

References

1. Zhao, Q.; Xu, Y.; Liu, Y. Soybean oil bodies: A review on composition, properties, food applications, and future research aspects. *Food Hydrocoll.* **2022**, *124*, 107296.
2. Liu, S.; Zhang, M.; Feng, F.; Tian, Z. Toward a "green revolution" for soybean. *Mol. Plant* **2020**, *13*, 688–697. [CrossRef]
3. Khamies, M.; Hagar, M.; Kassem, T.S.; Moustafa, A.H.E. Case study of chemical and enzymatic degumming processes in soybean oil production at an industrial plant. *Sci. Rep.* **2024**, *14*, 4064. [CrossRef]
4. Rizi, M.S.; Mohammadi, M. Breeding crops for enhanced roots to mitigate against climate change without compromising yield. *Rhizosphere* **2023**, *26*, 100702. [CrossRef]
5. Chatterjee, C.; Gleddie, S.; Xiao, C.-W. Soybean bioactive peptides and their functional properties. *Nutrients* **2018**, *10*, 1211. [CrossRef]
6. Preece, K.; Hooshyar, N.; Zuidam, N. Whole soybean protein extraction processes: A review. *Innov. Food Sci. Emerg. Technol.* **2017**, *43*, 163–172. [CrossRef]
7. Shaltouki, M.; Nazeri, V.; Shokrpour, M.; Tabrizi, L.; Aghaei, F. Phenotypic and genotypic assessment of some Iranian Ziziphora clinopodioides Lam. Ecotypes. *J. Agric. Sci. Technol.* **2021**, *23*, 645–660.
8. FAO. Food and Agriculture Organization (FAO). Available online: https://www.donorplatform.org/post/fao-statistical-yearbook-2023-world-food-and-agriculture/ (accessed on 1 January 2023).
9. Kong, W.; Baeyens, J.; De Winter, K.; Urrutia, A.R.; Degrève, J.; Zhang, H. An energy-friendly alternative in the large-scale production of soybean oil. *J. Environ. Manag.* **2019**, *230*, 234–244. [CrossRef]
10. Aussanasuwannakul, A.; Boonbumrung, S.; Pantoa, T. Valorization of soybean residue (Okara) by supercritical carbon dioxide extraction: Compositional, physicochemical, and functional properties of oil and defatted powder. *Foods* **2023**, *12*, 2698. [CrossRef] [PubMed]
11. Wilcox, J. (Ed.) Breeding soybeans for improved oil quantity and quality. In *World Soybean Research Conference III*; CRC Press: Boca Raton, FL, USA, 2022.
12. Say, M.; Kong, S.; Nat, Y.; Tan, C.P.; Tan, R. Oil extraction through hydraulic pressing from Cambodian soybean seeds and analysis of its physicochemical quality. *J. Food Technol.* **2023**, *10*, 93–102.
13. Cheng, M.-H.; Rosentrater, K.A. Economic feasibility analysis of soybean oil production by hexane extraction. *Ind. Crops Prod.* **2017**, *108*, 775–785. [CrossRef]
14. Zhang, H.; Yuan, Y.; Zhu, X.; Xu, R.; Shen, H.; Zhang, Q.; Ge, X. The effect of different extraction methods on extraction yield, physicochemical properties, and volatile compounds from field muskmelon seed oil. *Foods* **2022**, *11*, 721. [CrossRef] [PubMed]
15. Rostami, M.; Farzaneh, V.; Boujmehrani, A.; Mohammadi, M.; Bakhshabadi, H. Optimizing the extraction process of sesame seed's oil using response surface method on the industrial scale. *Ind. Crops Prod.* **2014**, *58*, 160–165. [CrossRef]
16. Potrich, E.; Miyoshi, S.C.; Machado, P.F.; Furlan, F.F.; Ribeiro, M.P.; Tardioli, P.W.; Giordano, R.L.; Cruz, A.J. Replacing hexane by ethanol for soybean oil extraction: Modeling, simulation, and techno-economic-environmental analysis. *J. Clean. Prod.* **2020**, *244*, 118660. [CrossRef]
17. Lavenburg, V.M.; Rosentrater, K.A.; Jung, S. Extraction methods of oils and phytochemicals from seeds and their environmental and economic impacts. *Processes* **2021**, *9*, 1839. [CrossRef]

18. Taticchi, A.; Esposto, S.; Veneziani, G.; Minnocci, A.; Urbani, S.; Selvaggini, R.; Sordini, B.; Daidone, L.; Sebastiani, L.; Servili, M. High vacuum-assisted extraction affects virgin olive oil quality: Impact on phenolic and volatile compounds. *Food Chem.* **2021**, *342*, 128369. [CrossRef] [PubMed]
19. Ferreira, M.C.; Gonçalves, D.; Bessa, L.C.; Rodrigues, C.E.; Meirelles, A.J.; Batista, E.A. Soybean oil extraction with ethanol from multiple-batch assays to reproduce a continuous, countercurrent, and multistage equipment. *Chem. Eng. Process. Process Intensif.* **2022**, *170*, 108659. [CrossRef]
20. Abad, A.; Shahidi, F. A robust stripping method for the removal of minor components from edible oils. *Food Prod. Process. Nutr.* **2020**, *2*, 1–9. [CrossRef]
21. Comerlatto, A.; Voll, F.A.; Daga, A.L.; Fontana, É. Mass transfer in soybean oil extraction using ethanol/isopropyl alcohol mixtures. *Int. J. Heat Mass Transf.* **2021**, *165*, 120630. [CrossRef]
22. Chakraborty, D.; Das, J.; Das, P.; Bhattacharjee, S.; Das, S. Evaluation of the parameters affecting the extraction of sesame oil from sesame (*Sesamum indicum* L.) seed using soxhlet apparatus. *Int. Food Res. J.* **2017**, *24*, 691–695.
23. Farzaneh, V.; Bakhshabadi, H.; Gharekhani, M.; Ganje, M.; Farzaneh, F.; Rashidzadeh, S.; Carvalho, I.S. Application of an adaptive neuro_fuzzy inference system (ANFIS) in the modeling of rapeseeds' oil extraction. *J. Food Process Eng.* **2017**, *40*, e12562. [CrossRef]
24. AOCS. AOCS Official Method Cd 8-53. In *Official Methods and Recommended Practices of the AOCS*; AOCS: Champaign, IL, USA, 1993.
25. Cunniff, P.; Washington, D. Official methods of analysis of aoac international. *J. AOAC Int.* **1997**, *80*, 127A.
26. Bakhshabadi, H.; Rostami, M.; Moghimi, M.; Bojmehrani, A.; Bahelkeh, A.; Toorani, N. Optimizing the operating parameters of cooker during oil extraction and production of sunflower meal on an industrial scale. *Iran. Food Sci. Technol. Res. J.* **2017**, *13*, 27–37.
27. Moghimi, M.; Farzaneh, V.; Bakhshabadi, H. The effect of ultrasound pretreatment on some selected physicochemical properties of black cumin (*Nigella sativa*). *Nutrire* **2018**, *43*, 18. [CrossRef]
28. Lee, Y.-C.; Oh, S.-W.; Chang, J.; Kim, I.-H. Chemical composition and oxidative stability of safflower oil prepared from safflower seed roasted with different temperatures. *Food Chem.* **2004**, *84*, 1–6. [CrossRef]
29. Bakhshabadi, H.; Mirzaei, H.; Ghodsvali, A.; Jafari, S.M.; Ziaiifar, A.M. The influence of pulsed electric fields and microwave pretreatments on some selected physicochemical properties of oil extracted from black cumin seed. *Food Sci. Nutr.* **2018**, *6*, 111–118. [CrossRef] [PubMed]
30. Mitra, P.; Ramaswamy, H.S.; Chang, K.S. Pumpkin (*Cucurbita maxima*) seed oil extraction using supercritical carbon dioxide and physicochemical properties of the oil. *J. Food Eng.* **2009**, *95*, 208–213. [CrossRef]
31. Ma, Y.; Wu, X.; Zhao, L.; Wang, Y.; Liao, X. Comparison of the compounds and characteristics of pepper seed oil by pressure-assisted, ultrasound-assisted and conventional solvent extraction. *Innov. Food Sci. Emerg. Technol.* **2019**, *54*, 78–86. [CrossRef]
32. Anjum, F.; Anwar, F.; Jamil, A.; Iqbal, M. Microwave roasting effects on the physico-chemical composition and oxidative stability of sunflower seed oil. *J. Am. Oil Chem. Soc.* **2006**, *83*, 777–784. [CrossRef]
33. Bruhn, C.M. Consumer attitudes and market response to irradiated food. *J. Food Prot.* **1995**, *58*, 175–181. [CrossRef]
34. Osséo, L.S.; Caputo, G.; Gracia, I.; Reverchon, E. Continuous fractionation of used frying oil by supercritical CO_2. *J. Am. Oil Chem. Soc.* **2004**, *81*, 879–885. [CrossRef]
35. Bakhshabadi, H.; Mirzaei, H.; Ghodsvali, A.; Jafari, S.M.; Ziaiifar, A.M.; Farzaneh, V. The effect of microwave pretreatment on some physico-chemical properties and bioactivity of Black cumin seeds' oil. *Ind. Crops Prod.* **2017**, *97*, 1–9. [CrossRef]
36. Alimentarius, C. Codex standard for named vegetable oils. *Codex Stan* **1999**, *210*, 1–13.
37. O'brien, R.D. *Fats and Oils: Formulating and Processing for Applications*; CRC Press: Boca Raton, FL, USA, 2008.
38. Velasco, J.N.; Andersen, M.L.; Skibsted, L.H. Evaluation of oxidative stability of vegetable oils by monitoring the tendency to radical formation. A comparison of electron spin resonance spectroscopy with the Rancimat method and differential scanning calorimetry. *Food Chem.* **2004**, *85*, 623–632. [CrossRef]
39. Farhoosh, R. Critical kinetic parameters and rate constants representing lipid peroxidation as affected by temperature. *Food Chem.* **2021**, *340*, 128137. [CrossRef] [PubMed]
40. Emmons, C.L.; Peterson, D.M.; Paul, G.L. Antioxidant capacity of oat (*Avena sativa* L.) extracts. 2. In vitro antioxidant activity and contents of phenolic and tocol antioxidants. *J. Agric. Food Chem.* **1999**, *47*, 4894–4898. [CrossRef] [PubMed]
41. Holser, R. Properties of refined milkweed press oil. *Ind. Crops Prod.* **2003**, *18*, 133–138. [CrossRef]
42. Matthäus, B. Utilization of high-oleic rapeseed oil for deep-fat frying of French fries compared to other commonly used edible oils. *Eur. J. Lipid Sci. Technol.* **2006**, *108*, 200–211. [CrossRef]
43. Navarra, G.; Cannas, M.; D'Amico, M.; Giacomazza, D.; Militello, V.; Vaccaro, L.; Leone, M. Thermal oxidative process in extra-virgin olive oils studied by FTIR, rheology and time-resolved luminescence. *Food Chem.* **2011**, *126*, 1226–1231. [CrossRef]
44. Spielmeyer, A.; Wagner, A.; Jahreis, G. Influence of thermal treatment of rapeseed on the canolol content. *Food Chem.* **2009**, *112*, 944–948. [CrossRef]

45. Hosseini, S.M.; Bojmehrani, A.; Zare, E.; Zare, Z.; Hosseini, S.M.; Bakhshabadi, H. Optimization of antioxidant extraction process from corn meal using pulsed electric field-subcritical water. *J. Food Process. Preserv.* **2021**, *45*, e15458. [CrossRef]
46. Samaram, S.; Mirhosseini, H.; Tan, C.P.; Ghazali, H.M. Ultrasound-assisted extraction and solvent extraction of papaya seed oil: Crystallization and thermal behavior, saturation degree, color and oxidative stability. *Ind. Crops Prod.* **2014**, *52*, 702–708. [CrossRef]
47. Regulation (EC) No 1333/2008 of the European Parliament and of the Council of 16 December 2008 on Food Additives (Text with EEA Relevance). Available online: https://eur-lex.europa.eu/eli/reg/2008/1333/oj (accessed on 11 December 2008).
48. Laoretani, D.; Fernández, M.; Crapiste, G.; Nolasco, S. Effect of drying operating conditions on canola oil tocopherol content. *Antioxidants* **2014**, *3*, 190–199. [CrossRef] [PubMed]
49. Subroto, E.; Manurung, R.; Heeres, H.J.; Broekhuis, A.A. Optimization of mechanical oil extraction from *Jatropha curcas* L. kernel using response surface method. *Ind. Crops Prod.* **2015**, *63*, 294–302. [CrossRef]
50. Rezzoug, S.-A.; Boutekedjiret, C.; Allaf, K. Optimization of operating conditions of rosemary essential oil extraction by a fast controlled pressure drop process using response surface methodology. *J. Food Eng.* **2005**, *71*, 9–17. [CrossRef]

MDPI AG
Grosspeteranlage 5
4052 Basel
Switzerland
Tel.: +41 61 683 77 34

MDPI Books Editorial Office
E-mail: books@mdpi.com
www.mdpi.com/books

www.ingramcontent.com/pod-product-compliance
Lightning Source LLC
Chambersburg PA
CBHW061553210926
51850CB00009B/2089
* 9 7 8 3 7 2 5 8 7 7 7 3 7 *